BRIGHT START

DR RICHARD C. WOOLFSON

hamlyn

Contents

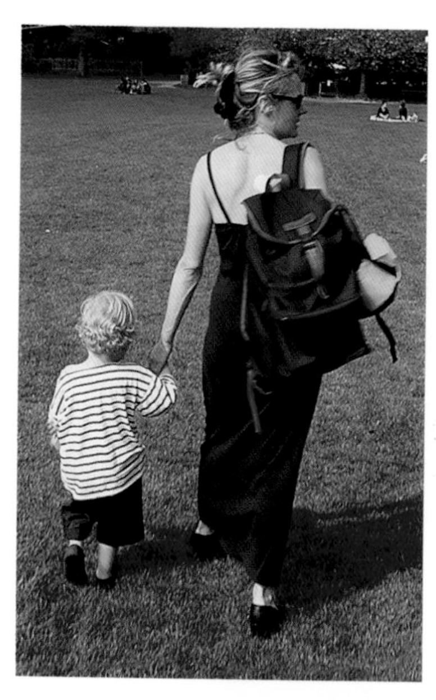

Using this Book

The more you understand the nature of your child's development over her first five years, the better placed you'll be to promote her progress. This book helps you along this road of understanding by identifying the key areas of development that your child experiences during this fascinating period in her life – but try to take a broad view, rather than considering each area of development in isolation, because all of these different aspects of your child's growth interact. When using the suggestions given throughout this book as a source of ideas for stimulating your child, take a holistic approach, as this balanced way of promoting your child's development is more effective than concentrating on one feature alone.

How to Use this Book

There are many ways to categorize aspects of child development. This book focuses on five main dimensions, although they all interact with one another:

• **movement.** At birth, your child's physical movement is extremely limited, but by the age of just 15 months she can walk independently and go wherever she wants, even up and down stairs. At 2½ years old she has barely mastered the skills of jumping into the air and landing steadily on her feet, whereas by the time she is 5 years old she can hop, run and balance on one foot.

• **hand-eye coordination.** Your new-born baby's hand control is minimal, but over the next year her coordination extends to the point where she can put her hands out intentionally towards a toy and then pick it up. During her second year she begins to make marks on a piece of paper with a crayon, and by the end of her third year she can copy a circle that you draw for her. From 3 to 5 years hand control develops rapidly until she is able to copy her own name, and perhaps even write it herself.

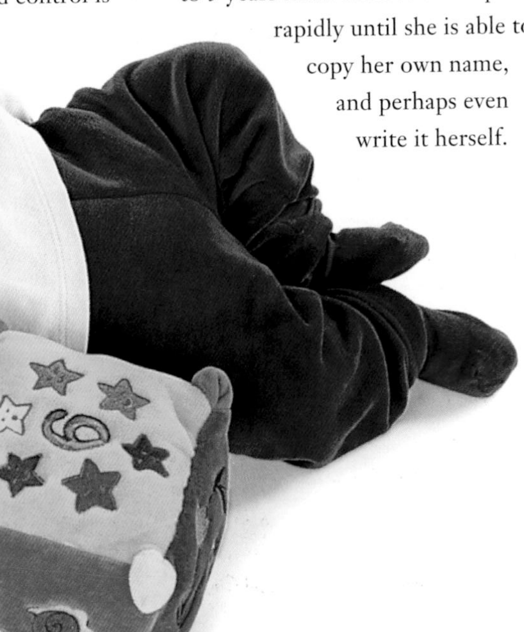

Above: As soon as they can grasp, babies instinctively explore objects with their hands and mouth.

• **language.** For at least a couple of months, crying is your baby's only verbal means of communication. Over the next year, she progresses from gurgling sounds, to random vowel and consonant sounds, until she says her first word. By her third birthday she probably uses well over a thousand words and begins to understand grammatical rules, and by the time she is 5 her ability to use more complex sentences enables her to take part in conversations with children and adults.

• **learning.** Your new-born baby is pre-programmed to learn, although she is at a very early stage in the process of understanding. By the start of her second year, however, she has learned a great deal, and the thirst for learning continues unabated through the toddler stage. At 1 year old, her memory is just good enough to recall where she placed her last toy; by the time she reaches her third birthday she can tell you all about some special event she experienced days ago. As she approaches the start of school, your child can already count at least up to five, compares objects using a number of different characteristics, and has good concentration when trying to solve a problem.

• **social and emotional.** Your young baby is such a sensitive individual, totally dependent on you for all her emotional needs. Throughout the first 15 months, you will see her confidence improve; she continues to have a close emotional attachment to you throughout her second and third years, but she also forms relationships with other children. From then on friendships are important and social skills improve. Her independence grows, too.

Top Tips

1. Establish an overview. Make a point of dipping in and out of all the chapters regularly, to help you maintain a general overview of your child's development. You'll help her more effectively if you keep a broad view.

2. Use trial and error. If a planned activity doesn't prove popular with your child, be ready to try something new. There are always several ways to help your child acquire the same skill, so be prepared to try a different approach.

3. Pick 'n' mix. You and your child will have much more fun together with a varied programme of stimulation, involving activities that cover as many different areas of development as possible. Avoid focusing on one area exclusively at a time.

4. Be creative. The activities suggested in this book are not exhaustive. You'll be able to think of additions. That's great – create your own set of activities to use in conjunction with those offered here.

5. Avoid pushing her too hard. The activities given in this book are not tests that she must pass at a particular time. When she can't manage a particular activity or game, come back to it in a few weeks when she is ready or skip it altogether.

Be Flexible

This book provides you with lots of ideas for promoting your child's development, but it is not a checklist that should be worked through in a rigid, inflexible way. Remember that she is unique – a programme of stimulation that benefits your best friend's child might not have the same effect on yours. So use this book as a flexible range of suggestions, some of which will be more appropriate for your child than others.

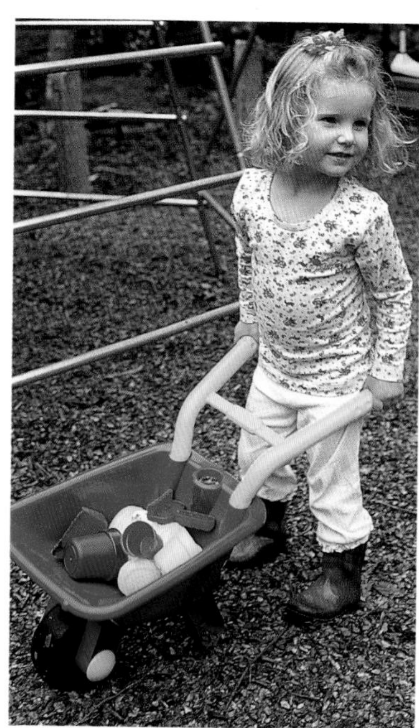

Above: To maximize your child's interest ensure that you provide her with a wide range of toys and activities, both indoors and outdoors.

Each section in this book can be read on its own or in conjunction with any other. Feel free to take one activity at random or to use it as part of a planned programme of stimulation for your child.

Bear in mind, too, that all these areas of development are linked to each other. Every activity given in this book has an impact in several areas and therefore makes a multifaceted contribution to your child's progress.

The Importance of Stimulation

Your child's first five years are an amazing time for him and for you. At birth, he arrives in this world with an enquiring mind, ready to explore and discover, and you can help this process along by providing him with love, care and stimulation, so that he becomes a bright baby. As a toddler, your child develops at an impressive rate, and his curiosity and thirst for knowledge seem insatiable. By providing appropriate stimulation you will encourage him to discover himself and the world around him, so that he becomes a bright toddler. Then, during the pre-school years from 3 to 5, development continues to move at an astounding pace. Every day he has many challenges to face and lots of obstacles to overcome – that's part of growing up. Your active support, stimulation and encouragement will ensure that he develops into a bright child.

A Journey of Discovery

Right from birth, your baby demonstrates his desire to learn. He wants to make sense of the world around him, and he does everything he can to reach out and explore. He is an active learner who uses every skill he has to extend his understanding, no matter if he is 1 week old or 1 year old. Yet that doesn't mean that as a parent you should sit back and leave it all to chance – on the contrary, if this is what he can do on his own, imagine what he could achieve with your help!

From 16 months onwards, your growing toddler has an innate desire to explore uncharted territory, and he does everything he can to learn new things all the time. This determination to understand his surroundings, to interact with other children, and to have more control over himself and his environment continues throughout his second and third years. Yet the knowledge and new skills he acquires at this stage, learned through his own efforts, are based on the stimulation you provide.

By the age of 3, your child's zest for getting more involved in life around him drives him every single day. His new skills bring him success because he can achieve much more than he did before, and his enthusiasm for new experiences is limitless. Now he is also able to seek his own stimulation and search out many more new activities on his own, without relying on you so much. Motivation will take your child so far – but your support, stimulation and guidance can open entirely new horizons for him.

Partners in Progress

Your stimulation will provide your child's development with a further boost. Using the activities and ideas suggested throughout this book enhances and extends his innate desire to learn, and gives you an opportunity to make his early

Left: This little girl's fascination with pouring water shows how easy it is to make everyday events like bathtime stimulating for your baby.

BRIGHT START

years more interesting, more rewarding, more challenging...and, of course, more fun. And that's what makes a bright, dynamic child.

Think of yourself as your child's 'learning partner': his progress depends on the interaction between his unique abilities, your unique personality and his everyday life. Your role is to work with your child, matching the level of stimulation to his current stage of development – not to take over, or to provide so much structure that his natural spontaneity is lost.
But it's not just about promoting his learning: there are emotional benefits, too. After all, even as a baby every child thrives on love and attention from a parent. He adores your interest and probably tries that little bit harder when he knows you are watching.

You benefit as well. Interacting with your child in a positive way – not just when he misbehaves or needs to be fed – enhances your relationship with him. The emotional connection between the two of you strengthens as a result of working together, because each of you gets to know the other in new ways. He learns that you can be a source of fun and support, and you learn about his abilities. This increased closeness builds his confidence – in this frame of mind, your child will be ready to tackle the challenges of his first five years.

Top Tips

1. Don't dominate. The challenge facing you as his parent is to provide a high level of stimulation without taking over from him completely. Remember that the two of you are working together to promote his development.

2. Enjoy playing with him. If you don't enjoy playing with him and if he doesn't enjoy being with you, his rate of learning will slow down. So look on the activities you provide as fun, not learning, and make sure there is plenty of laughter every day.

3. Give appropriate activities. Strike a balance between encouraging him to progress and pushing him so hard that he gives up altogether. Tune in to his level of understanding and abilities, and then give him suitable toys and activities.

4. Give your child space. You don't need to hover over him all the time in an attempt to ensure that he learns at every opportunity. He loves stimulation from you, but he also enjoys having room to explore and learn on his own.

5. Delight in his achievements. Whatever his talents and abilities, your child is very special. He's wonderful and he needs you to tell him this. Show your pleasure at every new skill he acquires.

Above: The activities you share should be fun – the more pleasure you both get, the more motivated your child will be.

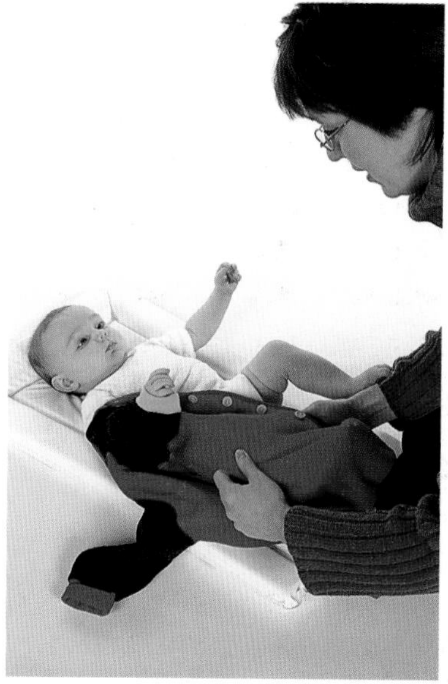

Above: Eye contact and talking to your baby are very important – changing time provides a good opportunity.

Your Attitude

Your attitude towards stimulation determines the impact and success of your involvement in your child's development. Push her too hard to achieve the milestones for her age group, spend too much time on a programme of activities designed to promote her skills, get too intense about her achievements – and you'll soon find that her natural enthusiasm for play evaporates. On the other hand, show no interest in your child's progress, spend no time playing with her, have a completely relaxed attitude when it comes to acquiring new skills and you'll soon find that she's lethargic. Try to find a suitable balance.

Getting the Balance Right

The best way to determine whether or not you are achieving a suitable level of stimulation is to note any significant mood changes. Typical signs of under-stimulation, even in a baby, include a general level of passivity in which she shows little interest in her toys, a lack of animation in her body language and facial expression, and a higher than usual level of tiredness. You may also find that she is unusually quiet and becomes easily upset over things that she usually takes in her stride.

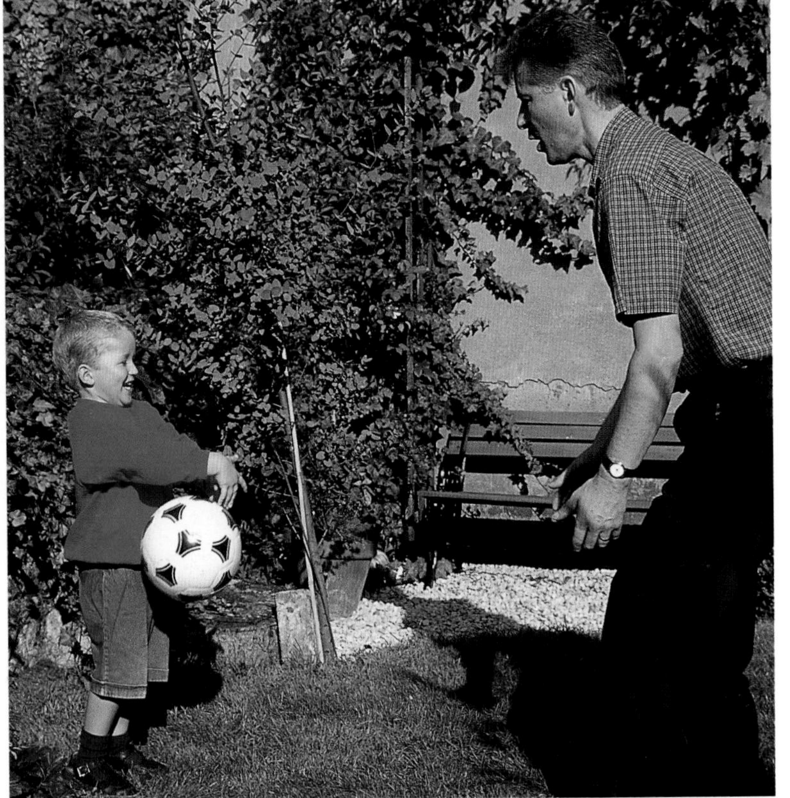

Typical signs of over-stimulation include a high level of activity because she feels the need to be on the go the whole time, a disrupted sleep pattern, irritability, and fluctuating and unpredictable levels of concentration. Be on the lookout for these warning signs to ensure you get the balance right. In most instances, there is a greater danger of over-stimulation than under-stimulation. There are a number of reasons for this.

First, you have a natural desire to encourage your child to achieve her highest potential and this may drive

Left: Your participation in games will encourage your child, and as he gets older you can let him make the rules sometimes.

you unwittingly towards providing her with a higher level of stimulation than she actually needs. Secondly, you may believe that stimulation, no matter how much, can only benefit your child because there is always more to learn. Of course her capacity to absorb new information is never used up, but stimulation has to be paced appropriately for your child or her motivation will soon ebb away. Thirdly, you probably compare her to other children of her own age, matching her rate of development against theirs. Any indication that she is less advanced than other children of her age (and there's always someone more advanced than your child) may make you feel under pressure to push her more.

Do your best to resist these pressures towards over-stimulation. As long as you are aware of the risk and occasionally step back and think about what you are doing with your child, the chances of over-stimulating her remain low.

There's no ideal amount of time you should spend on the activities in this book. Much depends on your and your child's inclinations, your family routine, and her level of development. Also remember that she is receiving stimulation for much of the time anyway, just by watching what goes on around her and by being involved in daily activities around the home, such as washing, dressing, eating, going to the toilet, and so on. The best arrangement is to integrate the suggested activities into her normal play pattern so that they appear natural rather than contrived.

To help develop a consistently positive, supportive attitude towards stimulating your growing child, ask yourself the following question: what do I mean when I say I want a 'bright' child? In this book, the word 'bright' does not simply mean 'clever'. Developing your child's learning is one aim of some of the activities presented here, but not the sole aim. A truly bright child is one who is dynamic, interested and responsive, and who interacts spontaneously with her surroundings; she is also sociable, contented, has a high level of self-confidence and is comfortable in her relationships with others.

Top Tips

1. Be honest with yourself. You're only human; there will be plenty of times when playing with your child is the last thing you feel like doing. If you reach this stage, just stop and rest. Stimulating activities work best when you are both in the mood for them.

2. Avoid comparisons. Continually remind yourself that every child develops at her own pace. There will be times when her development seems either to slow down or to speed up – don't worry about these individual variations.

3. Avoid too much structure. Free time is important for your child. It allows her the space to make choices for herself. If you plan every activity for her, she could soon lose the confidence to keep herself amused when you don't organize her play for her.

4. Be spontaneous. Keep in mind that your child's development is boosted by her normal, unplanned everyday experiences, such as playing with water in the bath or studying the products on supermarket shelves. Learning goes on all the time.

5. Talk to others. Many parents like to swap stories about their child's progress – both successes and problems – with friends. This helps them to maintain a balanced outlook. Sharing proud moments as well as your anxieties may be good for you.

Right: A happy and animated child who is absorbed in her activities is the best indication that you are providing the right level of stimulation.

Nature or Nurture

Your position regarding the nature/nurture debate affects your interactions with your child. If you believe in the 'nature' argument, then you'll assume that his inborn characteristics, learning abilities and personality determine what sort of person he becomes, and that your own individual input as a parent does not have much to do with it. If you believe in the 'nurture' argument, however, you'll assume that his development is dependent entirely on the way you raise him and the level of stimulation he experiences during his childhood. You might take a middle-of-the-road approach, recognizing the importance of both your child's innate talents and also the environment in which he is raised.

Opposing Viewpoints

Here are some examples of the ways in which your own attitude towards the different roles of heredity and environment in your child's life can influence his development.

If you believe firmly in the 'nature' argument (namely, that your child's talents are inborn), then it is probable that you:

- don't place a great amount of importance on providing stimulation for him because you expect his abilities to develop no matter what happens.
- take a relaxed and fatalistic approach to his development, on the basis that there is not much you can do to affect it anyway.
- accept his strengths and weaknesses without challenge, and do not feel the need to stretch his abilities in any specific direction.
- assume that all similarities between yourself and your child are due to inherited characteristics and that this has nothing to do with learned behaviour.

Left: Whatever her inherited traits, loving parental attention will increase a baby's sense of enjoyment and security.

If you strongly support the 'nurture' argument (namely, that your child's abilities are determined by his environment), then you probably:

- regard a well-structured programme of stimulation as the vital key to your child's satisfactory development.
- are ready to get involved with a plan of stimulation whenever you

Above: At around 4 years of age these two boys are learning a great deal by doing some simple planting in pots in the garden.

detect any area of his development that could be improved.
• assume that playing with your child and providing challenges for him to tackle is a necessary part of your parental responsibilities.
• think that perceived similarities between you and your child arise through imitation, because he unintentionally copies you.

Fortunately, few parents and professionals take either of these extreme approaches. Common sense and everyday experience tell you that your child's progress isn't as simple as either 'nature' or 'nurture' alone. True, there are many skills which a child shows early on that undoubtedly are innate (such as musical ability), but there are also many skills that improve rapidly just with practice (such as learning to read). It's more a question of how much both influences contribute to his overall development than of its being entirely one or the other.

Maximize Potential

The picture of development is even more complex. The reality is that your child's progress is a dynamic, constantly changing process that is more than a simple combination of the abilities he was born with and the stimulation he receives as he grows during his early years. For example, every time you respond with excitement when he learns something new or acquires another skill, his confidence and motivation are heightened, which makes him try harder, which in turn makes you even more delighted with him. So your interest, his curiosity, your support, his willingness to take a risk, your guidance when success eludes him, are just some of the many other factors that play a part in his development.

What matters most is that you try to maximize your child's full potential, and that you create an environment at home in which his natural talents are nurtured and extended as much as possible. Of course you will find that there are limits to what he can do, yet you should help him to go as far as he can, whether it's teaching him how to dress himself or helping him to finish that difficult jigsaw puzzle. So get involved, use the activities suggested, and don't be restricted by the nature versus nurture debate.

Top Tips

1. Play with your child. There is an emotional dimension to development, irrespective of your child's current skills. The fact is that he loves attention from you whatever the time of the day, and this puts him in a positive, enthusiastic frame of mind.

2. Expect variations in rate of progress. You'll find that some months your child leaps forward in his development and yet at other times he appears to make no progress whatsoever. Surges and plateaux in progress like this are normal.

3. Identify his interests. Discover the activities, toys and games that usually grab his attention and use these as the starting point for further stimulating activities. Introduce new ones periodically in order to broaden his interests.

4. Accept his individuality. He's not the same as his brother, or his sister, or your friend's child – he is a unique individual who will develop during the early years at his own pace. He needs you to love him for who he actually is and his own special achievements.

5. Affect what you can. In the end, you can't do much about your child's inherited characteristics as they are fixed, but you can do plenty about directing these innate skills and providing stimulation to encourage the development of new skills.

Below: Tailor your parental input to each child's personality and aptitude; even within the same family children often develop different skills at very different rates.

Building Self-confidence

The foundations of your child's self-confidence are laid during the first year of her life. She may only be a young baby but she already has a sense of self, a sense of what she can and cannot do. Her confidence is affected by the achievements she makes as she grows and develops, and continues to expand throughout the first five years of her life, as she learns new skills every day. The way in which others react towards her also has an impact on her confidence – your love, praise and interest all boost your growing child's belief in herself.

Components of Confidence

Self-confidence has a significant effect on your child's development because it influences her drive to achieve and her relationships with others. There are three aspects of your child's confidence to consider:

- **self-belief.** This is the extent to which she believes that she has the ability to meet the challenges that face her. A child who has little self-belief won't even try to master a new skill because she thinks that it will be too difficult for her. As a result, she would rather avoid an activity altogether than run the risk of failure.
- **self-value.** This is the extent to which your child values herself, and you'll see examples of this every day. Watch your child trying to master something – when she succeeds, she will probably turn to you and give you a huge grin. A child with a low self-value is completely unimpressed by her own achievements.
- **self-reflection.** This is the extent to which she receives positive feedback from other people around her. When you tell her how much you love her and give her a big cuddle because, say, she managed to go further up on the climbing frame than she has done before, this gives her a positive self-reflection and consequently makes her feel good about herself.

A child with low self-confidence has less enjoyment in life, prefers to take a more passive role, and may have difficulty giving and receiving love from others. Challenge and adventure threaten her rather than excite her, making her reluctant to discover and learn.

Determination

Findings from psychological research suggest that a young child usually has strong determination and wants to achieve her goals. She is willing to explore and venture into new areas, convinced that there can be no challenge that is beyond her grasp. It's almost as though your child holds an innate positive sense of self-belief.

And this positive self-belief extends to most areas of her life. For instance, as a toddler she makes valiant attempts to climb the stairs in your house before she eventually succeeds, she tries to run long before she is

Right: A reassuring hug can make all the difference at times when your child is upset.

steady enough to do this safely, and she tries to communicate with you even though she has barely started using single words. In other words, she is confident enough to try anything.

Yet her belief in herself is easily dented by experience. The sudden realization that, for example, she can't place all the shapes into the shape-sorter can dampen her interest in the toy. The same thing can happen when your child tries to propel her three-wheeler using the pedals, discovers that she hasn't moved it at all, and then cries in frustration. If failure of this sort occurs often enough, your child's self-confidence dips and she'll give up trying.

Top Tips

1. Have plenty of loving physical contact. A warm, loving hug is a very fundamental way of telling your child that you love her and that you think she is marvellous. This sort of contact with you boosts her self-belief.

2. Reassure her. If she explodes with frustration because, for example, she can't fit all the pieces of the jigsaw together, try to calm her. Reassure her that she'll soon master it, and then on this occasion solve the puzzle for her.

3. Break challenges into small stages. Your child wants to do everything, even when the task is beyond her. Help her complete a new activity in stages, each of which is a separate achievement. For example, encourage her to run a few steps at first before she attempts to race across the room.

4. Tell your child what you feel about her. Your praise and encouragement have a huge positive effect on her self-confidence. She values your attention and is proud when you comment on her achievements. She never tires of receiving your praise.

5. Avoid obvious pitfalls. There is no point in deliberately letting your child learn through failure. If you know that she is heading for a disappointment, steer her away from that activity before she gets fully involved.

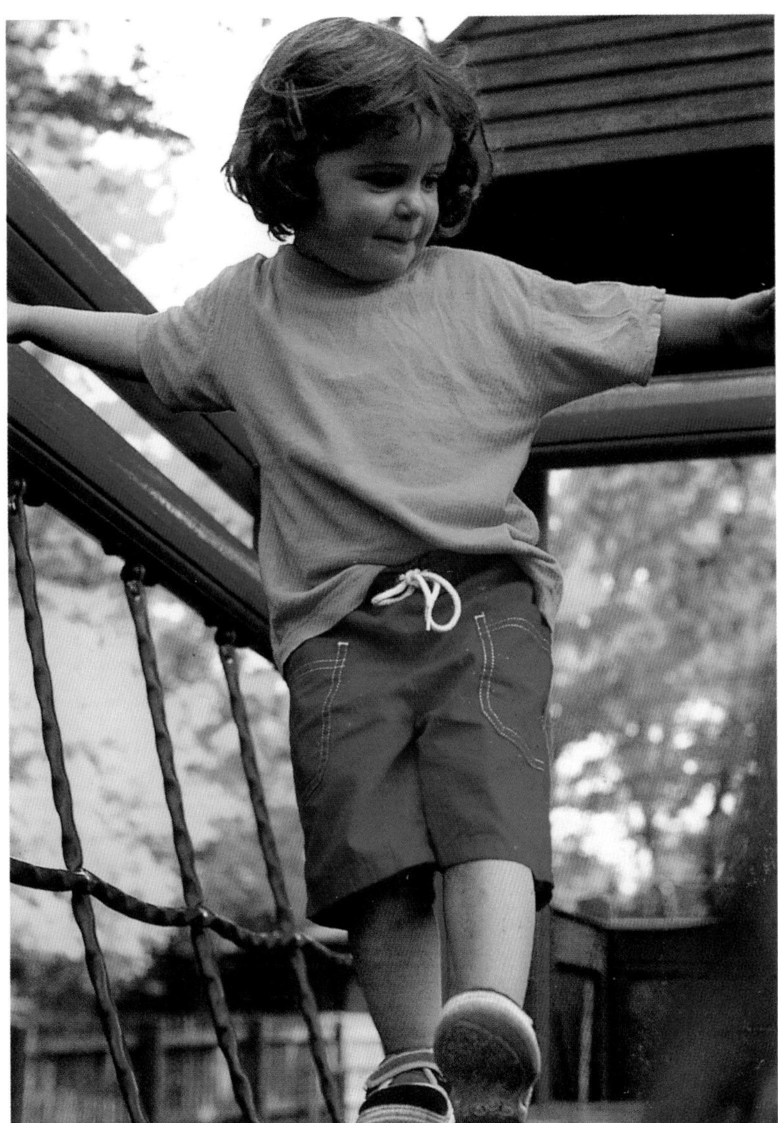

Above: This toddler's relaxed stance and confident stride show her self-belief as she tries a new piece of playground equipment.

So watch her closely when she plays. Give her the freedom to play on her own in order that she feels the success of achievement, yet at the same time be ready to step in if you see disappointment and frustration building up. And if your child does lose her temper or let frustration get the better of her, cuddle her, cheer her up and direct her towards another toy or activity that you know she has already mastered. She can always return to the original activity at a later stage when she is in a more positive frame of mind.

Special Needs

Up to 20 per cent of children have difficulties with their development. Sometimes these difficulties are minor and are easily overcome by extra stimulation for a short period. In a small minority of children, however, the developmental problems are long lasting, causing them to have long-term special needs. For instance, a child could have persistent slow speech development and not be able to talk in phrases when others his own age already use sentences, or perhaps he experiences difficulty when trying to learn new concepts such as colour names. A child with special needs typically requires extra help once he starts school.

Identification

Most major conditions resulting in special needs – such as cerebral palsy, spina bifida, Down's Syndrome and severe learning difficulties – are spotted during a baby's first year. Yet other developmental difficulties may not become apparent until your child is between 2½ and 5 years old, because that is the time when new skills are expected to emerge. Speech and language problems, for example, are often not regarded by professionals as serious until a child is around 3 years old. Hearing difficulties might not be accurately pinpointed until this age as well.

The developmental checklists given throughout this book offer a guide to typical progress made between birth and 5 years. Do remember, however, that if your child does not pass the stages by the suggested times, it does not mean he has special needs. He'll probably be ready to progress to the next skill very soon and just needs a little time to develop his potential.

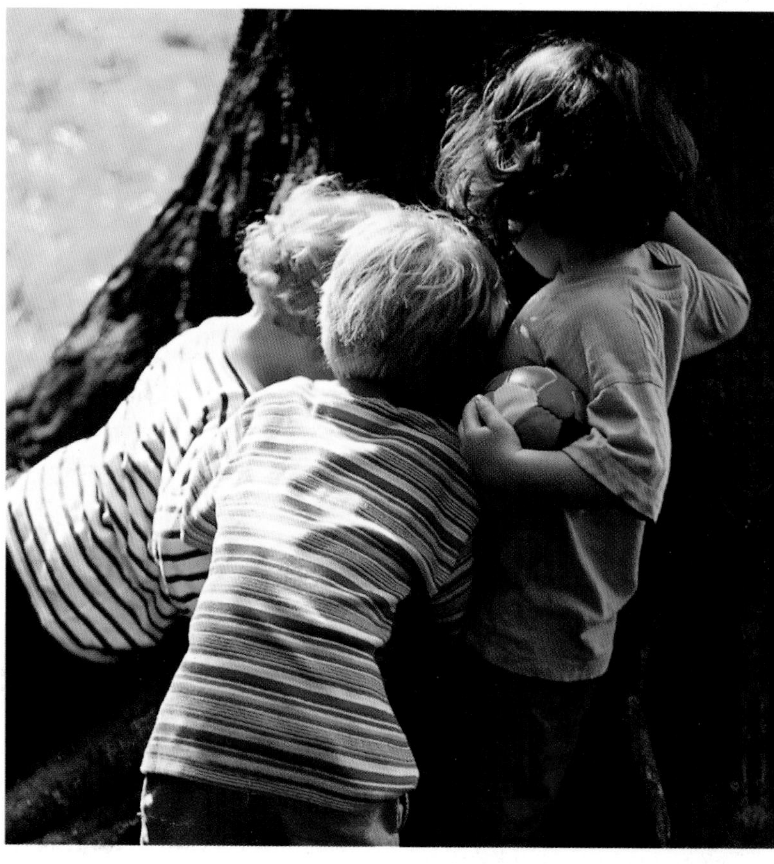

Right: Even though a child with special needs may not progress at the same rate as other children of his age, he will enjoy and learn from social contact.

If you have any doubts at all about your child's development, speak to your family doctor or other health professional. The chances are that you have no need to be worried, but you'll feel reassured by an informed opinion from someone else.

Top Tips

1. Emphasize similarities, not differences. Keep thinking about the similarities between your child and other children, instead of focusing on the differences. Your child has special qualities and he thrives best when you have a positive attitude.

2. Gather information. The more you know about the particular developmental difficulty your child is experiencing, the better. Read about it, talk to the professionals involved with your child, and try to learn from listening to the experiences of other parents, too.

3. Expect change to be slow. He is likely to move forward in very small, steady steps, but he will progress. By all means, expect the most from him and encourage him to try hard, but have expectations that are realistic.

4. Be proud of him. Routine achievements that other children and parents take for granted may require a big effort from your child. So you are entitled to be very proud of him when he, say, learns to count or learns the names of letters.

5. Be prepared to challenge professionals. Although professionals have experience of many children, you are the one who knows your child best of all. Do not be afraid to challenge the views of any professional who is involved with your child.

Your doctor may advise you on suitable specialist assessment for your child. Whatever the nature of the problem, always bear in mind that your child is the same as he was before the assessment. He has not changed in any way as a result of his difficulty being identified – he's still the same wonderful, unique individual with his own range of characteristics and abilities. The challenge facing you is to ensure that he receives stimulation to achieve his maximum potential.

Help for You and Your Child

A child with special needs will be offered a range of services, all aimed at promoting his development. Much depends on the individual child and the nature of his difficulties, but the type of professional support offered could be speech therapy, physiotherapy, a play programme, or even extra nursery classes. Take advantage of any help like this, as it all benefits your child.

In addition, provide lots of stimulation for him at home. Virtually all the activities presented in this book are just as suitable for your child with special needs, though they might need to be adapted occasionally and your child may need extra encouragement. He has special needs, but like any other child he also has the basic need to be loved, valued and cared for, to experience success and to have his abilities stretched to the limit.

It is obviously a source of worry to discover that your child has special needs. Some parents blame themselves even though they are clearly not at fault and may feel guilty. It's helpful to share these feelings with a friend or partner who can lend a sympathetic, understanding ear. Professional counselling may be appropriate for families of children with severe developmental problems.

Above: It is important for all children, whether with special needs or not, to be allowed to progress at their own pace.

Special Needs at School

Every infant classroom includes children with a wide range of abilities. Don't assume, therefore, that all the other children are brilliant and yours is the only one who struggles with some aspects of the curriculum. The best help you can give is to ensure that the school – and the class teacher in particular – has all the necessary information about your child's difficulties and his associated special needs. Additional help given to a child with special needs ensures that he thrives in the classroom despite his difficulties.

Non-verbal Communication

Until your baby develops meaningful spoken language (usually by the end of the first year), she relies on non-verbal communication – including facial expression and body movements, as well as crying – in order to express her feelings and ideas to you. As spoken language gradually becomes her preferred means of communication over the next two years, she also continues to use body language in order to express her feelings and ideas to you. Both forms of communication run side by side. Even once your child can express her views clearly using words, this doesn't diminish the importance of her non-verbal communication – she continues to convey subtle messages about her feelings and attitudes through body language. It's more sophisticated, varied and complex than in earlier years, so you have to work harder in order to interpret it.

Dimensions of Your Child's Non-Verbal Communication

The main features of body language at various stages during the first 5 years are:

- **crying.** This is your child's instinctive way of letting you know that she is unhappy.
- **facial expression.** Your child can convey a whole range of emotions simply by changing the expression on her face. Just by looking at her appearance, you can tell when she is, for instance, happy, sad, contented, uncomfortable, tired, afraid, hurting or angry.
- **arm and hand movements.** When she's relaxed and contented, her hands will probably lie open by her side, fingers spread out. However, clenched fists, for instance, silently tell you that she's tense or raging about something.
- **leg and feet movements.** When she is lying in her cot as a young baby, vigorous leg movements could indicate she is happy and excited, or they could mean she is upset and in pain. When more mobile, she walks away from something she dislikes.

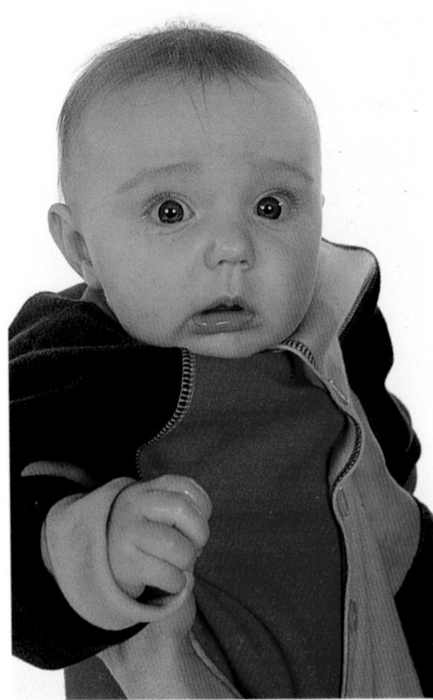

Above: At 5 months this little girl's startled look reveals exactly how she is feeling.

- **posture and head position.** When your toddler stands or sits with slumped shoulders and head hanging down, she is probably troubled, even though she hasn't said a word to you about whatever is worrying her. But shoulders held back and head held high are an indication of self-confidence. As she gets older, observe her head position further: it may, for instance, be nodding or shaking, which indicates whether or not she agrees with you; or it might be pushed forward at a rather menacing angle, which lets you know that she's angry about something.
- **physical contact and body distance**. Snuggling up to you for a warm, cosy cuddle tells you immediately that your child is at ease with you and likes your company. She tells you exactly the opposite when she struggles

furiously in your arms. When she is older, if your child stands close and presses herself against you, the chances are that she feels very insecure, or very afraid, or very angry with you – you'll be able to identify the real emotion by studying other aspects of her body language at the same time, such as hand grip and breathing.

Top Tips

1. Practise interpreting. Make a specific point of noticing her body language, which you can only do by looking at her when she speaks to you. The more you do this, the easier it becomes, and you will gradually become more adept at it.

2. Use her gestures yourself. This is one way to work out the meaning of her non-verbal communication. Breathe the way she breathes, scratch your head the way she does. What do you feel when you do this?

3. Look for groupings. Hand movements, for example, won't tell you as much on their own as they do when combined with facial expression and posture. Look at the whole picture of her body language, not just one element.

4. Act on your assessment. There's no point interpreting her non-verbal communication unless you intend to do something about it. If you think she is upset, give her a cuddle; if you think she is afraid, give her extra reassurance.

5. Watch other children. Look at other children and the ways in which they convey meaning non-verbally. You'll probably see different gestures, ones that are not used by your own child, but this broadens your general understanding of body language.

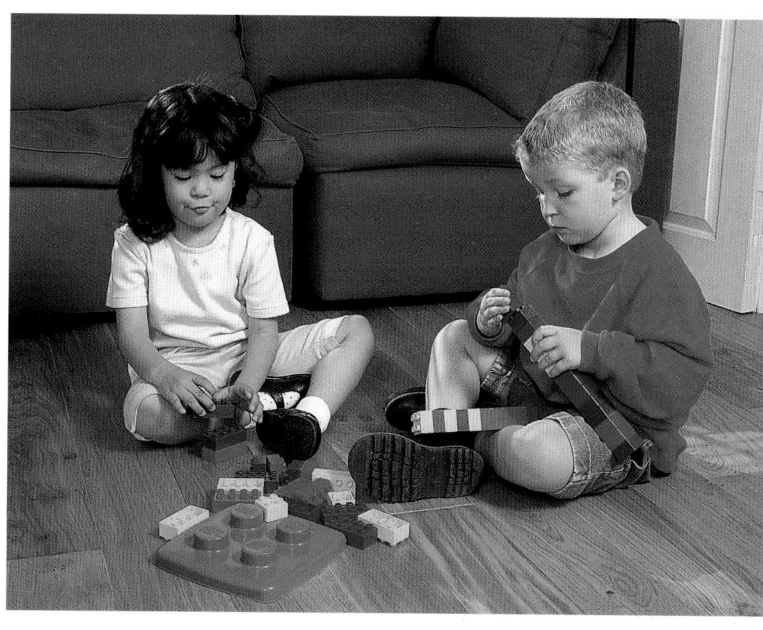

Above: At 3½ this little boy is protecting his bricks with his legs; he regards them as his and signals that they are not for sharing.

It's important to respond to your child's body language as well as to the words she says to you. Non-verbal communication usually happens without any thought behind it and is less controlled, and therefore may indicate more genuine emotions than verbal communication.

Moments may arise when your child tells you one thing using spoken language but something completely different using her body language – like the time your 3-year-old assured you she wasn't upset by the fight with her best friend, but the next minute her facial expression crumpled and she burst into tears.

Other clashes between verbal and non-verbal communication could be more subtle – like the time your 5-year-old insisted she wasn't afraid of visiting the dentist, but you noticed that she nervously rubbed her fingers together in the waiting room. In most instances, non-verbal messages are more genuine than verbal ones precisely because they are less deliberate.

Bear in mind that the same gesture can have a different meaning in different contexts. So look for clusters of gestures, those that involve a combination of facial expression, arm and leg movements, and body movements. You'll get a more accurate picture of her communication when you interpret a cluster of body language rather than a specific gesture on its own.

Gender Differences

There are well-documented developmental differences between boys and girls, both physical and psychological. For instance, girls tend to pass through the major developmental stages earlier than boys, including walking, talking, potty training and self-help skills. Major gender differences in behaviour, clothes and play patterns then emerge during the pre-school years from 3 to 5, by the end of which your child also has fixed views about 'boyness' and 'girlness'. The challenge facing you is to encourage your child to develop as an individual, irrespective of gender – and the best way to achieve this is through awareness of potential gender-related influences.

Facts about Gender

Here are some other facts about gender differences in young children:

- boys tend to be more adventurous than girls; they are more likely to take risks. But this slight tendency may be reinforced by parents who tacitly accept this type of behaviour from boys but discourage it from girls.
- girls are quicker at learning how to cooperate with each other. By the age of 3, they are able to play games quietly together, while boys of the same age are more likely to bicker with each other in that situation.
- parents tend to react differently to boys and girls. For example, they are more likely to tolerate aggressive behaviour from a boy than from a girl – in most families, aggression is discouraged when shown by a girl.

Your baby's awareness of gender differences emerges very early on. At the age of only 3 months, he can tell the difference between a woman's face and a man's face. By 6 months, therefore, your baby differentiates between men and women just by voice tones.

Left and right: Girls and boys naturally split into gender groups. These 3-year-old girls are dancing together while the little boy is standing on the sidelines.

Your child's awareness of gender differences is firmly established by the age of 15 months. By then, if your boy of this age mixes with children wearing unisex clothing he will tend to stay beside the boys (and a girl will tend to stay beside the girls), despite the fact that he probably couldn't say why he does this.

Top Tips

1. Be self-aware. Think about your own attitudes to boys and girls. For instance, be prepared to give as much encouragement to your girl when she shows signs of being adventurous as you would to your boy in the same situation.

2. Encourage individuality. Try not to be limited by society's views on gender. Let your child play with a toy even though it's normally for girls, if that's what he wants. He is entitled to express his individuality through toys, games and clothes.

3. Don't fuss over gender issues. The moment your child realizes that you are concerned about his choice of clothes or toys, he'll probably use this as a means of grabbing your attention. Try to adopt a relaxed approach.

4. Have confidence in your parenting ability. Rely on your instincts, and don't be concerned over what others tell you about the way boys should behave and the way girls should behave. There is no 'should' about it – it really is entirely up to you.

5. Provide a good role model. Since your child is strongly influenced by your own attitudes and behaviour, try to ensure that in your family home chores are not allocated on a gender basis. This broadens his perspective.

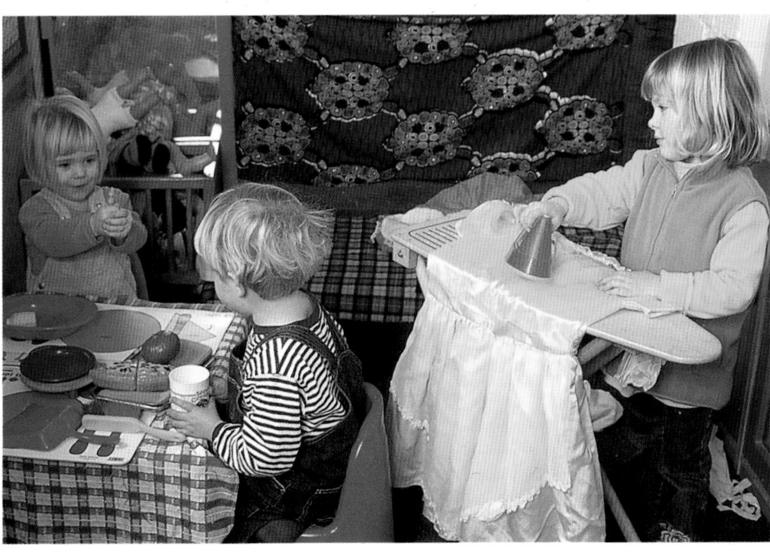

Over the next six months or so, you'll begin to see a pattern of gender preferences for toys emerge, though this may be influenced by you and your values. And by the end of the third year, your child's view of gender usually follows the sex-stereotypes that are found in society as a whole.

Between the ages of 3 and 5 your child may begin to express his gender identity through what he wears and the games he plays. By this time, girls will tend to be more self-reliant and able to express their feelings verbally. Girls will also tend to behave differently as soon as boys appear in the same room, becoming quieter and moving closer together.

Breaking the Barriers

It stands to reason that there is a biological component to gender differences, but it also makes sense to accept that the influence of parents must also play a part. These separate factors interact powerfully to create your child's overall views on gender.

Above: Regardless of gender, all children enjoy copying the everyday tasks that they see adults perform.

Although gender differences and stereotypical views on gender develop early in childhood, the fact is that there is no good reason why a girl should not play football or a boy should not play with a doll. Of course, others might look disapprovingly at such unexpected behaviour, but that is simply an expression of their own fixed views. Your child should be allowed free choice in play and should not be limited by gender barriers.

In fact, breaking these barriers could be good for him. Since play is crucial to your child's development, it stands to reason that the more varied his play experiences, the more likely he is to enhance his development. If he is able to play with toys and activities traditionally associated with girls, he simply broadens his experience. Diversity is good for your growing child, whether girl or boy.

Birth Order and Personality

There is a link between your child's birth order and her subsequent development. In other words, her progress during childhood is to some extent affected by her position within the family (that is, for instance, whether she is your first born, your middle child, an only child or your youngest). Evidence from research confirms that some characteristics – including temperament, learning skills, problem-solving ability, social skills and confidence – are associated with each of the major birth positions. Remember, however, that birth order is only one of the many influences on your child's development, and that its effect can be offset by the way you raise her.

Typical Characteristics

Here are some key findings from psychological research:

• **first-born children tend to be more intelligent than their siblings, and they tend to think clearly and rationally.** They are likely to be the most successful in life, compared to their siblings.

• **second children frequently are less concerned with following rules.** They prefer to go against the grain and to challenge conventional thinking. Your second-born child may push your rules to the limits.

• **youngest children are the most able of all the children in the family to cope with the stresses and strains of everyday life.** Your youngest child is likely to be confident, and to be able to handle problems on her own without seeking help.

• **middle children are usually the most even-tempered, and are adept at solving disputes peacefully.** Your middle child is also likely to be protective towards her older and younger siblings – she may occasionally feel left out of things.

• **only children typically mix well with adults.** The chances are, though, that your only child is self-sufficient, and when she mixes with others she shows good leadership qualities.

How Birth Order Operates

When you think about it for a moment, you'll have no difficulty in working out why these various effects of birth order occur. Take your first-born child, for example. She has you all to herself for the first part of her life – she may be 2 years or older before the next one arrives – and this means you spend all your child-focused time with her.

Left: Once a younger sibling is mobile and can interfere in an older child's activities, tensions may occur and you will need to judge how long they can spend together.

The effort you put into stimulating her development doesn't have to be shared around with any other child. With that level of attention from you, it's hardly surprising that she's so bright, alert and highly motivated.

And the fact that later-born children like to bend the rules and seek the outrageous rather than the traditional is probably down to the fact that they want to be different from their older brother or sister. Your second-born child wants to carve her own destiny; she doesn't want to be in the shadow of her high-achieving older sister and the best way to avoid that trap, as far as she is concerned, is to follow a different path altogether.

The reason youngest children tend to be the most independent is largely due to necessity. There's nothing like living with the prospect of being always at the back of the family queue to sharpen your youngest child's survival skills!

Taking Control

Try to understand how birth order could mould your child's development because that will help you to ensure that she doesn't become unduly affected by this potential influence. Look at your child's life from her point of view and imagine what it must be like to have that particular family position.

Then do what you can to make sure that birth order doesn't have a disproportionate effect on her life. For example, make a specific point of spending time stimulating your second child even though you now have two to look after; don't always assume that your older child should be responsible for her younger siblings when they play together; let your younger child sometimes be the one to choose the television programme the family watches.

Below: Encourage your children to play together and cooperate with each other, including during their daily routine.

Top Tips

1. Take an interest in each of your children's progress. Every child needs to feel valued by their parents. Your youngest child's achievements are special to her, even though you have been through that stage already with her older siblings.

2. Let your child's natural characteristics show through. Your second born, for instance, might be desperate to achieve as good grades at school as her bright older brother. If so, she deserves your support in this.

3. Make turn-taking a hallmark of your family. Older children often think they have an absolute right to come first in the queue every time. But your youngest child can be the one who gets the new toy occasionally.

4. Listen to your children. Take your middle child seriously when she says that her older brother has more freedom and her younger sister is spoiled. Let her express her feelings and show that you are listening.

5. Praise effort as well as achievement. What matters is that each of your children tries their best. Of course you are delighted when one of them has high achievements, but that shouldn't detract from your pleasure at the others' efforts.

Sibling Rivalry

The moment you have your second child – in fact, the moment your first born realizes he has a little brother or sister on the way – you need to consider the possibility of sibling rivalry. Jealousy between children in the same family is so common that most psychologists regard it as normal, and it arises because each of your children has to compete for his own share of parental time and attention. The extent to which sibling rivalry occurs depends on many factors, including the age gap between your children, the techniques you use to help them resolve conflicts and the way in which you relate to them.

About Sibling Rivalry

Jealousy of brothers and sisters can show in a variety of ways. Your 2-year-old could become moody and withdrawn around the time his younger sister is born; or your 4-year-old might complain that his 2-year-old brother constantly takes his toys without asking. But sibling rivalry isn't just confined to the first-born child. There is evidence from psychological research that second-born and third-born children can resent a new baby, even though they are already used to living with others in the family. The youngest child can also be jealous of his older siblings; your 18-month-old toddler might burst into tears when he sees you cuddling his older sister because he wants all your love for himself.

Don't be surprised, however, at the individual differences between your children when it comes to sibling rivalry; one might be very concerned about everything his brother does while another might not show any worry at all.

The age gap between your children can also have an effect. Research shows, for instance, that sibling rivalry tends to be at its highest when the age gap separating children is between 18 months and 2 years, and it tends to be lowest when the age gap is either much smaller or much larger. When the first born child is very young at the birth of the second baby, he will barely notice the new arrival because he is so concerned with

Below: Let your toddler touch her new brother or sister gently as she needs to feel involved in the baby's arrival as much as possible.

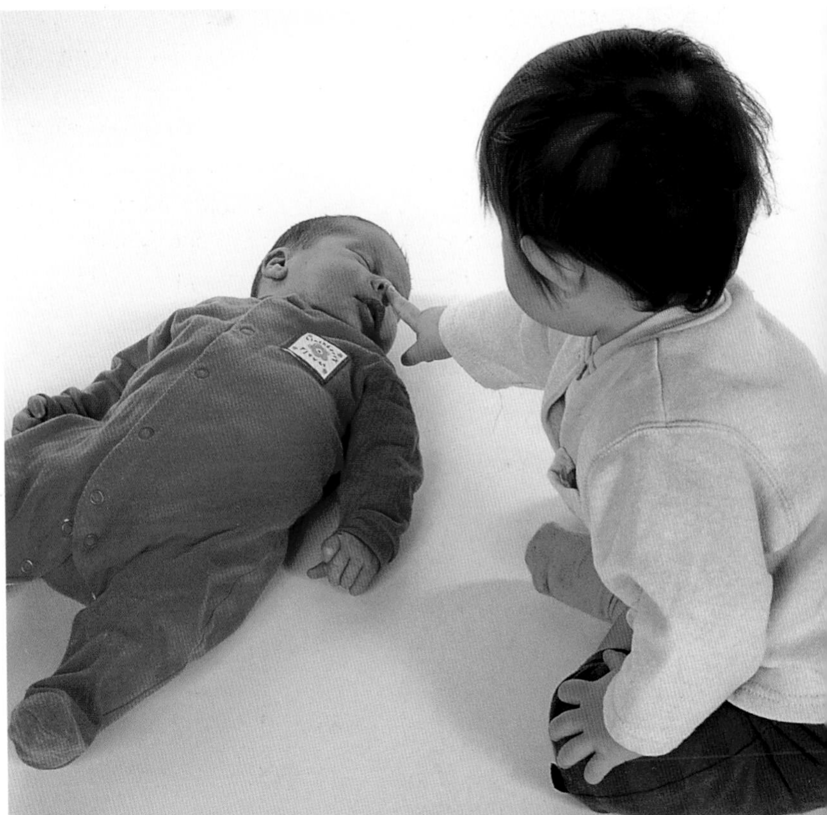

himself; and when the first-born is several years older when the second baby arrives he probably won't feel threatened by the presence of a new baby because he is secure in his relationships and has an established daily routine.

Top Tips

1. Avoid comparing one child to another. There are few things more likely to cause antagonism and resentment of siblings than pointing out to one child that his older brother is, for instance, cleverer, more responsible or more helpful.

2. Deal with rivalry as it arises. If your child shows signs of jealousy towards the new baby, deal with it at the time instead of leaving it for later. Explain that it's normal to be jealous sometimes, but you love them both the same.

3. Buy games that require cooperation. Although there may be a couple of years' age difference between your children, try to find a game that they can play together, such as football or a simple card game. Cooperation in play eases tension.

4. Go on family outings together. Such outings with young children under the age of 5 can be very stressful for everyone concerned – but they can also be great fun. Spending time together doing something enjoyable like this often adds strength to sibling relationships.

5. Praise them when they do play together. If your children get on well with each other, let them know that you are pleased with their behaviour. Tell them that the atmosphere is a lot more pleasant when they don't bicker.

Identity

Sibling rivalry between your children is normal – it is extremely common and is not a sign that there is something wrong. Fortunately, there's lots you can do. Don't simply sit back and let your children sort it out – that just won't happen.

Basic practical techniques such as giving each of your children time with you on their own, making each one feel special, showing an interest in their individual lives and avoiding comparisons all help to reduce potential tensions. Yet you need to do more than that. Bear in mind that sibling rivalry occurs not just because your time, attention and resources are limited, but also because each child has a psychological need to develop their own unique identity.

Of course, you need to encourage your children to share, to have a caring relationship and to take responsibility for each other. Yet they should be allowed to establish themselves as unique individuals.Your children are less likely to resent one another when they feel secure in their own identity.

Sorting Out the Fights

When your children do fight, give them a minute or two before getting involved – you may find that the argument is resolved. If, instead, the bickering just gets worse, intervene calmly, sit each child down in a chair so that they face each other, do your best to settle them until they are both silent, and

Above: It will help a toddler to accept a new baby if you spend time before the birth explaining what is going to happen.

then ask one of the children (the one who wasn't first the last time you did this) to express his point of view. Make sure the other looks and listens while he talks. When he has finished, give your other child a turn to speak. Then help them to reach a resolution of their argument and let them return to play. Eventually your children will be able to settle more and more of their differences without relying on you to sort things out for them.

Grandparents and Carers

Your child's grandparents can play such an important and special role in her life. They'll probably be delighted to have the opportunity to devote their love, attention and resources to her, savouring any chance at all to spend time with their grandchild. This relationship adds to your child's development. Equally, you cannot expect them to act as unpaid childminders, so if you are returning to work you will have to make satisfactory arrangements for childcare. You need to think carefully about the options available. Whatever care arrangement you make, be sure that it is one that suits you and your child and that it is of a high quality – if not, you will both lose out.

Getting Grandparents Involved

Nowadays, grandparents tend to be younger than previously (in their forties or early fifties) and are likely to be fit, active and in full-time employment themselves. They are, therefore, less likely to have as much free time to spend with their grandchild. On the other hand, more children than ever before live with their grandparents (not always with their parents too), and in these instances the grandparents are the ones who look after the child.

Your child loves it when your parents come to visit – her excitement at their arrival is clearly visible. However, she will form a stronger emotional attachment to her grandparents when she also spends time alone with them, when you are not there. It's not that grandparents are inhibited by their own children's presence, just that their grandchild is more likely to give them all her attention. They need to spend time together in order to cement this special connection.

It is best to resolve any points of tension between you and your child's grandparents as soon as they arise. In families, little misunderstandings can easily grow into huge disagreements if they are not addressed properly, and before you know it, you and your child's grandparents may have fallen out. Honest communication is the best way to reduce tension.

Right: Grandparents are often in a position to give a child concentrated love and attention away from the stresses of everyday family life.

The Right Childcare Option

Some parents are lucky enough to have a trusted relative who lives close enough to look after their young child while they are out at work. In cases when this is not possible, the most popular childcare options are nannies, who look after the child in the home, or childminders, who look after one or more extra children in their own home, perhaps alongside their own children. There are also various types of nurseries and crèches, in which several carers look after children in a separate premises, though not all of these cater for under-3s on a full-time basis.

Above: When selecting childcare, talk to other parents who have resumed work to help you weigh up the various options.

When selecting someone to care for your child while you work, there are specific criteria to consider:

- qualifications in childcare and education.
- previous experience in childcare and education.
- references from other parents.
- registration.

Having considered the above factors and having met the potential carer, ask yourself these questions:

- am I at ease with this carer?
- if I was a child, would I want to spend time in the company of this person?
- do the carer's views on child development coincide with mine?
- what will the carer offer my child?
- how does the carer interact with parents?
- what kind of social life will the carer provide?

Your child is a very precious part of your life and she deserves the best care possible while you are elsewhere. Check out the options carefully and thoroughly before making a decision.

Once you are satisfied on all these points – and assuming the hours, location and cost suit you – make the commitment. By approaching the selection meticulously you can return to work knowing that your child is in good hands.

Top Tips

1. Make grandparents welcome in your home. Grandparents won't visit where they are not welcome; they don't want to be thought of as pushy or intrusive. Make your invitations to them very clear so that they know you want them to call.

2. Listen to their advice. Of course you are the parent and they are the grandparents, and decisions about the way your child is cared for rest with you. Yet there is no harm in at least listening to the grandparents' comments.

3. Explain about the carer beforehand. A week before she is due to start with her carer, tell your child about the arrangements you have made. Be ready to answer any questions she might have, and adopt an upbeat attitude about it.

4. Make a visit. A few days before your child is due to start with the carer, arrange for the two of them to meet. This lets your child grow accustomed to the idea. Meeting her carer in advance reassures and excites her.

5. Talk regularly with the carer. It's important that you have a regular report of your child's progress from the carer. That way you can make sure that any minor difficulties are resolved before they turn into major problems.

baby

0–15 months

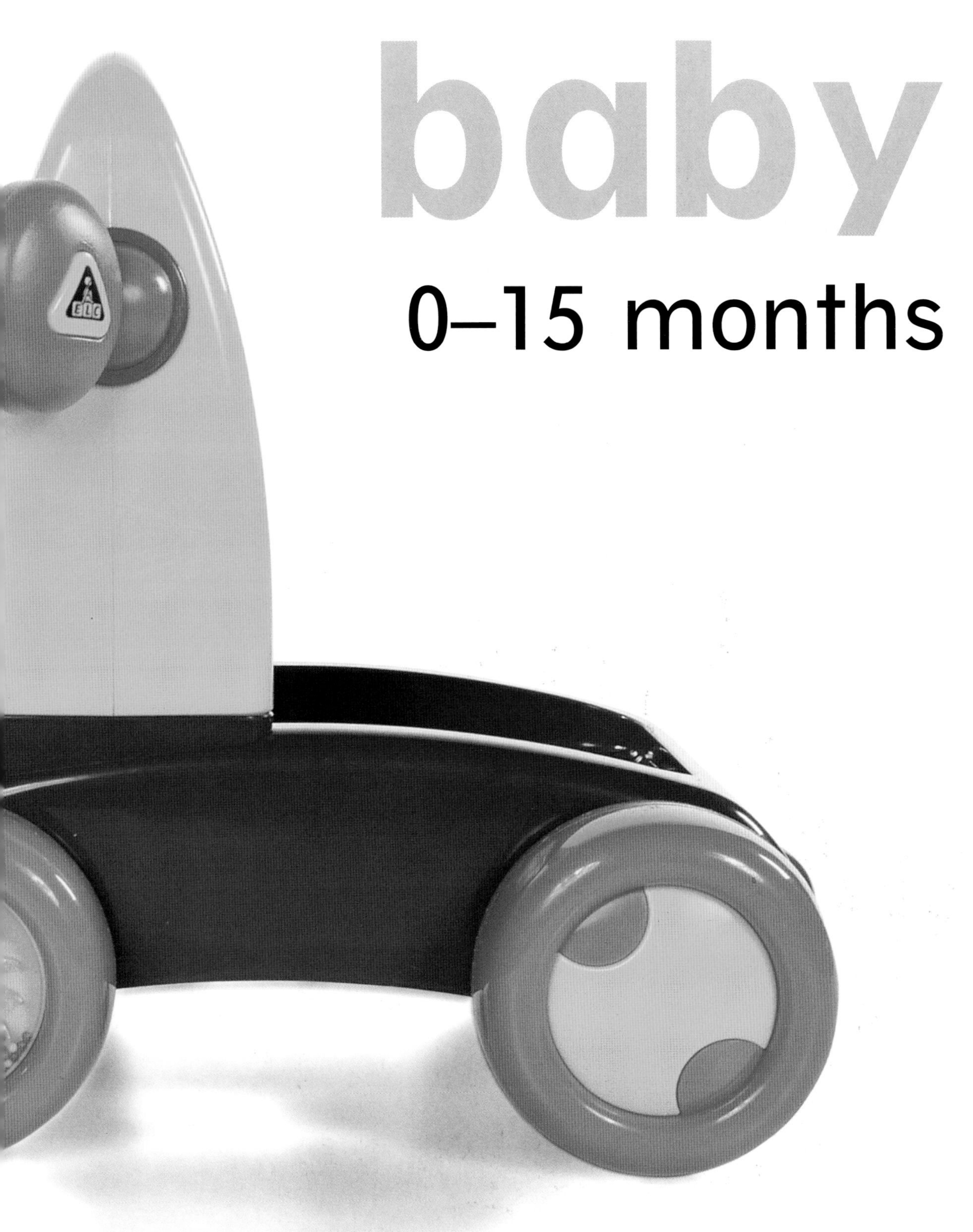

Crying

All babies cry from time to time, though some cry more than others. Crying is your baby's way of telling you that she is troubled about something: for instance, she could be uncomfortable, in pain, cold, hungry, tired, bored or thirsty. It is her natural mode of communication before she can use spoken language. At first all her cries sound the same but you will steadily get to know what each type of cry means. Your baby cries most frequently during the first 3 months, and then her crying tails off. Research has also found that many babies cry without any explicit source of discomfort.

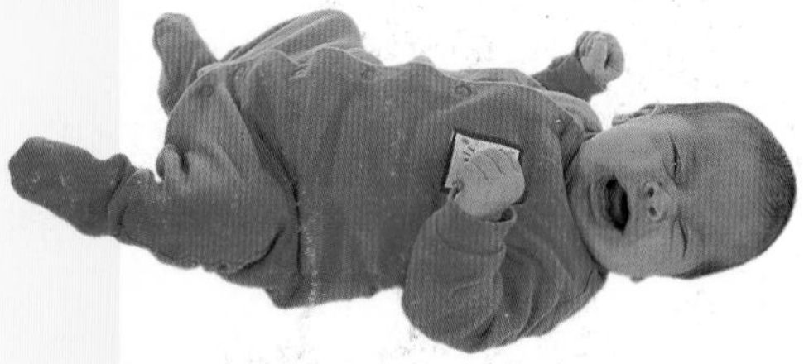

Left: Crying is one way a new-born baby has of communicating her needs.

What to Do

When your young baby cries, always check out the obvious possibilities first. Perhaps she needs a feed, or maybe she is too cold. Also consider the possibility that she simply wants attention, or that she doesn't feel well. Once you have ruled out these options, give her a big reassuring cuddle – that might not stop her crying immediately but it will help. The warmth of loving physical contact, and the vibrations of your beating heart, reassure your sobbing baby. You'll feel happier, too, knowing that you are holding her close to you.

Although you may become agitated by her tears, don't let persistent crying get you down. Between birth and the age of 3 months, she probably cries for around a total of two hours every single day (although not all at once). After that, the amount of crying she does each day is cut by half, though even one hour a day of crying can pull at your nerves. There is absolutely no evidence to support the popular myth that, as babies, boys cry more than girls.

Soothing Techniques

Try the following strategies for settling your crying baby:

- **movement.** The simple act of gently rocking her back and forth in your arms or in her buggy could have a calming effect. Sometimes she will stop crying if you just change her position in the cot.
- **touch.** She may stop if held gently but firmly in a warm bath. Hugging her close to you could have the same effect. If she is really agitated and doesn't want to be lifted, let her lie in her cot while you gently stroke her cheeks and forehead.
- **sounds.** You'll be amazed how your singing soothes her – it's the sound of your voice, your loving tone and the familiar rhythm of the words that she concentrates on. Some babies like a steady background noise such as the sound of a washing machine.
- **amusement.** Sometimes your crying baby can be brought out of her tears by the sight of a toy brought close to her. Her interest in the object makes her momentarily forget her distress and so she suddenly stops crying.

Whatever technique you use with your crying baby, use it consistently before changing to something else. It's very easy to panic when you are faced with a baby who cries regularly for no apparent reason, and to try one thing after another. The problem with that methodology is that your baby can't get used to any of the techniques because you didn't use them for long enough. Persist until you are absolutely sure it has no effect on her tears.

To Lift or Not to Lift

Almost certainly you will be given conflicting advice about comforting a crying baby – one person will tell

Right: By the time your baby is 4 months old you will have a good idea whether his cries mean he is hungry, tired, uncomfortable or just wants your attention.

you to leave her when she cries (otherwise she will learn to cry in order to get your attention) while another person will tell you to cuddle her every time (otherwise she will feel lonely and neglected). Both of these suggestions are too extreme, however.

Top Tips

1. Stay calm. The persistent screaming of a baby can make you want to scream yourself. That would only make your baby more agitated and tearful. Make a big effort to keep control of your temper.

2. Get help. If possible, let another person spend time with your crying baby. This could be your partner, a friend or a relative, as long as it is someone you can trust. You'll be more able to cope after you've had a break.

3. Don't feel guilty. The fact that she cries every night does not mean you are an inadequate parent. As long as you can eliminate the typical sources of distress, then her tears are probably not related to the way you care for her.

4. Take a long-term view. If your baby cries regularly during her first 15 months, reassure yourself that this is a temporary phase. Crying usually eases off markedly soon after the age of 1 year.

5. Have confidence. Your level of confidence in your parenting skills affects the way you handle your baby – she can sense when you are unsure and tense. So tell yourself that your techniques for soothing her will work. Be positive.

Use your judgement when it comes to deciding whether or not to lift your crying baby. Be prepared to be flexible; sometimes it may be appropriate to leave her a little longer while at other times what she needs is a reassuring cuddle. It really is up to you to do what you think is best.

Below: Babies often cry before they go to sleep – as a parent you are best placed to judge whether your baby is in distress or whether her cries will subside into slumber.

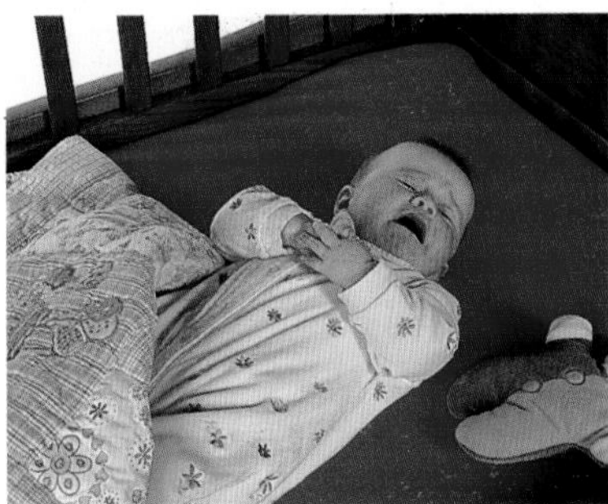

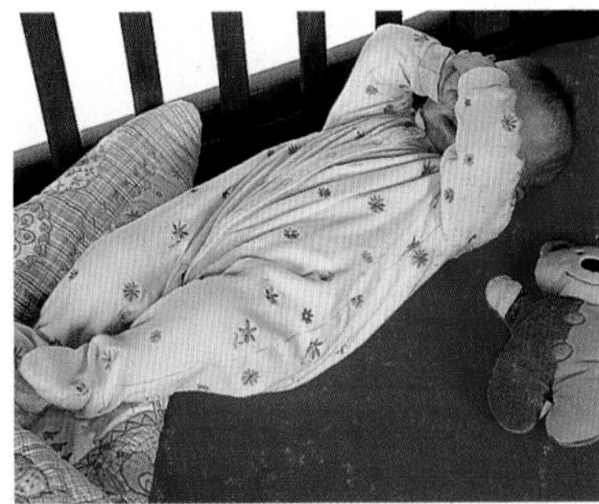

Feeding and Weaning

The decision to either bottle-feed or breast-feed your baby is entirely up to you – choose the method with which you are most comfortable. Whatever method of feeding you select, however, the point will arise when you realize that your baby is still hungry after each feed and that he needs to eat more than milk alone. And that's when weaning begins, when he progresses from just drinking milk to drinking milk and eating solid food. Although your baby's body is telling him and you that he requires solids, he may find the transition difficult because he is so used to his current method of feeding. Take a planned approach to weaning in order to help him through this phase.

Left: Feeding is a natural process.

Early Feeding

Your baby's ability to suck milk from a breast or bottle is instinctive. He is born with two reflexes which make this possible, namely, the sucking reflex (which makes him automatically suck at any object placed in his mouth) and the swallowing reflex (which makes him automatically swallow any fluid in his mouth). Feeding is a completely natural process.

Some parents feed their baby on demand, others do so according to schedule. There are advantages and disadvantages with each method:

- **feeding on demand.** The big plus to this technique is that your baby never really has to go hungry – you simply feed him when you think he is ready to eat. You give your baby control over his feeding schedule. The big minus is that you can end up feeding him many times throughout the day and night, without any lengthy break, and one feed can run on into the next. Feeding on demand, however, is widely recommended by health professionals especially when babies are young.
- **feeding on schedule.** On the positive side, feeding him on a fixed schedule enables you to plan your day (and your baby's) more effectively – it gets him used to managing his basic needs. On the negative side, however, the schedule might mean that he is hungry and distressed in between each feed, and if he isn't satisfied after one feed he has to wait for the next one.

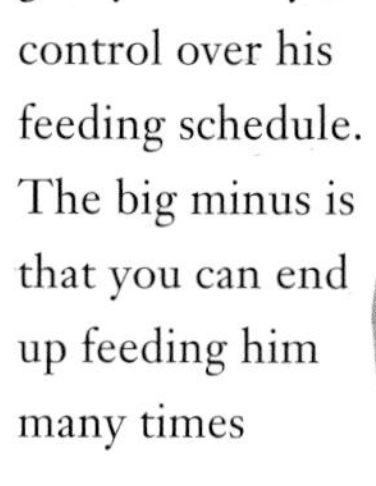

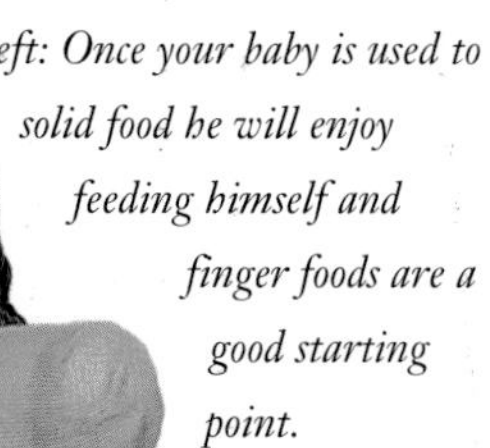

Left: Once your baby is used to solid food he will enjoy feeding himself and finger foods are a good starting point.

As with the type of feeding, the feeding strategy itself is your choice. Select the one with which you are most comfortable. Once you have chosen to feed either on schedule or on demand, try to stick with it rather than changing from one to the other and back again. Have confidence in your feeding strategy. Constantly changing from demand to schedule or vice versa can confuse your growing baby.

Top Tips

1. Relax about feeding. Of course you want your baby to eat enough and of course you are anxious that he should transfer happily from milk alone to solids and milk. But if you are tense during feeding, he'll experience tension, too.

2. Think before you feed. Don't automatically assume that your baby cries between feeds because he is hungry. He could be uncomfortable or bored. Check other possibilities before rushing to organize his next food intake.

3. Make hygiene a priority. Cleanliness is important for both breast- and bottle-feeding. Unfortunately, the combination of your tiredness and the pressure of feeding a hungry baby can quickly result in lapses of hygiene.

4. Persist with weaning. Your baby's initial reaction of distaste to solid food might put you off the whole process. Don't give up so easily. Instead, take a consistent, regular approach when introducing solids into his diet.

5. Encourage your baby. As he takes his first taste of solid foods, let him know that you are delighted with him. Smile at him, talk to him, and give him a big cuddle. This reassures your baby and puts him in a more positive mood.

Weaning

Eventually your baby will reach the stage where he simply can't satisfy his hunger from either breast or formula milk alone. This is because the store of minerals he was born with (for example, iron) begins to run out and he instinctively searches for something more substantial; his body size is also larger and this means he needs more nourishment to keep going.

Above: By 11 months your baby can enjoy a wide range of foods, and drink from a trainer cup.

There's no specific time to wean your baby from milk to solids. If he seems satisfied with milk meals every day then he probably gets all the food intake he requires – certainly he'll not gain any special nutritional benefits from eating solids before the age of 4 months. Let your baby set the pace. If he starts to demand additional feeds or begins to wake more often at night from hunger then he may be ready for solid food. This will probably be between 4 and 6 months.

Do this gradually. To get him used to the new taste, put a tiny amount of solid food on the tip of a clean, plastic baby-sized spoon and put it in his mouth. Remember that your baby is used to tasting only milk and so his face is likely to screw up with displeasure when he first tastes solids. Give him a drink of milk immediately afterwards. Later on during the same feed, let him taste the solid again, then give him some more milk. In this way, his familiarity with the taste of solid food slowly builds up, as does the amount of solids that he takes with his milk during each feed.

Right: At 5 months your baby will still need her food puréed but between 6 and 9 months you can introduce foods with lumpier textures.

Sleeping Patterns

Your baby needs sleep in order to stay bright, but you'll find that she doesn't always sleep precisely when you want her to. In the first few weeks her sleep pattern is irregular, though by the age of 6 to 8 weeks her naps are more predictable and she starts to sleep for longer periods through the night. Some babies resist sleep at all costs, even when they are tired, while others settle down to sleep without any complaint whatsoever. Evidence from psychological surveys confirms that the majority of parents are troubled at some stage because their baby likes to stay awake at night.

Facts about Sleep

Here are some facts about sleeping patterns during your baby's first 15 months:

• your first-born child is more likely than your other children to have sleep difficulties.

• a baby weaned on to solid foods later than normal is more likely to be a poor sleeper (but early weaning can cause health problems).

• gender difference has no effect on sleeping patterns; boys and girls develop a stable sleeping routine at the same rate.

• it is not until around the age of 3 or 4 months that your baby sleeps more during the night than she does during the day.

• during sleep, your baby's pupils decrease, she breathes less air, her heartbeat slows, and she produces urine at a slower rate.

• your baby needs sleep; if she doesn't sleep well she eventually becomes irritable and moody, and will lose interest in both feeding and playing.

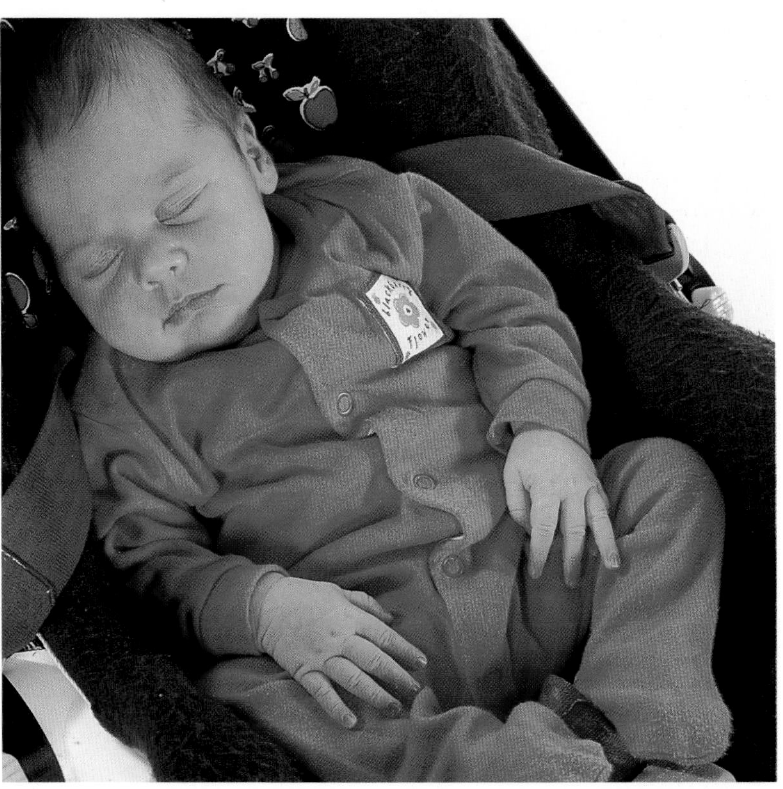

Above: A new-born baby's sleep pattern is unpredictable and will often remain so for the first 3 or 4 months.

During the early months, your baby probably sleeps in total for about 19 hours every day, although she sleeps very lightly and at times you may not even notice that she is no longer awake. On average, she will fall asleep up to eight times per day.

Once she is a year old, however, your baby sleeps for only around 13 hours every day. Your own sleep pattern as an adult is quite different from your baby's, so be prepared for early parenthood to be tiring! But don't worry – her sleeping habits will begin to match yours as her first year progresses.

When She Won't Sleep

Your baby's sleep habits are extremely variable during the first four or five weeks, and you may find she sleeps and wakes according to her own timetable, no matter how hard you try to influence her. If you are sure that she is comfortable, well fed and much loved, then accept her sleeping pattern for what it is because it isn't linked to your management of her.

Top Tips

1. Check the bedroom for comfort. A pleasantly warm room, that is neither too hot nor stuffy, with subdued lighting creates an atmosphere for sleep. Reduce loud background noise if at all possible.

2. Stick to a routine. Your baby responds best to routine. A regular time for a morning or afternoon nap, and her night-time sleep, helps her achieve a stable sleeping pattern.

3. Bath her before bedtime. She'll be soothed and relaxed by a warm bath, a fresh nappy and a clean change of clothes. Once this routine is complete, place her in her cot and read her a story, using a gentle and relaxed voice tone.

4. Time her naps. It is not always possible to keep your baby awake when she decides to have a nap. Yet she may want to stay awake during the evening and night if she had a long sleep just before her last feed of the day.

5. Don't panic. A baby who lies awake during the night seeking parental attention can exhaust and worry you. But if you let anxiety take you over, this will have a negative effect on your baby, making her even less able to fall asleep.

Right: At night try to re-settle your baby without putting on the light or getting her up. Keep the environment as calm and unstimulating as possible to reinforce that night-time is for sleeping.

Yet there are lots of techniques you can try to help your baby sleep. Every baby is different and what works with your best friend's baby might not work with yours. Some babies nod off when rocked gently or in response to soft background noise, others when wrapped snugly in a blanket or stroked gently. Be prepared to use different techniques when trying to soothe your baby to sleep. You'll eventually find a method that suits her – though that same method might not work with her next week.

If your baby aged 3 months or older wakes up during the night, check that she is not in pain and doesn't need a change of nappy, and then try to encourage her to go back to sleep. Don't be tempted to make a big fuss of her as this is effectively a reward for waking up and she is likely to do the same the next night.

Below: If all else fails, most babies will drop off to sleep in the car.

Discipline

The chances are that your baby is wonderful, but there will still be moments when you have to lay down rules for him to follow: for instance, when he grabs the glasses from your face then twists them in his little hands, or when he screams with rage because you won't give him that extra treat. Discipline is not simply about punishment – on the contrary, if punishment forms part of your discipline, it should have a very minor role. Instead discipline encourages your infant to take control of his own behaviour, and to think of others. From this perspective, it can only be good for him.

Above: It may sometimes help to calm an upset child if you pick her up and reinforce your point quietly and firmly.

Understanding

Your baby's understanding of discipline develops gradually during the first 15 months. Certainly, there is absolutely no point in accusing a young baby of being naughty, because until the age of 6 months at the earliest he can't possibly understand rules. Likewise, it makes little sense to warn your 3-month-old baby to stop crying or he will be in serious trouble. True, there are some people who tell you that you have to set rules eventually and that it is better to start the process when your baby is young than to leave it until later when it might be too late. But that's a rather harsh approach. In general, your baby can't begin to grasp the meaning of rules until he has a better grasp of the world around him.

The situation changes, however, during the middle of the first year. Between the ages of 6 and 12 months, he begins to understand when you say the word 'no' to him – you can tell this by his negative reaction. The instant he glares at you and deliberately tries to do something that you have told him not to, that's the time to take discipline seriously. From that moment onwards, the process of establishing rules with him begins.

Right: Uncooperative behaviour can often stem from tiredness or frustration rather than deliberate disobedience.

Remember, however, that discipline with your growing baby is not about coercion. In fact, the source of the word 'discipline' lies in the Latin word meaning 'learning' – in other words, your baby

should learn through discipline. He should not be afraid of it. Try to create a caring atmosphere at home which encourages him to learn rules, rather than a system that tries to force him into good behaviour.

Styles of Discipline

You'll make your own decision about the type of discipline you want with your child. A lot will depend on your attitudes, on your childhood memories of the way your own parents established discipline with you, and the relationship that you and your baby have together. Expect your baby to challenge you occasionally, despite his charming personality. That's a normal part of the learning process. Remind yourself if necessary that he is just the same as every other child, and that you are just as effective as every other parent.

Above: Long-term success is more likely to be achieved with a consistent democratic approach to discipline.

The most common styles of parental discipline are:

• **authoritarian.** This type of parent is extremely inflexible: they set rules which have to be followed on every single occasion, without exception. Their baby must conform at all times and breaches of rules are always punished.

• **democratic.** This type of parent has rules too, but the rules are fair, they are in the baby's best interests and they often involve basic safety. Breaches of rules are usually dealt with firmly, but using explanations rather than punishments.

• **permissive.** This type of parent takes a hands-off approach to discipline, based on the assumption that their baby will learn rules through experience as he grows. There is no punishment because there are no set rules.

Most parents have a mixture of styles with one type dominating. Research suggests that babies and young children don't thrive best in extremes, so authoritarian and permissive styles are rarely the most effective. In providing discipline for your baby, you aim for him to reach the stage of self-discipline in which he doesn't need you to tell him how to behave.

Below: There are times when you need to be very firm to get your message across.

Top Tips

1. Keep calm. Try to stay calm when your baby or toddler breaks the rules. If you lose your temper with him, he'll just become upset too and won't learn anything in that state. Deal with him firmly, but without getting angry.

2. Explain rules to him. You know that, for instance, your 9-month-old baby can't fully understand an explanation about the importance of a particular rule, but say it to him anyway. At some point he will start to grasp its meaning.

3. Avoid physical punishment. Smacking doesn't work as a deterrent and has only a short-term effect. In the long term smacking your toddler makes him frightened of you and may actually make him more defiant and determined.

4. Use positive reinforcement. One of the best ways to encourage your baby or toddler to follow rules is to praise him, cuddle him and generally show approval when he does behave well. That's better than punishment.

5. Be firm but flexible. For every rule there is an exception. Although you should usually stand your ground, there are also times when you can let your toddler misbehave without reprimand, perhaps because he is just over-excited.

Development

First Week Skills

Movement
- Sucks in reflex when a soft object is placed in his mouth.
- Automatically swallows milk on his tongue.
- If startled he will arch his back and throw his arms and legs in the air (Moro reflex).
- Moves legs in a reflex stepping action if his feet are lowered on to a flat surface.
- When his cheek is stroked he turns his head to find the nipple ('rooting' reflex).
- He cannot hold his head without support or raise it from the mattress.
- While sleeping he often lies with arms and legs in the foetal position.

Hand–eye Coordination
- Grasps items placed in his hand in a reflex reaction but is unable to hold on to them.
- Focuses on an object that is roughly 20–25 centimetres from his face.
- Often holds his hand in a fist.
- Blinks in reflex when an object approaches his face quickly.

First Month Skills

Movement
- She can raise her head a couple of centimetres when lying face down.
- Moves her head from side to side but mostly lies with her right cheek on the mattress.
- Screws up her face when she experiences a bitter taste.
- Tries to turn on to her side when lying on her back.
- Kicks her arms and legs in the air.
- When startled will still arch her back and fling out her arms and legs in the Moro reflex action.

Hand–eye Coordination
- Stares at objects about 20–25 centimetres from her face.
- She will follow objects which are moved a few centimetres from side to side.
- Moves her hands without much control but can connect her fist with her mouth.
- She may pull her blanket towards her.
- The grasp reflex is still strong when something is placed in her palm.

Language
- Conveys mood through agitated arm and leg movements, and facial expressions such as mouth twitching or staring.

Second Month Skills

Movement
- Limited control over arms and legs.
- Holds a small object for a few moments.
- Holds his head off the mattress for a couple of seconds.
- Neck control increases and is beginning to support the weight of his head when he is carried.
- Early reflexes (Moro, grasp reflex) are fading.

Hand–eye Coordination
- Hand control begins; his hands are mostly open with fingers becoming more flexible.
- Peers with interest at his fingers.
- The grasp reflex fades.
- He will close his fingers around a small object placed in his palm and move the object towards his face.
- Tries but cannot reach accurately for a small toy.

Language
- Makes a cooing, repetitive vowel sound, when relaxed.
- Uses a couple of identifiable but meaningless sounds.
- Goes quiet when he is lifted up.
- Moves his eyes to look for the source of a noise.
- Watches the gestures and body language of those talking to him.

Third Month Skills

Movement
- Improved head control means she can hold her head off the mattress for longer whether lying on tummy or back.
- Enjoys being held upright, and head and neck movements become more varied.
- Leg movements become quite vigorous when kicking.
- Better at moving her body around her cot.

Hand–eye Coordination
- Watches an object as it moves around the room.
- Stretches out her hand towards an object close to her.
- Grabs a toy firmly when it is placed in her hand.
- Thrusts her hands towards source of food.
- Will stare at pictures in books and try to touch them.
- Peers at objects and tries to put them in her mouth to explore their properties.

Language
- More attentive to distinctive sounds she hears.
- Listening skills have improved and she goes quiet when she hears a small noise.
- Enjoys hearing you sing to her.
- Gurgles and coos in response to sounds,

From Birth to 3 Months

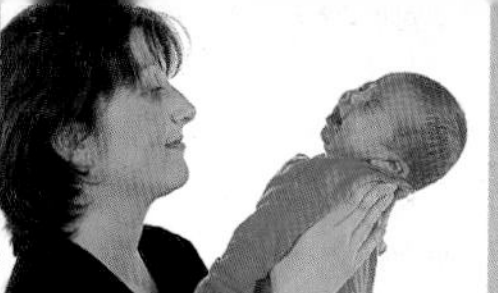

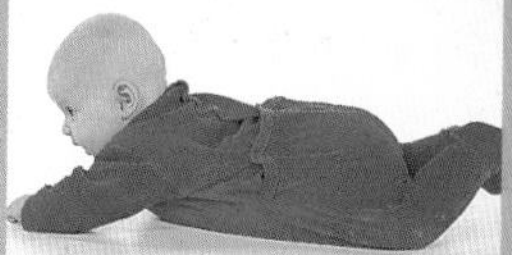

Language
• Tries to look at you when you speak to him.
• Reacts to sounds such as a sudden noise.
• Recognizes his parents' voices and can distinguish high and low pitches.
• Makes eye contact if held close to your face.

Learning
• Is able to focus his attention on you.
• Can distinguish the faces of his parents from those of strangers.
• Recognizes his parents' scent within days.
• Is sensitive to touch and is calmed by being held.
• Has varying periods of alertness but sleeps 80 per cent of the day in about eight naps.

Social and Emotional
• Enjoys your company and responds positively to your voice.
• Stares at your face when it is within 20–25 centimetres of his.
• Cries when he is unhappy or uncomfortable.
• Moves his arms and legs about in excitement.

• She makes sounds when she is happy.
• Responds positively to soothing words.• Uses a wider range of cries and parents can begin to distinguish the difference between cries of hunger, boredom, tiredness, discomfort.

Learning
• Loves to look at anything in her surroundings.
• Will stare for longer at blue and green objects than red ones.
• Is fascinated by objects placed near her.
• She will remember an object that reappears within a few seconds of moving.
• Begins to recognize her parents' voices as distinct from others.
• She is alert for about one in every ten hours.

Social and Emotional
• Enjoys a cuddle and being smiled at.
• Responds positively when you talk and sing to her.
• Makes eye contact.
• Is able to relax at bathtime, kicking and splashing in the water.
• Cries from hunger, thirst, discomfort.
• May mimic if you stick your tongue out at her.

• Is encouraged to repeat sounds when people smile and talk back to him.

Learning
• Can control vision more accurately and peers at an object moved in a pattern in front of him.
• Likes listening to music and is comforted by background sounds such as the washing machine or car engine.
• Becomes excited in anticipation, for example when he sees the bath.
• Begins to coordinate his senses by looking towards sounds.
• Clearly distinguishes between people, voices, tastes.

Social and Emotional
• He has shown you his first smile and is likely to smile if you beam at him.
• Enjoys attention from you and others.
• Stays awake for longer if people interact with him.
• May begin to sleep through the night.
• Begins to amuse himself when left alone by looking around, tracking and batting at objects.
• Feeding becomes a social experience: he looks at you while you feed and talk to him.

will gurgle to herself for several minutes.
• Makes at least two distinct sounds such as 'oooh' and 'aaah'.

Learning
• Sees a link between her hand movement and the toy's reaction, for example a toy might rattle when she moves it.
• Improved memory allows her to anticipate events such as feeding, and reappearance of a person playing peek-a-boo.
• Recognizes familiar music.
• Will imitate actions such as opening and closing mouth, sticking out her tongue.
• Fascinated by her hands, which she fans in front of her face.
• Begins to differentiate family members by sight and the sound of their voice.
• Can tell the difference between a woman's face and a man's face.

Social and Emotional
• More responsive to any adult who shows interest in her.
• Thrives on attention, even tries to attract attention when a parent is near her.
• Has a broad range of facial expressions to express her moods.
• Smiles a lot more readily, and her crying decreases.

Development

Fourth Month Skills

Movement
• Sits in an upright position with support.
• Turns from left side to right, and vice versa, without help.
• May start to roll over from front to back and vice versa.
• Pulls himself around the cot.
• Head doesn't flop around when you hold him.
• Can turn and move his head in all directions.
• Grasping is deliberate and no longer a reflex.

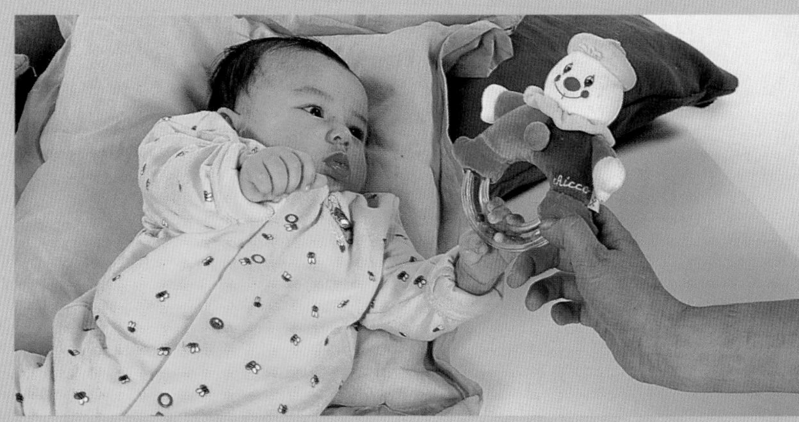

Fifth Month Skills

Movement
• Pushes feet firmly against surfaces such as the bottom of the cot.
• Moves around the floor by rolling and turning her body.
• Can keep her legs in the air and kick them about freely.
• Holds her head confidently when she is supported in an upright position.

Hand–eye Coordination
• Watches you as you move around the room.
• Starts to look for an object that has slipped from her grasp.
• Lifts her hand towards a nearby object and reaches for it more accurately than before.
• Can hold a small toy in her hand.
• Has a firm grip and doesn't like to let go.

Sixth Month Skills

Movement
• Sits up on his own without requiring any support.
• Pushes his head, chest and shoulders off the floor when face down.
• Shows first signs of crawling by drawing one knee to his tummy.
• Makes energetic body movements to propel himself on the floor.
• Becoming more adept at rolling from front to back and back to front.
• Twists and turns in all directions.

Hand–eye Coordination
• Uses both hands in synchrony and can pass objects from one hand to the other.
• Keeps watching a toy that falls from his grip.
• Plays with toys more purposefully instead of just mouthing them.
• Enjoys dropping a toy and picking it up again repeatedly.
• Tries to feed himself by putting food to his mouth with his fingers.
• Grabs hold of the bottle or spoon while having his meal.

Language
• Synchronizes his speech with yours as though in conversation.
• Produces more different vowel and consonant sounds such as f, v, ka, da, ma.
• Laughs when happy and now screams when angry.
• Makes gurgling noises when playing contentedly.
• Begins to react to the mood of music that he hears.

From 4 to 6 Months

Hand–eye Coordination
- Reaches out when you place him in the bath and slaps his hand in the water.
- Tries to grab objects near him.
- Stares at the place from which an object has dropped.
- Waves small toys held in his hand.
- His eyesight has improved and he can focus on near and distant objects as well as an adult can.

Language
- Gives a definite laugh when something entertains or amuses him.
- Makes vocalizations to attract your attention.
- Listens keenly to distinct noises.
- Shows pleasure through excited movement and delighted facial expressions.

Learning
- Recalls how to play with a familiar toy in a particular way.
- Peers at his own reflection in a mirror.
- Looks curiously at objects.
- May have two or three naps in the day, and can be alert for up to an hour at a time.

Social and Emotional
- Uses facial expressions to keep your attention.
- Chuckles spontaneously when he feels happy.
- Enjoys familiar situations such as feeding, bathing, dressing.
- Laughs loudly when he is tickled.
- Relaxes when you sing gently to him.

Language
- Makes an increased range of sounds with consonants such as d, m, b.
- Uses three or four babbling sounds at random, combining vowels and consonants; for example, 'nanana'.
- Vocalizes when you talk to her and may babble to you during gaps in your speaking.
- May imitate your facial expressions and observes your reaction to her.
- Tries to imitate sounds she hears.
- Listens intently and can hear almost as well as an adult.

Learning
- Likes to explore whenever she has the opportunity.
- Focuses well but prefers to look at objects within 1 metre of her.
- Is curious enough to handle any object near to her.
- Detects a sound source accurately by turning towards it.
- Drops one object when another attracts her interest.
- Weaning begins with the introduction of solid foods.

Social and Emotional
- May form an attachment to a cuddly toy or other comforter and likes to have this object close to her when going to sleep.
- Can play on her own for short periods.
- Shows interest in new surroundings.
- Complains when you try to remove a toy from her hand.
- Can be shy in the company of strangers.
- Smiles and vocalizes to attract attention.

Learning
- Recognizes himself in a photograph or mirror.
- Switches his stare from one object to another as though comparing them.
- Holds a toy in each hand without dropping them.
- Actively reaches out for toys that attract his curiosity.
- May start to understand the meaning of 'no'.
- Can differentiate between men and women by their voice tones.

Social and Emotional
- May become anxious in strange company and begin to cry.
- Chuckles in anticipation when you come towards him.
- Playfully holds on to a toy when you try to remove it.
- Coos or stops crying in response to familiar music.
- Turns when he hears his own name.
- Becomes anxious in some situations, for example when he has manoeuvred himself into an awkward position.

Development

Seventh Month Skills

Movement

- Rolls competently from back to front and vice versa.
- More consistently draws one knee towards her tummy in a crawling movement.
- May be able to move along the floor with her tummy raised.
- Takes her own weight when supported under her arms.
- Often brings feet to her mouth to suck on her toes.

Hand–eye Coordination

- Explores toys in new and interesting ways, by rattling, shaking and banging them.
- Pulls at different parts of a toy.
- Has a good firm grasp and is less likely to drop a held object.
- Is more accurate when using her fingers to feed herself.
- Begins to use finger and thumb in a pincer movement.
- Uses her hands to explore her own and other faces.

Eighth Month Skills

Movement

- Has improved leg and foot strength so tries more adventurous balancing.
- Takes his own weight, gripping a chair for support.
- Able to crawl forwards and backwards.
- Pulls himself to standing, although he finds it hard work.

Hand–eye Coordination

- Uses finger and thumb together in a pincer grip.
- Opens and closes hands voluntarily.

Ninth Month Skills

Movement

- Can turn around while crawling.
- Moves her entire body comfortably around the room.
- Makes a stepping response when held under the arms.
- Shows interest in climbing up stairs.

Hand–eye Coordination

- Uses a firm pincer movement to feed herself finger food such as peas and raisins.
- Hand movements are more coordinated: she may be able to build a two-brick tower.
- Brings her hands together deliberately.

From 7 to 9 Months

Language

• More responsive when you talk to her and will respond to comments such as 'Look at that'.

• Likes to hear songs and to babble along with them.

• Seems to understand your different voice tones, such as happy, serious, surprised.

• Has a clear understanding of a firm 'no'.

• Enjoys blowing raspberries.

Learning

• Remembers faces of familiar adults she does not see very frequently, such as a baby-sitter.

• Continues to look for an object that goes out of her vision.

• Knows how to move toys to make them noisy.

• Understands that she can make objects move.

Social and Emotional

• Lets you know when she's miserable or happy.

• Gets annoyed if you stop her from doing something.

• Is very aware of verbal praise and enthusiasm.

• Skilled at attracting attention when she's bored.

• Enjoys the familiarity of routines such as bathtime and bedtime.

• Likes to drop objects when sitting in his high chair.

• Tries to pull at a string attached to a toy.

Language

• Tries to imitate the sounds you make.

• Repeats the same sound over and over, such as syllables of words you use.

• Opens and closes his mouth when he watches you eat, imitating your jaw action.

• Shouts to attract your attention.

Learning

• Looks for a concealed object.

• Facial expression shows he recognizes a toy not seen for a couple of weeks.

• Plays with two or more toys together.

• Curious about new items.

• Discovers new properties in familiar toys: the ball he chews will roll away if pushed.

• Makes an effort to reach objects some distance away.

• Begins to mimic actions such as waving.

• Is alert for longer and may manage with only one nap during the day.

Social and Emotional

• Initiates social contact with other adults.

• Clings to you in crowded places.

• May be shy and reluctant to be picked up by strangers.

• Fascinated by mirror images and family photographs.

• Enjoys being in presence of other babies but does not play cooperatively with them.

• May answer simple questions by facial expression, body movements and sounds.

• Scans her surroundings and attends to small details.

• She may be able to point to an object she wants.

Language

• Uses two-syllable babbles consistently, such as 'dada', 'mama'.

• Says her first word, though it may be unclear.

• Listens when you speak to her and can understand simple instructions such as 'Come here'.

• Will interrupt play to locate the source of a particular sound such as a ringing bell.

• May be able to imitate animal sounds you make to her.

Learning

• Loves to feel the texture of objects.

• Arranges small toys into different patterns and shapes.

• Bangs two small toys together to make sounds.

• Waves her hands in response to someone waving at her.

• Enjoys familiar games and rhymes and laughs at appropriate times.

• Makes connections between actions, for example if she pulls the rug the toy on it will come closer.

Social and Emotional

• Is curious about other babies her own age and may stare or poke at another child.

• Covers her toys if another child approaches.

• Gets upset when she sees that you or other children are upset.

• Looks up at you as she plays on the floor.

• Reacts to an audience and will repeat an action that is applauded.

Development

Tenth Month Skills

Movement

- Likes looking at the world from an upright position.
- Good at crawling and able to propel himself along the floor.
- Climbs up the first step and slides down from it.
- Stands on his own two feet, gripping something for support.

Hand–eye Coordination

- Likes playing with toys that move across the floor.
- Likes to explore boxes, cupboards and drawers.
- Grips two small blocks in one hand.
- Hand preference may begin to show.
- Enjoys rhymes involving hand coordination such as 'Pat-a-Cake'.

Language

- Combines different syllables in one utterance, for example 'ah-leh', 'muh-gah'.
- Stops what he is doing and listens when you say his name.
- Says one or two words consistently, not always clearly.
- Chatters in the rhythm of speech but without meaning.
- Moves his body along to the rhythm of music.

Eleventh Month Skills

Movement

- Moves swiftly around the room, supporting herself with the furniture.
- Slowly and gently lowers herself to the ground, landing with only a small bump.
- May bottom-shuffle around the room.
- May lean towards an object on the floor while standing against support.

Hand–eye Coordination

- Is fascinated by containers and shakes them in the air.
- Tries to pull lids off boxes to find whatever is inside them.
- Shows good coordination of thumb and index finger.
- Turns pages of a book as you sit with her.
- Enjoys putting one thing into another.
- May be able to build a small tower of stacking cups or blocks.

Language

- Listens to you very carefully when you talk to her.
- Follows simple instructions, for instance to give things to you and take them back.
- Occasionally utters single words but much of her language appears meaningless.
- Enjoys playing with musical toys and experimenting with her own sounds to accompany these.
- Will point to an object in a picture book when you say its name.

Twelfth Month Skills

Movement

- Shows the early signs of independent walking.
- More confident climbing up the stairs.
- Has better body control when lowering himself from standing.
- Crawls effectively on his hands and knees.
- May walk if you hold his hands or when he is pushing a wheeled toy.

Hand–eye Coordination

- May use a spoon for stirring rather than banging.
- Spends time building with small wooden blocks.
- Enjoys water games and can pour from containers held in either left or right hand.
- Can slot simple shapes correctly into a shape-sorter.
- May be able to make a mark on paper with a crayon.
- Hand preference is more obvious.

From 10 to 12 Months

Learning

- Tries to imitate your actions.
- Is interested in things which go together, such as cup and saucer and parts of puzzles.
- Listens to and follows basic instructions such as 'Give me the cup'.
- Likes trying to push shapes into a shape-sorter.
- Spends up to a fifth of his waking time staring and observing.

Social and Emotional

- Gives cuddles as well as receiving them.
- Loves interactive games, like peek-a-boo.
- Is happy to spend time amusing himself.
- May be anxious when visiting unfamiliar places.
- Snuggles up to you when you read him a story.
- Has no understanding of the effect of his actions on other children.

Learning

- With better concentration she can focus on an activity for at least a minute.
- Can place a small block in a plastic cup.
- Imitates more of your actions as you move around the house.
- Tries something, then reflects on her actions for a few moments.
- May attempt the next action in a familiar routine that you have begun.

Social and Emotional

- Is frustrated when her wishes are blocked and loses her temper quite easily.
- Swings from positive to negative moods very quickly.
- Stares at other children but does not interact with them.
- Likes to do things that gain your approval.
- Feels very secure with you but anxious with unfamiliar people.

Language

- Has said his first word: 'Dada' is commonly first, or 'bye-bye'.
- May be able to use three or four words to name familiar objects, for example 'dog'.
- Follows basic instructions consistently.
- Has good hearing but loses interest in repetitive sounds.
- Knows the names of other members of the family.

Learning

- Understands basic directions involving one familiar action, for example 'Wave bye-bye'.
- Copies you when you bang two wooden blocks together.
- Is curious about objects which rattle when shaken.
- Makes a good effort to put the pieces of an inset board in place.
- May hesitate when given a new puzzle but will then apply existing knowledge.
- Needs less sleep and may be awake for about 11 hours every day.

Social and Emotional

- Plays any games that involve social interaction between you and him.
- Is very affectionate towards you and others in his family.
- May show temper when he doesn't want to cooperate.
- Has a preference for playing with a child of his own gender when in mixed groups.
- Will play next to another baby his age, but will play actively with an older child.
- Has tremendous belief in his own abilities and is increasingly frustrated when he finds he can't achieve his goals.

Development

Thirteenth Month Skills

Movement

• Spends a lot of time trying to climb up stairs but finds coming down is harder.
• Steadier on her feet, though still topples easily.
• Might rely on a chair or wheeled toy for support when walking.
• Is determined to walk on her own, despite frequent falls.

Hand–eye Coordination

• Uses her hand to indicate to you that she wants a particular object.

Fourteenth Month Skills

Movement

• Totters about the house, tripping over objects on the floor.
• Is able to stop and change direction when walking.
• Insists on walking unaided when outside with you.
• Climbs stairs on all fours or by shifting his bottom one step at a time.
• May still crawl occasionally although he can walk.

Hand–eye Coordination

• Knows how to use crayons appropriately instead of mouthing them.
• Can build a tower of two or three bricks.
• Is more adept at fitting difficult pieces into a shape-sorter.
• Puts his hands and arms up when you bring his jumper towards him.
• May be able to throw a medium-sized, lightweight ball.

Fifteenth Month Skills

Movement

• Moves confidently through the house.
• Has better balance as she walks, keeping her arms closer to her sides.
• Can stop when walking and bend to pick up an object from the floor.
• Attempts to stand still and kick a ball if encouraged to do so – but she will probably miss or fall backwards, though she still enjoys trying.
• Masters the challenge of climbing in and out of her high chair.
• May be able to kneel on a chair while at a table.

From 13 to 15 Months

- Enjoys making marks on paper with crayons and pencils.
- Hits pegs into a peg board with a hammer.
- Plays with a toy telephone, putting the receiver on and off it.

Language

- Recognizes her own name but probably cannot say it.
- Says five or six words in the appropriate context.
- Shouts out at you when she doesn't like what you are doing.
- Makes tuneful sounds when hearing familiar music.

Learning

- Will try to use a spoon to feed herself.
- Has fun pointing to pictures of familiar objects in books.
- Will concentrate for longer periods on puzzle toys.
- Interested in video tapes and television programmes.
- Begins to show imagination in play.

Social and Emotional

- Innate desire to become independent begins to show, for example she tries to help when being dressed.
- Is less inclined to go for an afternoon nap.
- Will give you a big cuddle when she is happy.
- Holds a cup and drinks from it, with some help.
- May pass toys to another child.
- Plays alongside rather than with a child of her age.

Language

- Tries to sing along with you.
- Begins to learn the names of body parts.
- Listens avidly to other children when they talk to each other.
- Enjoys making sounds with musical instruments.
- His babbling has all the rhythm of language.
- Is fascinated by the language use of other children the same age.

Learning

- Can complete a simple but lengthy task with encouragement.
- Can look away from what he is doing, then go back to it.
- Is keen to explore the whole house but is oblivious to danger.
- Has a serious facial expression while you read him a story.
- Is developing the use of imagination in play, for example with pretend tea parties.

Social and Emotional

- Is more socially confident yet is sometimes terrified of strangers.
- Has increased sense of self and awareness that he is an individual with his own likes and dislikes.
- Recognizes that his name is different to other people's.
- May develop a minor fear, eg of animals.
- Loves to be independent and to cope without your help.
- May have a temporary phase of attachment to one parent in particular.

Hand–eye Coordination

- Is able to hold an item in each hand at the same time.
- Has a firm hand grip and rarely drops objects accidentally.
- Likes playing with moving objects, watching them as they roll.
- Enjoys fitting pieces into an inset board puzzle.

Language

- Can say five or six single words.
- Understands many more words than she can say.
- Has great fun when you recite familiar rhymes and songs to her.
- Can follow a broader range of basic instructions: 'Let go of the toy', 'Take the biscuit'.

Learning

- Concentrates well until she completes an activity.
- Enjoys pretend play, either alone or with you.
- Will try to tidy her toys if instructed to do so.
- Enjoys sand and water play.

Social and Emotional

- Is very determined to get her own way.
- Has a tantrum when her frustrations become too much.
- Wants to feed herself though can't manage entirely on her own.
- Is keen to explore everything whether it is safe or not.
- Begins to show signs of jealousy when you give attention to others.
- Loves the social nature of a family meal.
- Can begin to learn social skills such as greeting another person by saying 'hello'.

Movement

The Development of Movement

Your baby's transformation from an infant who has almost no control over her head, hand, leg and body movements at birth into someone who has probably taken her first step by the fifteenth month is one of the most visible signs of development you will ever see. The enormous progress in physical maturity that occurs during this very short period in your baby's life is visibly striking.

Above: A new-born baby has surprising strength, though her movements are random.

What is even more amazing is that some of the remarkable changes in your baby's control over her movements seem to occur spontaneously, without any prompting, alongside her physical and neurological maturation. Take that all-important first step. No matter what you do to encourage her to walk early she won't be able to do it until she is in a natural state of physical readiness; walking is one of those movement skills that you can't really hurry along. No matter how much walking practice you give a baby who is, say, 4 months old, she won't be able to coordinate her leg and body movements at that age to enable her to walk.

In contrast to the skill of walking, there is evidence that practice in other aspects of movement does have an impact. A child who is allowed lots of opportunities to crawl will probably be better at crawling than a child who is denied this form of activity. The same applies to moving up and down stairs. Perhaps the best strategy to take when it comes to encouraging your infant's movement is to remember that the pace of her physical and neurological development has a big impact and that this will limit the effect of practice in some areas.

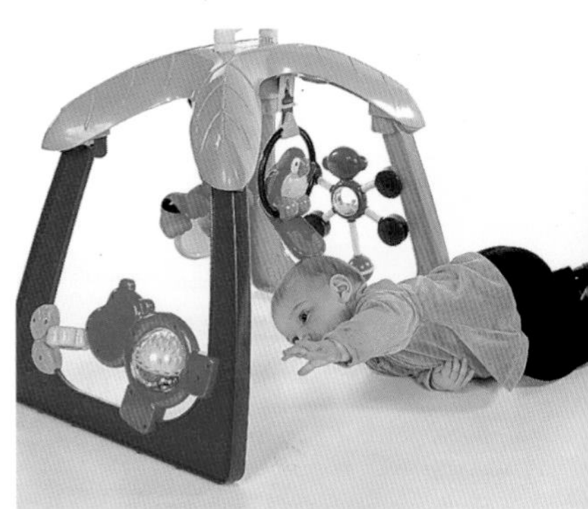

Above: At 6 months your baby may be able to shuffle or roll to reach what he wants.

Of course, the blueprint for walking is present almost at birth. If you hold your new-born baby firmly under her arms (while gently supporting her head with your thumbs) and lower the soles of her feet on to a flat surface, she will automatically move

Right: Once your baby can support her upper body on her arms she is part of the way towards crawling.

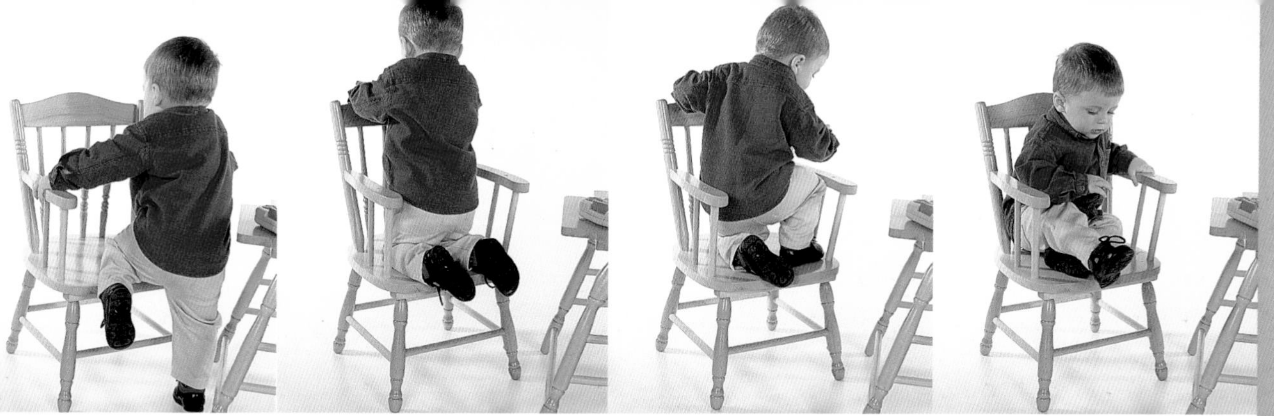

her legs in a reflex stepping action. This looks as though she is walking but she is not. Yet within the next 12 months, this innate, involuntary reaction becomes part of her deliberately controlled movements.

Direction of Control

Every baby is different in terms of rates of movement development, but in general, your baby's ability to gain control over her body movements in the first 15 months follows two distinct directions:

- **from the head down.** She establishes control at the top of her body before lower down. For instance, she will be able to hold her head up independently before her spine is strong enough for her to sit up on her own; and she will sit upright long before she can walk.
- **from the chest out.** Your baby gains control over the middle of her body before her hands and feet. For instance, she can raise her chest off the floor before she can reach out accurately with her hands; and she will be able to pick up something with her fingers before she can kick a ball with her toes.

Scientific research suggests that these two directions in movement development match the sequence of your baby's brain development. In other words, the part of the brain that is responsible for her head and chest control grows faster than the part of the brain in charge of her arm and leg movements – hence the two-directional pattern in movement progress.

It's also interesting when you consider that movement control develops in a sequence which builds up logically towards the ability to walk. An infant who didn't have, say, control over her head and who couldn't hold it upright would not be able to walk even if her legs were strong enough. In the same way, your baby needs chest and hip control in order to balance while walking or she would topple over. So she's learning to walk long before she stands on her own two feet. In fact, the moment your new-born baby tries to lift her head to see what's going on around her, she has started a developmental sequence which will eventually lead to your buying her her first pair of shoes!

Her Own Way

Another amazing aspect of movement in babies is that although the majority of them pass their physical milestones at roughly the same age (for instance, most can sit up on their own by the age of 6 months), there is huge variation in the way that each stage is achieved.

Above: At 15 months this little boy has mastered the complex manoeuvre of sitting on a chair.

Crawling and walking are good examples of this. Your baby might be one of those who likes to crawl with her hands and knees touching the floor, while your best friend's infant of the same age might prefer to crawl with her bottom high in the air and her knees raised off the ground. But they are both crawling, in their own distinctive ways. There are even some babies who dislike crawling so much that they show no interest in it, and make a smooth transition from sitting to walking with almost no crawling in between. The same applies with walking. Your baby might have gone from sitting up, to crawling, to standing, to walking. Yet there are other infants who have an intermediate stage of bottom-shuffling in which they sit upright on the floor, gently raising and dropping their bottoms as they propel themselves along.

Allow your baby to find her own way of expressing her innate desire to gain control over her body movements. Don't be alarmed if she does not follow the exact same pattern of movement development as others her own age. They usually all get there in the end, anyway.

Stimulating Movement: Birth to 3 Months

Although your young baby has an inborn need to explore his surroundings, control over his body movement during these early months is extremely limited. At birth, for instance, he cannot hold his head without support and he can't roll from his back to his side or tummy. That doesn't stop him from trying, however. You'll see many instances of your new baby straining unsuccessfully to move himself into a new position.

SUBTLE CHANGES

Progress in head and body movement is visible if you know what to look for. When your baby is a few weeks old, his head can move to the left or right, but it will mostly be turned towards the right with his right cheek resting on the surface of the cot. That's a perfectly normal reflex action.

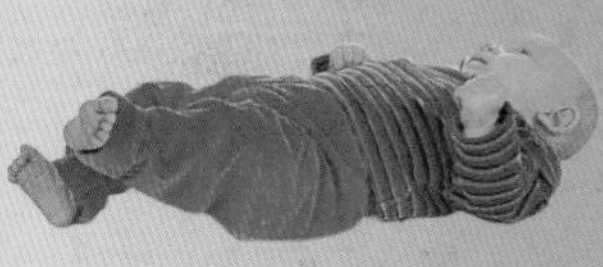

As he nears the age of 3 months, however, he spends much more time with the back of his head flat against the cot surface. This increased control lets him have more choice about where he can look. The strength of these early reflexes diminish, and learned movement takes over.

Suitable Suggestions

The most relaxed position for your young baby when lying in his cot is to be on his back. This provides constant opportunities for him to move his legs in the air and to flap his arms freely. In time, these limb movements will become stronger and more coordinated but for the moment he needs time to be allowed to lie on the mattress, without being weighed down by heavy cot blankets. As long as the room is comfortable and he is warmly dressed he will enjoy these unconstrained movements.

Of course, if his surroundings stimulate his interest, he will make more of an effort to move from a static position. That's why you should place toys within his line of vision so that he will be encouraged to shift himself

Below: Babies love being propped up, but ensure there is adequate support for head, neck and back.

towards them. Even a cot mobile hanging directly above him acts as an incentive to move. Babies are easily bored so do your best to vary the play items in his cot – a change of scenery keeps his interest strong. His neck muscles are under-developed, which means that he doesn't have much control over his head and chest movements, but he will manage somehow to move in order to see attractive toys.

As well as lying on his back, your baby likes to be placed face down on the mattress or on a clean floor. When he is in this position, his natural inquisitiveness makes him want to lift his head up. Until

Above: When a new-born baby is held upright with a foot on a flat surface she will automatically lift her leg and put the other down as if walking. This reflex disappears after about six weeks.

the age of 5 or 6 weeks, he won't be able to do this exercise even for a couple of seconds, but from that time onwards his maturing neck muscles allow him to raise his head from the resting position for a moment or two. It's a bit like the way an unfit adult might do press-ups! This is good practice for him. As well as making his day more stimulating, it's another opportunity to develop those very basic movements.

Once your baby is a few months old, another suitable activity is to hold him upright, although you will need to have a firm grip on him because his back can't take the strain on its own. He loves seeing the world this way and the moment he is propped up, perhaps as you hold him on your knee, his head and neck movements become much more varied and active.

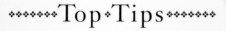

Top Tips

1. Let him kick as much as he wants when you change his nappy. He revels in the sense of freedom from constraint, and may suddenly kick his legs in excitement. Keep him stable on the changing mat while he kicks furiously.

2. Lie on the floor with him. The fact is that he adores you and wants you to be with him whenever possible. When you are close to him, he tries to look at you or to move towards you.

3. For safety reasons, keep a close eye on him if he is not in his cot. You'd be amazed how much a young baby can inch his way from one position to another. Despite his poor coordination, he will somehow manage to move.

4. Place toys on one side of his cot today and then on another side tomorrow. Altering positions in this way encourages your baby to use different body muscles when reaching for them.

5. Gradually reduce the amount of support you give his head when lifting him to an upright position. Use your judgement. You certainly shouldn't let his head lag behind but neither should you do the job when his muscles can do it.

Q&A

Q Why do my baby's leg and arm movements become more agitated when he is upset?

A This is your baby's way of telling you that he's miserable. He can't express his distress through words, so he uses non-verbal communication to let you know what he is feeling. His tears accompanied by rapid limb movements give you an unmistakable message that he is unhappy.

Q Could I damage his legs by bending and stretching them to strengthen them?

A As long as you do this gently, without causing any discomfort, his leg muscles will probably benefit from this exercise. However, don't force him. If you make the leg movements very soft, and you talk happily to your baby as you do so, then he will probably have a great time.

Toys: plastic blocks, rattles that can be held in a small hand, cot activity centre, floor-based multi-gym

Stimulating Movement: 4 to 6 Months

Most of the early reflexes governing movement have gone and your baby now exercises a lot more control over her arms, legs, chest and head. Probably the most significant change in movement in this period is your growing baby's ability to sit up with a decreasing amount of support. And by the age of 6 months, it's a case of 'Look at me – I can do it on my own!'

I Can Roll

When your baby is around 4 months old, you'll notice that she turns from one side to the other. One moment she was side-on to the left, yet a few seconds later she faces the right. This is a remarkable feat of coordination, involving head, neck, chest, hips, arms and legs. She can change her position without waiting for you, which provides a huge boost to her independence.

Similarly, your growing infant can turn from her back to her tummy completely on her own. As well as giving her more ways to explore and discover, this demonstration of body strength proves that she is getting ready for sitting up, crawling and walking.

Suitable Suggestions

The tendency for your infant's head to lag behind the rest of her body disappears gradually, enabling her to experience movement without losing control over her head altogether. This makes her feel more secure and consequently she just loves those games in which you sit her on your knees facing you while you gently bounce her up and down. Of course she totters about and she needs you to stop her from falling over, but she thinks this activity is good fun – she'll chuckle loudly with delight!

Other movement games are suitable too, such as softly swinging her from side to side while holding her firmly. You'll notice her balance steadily improving between the

Right: Once your baby can sit independently a more varied range of toys and activities are available to him.

Above: Putting a favourite toy just out of reach will encourage your baby to push himself forward.

fourth and sixth month; and her confidence with movement also builds up as a result.

Top Tips

1. Tickle her under her arms and along her body. Her little legs and arms will show a flurry of activity when you gently tickle her. Don't overdo it or she will burst out crying with too much excitement.

2. When she is face down, put her favourite toys just out of her reach. Now that she knows she can move towards them, she will try very hard to reach them. Avoid placing the toys too far away or she will give up trying to get them.

3. Move around the room as you talk to her. When she is in a steady sitting position, talk to her. After a few seconds, gradually walk to the other side of the room so that she turns her head to follow. This enhances her head control and balance.

4. Don't tuck her up too tightly at night. She needs room to move while lying in her cot waiting to go to sleep. Covers should be resting on her, rather than tightly tucked in under the mattress. Like you, she wants freedom to change position.

5. Give her small toys to hold while she sits on your lap. Your child's balance skills will improve even more when she concentrates on another activity at the same time. You'll find that while gripping a toy she can sit without toppling.

Easy exercises to strengthen her back, chest and neck muscles can play a bigger part in her daily activities now, though always be careful not to push against her if she resists. Try this: let your infant lie stretched out on the floor and kneel at her feet, so that she can focus on your face without difficulty, then engage her attention and put your index fingers out towards her hands so that she can grip them; once you feel her hands locked around your fingers, raise them a few centimetres from the ground.

By the age of 4 or 5 months your baby will probably be able to roll over from her stomach to her back – this is easier than the other way round because she is able to use her arms in a pushing action in order to start the movement off.

Your infant still needs regular periods of lying face down. It's only in that position that she can push herself against the floor, strengthening her upper torso. By the time she's 6 months old, she can raise her head, shoulders and chest off the floor, so that only her hips and legs remain in contact with the surface. And if your beaming face is there to greet her, she tries even harder to achieve this target. Don't forget her leg muscles. She may be able to bear her own weight on her feet if you hold her securely under her arms while she is in the standing position. Practise this with her.

Q&A

Q Why does my 5-month-old usually keep her legs off the cot mattress whereas before she used to rest them on it?

A This is just the effect of the growth in her leg muscles, and the fact that she's no longer as passive. Keeping her legs in the air like this is more comfortable for her and she can move around more freely without knocking anything.

Q Should I restrain her when she wriggles around during bathtime?

A Your first priority must always be to keep her safe. But if you hold her steady, you can just let her wriggle and splash about. The sensation of warm water against her legs, coupled with the noise of splashing, excites her. Allow an extra few minutes for her bathing routine so that she has this special time to practise her movement skills.

Toys: soft play-mat, soft story book, soft building blocks, bath toys, cushions, wooden shapes, door bouncer

Stimulating Movement: 7 to 9 Months

Having gained more control over his upper body movement so that he sits up easily, it is the turn of your child's lower body to become more responsive in this next three months. As the early stages of crawling emerge, and perhaps also his first intentional stepping response, he finds totally new ways of moving himself around the house. This opens up new play opportunities and further sharpens his desire to investigate and explore.

Frustration

Your infant's ambition outstrips his ability when it comes to movement. In other words, he has lofty aims and is none too pleased when reality takes over and he discovers that he can't reach the soft toy that is a metre away. Tears of frustration flow freely at this age.

Calm him, reassure him, and be prepared to bring the object of his despair over to him. The next time you hear his moans of frustration, try to settle him before he reaches explosion point. He is less likely to become agitated and give up when you are there with him. You need to find a balance between encouraging him to move towards the source of interest and causing him too much frustration.

Suitable Suggestions

From the age of 6 months onwards, help your child to practise the sitting and balancing ability he has already acquired. For instance, when he is in that position, place a wide range of attractive toys around him, some on either side, and some outside his range of reach. If allowed to play on his own, he will grab one toy, then put it down to pick up a different toy on his other side. Each time he reaches, grabs, places, turns and stretches, your infant improves his upper body movements as well as his balance.

And it's in this phase that crawling begins. Bear in mind that there are several stages in the development of crawling – he doesn't go from having no crawling skills one day to confidently crawling the next. In fact, one psychological study confirmed that there are up to 14 different progressions that your child has to go through before he can crawl competently! This means he needs encouragement and practice.

Don't be impatient with him because, say, he doesn't yet lift his tummy off the floor when crawling: his crawling movements are simply not mature enough yet. He will improve his crawling ability spontaneously, and there are no specific exercises you should do to hurry the process along. However, make sure he has plenty of opportunities to lie face down on the floor so that he can use his crawling ability and extend it through practice. You will also find that around the seventh month your baby is competent at rolling from his back to his tummy, as well as the other way

Above: This 7-month-old is starting to make crawling motions though she cannot yet raise her whole body off the floor.

round. This makes life much more interesting for him!

Although your 9-month-old won't have achieved the ability to walk on his own, he will probably have the physical skills and the self-confidence to support himself once he stands up. Every day, put your child in a standing position a couple of times and let him take his own weight by gripping on to a low table or solid, heavy chair that won't topple over.

Bear in mind that he will probably fall over if he lets go, so try not to distract

Above: Supporting your child standing up helps build up the muscle strength and balance she needs for walking.

his attention while he stands. Be ready to catch him should he accidentally lose his grip and balance, reassure him and then return him to the previous position. Give him lots of cuddles and praise when he manages this particular challenge.

Below: At 9 months this baby is a confident crawler.

Top Tips

1. Allow him time in the baby walker. He will be happy to sit in a baby walker, although he may not be able to propel it in the desired direction at this stage. If he appears to lean too far over to one side, sit him back in the centre once again.

2. Tickle his bare feet. The soles of his feet are very sensitive to a tickling touch. Keep your hand still as you tickle him, so that he can choose whether to draw his legs away or to keep them in that position.

3. Give him simple directions or questions. For instance, when he is sitting surrounded by his toys, ask him 'Where is teddy?' He may turn round to look for it, and try to reach it.

4. Play 'facing' games. Sit on the floor facing your baby and pass toys to him. Once he is into the rhythm of this passing game, hold the toy a few centimetres from the normal passing point so that he must lean his body and arms to get it.

5. 'Accidentally' drop toys. A good way of encouraging him to use his full chest and hip control is to make as though you intend to hand him a toy but then deliberately let it slip from your grasp. Let him pick it up from where it has fallen.

Q&A

Q My baby is 9 months old. I'm worried he'll hurt himself one of these days when he tries to pull himself up. How can I keep him safe?

A The only way he can learn new movement skills is by tackling new challenges and there is always a minor risk of injury in that situation. Instead of restricting his movements, stay close to him when he manoeuvres – that way you are better placed to prevent a potential accident.

Q While other infants seem energetic and active throughout the day, mine just sits there most of the time. Is there something wrong with him?

A His lack of activity is probably more to do with his personality than lack of ability. As long as he is interested in toys and is alert when you talk to him, you have nothing to worry about. He'll probably be one of those children who goes from sitting to walking, without the crawling stage in between.

Toys: baby walker, rattles that are easy to grip, floor-based activity centre, soft ball, small toy on wheels, solid ride-on toy

Stimulating Movement: 10 to 12 Months

It's as though your baby's improved balance and body movements, coupled with her increased chest, hips and leg strength, have all been aiming towards this last section of the first year, because it is in this phase that she might actually take her first independent steps. And even if she hasn't started walking by the age of 12 months, she will almost certainly be well on the way to that achievement.

Safety Rules

With your infant at a more mobile stage, she is potentially at greater risk of injury in the home. Active children of this age have an amazing capacity to jam themselves into small, fascinating little places that you wouldn't have expected them to notice, let alone access. And stairs have a particular lure for crawling infants who are desperate to see what lies at the top.

Try to make your home child-proof. Aside from placing a safety gate at the top and bottom of the staircase, put child-proof locks on every low cupboard in your kitchen and bathroom. Remove potential hazards where you can because if your child can get to it, she almost certainly will.

Suitable Suggestions

Your child's crawling skills remain important and you should continue to encourage them in new ways. For instance, you can put your child in one corner of the room and then attract her attention when you are in the opposite corner. This is good exercise for her and she likes the experience of moving over relatively longer distances. You can also build mini obstacle courses for her to negotiate – a thick cushion placed strategically between you and her means she has to climb over it in order to reach you. If her motivation is high enough, she'll cross that hurdle without too much effort.

Right: At about a year your child is likely to be supporting herself with one hand and cruising the furniture.

Do your best to get her to move while on her feet. One way is to help her to a standing position (or let her get there herself) and hold her hands firmly in yours so that she can't fall backwards, forwards or

Left: You can help your child to take her first steps by holding her hands and giving lots of verbal encouragement.

sideways. As she watches you slowly edge backwards away from her, she may try to take a step forward. If she stays rooted to the spot, give her lots of verbal encouragement to come towards you; you can even gently pull at her hands to indicate the direction in which she needs to move.

Another way is to let her rest in the standing position while holding on to a long range of furniture for support. This gives her the confidence to side-step her way along. For instance, you could place her at one end of a long sofa and wait at the other end for her. Or you could put a series of small chairs in a row so that she can edge her way along from one end to the other without having to sit down in between.

Above: Most children love to be swung, but always support them under the arms; never swing them by the arms.

Top Tips

1. Use her playpen as a support frame. If she is inside her playpen as you approach, lean over the top and put your hands part of the way down towards her. Wait until she pulls herself to standing using the pen bars before taking her hands in yours.

2. Make movement games fun. Of course you want your 1-year-old to walk. Getting irritated with her won't help and will only make her grumpy; this reduces her confidence and makes her reluctant to try. Keep it fun.

3. Allow success. There's no point in asking too much of your child. She needs to achieve success in challenges involving movement or her enthusiasm will diminish. When she does achieve at a new level, let her know you are delighted.

4. Steadily increase the spaces between the furniture. Once she starts to cruise around the room using the furniture for support, gradually extend the gaps between each item so that she almost has to lunge at the next one.

5. Expect episodes of little progress. There may be periods of development where progress seems to be at a standstill or even goes backwards. That happens with many children. Her progress will start again when she is ready and confident.

Remember that the act of walking requires not only good balance and body movements but also bags of confidence. Often it is this lack of self-belief which stops a child from taking her first independent step – she is afraid of falling over. That's why she needs you to be patient and supportive. Do everything you can to relax and encourage her to walk, but don't make her anxious about it or else she will prefer to remain in the safe stage of sitting.

Below: Babies often first pull themselves to a standing position using the bars of the cot or playpen.

Q&A

Q Should I let go of her hands suddenly so that she is left standing alone and is compelled to take a step?

A That could in theory motivate your child to walk, though it is more likely to terrify her. Dramatic gestures like that can backfire, making her less willing to trust you next time.

Q Since my toddler fell a couple of times trying to walk, she doesn't try any more. What should I do?

A Give her time to restore her confidence in her walking skills. You'll find that her natural drive to walk independently will surface again after a few days, once she has recovered from this temporary upset. In the meantime, don't pressurize her into walking.

Toys: wooden toddler trolley with bricks, large sit-and-ride toy, large wooden cubes for side-stepping, child-sized chair

Stimulating Movement: 13 to 15 Months

The majority of children take their first few walking steps before they reach the age of 15 months (the average age is 13 months). And what a surge of excitement this brings your child. No longer restricted to a particular area, he can launch himself into totally new adventures of discovery. His steadiness while walking rapidly increases and he toddles about the place, totally fearless and full of his own importance.

He's Still Not Walking

If your 15-month-old child hasn't taken his first step yet, don't worry. There are some children who don't walk until a few months later and yet whose subsequent development proves to be perfectly normal. It's just that their genetic blueprint has pre-programmed walking to occur at a later time than usual.

What matters is that the other positive signs of movement progress are there, such as he tries to crawl, he kicks his legs when lying in his cot, he pulls himself to standing, and he reaches out for toys. If these positive features are present, you can be sure he'll walk very soon. If you are concerned, talk to your health visitor or family doctor, who can reassure you.

Suitable Suggestions

The most important help you can give your child at this stage is to increase his confidence and stability when walking. Despite his determination to stand on his own two feet, he may be nervous about being in such an exposed upright position – the world certainly looks different from up there! And all it takes is a minor fall or bump to give him a little setback. That's why he needs bags of praise and encouragement from you when he starts to walk. Be there with him when you can, smiling at him, telling him how terrific he is and giving him a big cuddle when he manages on his own.

At first, he will probably walk with his arms stretched out on either side, rather like a poorly coordinated tight-rope walker, and his body movements will be very jerky. That's fine; he's just feeling his way very carefully and letting his balance system adjust to the new sensations. Within a month or so you will find that his arms are closer to his side and his forward steps are smoother, less shaky and altogether more relaxed.

Now that he is a toddler in the true sense of the word, you have to think seriously about keeping him safe without restricting him too much. When you take him shopping with you, for instance, he wants to hurry along the wide, flat aisles of the supermarket. That's a great opportunity for him to practise his movement skills.

Right: When your child first learns to walk she will often need to pause to steady herself.

But he can move fast and the last thing you want to happen is that he lunges for the items on the shelf before you can stop him or even that he disappears from your sight. You may find reins helpful (the type that fit round your child's upper body).

Left: At 15 months this little boy's balance is good enough to allow him to bend down to pick up a toy.

This is also the time when he extends his other movement skills, such as climbing. When he approaches stairs, he is unlikely to climb them in a standing position. Almost certainly, he still lowers himself to either a sitting or a kneeling position and ascends the entire flight that way. However, his increased leg strength and coordination allow him to progress upwards at a faster rate than before. He needs your supervision when climbing.

Top Tips

1. Comfort him when he falls. His unstable walking position renders him vulnerable to falls and this can upset your toddler. Comfort him, cuddle him and get him back on his feet straight away. He'll soon forget his moment of distress.

2. Let him climb in and out of his chair without help. This is a very complex challenge, but is one he can master given enough time. The twisting, kneeling and turning involved provides excellent practice for his balance and movement skills.

3. Ask him to pick up toys from the floor. When toddling about, your child will be willing to lift a toy from the floor. He stops beside it, slowly bends his knees with his bottom pushed right back, then picks it up. He improves with practice.

4. Play kicking games with him. He will not be able to stand still and kick the ball very well – the chances are that he will miss or fall backwards, or both! Yet he enjoys trying this new play opportunity.

5. Give him space. Your toddler is a dynamic explorer and he doesn't need much encouragement to go wherever his curiosity takes him. Make sure he also has lots of time to develop his walking and balance skills spontaneously, without direction.

Below: Some children are fearless climbers and will try to escape their cots at a surprisingly early age.

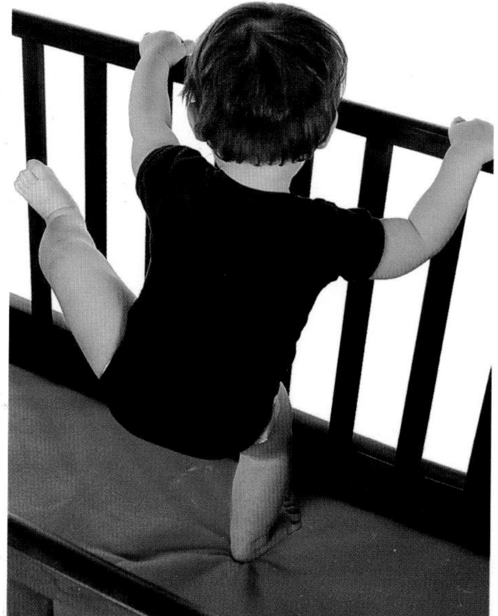

Q&A

Q Is it normal for a toddler to walk a bit, then crawl, then walk another bit, then crawl?

A Yes. A child rarely abandons his earlier mode of travel as soon as he learns to walk. After all, he knows that crawling is a very efficient and rapid form of movement which isn't tiring. Walking, however, is slower and more exhausting to start with. That's why he still uses crawling to cover longer distances.

Q Should my toddler wear shoes inside the house as well as when he is outside?

A The main purpose of shoes is to provide protection for his feet, not to give him better balance. At this stage, therefore, he should still be allowed to walk around carpeted areas in bare feet so that his toes and foot muscles are fully exercised.

Toys: pull-along toy, sit-and-ride toy, small and large soft ball, child-sized table and chair, inflatable paddling pool

Hand–eye

Coordination

The Importance of Hand–eye Coordination

The world is a fascinating place for your young baby. There is so much he wants to learn, so many things he wants to discover – and between birth and 15 months, his main means of exploring is through looking and touching.

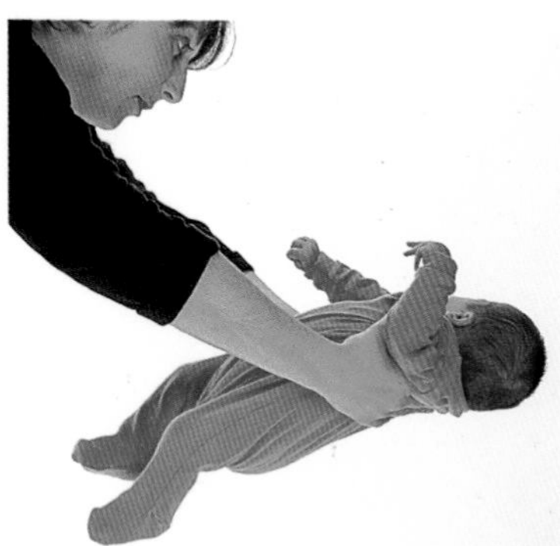

Left: Most of your new-born baby's movements are instinctive, not deliberate.

Right from birth, he spends time watching the world around him, sometimes just taking in the information he sees, sometimes reaching out to get directly involved, and often combining both vision and touch. It is this process of hand–eye coordination (which involves many aspects, such as focusing, looking, reaching, touching, grabbing, lifting and throwing) that occupies so much of his time.

That's why you'll find he constantly reaches out for any object that is within range. To you, that small cardboard box is a boring bit of old rubbish just waiting to be thrown out, but to your young curious baby it's an exciting treasure just waiting to be explored by his eager little fingers – he wants to know how to get the lid off in order to see what lies inside. Likewise, you know that an electric socket must be avoided by little fingers at all costs, whereas your baby can't believe his luck when he finds such a treasure chest within his reach.

Your infant's ability to control his hands and fingers – and to watch these movements closely – allows him to explore, to discover, and to learn about the world around him. For instance, using hand–eye coordination, he tries to pull the rattle close so his face to that he can peer closely at it, shake it, and even put it in his mouth! Early hand–eye coordination boosts his progress with learning.

Reflexes

As you will have already discovered, however, your baby appears to have virtually no control over his hand movements at birth and for several weeks after. It's as though his hands have a will of their own; you may find, for instance, that during feeding one of his hands suddenly arrives from nowhere and hits against you! Rest assured, he is not doing that deliberately.

The fact is that your baby's early vision and touch skills are dominated by a number of reflexes with which he was born. These are physical reactions over which he has no control and which happen automatically without your baby thinking about them at all. It is instinctive behaviour. Many reflexes are connected with survival (such as the sucking reflex which causes your baby to suck whenever a nipple is placed in his mouth). Some early reflexes, however, are connected with hand–eye coordination. These include:

- **blinking.** If your baby hears a sudden loud noise, or if an object approaches his face very quickly, his eyes automatically close. This is a very primitive form of self-protection that is present at birth and lasts throughout life. At the end of the first year, for instance, he'll still blink when a toy slips from his grasp and crashes on to the floor.
- **palmar grasp.** When your young baby is lying on his back with his

Below: Once your child is on the move, keep anything hazardous well out of reach.

Above: A 7-month-old baby is able to target an object, pick it up and move it, very often to her mouth.

hands in the air, gently place your index finger in the palm of his hand so that he can feel the pressure of your touch. His hands will automatically grasp your finger very tightly and he seems unable to let go. This reflex is present at birth but usually disappears by the time he is 3 or 4 months old.

- **Moro reflex.** Be very gentle when testing this reflex. Hold your baby firmly in your hands so that he faces you. Then quickly lower him 15 centimetres (while still gripping him securely). The Moro reflex (also known as the startle reflex) forces him to arch his back and to throw his arms and legs into the air, as though he is trying to grab on to something. This vanishes by the age of 4 months.

Action without Understanding

At the same time as your infant grows out of these early primitive reflexes, his hand–eye coordination develops in a more structured way. But remember that he doesn't yet understand the implications of his actions. That's why, for instance, he happily grabs the spectacles from your face and cheerfully twists them till they fall apart. It's genuine curiosity that drives his behaviour, nothing else.

So try not to get annoyed with him when you realize your 6-month-old has scrunched up the letter you received earlier that morning, and then happily drenched it in saliva as he tried to chew it. Of course, you have to set limits on his behaviour or else within a few months your home will be totally chaotic, but do your best to achieve this without losing your temper at his explorations using vision and touch. If you do become continually angry with him for this sort of behaviour, you run the risk of making your baby afraid to reach out and investigate.

The same caution applies to safety. Exploration is the name of the game when it comes to hand–eye coordination during your baby's first year. Small beads are things to be lifted, chewed and swallowed, as far as he is concerned. Concerns about choking, vomiting, or eating dirt don't bother your inquisitive baby at all. His determination to discover is the only impulse he responds to, and hand–eye coordination enables him to interact with his surroundings. Simply keep an eye on him to make sure he remains safe.

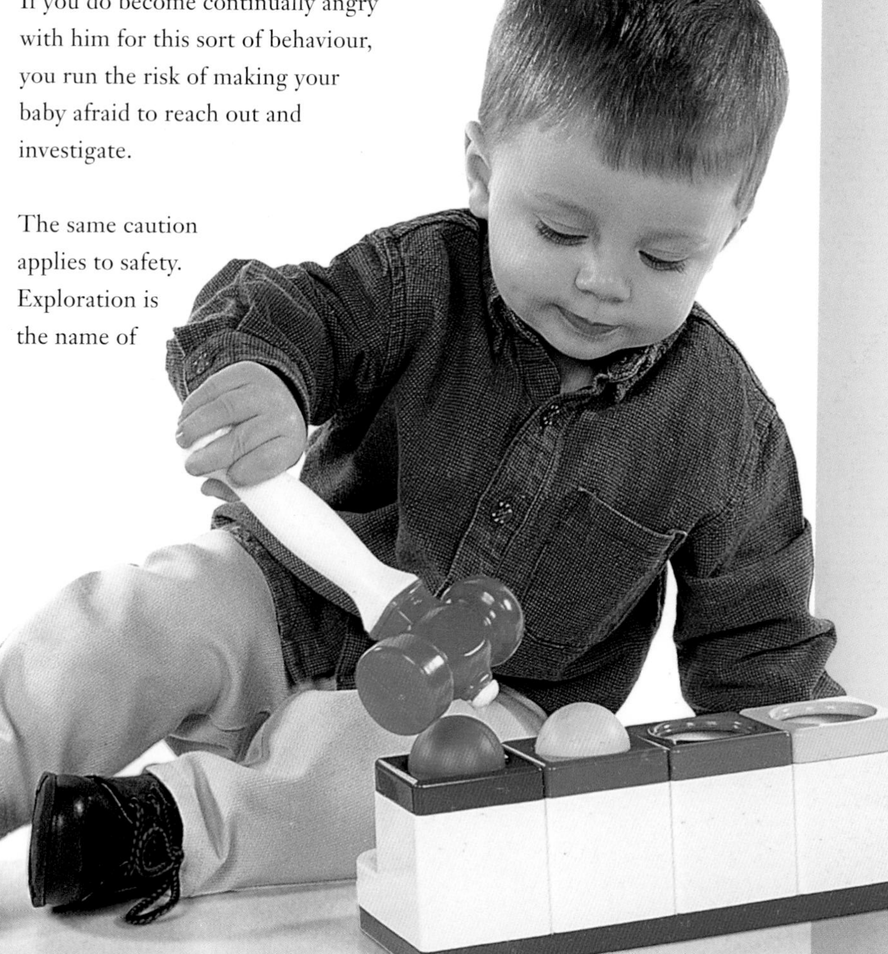

Right: By 15 months or so toddlers can exert good control over simple tools like a hammer.

Stimulating Hand–eye Coordination: Birth to 3 Months

Your young baby needs lots of time to watch what is going on around her. Her head moves from side to side as she lies in her cot, captivated by everything she sees, and she desperately wants to reach out and touch, even though her hand–eye coordination has barely started at this stage. Her innate need to discover and learn new things forces her to interact with her surroundings.

Grab Her Attention

To stimulate your baby's interest, place a hanging mobile above her cot. Position it so that it is well out of her reach (or else you can be assured she'll grab it) yet close enough to be within her vision (just above the highest point of the cot). If you choose a mobile that also makes a noise when activated, so much the better.

Let your baby watch you doing routine household chores. Filling and emptying the washing machine is a boring household task for most people. However, your young baby loves to watch you moving around the house like that. If possible, position her in such a way that she can see you easily.

Suitable Suggestions

During these first three months, your baby is very dependent on you to bring toys to her. Without your help and support, she'll soon become bored lying in her cot or pram because she isn't yet able to reach out in a coordinated manner. So be prepared literally to put toys into her hands until she grabs hold of them. And once she has the toy within her grasp, gently move her arm to and fro. The more you demonstrate these activities to her, and help her carry them out, the more likely she is to repeat them herself.

Below: Introduce your baby to toys with stimulating textures and colours when she is calm and alert.

Brightly coloured, noisy toys are the most suitable type during this period; babies find it easier to distinguish primary colours (red, yellow, blue) than combined colours (such as purple, green, orange). Their sights and sounds attract her attention, making her want to discover all she can about them. And don't forget to use picture books. Sure, she can't turn the pages or tell you the names of the objects shown in the pictures, but she will stare at them and try to touch them; because your baby doesn't realize the difference between a picture and the real thing, she tries to feel the objects displayed on the pages.

Change your baby's play position when possible. Interestingly, the same toy will have a different appeal for her when she lies flat, compared to its appeal when she is upright. For instance, your baby will smile happily when you hold her in your arms and show her a rattle, even though she showed no interest in the same toy a few minutes before while lying in her cot.

Above: A young baby will be fixated by a colourful hanging mobile.

Babies love a gentle tug-of-war over a toy, as long as they win! Dangle, say, a child's plastic ring above her until she grabs hold of it firmly. Then softly pull at the other side, while smiling at her. You'll notice her grip strengthen, and you can let the ring be rocked backwards and forwards in this mock tugging situation. Be warned, however: if by mistake you pull so hard that she lets the ring slip from her fingers, she'll almost certainly be furious and will burst into tears.

Below: Baby gyms provide lots of visual interest initially and your baby will find it very exciting once she can make the toys move.

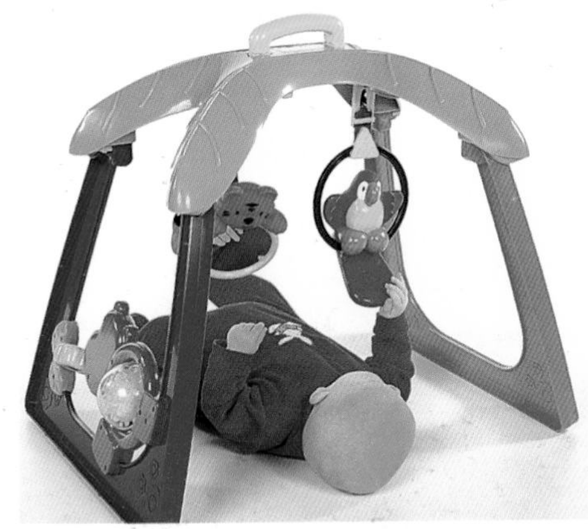

Top Tips

1. Buy her toys which can be gripped easily by small hands. Large toys are too difficult for her to hold and she will lose interest in them. She likes to grasp objects and then bring them close to her face so that she can peer closely at them.

2. By all means place a toy so that she has to make an effort to reach it. If you see that she struggles in vain, however, give it to her eventually: if you don't, she may lose interest and give up.

3. Provide her with a variety of toys, if possible. Although all rattles, for example, might seem the same to you, each one is special to your baby and she sees different qualities in them.

4. Be prepared to demonstrate hand movements to your baby if you see that she plays repetitively. This gives her an example of novel hand movements, which she may try to copy.

5. Assuming you buy her toys that are safe for young children, let your baby put them into her mouth to explore their properties. This is another dimension of hand–eye coordination.

Q Is it safe for me leave some toys in the cot so that she can play with them whenever she wants?

A As long as you are sure the items are safe for young children and do not need to be kept under adult supervision, it's fine to leave some toys at the side of the cot. Apart from staring at them, she will also reach for them. It's good to give her this sort of independence early on.

Q Should we choose curtains with patterns for our baby?

A Yes. You want your baby's bedroom to look attractive, and child-centred patterns on curtains (such as brightly coloured cartoon characters set against a white or light background) are great for your baby, too. She spends lots of time looking at her immediate environment and attractive colours and patterns will encourage her interest.

Stimulating Hand–eye Coordination: 4 to 6 Months

Your baby changes dramatically throughout this period. He is altogether more reactive to you and to his general surroundings. With more purpose behind his vision and touch, your infant becomes an active explorer, using his hand–eye coordination in a more focused and controlled way. This shift towards a greater level of control helps him become more actively involved.

Set Limits

He's still quite young but you could consider setting up some rules about touching. Make a point of warning him about small items. Your baby still likes to put things in his mouth, although he is more aware of the dangers this poses. When you see him about to put a small item in his mouth, firmly but quietly say 'no' and remove the object from his hand. You will have to repeat this process again and again and again.

Set some 'no go' areas in your home. Decide what objects you don't want him to explore (for instance, your china ornaments, electric sockets, electrical items) and tell him not to touch these. Of course he will forget and touch them anyway. You need to keep reminding him.

Suitable Suggestions

If he drops a toy you'll notice that he actively searches for it with his eyes and if he pinpoints it with his vision, he'll do everything he can to grab hold of it. Encourage him to look for objects that are not immediately to hand but are within his visual range. Your question 'Where's the ball?' prods him into action. He loves your attention and interest.

Below: In the early months all babies use their mouths as well as their hands to explore objects.

Use everyday opportunities as they arise naturally. Whatever you are doing while he is with you, talk to your growing child. He likes to watch you move around the room, and even if his attention is momentarily distracted, he quickly turns back to you when you start to talk to him again.

Bathtime is a great opportunity for letting your baby use his hands to splash the water. At first, he may give himself a fright: if the water sprays into his face he'll blink furiously and might even burst out crying,

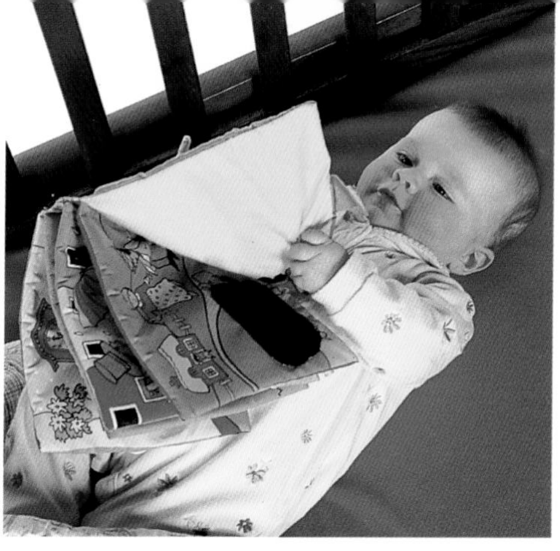

Left: Big cloth books are an ideal way of introducing your baby to the idea of turning pages.

but settle him, reassure him and calm him down. Soapy bubbles have a lovely texture, though make sure he doesn't rub any into his eyes. As long as you are relaxed while bathing him, he will thoroughly enjoy this special time of the day.

Top Tips

1. Show enthusiasm for his explorations. He wants to please you at every opportunity, so give him a big smile when you see him reaching, touching and exploring to heighten his enjoyment and enthusiasm for this activity.

2. Keep safety in mind at all times. Aside from the obvious worry about your child hurting himself, the reality is that injury or discomfort resulting from him touching or swallowing something will dampen his enthusiasm for exploring.

3. Show him how to pass from one hand to the other. Easy for you but difficult for your infant, passing a small toy from his left to right hand (or vice versa) is a skill he might achieve, especially if you demonstrate this to him.

4. Laugh when he makes a noise with rattles. Sit with him while he bangs them hard against the side of the cot or on the floor. When he sees that you are not at all upset by the noise, he will be happy to continue playing this way.

5. Let him reach for picture books. When he snuggles up to you while you talk to him about the pictures in his book, allow him to grab hold of the thick, cardboard pages if he wants to have a closer look by himself.

His increasing general physical maturity also helps to develop his hand–eye coordination. For instance, towards the sixth month your infant can sit up on the floor, while supported either by you or by strategically placed cushions. This changes his entire perspective and makes life more interesting for him. The typical child of this age loves to sit upright, legs splayed, while picking up and dropping toys from his hands on to the floor.

If your infant tries to grab hold of the bottle or the spoon while having his meal, let him (though don't let go yourself). Food is a great incentive for him to extend his hand–eye coordination skills! True, he's likely to make a terrible mess at this stage, but that's all part of child development. You may decide sometimes to give finger food as a snack, and this helps too.

Below: At 6 months your baby will still put most things to his mouth – this can be a good time to introduce finger foods.

Q Should I move ornaments out of the way of my 5-month-old baby or is that just giving in to him?

A It's best to remove possible temptations. Like it or not, you may have to change the way your household is organized in order to accommodate the increasing hand–eye coordination skills of your infant. It's far easier remove a fragile ornament altogether than to worry constantly that he'll get his hands on it.

Q What other strategies can I use to keep him safe?

A Praise him when he follows the rules. There is no bigger incentive for your baby to stick to rules about touching than your approval. He'll beam with delight when you cuddle him for not going near that hot radiator, and he'll feel very self-satisfied when you hug him for staying away from the electric socket.

Toys: baby walker, soft play-mat, soft story book, soft building blocks, bath toys, cushions, wooden shapes, door bouncer

Stimulating Hand–eye Coordination: 7 to 9 Months

Now that your baby's ability to sit on her own is well-established and she can make a good attempt to propel herself along the floor by crawling, there's no stopping her. She will do just about anything to get hold of that toy, even if it is under a chair or on top of a shelf. She has no fear of danger – all that matters to her is the enticing prospect of reaching the object of her desire.

She Gives Up Too Easily

You may not discover that your infant gives up easily until she turns to you one day in tears, distressed by her inability to stack the rings on the central pillar or to bring the food to her mouth the way she had intended.

If you think your child gives up too easily, give her gentle encouragement to complete the task, though don't force her. And make a point of setting a good example yourself. Let her see you struggle with a similar task while still smiling (for instance, pouring water from a jug to a cup) – this will persuade her to adopt a similar attitude.

Above: Stacking rings are an excellent toy for helping your child improve her coordination.

Suitable Suggestions

There is a wide range of suitable activities for stimulating hand–eye coordination now. For instance, you can encourage her pincer grasp. As she has better control over her hand movements, she can use her thumb and forefinger together in a pincer grip rather like a pair of pliers. Of course, a small object can easily slip from between her fingers, but this skill improves with practice. You can use small bits of food, or small toy blocks (though keep a close eye on her in case she tries to swallow them). She can do this while sitting in her high chair.

Practise action–reaction movements with her. Your child is more aware of the

Above: Songs with clapping actions are a great way to teach your child this skill.

Top Tips

1. Avoid comparisons. Every child is different, and you may find that your friend's child has more advanced hand–eye coordination skills than your child even though they are both the same age. Comparisons will de-motivate her.

2. Use pointing. When the two of you sit together, point to something in the room and say to her 'Look at that'; she will follow the line of your hand to the object. Then ask her to point to a specific object in the room.

3. Play with a wind-up car. Try to get one of those toy cars that is powered either by clockwork or battery. Take your child into a room in the house that does not have a carpet, and then let the car go. She'll watch it run all over the place.

4. Tickle her palms. Basic songs and rhymes which involve tickling her hands (such as 'This little piggy...') playfully force her to keep her hand in one position, then hurriedly remove it.

5. Leave toys in her cot. Your infant almost certainly wakes up earlier in the morning than you would like. That's why it's good to leave a pile of toys within reach so that she can play on her own without needing your attention.

connection between her hand movements and the world around her. You can help develop this skill. For example, sit your child on the floor and place a flat, clean tissue beside her so that one corner is a few centimetres away from her hand. Then place a small toy in the opposite corner and ask your child to 'pull the tissue towards you'. She may need several shots before she pulls the tissue to get the toy.

You can now have fun playing 'musical instruments' with your infant. Find a couple of old pots and pans and add a wooden spoon or two. Then pass this fine orchestral array to your enthusiastic 8-month-old. Before you know it she will be banging the spoon against the pot, the pot against the pan, and the lid against the spoon.

Your child will enjoy filling and emptying cups. Face her and let her see you put a wooden block into a plastic cup, and then turn the cup upside down so that the block falls out. Do this a couple of times then say 'You do this'. Hand the cup and block to her and give her lots of prompts to put the block back into the cup. She may have difficulty with this at first, so keep encouraging her until she completes the task successfully.

Below: This little girl is picking up banana pieces with thumb and forefinger in a pincer grip.

Q My baby is 8 months old and gets angry when she can't complete a puzzle toy. What should I do?

A React calmly to her frustration. When she simply can't manage that hand–eye coordination activity and consequently erupts with fury, don't let yourself get riled. Do your best to soothe her, then suggest she tries again. If she still doesn't succeed, put the item away and come back to it again later.

Q Is there any point expecting my infant to play quietly? She really likes to make a loud noise.

A Naturally you don't want to discourage her from playing, but now is as good a time as any to teach her that there are other people to consider. When she makes a particularly loud noise, speak quietly to her and ask her to be more gentle. She'll respond to you, at least for a few seconds anyway.

Stimulating Hand–eye Coordination: 10 to 12 Months

As he approaches the final quarter of his first year, your baby's self-confidence has vastly improved. Progress in all areas of his development including hand–eye coordination means he is a more independent and determined child. He likes to make his own amusement and isn't too happy when you tell him what he can and can't do. On the other hand, he remains desperate for your love and approval and doesn't like you to be angry with him.

When He's Passive

Children differ in their level of desire to explore, some are more dynamic than others. If yours is one of those who won't reach out for toys and isn't very keen to explore, then be prepared to bring toys to him, place them gently in his hands, and play with him. This will increase his motivation. He needs you to push him gently into more activities.

Also, check that he has toys suitable for his stage of development. If he only has toys suitable for a much older or much younger child, then he is unlikely to show much interest in them.

Left: Once your child can put a lid on a box this new skill will keep her occupied and give her tremendous satisfaction.

Below: Allowing a child to feed himself will help his coordination and make him more interested in his food.

Suitable Suggestions

Boxes with lids on fascinate him now. They don't need to be fancy or expensive in order to arouse his curiosity. All you need to do is take a small cardboard box with a reasonably tight-fitting lid, place a small object inside it, then put the lid back on. Bring the box over to your toddler and shake it backwards and forwards so that the object rattles around noisily. After a couple of seconds, hand the box to him without saying a word. He will immediately try to remove the lid in order to discover what's in it. Having achieved that, he will be content to spend a few minutes trying to fit the lid back on to the box.

His advanced hand–eye coordination means that he can attempt more complex tasks, such as ordering shapes of different sizes. He enjoys the challenge of nesting cubes, a series of boxes of diminishing size which fit neatly inside one another when placed in a specific order. Your child will find this hard

Left: At around this age your child may be ready to start some supervised scribbling with chalk or crayons.

to complete. However, he will rise to the demands of this toy and will be pleased to show you that at least two or three of the boxes fit inside each other.

Top Tips

1. Play lots of hand games with him. He enjoys action rhymes involving hand movements, such as 'Incy Wincy Spider', or games like 'Pat-a-Cake'. These games are great fun and also involve hand–eye coordination.

2. Get him involved in feeding. When you have a bit more time than usual, give your child the spoon to hold. He will make a good effort to bring the spoon to his mouth, though much of the food will already have fallen off.

3. Provide varied textures. If you can face the prospect of cleaning up a mess, give your toddler bowls containing different liquids such as custard, water and flour, and dried oats. Let him put his hands into each bowl to feel the different textures.

4. Offer solutions. If you see that he is stuck at a particular hand–eye coordination puzzle (for instance, putting a shape into the shape-sorter) suggest other ways he could try to do this. Stay with him as he tries out these suggestions.

5. Continue to support him. Despite his increased independence, he still has more fun playing when you are involved. By all means step back a little and give him space to explore on his own, but do remember he still needs you.

He loves sitting in the bath at the end of the day, playing with his toy water containers. Assuming he feels confident sitting in the bath (with you beside him), give him some plastic cups or jugs and suggest that he pours water from one container into another. This can turn out to be a particularly messy game but it's great for improving his hand control. He can pour from the left hand to the right, or the other way round. Encourage him to pour slowly and to take his time.

Your child's increased use and grasp of spoken language mean that you can give him direct commands involving hand–eye coordination. For instance, tell him gently 'Give me the cup'; he should be able to look round to see where the cup is, pick it up in his hand and then pass it to you. You'll see him concentrate very hard during this activity as he uses all his concentration to get it right.

Below: By this age your child is more likely to have the patience and dexterity to build a small tower of stacking cups or blocks.

Q Now that my child is very steady when sitting, is it safe to leave him playing alone in a shallow bath while I prepare a meal for his older brother?

A No. It is never safe to leave a child of this age alone in bath water. He could slip in a split second and be submerged in only a few centimetres of water. Far better for your older child to wait until his brother's bathtime is finished than to take such a risk.

Q No matter how often I show my toddler how to put the shapes in his shape-sorter toy, he still can't manage them all. Should he be able to?

A Shape-sorters are incredibly difficult for little fingers to manage. Your son probably manages the circle and square shapes but not the more complicated ones. Give him time to learn the solutions. As his hand control increases over the next few months, he will fit more shapes into the right holes.

Toys: nesting beakers, stacking cubes, shape-sorters, chunky crayons and some paper, musical wind-up toy, door bouncer

Stimulating Hand–eye Coordination: 13 to 15 Months

Your toddler's drive towards independence now increases. Her increased hand–eye coordination skills mean that she has much more control over her environment; it allows her to manipulate toys and other objects in any way she wants and she can play with a wider range of toys which are more challenging. You may find that her frustration increases and that she becomes angry with herself if, for instance, the building blocks won't lock together in the way she would like them to.

She Still 'Mouths' Toys

Most children this age play more purposefully with toys instead of simply putting everything straight into their mouths. However, if yours continues with this habit, do your best to avoid confrontation over this as toddlers can be determined to get their own way.

Because you run the risk of drawing her attention to the habit, which could make it persist even longer, attempt to distract your child with another activity when you see her about to mouth toys, and while she is distracted, gently remove the item from her hands. She will soon grow out of the habit anyway, even if you do nothing about it at all.

Left: Once past a year toddlers will be absorbed by toys that come apart and can be put together again.

Suitable Suggestions

Your child is especially fascinated by puzzles which draw on her increased learning skills and her hand–eye coordination. Give her a small wooden inset board, the type that has a piece cut out in a circle shape, for example, and your child then has to fit the missing piece back into its empty space on the board. She will enjoy trying these puzzles, though do remember that they are extremely difficult for her. Elementary shapes such as circles and squares are the best ones to go for. Your toddler may spend lots of time, sitting in silence with an intense expression on her face, as she tries to complete the puzzle. If you find that she almost gets the shape in the right place but can't quite manage it, give the piece a gentle nudge until it drops into the hole.

It's important not to de-motivate your child at this stage. Buy her inset-board puzzles that have only one or two pieces in them. She can't deal with more complex puzzles, and they may be so difficult that they put her off altogether.

The typical child of this age is also fascinated by building towers of things, usually of blocks. Until now, any attempts by her to place one block on top of another would probably have resulted in total failure: her immature hand–eye coordination skills would have meant that she couldn't balance the top block properly. At this stage in her development, though, the chances are that she can build a tower of two or even three blocks without it falling over. But she needs your encouragement. Practise this with her

Above: Copying real-life activities like using the telephone is great fun, and of course the actual thing is far better than a toy.

Left: Encourage your child to start to do things for himself. He will enjoy contributing to the dressing – and undressing – process.

Top Tips

1. Give her plenty of time to complete tasks involving hand control. Your child can't, for instance, pull her jumper on very quickly. So if you want her to achieve this target, avoid a time when you are in a rush.

2. Calm her if she becomes frustrated. She will almost certainly aim to master challenges that are much too difficult for her, and she needs you to calm her, to reassure her and to direct her to activities that are within her abilities.

3. Don't force hand preference. By now she may start to show preference for one hand over the other. Let this aspect of hand control develop naturally. Certainly, you should never force a left-handed child to use her right hand instead.

4. Play rolling the ball with her. Stand three or four metres back from her and softly roll a small ball towards her. Your child will love this game, either hitting it away when it comes near or trying to stop it and grab it.

5. Give her a toy telephone. She's seen you lift the telephone receiver to your ear often enough and wants to do this with her own phone. A small plastic or wooden toy phone will provide loads of amusement for your child.

regularly and let her look at a tower you have built as an example.

Many children of this age like to get involved with dressing and undressing. For instance, as you approach with her jumper, she may stick her hands and arms towards you in anticipation. That's terrific because she is proving to you that her understanding, vision and touch have advanced to the point where she can predict your actions and can try to help you with the task. And one day you are bound to discover that she has pulled her socks off and thrown them over to the other side of the room!

Below: Shape-sorters are ideal for this age group, though the more complex shapes may still prove quite a challenge.

Q My child is afraid to play with new toys. What can I do?

A Be patient with her. If you know that she prefers familiar toys to new ones, just place the new toy alongside her other toys without saying anything. Let her explore it in her own time. After a few days, sit with her and handle the new toy yourself without saying anything about it. Your interest will eventually encourage your child to play with it, too.

Q Is it better to give my toddler a large ball or a small ball to play with?

A She will be able to hold a small ball in her hands but will have difficulty trying to throw it. However, a large ball may block her vision when she holds it in preparation for throwing. The best solution is to go for an in-between size, one that she can hold firmly between both hands while still being able to see easily over the top of it.

Language

The Development of Language

Your baby's use of language changes so much during the first 15 months that it's hard for you to notice all the key changes that occur. From a new-born baby whose only method of communication with you is non-verbal because she can't actually make clear sounds, a year later she has become transformed into an active talker who has already spoken her first clear word.

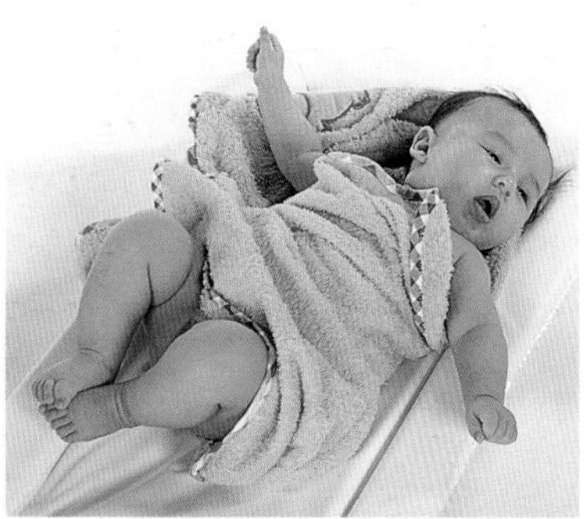

Left: Your baby's first identifiable step towards speech is a cooing sound.

What's even more amazing is that your child develops language in a systematic way. If you've ever tried to learn a foreign language you'll know what it is like to be confronted with millions of sounds and thousands of words. Well, that's what it is like for your baby; in fact, the challenge for her is even more difficult because she can't draw on any previous experience of learning a language. There are so many sounds in her environment, and yet she somehow manages to develop her own language skills without any special help.

That's one of the main reasons why most psychologists claim that your baby has an innate ability to learn language, that she arrives in the world already pre-programmed to pick out certain sound combinations from the whole array of environmental sounds that she hears. There is perhaps no other explanation that can satisfactorily account for how she spontaneously learns to speak amidst the noisy chaos of language around her.

Bear in mind, though, that there are other factors that also play an important part in your baby's language development. For instance, the actual language your baby hears has a direct effect, which is why a baby raised by English-speaking parents learns English and not, say, French, while a baby raised by French-speaking parents learns French and not German. And there is also plenty of evidence from psychological research that the pace and richness of your baby's language development will be affected by the amount of language stimulation she receives from you and others in her family.

Following a Pattern

Another startling feature of language development is that virtually all babies build their language skills in the same way, using the same 'building blocks' in the same order and usually at around the same time. This adds further support to the idea of the inborn nature of language.

Aside from the specific new skills that your baby develops each month in this early period of her life, you will also see her progress through linguistic phases, which include:

- **non-verbal.** For the first six weeks or so, your baby cannot make any identifiable sounds. Her only means of communication is through crying and other body language such as arm and leg movements, facial expressions and eye contact.
- **cooing.** This is a meaningless repetitive vowel sound that your baby utters, usually when she is settled and contented. Starting at around 2 months and disappearing a couple of months later, cooing does not follow a pattern.
- **babbling (random).** By 5 months your infant can produce a wider

Below: Once your baby starts to babble more hard consonant sounds will emerge.

range of sounds, largely because her voice and breathing have matured. Random babbling is the distinctive set of sounds your baby makes when she has your attention.

• **babbling (controlled).** For the next few months, she babbles in a more controlled way, almost as though she is taking part in a conversation with you. She may tend to use the same string of sounds regularly (such as 'papapa').

• **early speech.** Towards the end of the first year, your baby makes sounds as though she is talking – she looks at you, has a serious expression on her face and varies her voice tone – but she doesn't yet use any distinguishable words.

• **first word.** Around her twelfth month, your heart skips a beat with excitement on hearing her first word. Her vocabulary will increase by ten words or so in the next few months, extending to about 50 words by around 18 months.

There is no established link between early talking and intelligence. However, early language development will give your child a head start when it comes to communicating with other people and learning from them.

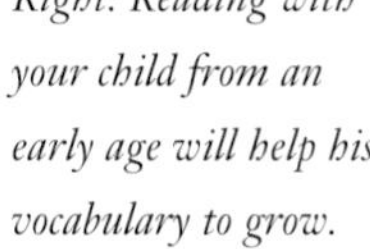

Right: Reading with your child from an early age will help his vocabulary to grow.

Listening and Speaking

Remember that your child uses language in two ways. First, she listens to the sounds she hears and interprets them in her own way. Known as receptive language, these analytical language skills enable her to make sense of the sounds she hears. Secondly, your infant also has expressive skills which enable her to make sounds of her own so that she can communicate verbally with you. When stimulating your baby's communication ability, focus both on her expressive language and on her receptive language.

Almost certainly your infant's receptive language will constantly remain far ahead of her expressive language. In other words, she will understand a lot more words than she can actually say. For instance, you'll discover that she smiles when she hears her name even though she can't actually say her name himself. This difference probably occurs because a growing baby typically hears language long before she is mature enough to speak (when, for example, she listens to you talking to someone else), and she is encouraged to respond to language even when she hasn't the ability to speak (when, for example, you ask her if she is happy after she has been bathed and changed).

Above: These two babies are clearly communicating with each other, despite the fact that they cannot yet talk.

Stimulating Language: Birth to 3 Months

Your baby cannot talk at birth. He can't even make any individual vowel or consonant sounds. But he can communicate using crying, facial expressions and body movements – through this non-verbal system, your baby is able to express his basic needs to you. The language stimulation you provide during this pre-verbal phase of his life, however, starts the long and exciting process of his own language development.

'Parentese'

You may find yourself instinctively talking to your baby using short sentences with large gaps between phrases and an exaggerated voice tone that you do not use when talking to another adult. This is known as 'parentese', and psychologists have discovered that using this style of language with young babies, in moderation, can be helpful in stimulating their language skills.

Yet it is important not to fall into the trap of constantly talking down to your baby, as that does not provide a good model on which he can base his own language skills. After all, he will have no incentive to develop a mature understanding of grammar and vocabulary if he only hears simplified 'parentese'.

Suitable Suggestions

The best way to encourage your baby's language skills is to talk to him at every opportunity, even though he can't understand the exact meaning of everything you say to him. By chatting to him while feeding him, changing him, playing with him, or while driving in the car with him, you provide a rich array of language sounds for him to listen in to and (eventually) to develop for himself.

Below: At only 1 month old this baby's attention is fixed on his mother's face while she talks to him.

Be animated when talking to your baby during these first three months. Make eye contact whenever possible so that he can see the broad smile that accompanies your happy words, as well as the more calm expression on your face when you to lull him to sleep. He watches your gestures and body language very closely, forming a link between the words you use, the mood you are in and your outward appearance. This sets the foundation for his own development of speech.

Don't worry that he can't possibly grasp the content of your conversation with him, especially when you talk about subjects not directly related to his immediate world. Don't feel silly speaking to your baby who is only a few months old. The fact is that every time he sees and hears you using words, he soaks up all these examples of purposeful

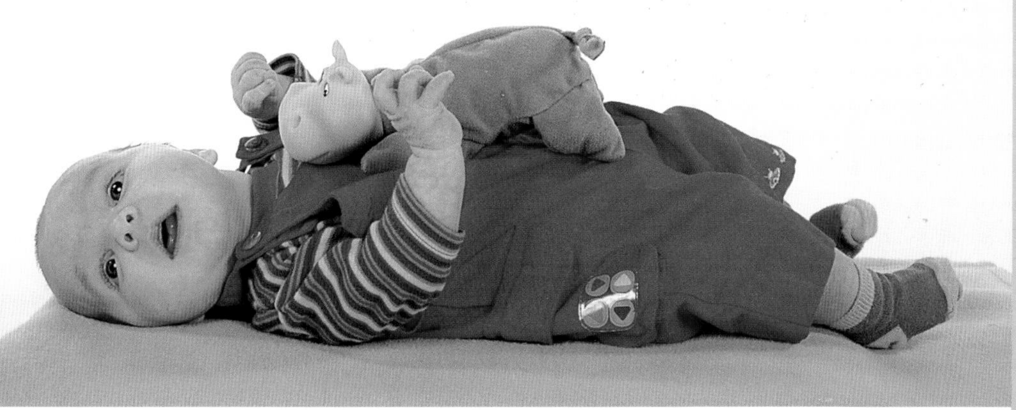

Above: At around 2 months this baby is responding to sound and beginning to vocalize.

language, preparing him for the time when he will eventually take part in conversations and express himself using the spoken word.

Top Tips

1. Interpret his cries to him. If you discover that he cried because, for instance, he needed a clean nappy, then you could say to him, 'You were crying because your nappy was dirty but you're happy now that I've changed it.'

2. At times hold him close when talking to him. Of course you should talk to him at every opportunity but try to ensure that there are lots of times when he is close enough to focus on your eyes, face and mouth.

3. React strongly to your baby's vocalizations. Once he starts cooing (probably around the eighth week), smile at him and talk back to him as though he is taking part in a conversation. This encourages him to continue.

4. Use play to encourage him to speak. Your baby is likely to make sounds to express his feelings when actively engaged in play. His relaxed and happy mood makes him want to vocalize.

5. Play listening games with your baby. When he lies in his cot, for instance, attract his attention by whispering to him, or by saying his name. Good listening skills are a crucial part of communication.

Songs are important, too, because they demonstrate a further use of language. They show him that words can be accompanied by a tune in order to create an atmosphere that is perhaps relaxed, happy or serene. Even if you have a dreadful singing voice, sing softly to your baby. As far as he is concerned, your voice is the most wonderful sound in the world. Its familiarity and its association with the love and care you shower on him are the factors that matter so much to your young baby. Sing him gentle lullabies sometimes to help him fall asleep, and sing him nursery rhymes that will grab his attention.

Below: Singing to your baby while you rock or jiggle her will also stimulate her response to language.

Q How can I learn the different meanings of my day-old baby's cries?

A Give yourself time to get to know your baby. With experience of caring for him, you'll soon be able to match a particular cry with a particular meaning; for instance, his cry which steadily builds up when he needs to be fed will be different from his more urgent, piercing cry when he is physically uncomfortable.

Q Is it all right to let my 2-month-old baby listen to the television?

A Sounds from your television set can play a part in encouraging your infant's speech and language growth. However, the beneficial effect is limited because the language he hears isn't accompanied by other non-verbal aspects of communication. Therefore long periods of listening to the sound of the television at this age provide little help for your baby's language development.

Toys: music box, rattle, toy that makes a noise when activated or moved, baby picture book

Stimulating Language: 4 to 6 Months

Your child passes from the cooing stage to the point where she begins to babble, and suddenly you realize that she is on the road to independent speech. Her need to make sounds becomes apparent at most times of the day, as she babbles when she's with you or while playing alone. Your growing baby loves the increased range of sounds that she can make.

Check It Out

When you think that your baby cries because she is hungry, for instance, your immediate reaction will be to give her a feed. And that's fine. But you'll help her language development a lot more if you pose a question to her between interpreting her cries and easing her discomfort.

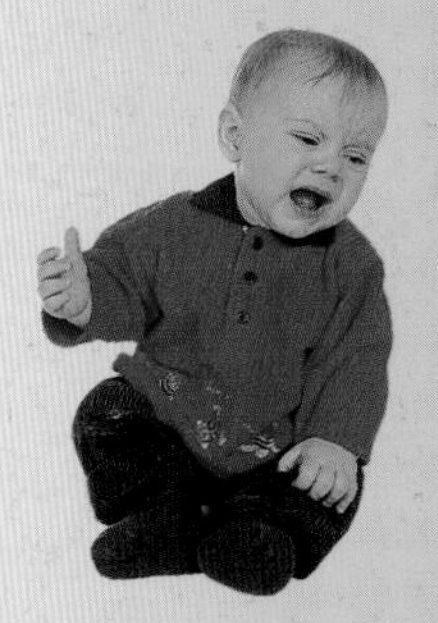

For instance, ask her, 'Are you crying because you want something to eat?' or 'Are you upset because your toy has slipped out of the cot on to the floor?' She can't answer you but she is at the point where she begins to understand more of the language she hears. Checking out the situation with your child encourages her interest in speech.

Suitable Suggestions

During this three-month period she becomes a more active participant in your conversations with her and she will give you the impression that she wants to join in the discussion (even though she still only makes random babbling sounds). That's why you should pause when talking to her, just as you do when chatting with an adult – you may be surprised when she gabbles away to you during these short gaps.

The same applies when asking her the sort of questions to which you know she is unable to give a coherent reply. For instance, you might ask her 'Do you feel better now that you've had your feed?' or 'Would you like me to take you to the park?' Of course she can't reply, but leave a short pause anyway and look at her as if you expect a response. Sometimes she will babble at that moment; even if she just stares at you in total

Right: Even when she is upset your baby will calm as you talk to her soothingly.

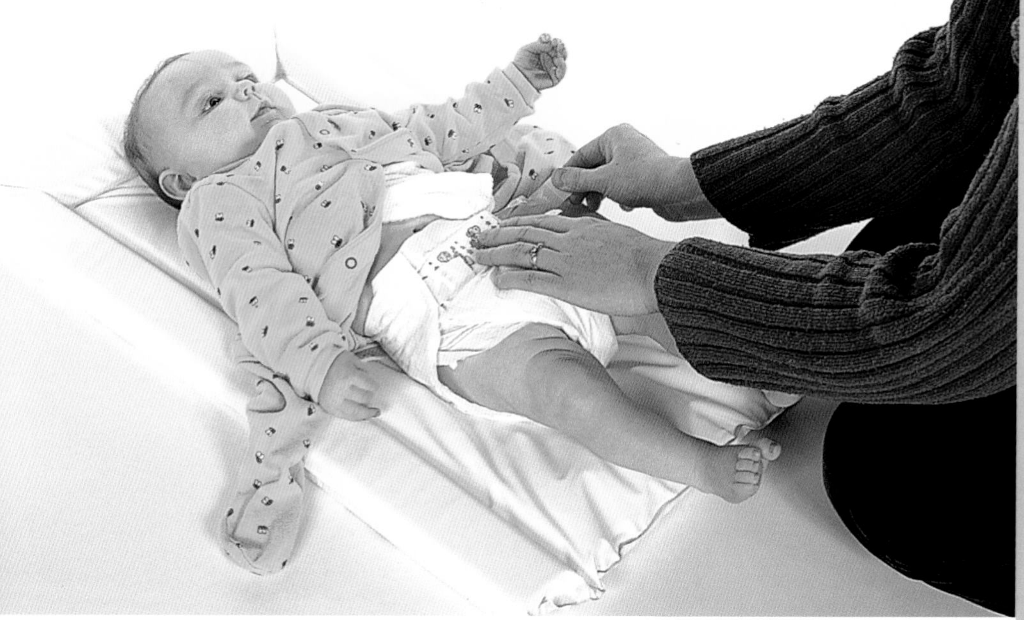

Above: Talk to your baby during your daily activities; animated conversation from you can be a good distraction if your child is getting fed up.

silence, your words and actions help develop her understanding of the concept of turn-taking in conversations.

You should also concentrate on encouraging her listening skills. When she plays in her cot, make sounds from different parts of the room, perhaps to her left, or to her right, or directly behind her. Each time you make the noise, wait for her to turn round to look at you, and give her a huge smile and a cuddle when she achieves this.

Listening activities like these sharpen her hearing and attention skills, which are essential for later speech and language development.

Reading her stories is another useful activity. The particular story that you read her between the age of 4 and 6 months doesn't matter too much (as long as it is suitable for a young child) – what matters more is that you should read the story with feeling and expression, that you should alter your voice tone appropriately during the story and that you should engage your infant's interest in it. Every few seconds look up from the story book and check that she is looking at you. If she is distracted, gently catch her attention and then proceed with the story.

Top Tips

1. Play her music with different tempos. She begins to react to the mood of the music she hears. Fast music might make her giggle while soft music may relax her and help her stop crying.

2. Sit her facing you as you talk. Hold her firmly on your knee and say (or sing) a rhyme to her. You can move your knees slowly up and down at the same time. She enjoys this activity more because she can see you clearly all the time.

3. When taking her out in the buggy, chat to her about the things she can see. Make a comment about the colour of the grass or the size of the bus that just drove past you. If she stares at something in particular, make a comment about it.

4. Talk back to her. Although her babbling is meaningless to you, speak back as though she is trying to convey some special thoughts or feelings to you. You'll be accurate some of the time.

5. Model sounds for her. To increase her range of babbling combinations, introduce a new sound by holding her so that she can see your face and then utter the sound again and again. She may start to imitate you.

Q&A

Q Is it possible that my 5-month-old baby recognizes her name when I say it?

A It is highly unlikely that she genuinely knows the sound of her name. She probably turns towards you when you say her name because she is attracted by the sound. Try saying a different name to her the next time – the chances are she will turn round and look at you this time as well.

Q Can my 6-month-old baby tell my voice apart from other people's voices?

A Almost certainly she can identify your voice from all the other voices that she hears. Your baby has spent so much time with you and has such a strong emotional attachment to you that your voice has a special meaning for her – and so her face breaks into a big smile.

Toys: plastic story books, cassette tapes with children's songs, voice tapes, noisy toys, play-mat with animal or shape patterns

Stimulating Language: 7 to 9 Months

As you listen closely to your baby's sounds, you'll notice that they seem to have a pattern to them. He might start to use the same sound combinations regularly and he might even use them in the same situation. And that's a clear sign that his babbling is controlled, not random, that he is using language in a more purposeful way than ever before.

Hearing

Poor hearing can slow down language development because it means the growing infant can't hear the sounds he makes himself, nor can he hear the sounds that others make to him. A child who misses out on this early auditory stimulation finds learning to speak more challenging than does a child with normal hearing.

Signs that your baby might have a hearing difficulty include his slowness to respond to your voice, his lack of reaction to your voice when you are not directly in his line of vision, and his startled response when you suddenly appear in front of him (because he didn't hear your footsteps as you approached).

Suitable Suggestions

As well as talking to your infant in your normal voice for most of the time, make a point of imitating his two-syllable utterances. Do this in a fun way as a game for a few minutes each day; he will thoroughly enjoy this activity.

When he sits in his high chair after he has had his lunch (and therefore he is in a good mood, ready to play with you), wait until he begins to babble, then pick one of the sound combinations he has just used and say it back to him ('la') using your usual tone of voice; smile as you do so and position your face within 25–30 centimetres of his. Your use of the same sounds makes him feel very good about himself.

Opinion is divided over the use of 'baby words' instead of the ordinary word. Some people argue that it is better, for example, to use the term 'bow wow' than the word 'dog' because that term is more akin to the speech that a child of this age uses and therefore will catch his attention quickly. But others argue that the danger with this strategy is that the child will learn the 'baby word' first and then will have to re-learn the proper word later on when his speech skills are more mature.

To be on the safe side, therefore, it is perhaps best just to use the proper word right from the start when talking to your infant. There is no need to use 'baby words'

Below: Repetitive hiding and 'peek-a-boo' games get an enthusiastic response.

Above: By repeatedly naming objects for your child, she will build up an understanding of words and meanings long before she can speak.

Top Tips

1. Let him blow bubbles. During the day, there will be moments when he blows bubbles with his saliva while making accompanying sounds. Although you might find this habit annoying, it actually helps strengthen his lip muscles.

2. Recite 'noise' rhymes. Tell your child a rhyme that has, for instance, animal sounds in it, such as 'Old MacDonald's Farm'. He'll have fun listening to you and may even try to copy sounds.

3. Play 'peek-a-boo' games. This enjoyable activity, which involves you suddenly appearing from behind your hands which are covering your face, enhances your child's concentration and attention skills as he tries to anticipate your appearance.

4. Watch his favourite video with him. Sit with him as he spends a few minutes watching the video. But make sure that you talk to him instead of just sitting there quietly. Discuss the characters and events of the video as they arise.

5. Use individual picture cards. Buy or make plain cards with a picture of an object on it. Show these to your infant, one at a time, and name each picture as he looks at it. Don't do this for more than a couple of minutes each day.

at all because he has the innate ability to pick out the key words from your speech.

Remember to name everyday household objects as you use them. It's easy to assume that there is no point in saying them because he is not yet ready to associate specific words with specific objects. Evidence from psychological research indicates that a 9-month-old child may in fact understand a lot more than he is generally given credit for. Try this out for yourself. Ask him 'Where is the spoon?' and watch his eyes – if he understands what you have said, he will start to look for the named item.

Below: Picture books are an excellent learning aid and your child will soon begin to recognize familiar images.

Q My son is almost 9 months old and I'm sure his language is developing more slowly than his sister's when she was that age. Is that normal?

A Evidence from research suggests that in general boys develop language at a slower rate than girls at every step along the way. This is a trend, however, and doesn't mean that every boy develops at a slower rate. However, it does suggest that your daughter's faster language acquisition is normal.

Q My son is 7 months old. When he babbles, he uses sounds that aren't part of our language. Why is this?

A Investigations have found that babies from countries with different languages tend to have the same range of babbling sounds (including speech sounds they haven't heard before). Your baby will eventually focus on the sounds that are relevant to your language.

Toys: child-safe mirror, soft chewy ball, stick-on rattle for high chair, soft story book, music tapes and CDs

Stimulating Language: 10 to 12 Months

Your child has now reached that period in her life when she will probably manage to say her first word. This is such a major step forward because it signifies her ability to use spoken language in a way that allows her to communicate meaningfully and precisely with you. Your child's first spoken word also marks the start of a rapid growth in vocabulary over the next couple of years.

Dummies

Sucking a dummy can make your child feel relaxed and contented. When she has this in her mouth, though, it prevents her from using her mouth muscles, lips and tongue to make sounds, and therefore it doesn't make any positive contribution to her speech and language development.

If your child likes sucking a dummy, try to decrease the amount of time she spends with it in her mouth during the day. There's no harm in her using it occasionally when she is distressed or when she wants to nod off to sleep. Bear in mind, however, that extensive use of a dummy stops her from making these all-important pre-speech babbling sounds.

Suitable Suggestions

Provide good examples of speech for her to copy. When you notice that she tends to use the same sound groupings to describe the same person or object – even though what she utters is nothing like the proper word – encourage her by saying the word she means. For instance, if she excitedly makes the sounds 'paneh' whenever she sees her grandmother, you could say to her 'Yes, that's right, it's grandma'. Although her utterance and your word might appear to be totally different from your point of view, your child might think they are the same. So your speech provides a model for her to copy.

But don't pressurize her into saying her first word, or you may end up discouraging her language development. At this age, your child's sounds should be spontaneous, not forced, and should be made because she wants to communicate with you, not because she thinks you will be disappointed with her if she doesn't speak. Of course, every parent of a child this age looks for the sound grouping that could be classed as a word. Yet there is a difference between waiting for a word in excited anticipation and making your child anxious because she hasn't yet managed to meet your expectations.

Songs and nursery rhymes should play an increased role in her daily routine. By now

Right: By 11 months your child will follow instructions, like giving things to you and taking them back.

she is totally familiar with the words and tunes and she tries to 'sing' along with you in her own way. This activity not only enhances her listening skills but also teaches her the sequential nature of language. In other words, that speech follows a sequence and isn't just a random series of sounds. Show her how pleased you are when she tries to join in.

Listen to her attentively, too. She needs to know that you focus on her speech sounds, just as you expect her to listen to you.

Above: Another milestone in your child's understanding is when she starts to enjoy the progression of a story rather than just picture books.

Make good eye contact with your toddler when she speaks, match your facial expression to hers, listen without unnecessary interruptions and then respond as though you fully understood the message she tried to convey. This is the precursor to genuine verbal conversation.

Below: Musical toys help your child's aural development and encourage her to experiment with different sounds.

Top Tips

1. Talk to her throughout the day. Your infant still benefits from hearing you use language purposefully in everyday settings, either addressed to her or when you talk to other people. This basic stimulation helps extend her vocabulary.

2. Give her toy musical instruments. She'll love crashing the toy drum with the sticks, and she will devise her own vocal accompaniment to go along with that activity. Making up songs of her own is good fun and she never tires of this.

3. Expect her to respond to basic instructions. Ask your year-old toddler to 'Give me the spoon'. Reward a positive response with a smile or hug; if she doesn't understand, repeat the question, then lift up the spoon to show her.

4. Cuddle up together when watching a video or television. As she snuggles up to you, talk in a gentle voice about the programme or video, perhaps describing the main characters. Her relaxed mood makes her listen closely.

5. Read her a bedtime story. Your toddler will settle better at night when you sit on her bed to read her a story. She concentrates on every word you say in that situation because she is happy and there are no other distractions.

Q Why is it that a young child's first word is nearly always 'mum' or 'dad'?

A That often happens simply because parents spend a great deal of time with their child, making them the most familiar adults in her world. However, a child's first word might easily be the name of the family pet or the term she uses to describe her favourite cuddly toy.

Q How aware is a 1-year-old of other people's names?

A As well as recognizing her own name when she hears it, she probably knows the names of other people in her family and the names of other familiar adults, such as her childminder or nanny. When she is with you and her brothers and sisters, speak one of their names – you'll find that she turns to look at that child before they speak.

Toys: wind-up music toy, story books with basic pictures, plastic toy animal, toy telephone, cuddly soft toy

Stimulating Language: 13 to 15 Months

If your child didn't start to speak before the end of his first year, he will almost certainly have achieved this milestone by the time he reaches his fifteenth month. He can say several words himself and understands the meaning of hundreds more, though there is one word that probably always results in a negative reaction from him – and that's when you say 'no'!

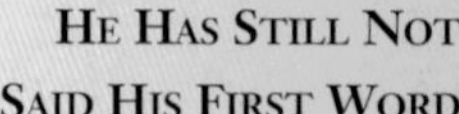

He Has Still Not Said His First Word

Every child develops at their own rate and although the majority of children have said their first word by the time they reach the age of 15 months, there are a significant number who don't achieve this stage until a few months later.

So there is no need to be unduly concerned about the non-appearance of the first word, especially if there are other signs that his speech is developing in a normal way. For instance, the presence of babbling is a positive sign that his language development is progressing satisfactorily, as is his active involvement in songs and nursery rhymes.

Left: At this age a child will enjoy familiar rhymes and action songs.

Suitable Suggestions

Now is a good time to introduce pretend play to your toddler, using his cuddly toys. Set them up in a circle and pretend to talk to them. At first, your toddler aged between 13 and 15 months might stare at you in amazement or he might burst out laughing. But he'll soon realize this is good fun and will join in as best he can. Do this with him a couple of times and you'll discover that he plays this game with his cuddly toys on his own – you'll hear him chatting away to himself and his toys.

When you bath or change your toddler, start to name his body parts. Make this a fun activity, perhaps by tickling his hand when you tell him 'This is your hand' or tickling the sole of his foot when you explain that 'This is your foot'. Do this each night, though try not to make it so routine that he becomes bored with it. Simple games like this help him learn the names of these body parts.

Right: Use everyday routines to name commonplace objects like shoes – your child will soon learn these words.

If possible, arrange for your toddler to spend some time in the company of other children who are approximately the same age (though it won't matter if they are a few months older). He won't play with them but he will be fascinated by their use of language. Most children this age want to be like other children and do every single thing they can to imitate them. So the company of other children can indirectly stimulate his language development.

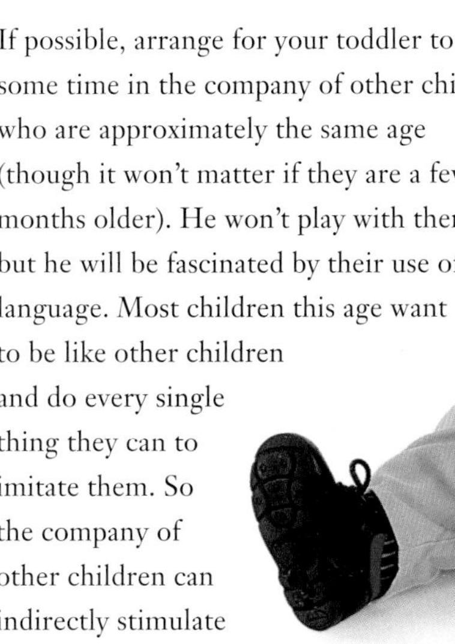

Left: At 15 months your toddler may well hold conversations with his soft toys.

Top Tips

1. Start to name individual colours. Your child is a long way from being able to identify and name the main colours. However, you won't do any harm by starting the process off now, and you may help him differentiate between colours.

2. Show excitement at every new word your toddler says. Pay close attention to the words he uses so that you know when a new word has crept into his vocabulary. He is delighted with your approval of his latest achievement.

3. Get your toddler actively involved with objects you name. Do this where possible because it is very effective. For instance, he'll learn the name of a ball quicker when he plays with it rather than just staring passively at it.

4. Use lots of repetition. Be prepared to say the same things over and over again. Of course you don't want your discussion with your toddler to be boring for him, but repetition of object names facilitates the language learning process.

5. Play with finger puppets. Your 15-month-old child loves finger puppets, especially when you move them about and make them talk to him. He will try to talk back to them. This is a fun, imaginative activity that stretches his language.

Your child will still use gestures as part of his communication, even though his verbal skills steadily increase. You can help his speech progress by resisting the temptation to respond to his gestures alone. For instance, should he point at his cup of juice, ask him 'Do you want the cup of juice?' or even better 'What is it you want?' Repeat the question if he continues to point. Eventually he will try to communicate his desire using spoken sounds instead of gestures alone.

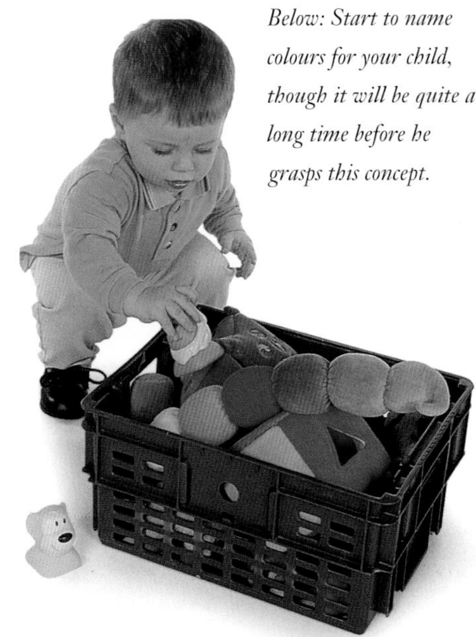

Below: Start to name colours for your child, though it will be quite a long time before he grasps this concept.

Q&A

Q My 5-year-old is very fond of his 15-month-old sister and he tends to speak for her. Should I discourage this?

A Yes. Gently explain to your older child that you are so pleased he wants to help his sister, but that she needs to learn to speak herself. Suggest that the best way he can help her is to let her try to speak, even if it isn't easy for her. Your 5-year-old will understand this.

Q Why do most children come out with single words to start with while others start with phrases from the outset?

A This is another example of the wide variations that can occur as part of normal development. Just as most children crawl before they walk while a few go straight to walking without crawling, the same stage-jumping can happen with language, too.

Toys: pop-up toy, toy musical instruments and musical toys, plastic train, tape of animal noises, soft toys and dolls

Learning

The Development of Learning Skills

Your baby learns so much in his first 15 months that you couldn't write it down, even if you tried! From a baby who knows absolutely nothing about the world into which he is launched, he becomes an active learner who interprets, thinks, makes decisions and remembers. The transformation is totally amazing.

Above: A baby's natural curiosity means he will constantly seek out new learning experiences for himself.

The main way in which he develops his innate learning ability is through play. It doesn't matter whether he plays with a rattle, with his cot blanket, with his feed, with his hands, with the bath water, or in fact anything at all – the fact is that when he interacts playfully with anything in his environment he learns new things. Look on him as a dynamic scientist who just can't wait to get out there in order to explore everything.

Below: Many quite ordinary objects provide an opportunity for a child to explore.

For your young baby, every new experience represents a new and exciting discovery. To you, for instance, emptying the washing from the machine into the plastic basin is so routine that you probably don't even think about it, but to your baby it is totally engrossing. He soaks up everything he sees and in doing so improves his learning skills every single day of his life.

A good way to define learning ability (also called 'intelligence', 'learning skills', 'thinking skills' and 'cognition') is your baby's ability to learn new skills and concepts, his ability to make sense of events that happen around him, his ability to use his memory accurately and his ability to solve small problems.

I'm Ready

When your baby is born, he already has a wide range of learning skills that ensure he is ready to explore and discover, for instance:

- **visual discrimination.** Within hours of birth, a new baby can tell the difference between your face and the face of a stranger. He can also tell the difference between a picture of a real face and a picture of a face in which the components are mixed up.
- **touch discrimination.** Soon after birth, he responds differently to hairbrush hairs of different diameters – in other words, he knows a thick hair feels different to a thin hair. As well as that, he will respond to a puff of air which is so gentle that even you couldn't feel it.
- **taste discrimination.** Your new baby also has a good sense of taste and smell. He makes a distinctive facial expression when he tastes foods that are sweet, sour or bitter. These facial expressions are the same ones that adults make when they experience these tastes.
- **reach discrimination.** Your new-born baby's movements of his hands and arms are not simply random movements. In one study, young babies wore special glasses which

Above: Toys which do lots of different things will fascinate an older baby – though they can lose their novelty quite quickly.

made them see an object that did not exist. Not only did the babies reach for the item, but they cried when they discovered it wasn't actually there.

- **hearing discrimination.** He can tell one cry from another. For instance, research has found that typically a new baby cries when he hears another baby cry, whereas he tends to stop crying when he hears a recording of his own crying. He also prefers the sound of a human voice to any other sound.

It's evidence like this that confirms your baby is ready to learn, right from birth. These (and other) basic learning skills provide the foundation for all his future learning, and from that moment and throughout his first 15 months, your baby's thirst for new knowledge, understanding and information never stops.

The Source of Learning Skills

Nobody knows for sure where your child's learning ability comes from, though there are two main competing explanations:

- **inherited.** Since your baby has many characteristics inherited from you (for example, his eye colouring, his height), it stands to reason that some of his learning ability is also inherited from you. Studies have found, for instance, that identical twins have levels of intelligence that are more closely matched than those of non-identical twins. However, it is impossible to quantify the exact contribution that heredity makes to your child's learning ability.
- **acquired.** There is endless evidence – both from scientific studies and from common-sense everyday life – that a baby learns through experience and that the quality of his learning ability depends on the quality of his learning experiences in the early years. This theory suggests that the level of stimulation provided for your baby in this initial stage of his life will greatly influence his learning skills; offering him a wide range of play opportunities enhances his learning ability.

The true explanation probably lies somewhere in between these two extremes. Your child's intelligence or learning ability is more likely to result from the interaction between the learning skills that he brings into the world at birth and the interesting experiences he encounters as he grows. That's why it is important to view your growing baby as an active learner, as someone who is ready to learn but who needs you to stimulate and challenge his existing abilities. The interaction between you and your baby boosts his learning skills.

Remember that your baby learns best in a relaxed atmosphere. A baby whose efforts at learning and discovering are greeted by an indifferent or over-anxious parent will soon lose his motivation to learn further. Playing and learning has to be fun for everyone involved.

Right: At around 15 months a child will quickly be able to work out how a simple toy operates – even if he has never seen it before.

Stimulating Learning: Birth to 3 Months

It's true that your baby spends much of her day either feeding or sleeping – or crying! But don't let that fool you. In these first three months, she is desperate to learn new skills and new information. She stares at everything she sees, trying to understand it; better still, she prefers hands-on experience because that's a more effective way for her to learn.

Colour And Shape Recognition

It's strange to think that your baby is such a sophisticated learner that she can tell the difference between colours, but she can! Experiments have found that when a new baby is shown various colours one at a time, she stares for longer at blue and green objects than she does at red ones. Colour preference is present early on.

The same applies with shapes. The length of time she stares at different shapes confirms that she can discriminate between a circle, a triangle, a cross and a square. Psychologists don't know for sure what she actually sees, but she definitely is able to differentiate between those four shapes.

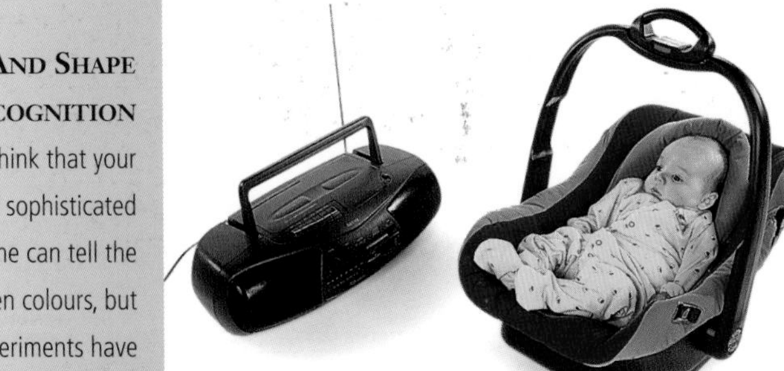

Above: Even small babies may be soothed by familiar music.

Suitable Suggestions

Take nothing for granted. Instead, assume that everything your baby sees and does actually develops her learning skills that bit further. Playing with her and talking to her as you clean and change her, for instance, engages her curiosity – she watches the nappy appear and tries to work out how it arrived there, she feels the sensation of the cleaning cream and talcum powder on her bottom, and she gasps in wonderment at the way her clothes are put on her. There's so much to learn from life's daily routines.

Her vision is already set to focus at around 18 centimetres. Hold her about that distance from your face, while resting her in one arm, then gently move a toy back and forth in the space between your face and hers. As well as encouraging her to focus on the toy, this also brings the object so close to her face that her natural inquisitiveness is stimulated. You'll find that she wriggles in your arms to indicate her interest, even though she isn't mature enough to reach out for the toy.

Make sure she has a wide range of brightly coloured noisy toys whenever she rests in her cot or pram. Obviously you shouldn't make her space too crowded (or she may not be able to focus on any one toy in particular) but she likes to have around two or three

Below: Although you won't be aware of it, babies can distinguish different colours and shapes from birth.

Right: One of the first signs that your baby is learning is when she smiles in response to your face and voice.

different toys close by her. And there's no harm in one of them being a cuddly toy – she learns just as much from that as from any other play object. Cuddly toys teach her about texture, size and movement.

Cot mobiles play a large part in the life of your baby at this age. Since many of your new baby's explorations are visual rather than tactile (because she isn't yet able to reach out for toys that attract her attention), she likes to look at an interesting array of toys hanging above her cot. She learns a great deal by peering at them, as they turn in different directions, showing her different perspectives each time. Choose a brightly coloured mobile, preferably one with lots of different attachments rather than one with several variations on the same theme. As it gently rotates on the supporting string, each new image delights your baby.

Below: Noisy, bright and textured toys are ideal for a small baby.

Top Tips

1. Spend time playing and talking with her whenever you can. Your baby learns from you playing with her just as much as she does from playing on her own. At this stage, she depends on you to initiate some play activities.

2. Don't worry about over-stimulating your baby. Obviously you want to avoid making her so excited that she bursts out crying, but that is unlikely. She wants as much stimulation and fun as you can have with her.

3. Remember that she is an active learner even at this age. No matter what you do with her, she will interpret your actions and reactions in her own way. She doesn't simply lie there passively, watching aimlessly as the world drifts by.

4. Let her play with the same toys the next day, too. Variety is important, but your baby learns new things each time she plays with the same toy as she holds it and looks at it in a different way.

5. Have confidence in yourself. Since your baby at this stage learns a great deal from everyday interactions with you, be confident that you are providing a satisfactory level of stimulation for her.

Q&A

Q Should my young baby be able to imitate some of my actions?

A To some extent, yes. If you stand at the foot of your baby's cot and complete an action which you know she is already capable of (such as opening and closing her mouth, or thrusting her tongue forward), the chances are she will carry out this action more frequently just after she has seen you do it.

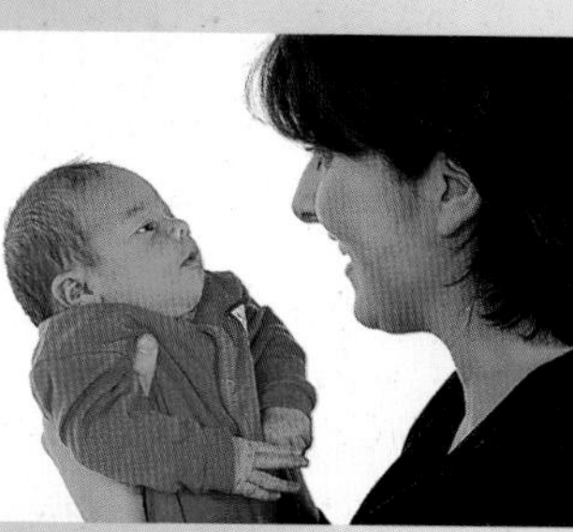

Q Should I talk and smile while I am playing with my young baby or will that distract her attention?

A Her attention will be momentarily drawn to you but that mild negative effect is greatly outweighed by the pleasure she receives from your attention. And if she is happy and contented because you show an interest in her, she is in a better frame of mind to discover and learn.

Stimulating Learning: 4 to 6 Months

One of the most noticeable changes in your infant's learning ability between the ages of 3 and 6 months is that he is more adventurous, with a keener interest in objects that are not immediately beside him. It's as though his perspective on life broadens as he realizes there really is a big wide world out there. And his increased hand and arm control allows him to reach out and grasp – this opens a whole new set of learning experiences.

Learning Behaviour

Your growing baby also learns to make associations when it comes to human behaviour. Resist the temptation to underestimate his abilities. For instance, by now he has learned that shouting or crying can be an effective way to get your attention; most parents respond instantly to a crying baby. And they are quite right to do so.

Yet sometimes it's worth waiting a couple of seconds or so before responding. That way your baby will also learn how to deal with situations on his own. Of course, if he is crying from hunger, he needs a feed. However, if he cries from boredom then a slight delay before you go to him helps your infant learn how to seek his own amusement actively.

Suitable Suggestions

Since the ability to concentrate is fundamental to learning (because even the brightest child won't learn unless he can focus long enough to absorb new information), you can begin to extend your infant's attention span. In the first few months, he used his attention passively, in that he would only look at an object when it was exactly in front of him. By the time he has reached 5 or 6 months, however, your growing infant has greater control and he can actively search for objects.

Practise this with him. Let him watch you, say, put his teddy on a chair that is in another part of the room but which he can see. Play with him for a few minutes, then

Below: An activity centre attached to the side of your baby's cot can provide valuable stimulation – even when you are not there.

Right: Once your baby is happy playing on his front, a toy placed just out of reach will encourage him to stretch for it.

ask, 'Where's teddy?'. He will actively scan for the object. If he can't locate it, try again. And if he still can't find teddy, repeat all the actions, making sure that he can see you place teddy on the chair.

Don't waste your time searching for so-called 'educational toys'. At this stage, every toy is educational in that your infant learns from anything he plays with. That's why the cardboard box that the expensive toy came in is of more interest to your child than the toy itself! Its bright colours, smooth surface, and moving cardboard lid teach him about shape, texture, colour and movement. You could end up spending a lot of money on toys that don't actually enhance your child's learning skills at all.

Above: Once your child can sit up, it is much easier for her to manipulate toys in a variety of ways.

Encourage him to explore once he gets his hands on a toy. Maybe he is one of those rather timid children who prefers a quiet environment – if so, demonstrate that the toy can be shaken, bashed against the side of the cot, or even thrown on the floor. Maybe he only holds the object in one position all the time – if so, regularly turn the toy gently in his hands so that he begins to see the value of taking a more active approach to his learning. Maybe he makes a fuss when you give him a new toy because he prefers the ones he already has – if so, take the new toy to him, play with him until he is comfortable with it, and then make sure he plays with that toy occasionally along with the other familiar ones. Stretch his learning horizons.

Top Tips

1. Let him play in a sitting position. Although he still needs support for sitting, he will play differently with toys in that position than when he lies down. His varied body posture allows him to use his hands and arms in different ways.

2. Give him age-appropriate toys. The manufacturers' age guidelines do not apply to every single child but they are generally accurate. There's no point in giving him a toy for a much older child – he won't know what to do with it.

3. Provide cause-and-effect toys. Your infant is now at an age when he begins to see the connection between his behaviour and a reaction from the toy (as long as that reaction is a reasonably loud noise or a bright light).

4. Reinforce his play with your smiles and attention. You'll notice that he looks up at you while playing, especially when he completes something new. In that situation, let him know how pleased you are with his achievement.

5. Make obvious start-of-routine actions. To encourage his ability to predict events, make the first step of a familiar routine very obvious (for instance, loudly get his bath towel from the cupboard) and watch his anticipatory reaction.

Below: If your child seems bored with his toys – improvise. Paper or a cardboard box will prove just as interesting to him.

Q&A

Q My 6-month-old loves to throw toys out of his pram. Is it a good idea to tie them on to a piece of ribbon?

A You need to be very careful when using this strategy because there is a potential danger that your baby could wrap the ribbon around his neck. So you would have to keep it shorter than 15 centimetres. A better idea is to give his toy back a couple of times, then put it away in your pocket.

Q When my baby plays, should I turn off the radio to avoid distractions?

A Certainly you could turn down the volume but there is no need to turn off the radio altogether. He needs to develop the ability to screen out distractions while learning, so this is good practice for him at the moment. Anyway, the background music may relax him and consequently could make his learning more enjoyable.

Toys: wooden cubes, baby gym, cot activity centre, nesting beakers, noisy blocks, wobbly toy, bath toy, box that rattles

Stimulating Learning: 7 to 9 Months

Your infant's new-found crawling skills mean that she can extend her sphere of learning and discovery to new territories. That's why you'll suddenly find that she has thrust her hand deep into the video player – it's not that she is being deliberately naughty, just that she is keen to find out what goes on inside that mysterious gap which takes the tape. Now she can move over to it in order to learn for herself.

Look, I'm Doing It

One of the hallmarks of this period in your child's life is that she gradually realizes she can have a direct effect on her surroundings and that something she does will influence an object which is not actually in her hands. She learns in an elementary way the nature of cause and effect and puts this into practice.

Don't be surprised, therefore, to see your 9-month-old infant pulling at a rug in order to obtain the toy that rests on the far side of it. In her mind, she has established the complex connection between pulling the rug and bringing the desired object closer. This new learning concept gives her more control over her environment.

Suitable Suggestions

Your 8-month-old baby often finds objects more interesting when they are further away from her. The unknown aspect of that far-away toy grabs her curiosity, making her want to learn more about it – that's why you find her straining herself to reach an ornament situated on a raised shelf. She can't resist the lure of the unknown. So play 'come and get it' games to encourage her thirst for learning. You could shake a box with a toy inside, making it rattle, then place the box a couple of metres away from her. Her desperation to find out what's inside motivates her to crawl and open the box.

Of course your infant likes to sit on the floor surrounded by her toys, but her innate need to learn means that she is always ready to look further afield for new discoveries.

Below: It is intriguing to watch a baby responding to an image that she does not yet recognize as being her own reflection.

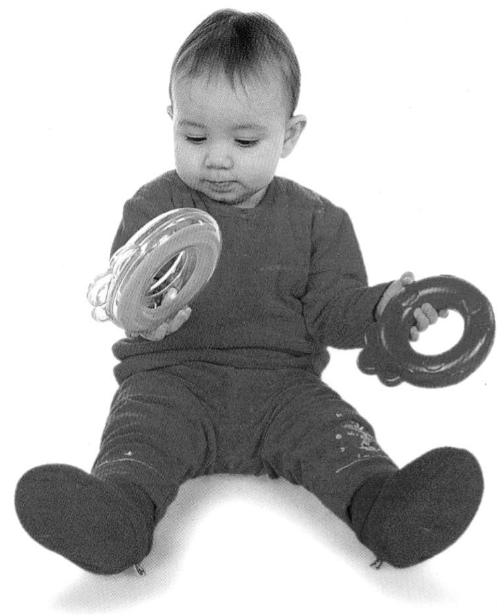

Right: A baby is learning about sound, texture and coordination when she does something as simple as banging two plastic rings together.

When you do try to stop her from exploring, she will probably be furious with you. Clearly you have to set limits, but you also have to be careful not to discourage her from developing her learning skills. This isn't always easy. Sometimes a compromise can be reached. For instance, you could let her hold the clock so that she can look at it closely, while making sure that you retain a firm grip on it, too. Then put it back in its usual place. That way her curiosity may be satisfied, without giving her a free rein to explore wherever she wants.

Remember, too, that your infant still learns from playing with familiar toys. Perhaps she has had a large soft ball for a couple of months and whenever she gets hold of it she simply chews it or drops it out of her hands. At the age of 8 or 9 months, however, she might learn something new: for instance, that she can hit it against the wall and it comes back to her, that it bounces if dropped from a height, that unless the surface is perfectly flat the ball doesn't sit still when placed there. In other words, she learns new things from old toys. So encourage her to play with all her toys, not just the ones you bought her most recently.

Below: Let your baby experiment with her food from time to time.

Top Tips

1. Don't restrict her too much. Of course there are safety issues to consider but allow your baby to explore freely under supervision. If she aims for forbidden territory, gently redirect her on to safer ground.

2. Play with mirrors. Even though she doesn't actually know that the image she sees in the mirror is her own, your infant still has great fun looking in a child-proof mirror. She'll squeal with delight when she sees your face appear there, too.

3. Let her sometimes make a mess when feeding. Food fascinates your child because it can be moulded and smeared into all sorts of shapes. At times, allow her to play with her food if she wants instead of eating it straight away.

4. Continue to challenge her memory. For instance, putting her teddy behind your back and asking her to find it enhances her recall. And if you bring out your hand without the teddy in it, she will probably try to crawl behind you to get it.

5. Put her in the baby seat in the supermarket trolley. Shopping without a grumpy infant is easier, yet she learns lots from cruising the aisles with you. Steer a middle course with the trolley, though, to avoid her grabbing things off the shelves.

Q When my baby plays with beakers in the bath, does she really learn anything?

A Yes, she does. If you observe her playing with these items, you'll see that she stares intently as she fills the beaker, then empties it, then fills it again. This is the first stage in learning about volume and about the way liquids change shape depending on the containers that hold them. It's another example of free play enhancing your infant's thinking skills.

Q My child is 8 months old and doesn't seem to see very small items. Is that normal?

A Her vision is maturing all the time, but it is still not as refined or sophisticated as yours. Evidence from research suggests that at this age she can probably see an object the size of a shirt button, but anything much smaller than that is not visible to her. In the next few months, her visual skills develop further.

Toys: toy with smaller pieces fitting into the main part, water toys, rings that stack on a pillar, balls of different sizes, empty containers

Stimulating Learning: 10 to 12 Months

What a difference a few months make to your child's learning skills! He has been able to move around and search actively for a couple of months already, but at this point he is ready to take a more focused approach to learning. Although exploration is still crucial to his learning, he spends more time playing with each individual toy than he did before, studying it more closely.

Bright First Born

There is a plethora of evidence which confirms that the first-born child in a family tends to be the brightest of all the children, and the effect lasts throughout childhood and into adulthood. This doesn't apply to every single first-born child, of course, but is nevertheless an identifiable tendency.

The most likely explanation for this finding is that the first-born child is the only one in the family to have parental attention all to himself (at least for a couple of years before the next one arrives). He has undivided parental interest, time and resources, and this probably results in a high level of stimulation which is hard to replicate when there are two or more children to be cared for.

Suitable Suggestions

His concentration and attention become more systematic. Previously he would have been all over the place, flitting from one toy to the next, scanning it briefly, playing with it briefly, then discarding it. Your child's maturity allows him to look at objects systematically rather than randomly. You can encourage this through instructions.

Above: At this age your child is likely to recognize animals and objects in her picture books.

Sit him on your knee as you read through a picture book. Instead of flicking over the pages, one after the other in quick succession, point out the different objects and draw his attention to them. Directions such as 'Look at the doll' or 'Look at the cow' help train your infant to scan the entire page not just look at the first things he sees. And if he points out an object on the page, then another object, give him a big cuddle and lots of praise. Even if he doesn't pick out the images in a systematic way, wait several seconds before you turn the page.

Give him opportunities to practise existing learning skills in new situations – he is at the

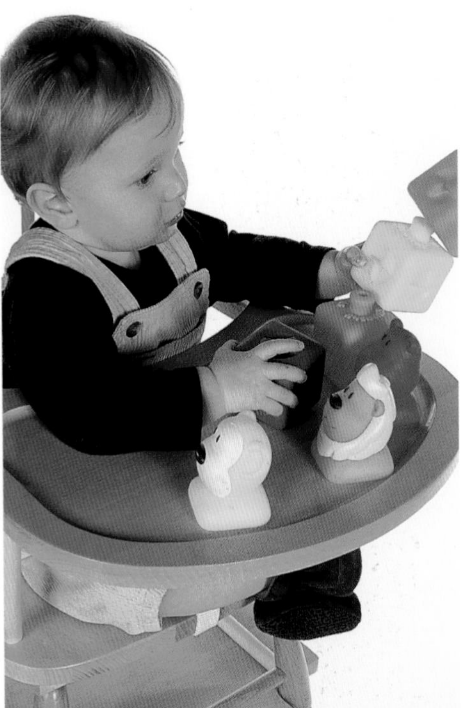

Left: This 11-month-old is deliberately stacking blocks in order to knock them over.

Above: Pretend play is likely to start with an action that your child sees you do frequently.

Top Tips

1. **Keep some 'special' toys.** At those times when your toddler is very bored, fed up and whining, bring out a toy that you have kept concealed in a cupboard. The sudden introduction of this toy cheers him up and stimulates his learning.
2. **Name basic body parts.** Playfully shake his hand and say 'This is your hand'. Do this for his feet, ears, nose, mouth and tummy. He starts to associate the word with the appropriate body part.
3. **Play along with him.** Research studies have found that the presence of a parent during play usually has a number of positive effects – the child plays for longer, is more willing to try unfamiliar toys and is more adventurous in his explorations.
4. **Start a routine, then let him continue.** This strengthens his memory. Complete the first stage of a familiar routine (for example, take out the bath towel) but stop there. Give your toddler time to continue, perhaps by starting to pull his socks off.
5. **Provide access to household utensils.** A small plastic bottle and a basin of water lets him learn from water play, and a piece of dough allows him to make different shapes. He learns from playing with ordinary (but safe) household items.

stage where he can adapt old strategies to novel problems. For instance, suppose he likes to play with toy nesting boxes and he is able to fit them into each other properly. Try to find other items that fit this way too, such as plastic cups of various sizes or small plastic barrels. At first, he may hesitate when faced with the new puzzle but he will soon apply his existing knowledge. Experiences like this build his confidence as a learner, making him a motivated problem-solver who can adapt and apply his learning concepts.

Encourage him to persist with those puzzle toys that he couldn't complete before, but remove the easy pieces. Shape-sorters, for instance, often contain some parts that can be fitted by a younger child (because they have the same outline no matter how they are rotated) as well as some that are usually not mastered until the child is older, by which time he may be bored with the toy altogether. So give him the shape-sorter without the easier shapes (such as the square, circle and triangle), and suggest that he puts the remaining shapes into the right places. Calm him if he becomes frustrated; jolly him along until he succeeds.

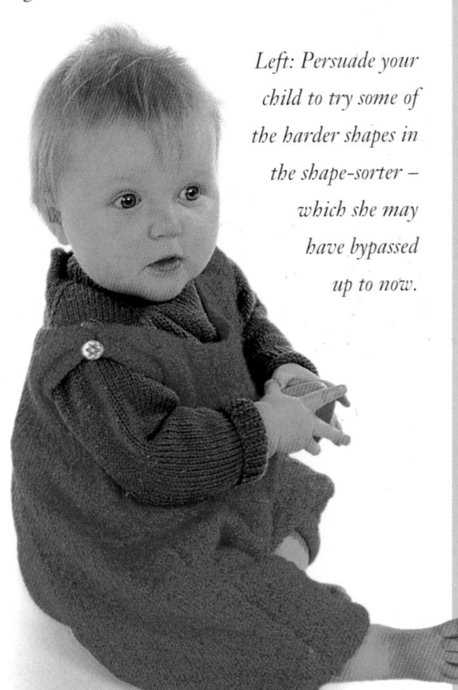

Left: Persuade your child to try some of the harder shapes in the shape-sorter – which she may have bypassed up to now.

Q&A

Q Exactly what is an intelligence test?

A This is a series of items which claim to measure important learning skills, such as reasoning, short-term memory, long-term memory, and pattern recognition. A child's performance on these various tests is then compared against the average scores which have been previously obtained from a very large sample of children his own age.

Q Should I arrange for my child to have an intelligence test to see how bright he is?

A The problem with intelligence tests is that they don't give an accurate picture of how a child will perform in a real-life problem-solving situation – they are too artificial and may be inaccurate. That's why it is far better for you to continue stimulating your child's learning skills each day than to arrange for an intelligence test.

Stimulating Learning: 13 to 15 Months

Your child's increased hand–eye coordination skills, along with her ability to toddle all over the place, gives her the confidence to investigate the entire house. You come into the kitchen one day, only to find her sitting quietly on the floor as she empties all the containers in your food cupboard. Unperturbed by the mess, her desire to learn blots out all worries about the consequences of her learning adventure.

Use Her Name

Help develop your child's listening skills by using her name when talking to her. For instance, if you want her to play with a puzzle toy, instead of saying 'Here's a toy for you', start the sentence with her name and then wait until she has turned towards you before completing it.

The same applies to simple requests. You might have to repeat everything to your toddler, almost as though she can't be bothered listening, yet it's more likely you have to do this because she doesn't tune in to your instruction until you are half-way through it. Saying her name at the start gains her attention, and gives her time to concentrate on what you have to say.

Suitable Suggestions

Imagination starts to play a role in your child's life for the first time and this begins a major shift in her thinking skills. Between birth and 12 months, she could only think in terms of what she saw directly in front of her – if the toy wasn't in her line of vision she couldn't pretend it was there, and that clearly limited her learning potential. Around 12 to 15 months, she becomes capable of symbolic thought and as a result can use one object to represent another; for instance, a wooden block can be a cup that she tries to drink out of. Imagination is an important part of learning.

Start playing 'pretend' games with your toddler. Reading her stories with an animated expression is one way to enhance her imagination. You can also pretend to have a tea party for her cuddly toys. She has terrific fun pretending to pour cups of tea for her guests, enabling her to practise actions that she has seen you carry out. Provide opportunities for her to use learned information in practical ways. Take tidying up, for example. This is good from several points of view, such as encouraging

Left: Include your child in the household routine. You can make tidying up fun by encouraging her to put some of her own toys away.

Left: Most toddlers will consider it a great privilege to be allowed to use some of your equipment and copy what you do.

independence and responsibility, but it also has value in developing her organizational skills. Tidying up her toys requires her to search the room systematically, to remember to place toys in the same box each time she picks one up from the floor, and to concentrate on the task until it is completed. She loves helping you with this, so resist the temptation to do it all yourself even though that would complete the job at a faster rate.

You can also stimulate her creativity by setting up a small tray with a thick mixture of sand and water, though watch her closely in case she thinks it would be a good idea to taste the mixture. Make the texture solid enough to stick together, roll up your toddler's sleeves and let her immerse her hands in the substance. At first she probably just picks up the mud, then lets it drop. Once the initial excitement is over, however, she may start to use her memory and background knowledge to create shapes, models and patterns.

Below: Sand and water play will fascinate your child but will need supervision.

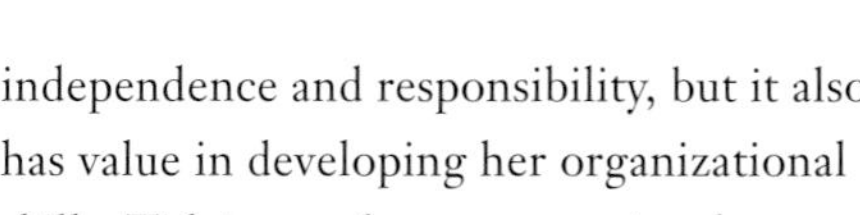

Top Tips

1. Extend her play. Help her learn how to extend the way she plays. For instance, if she makes one shape with the play dough, ask her to make another shape. If she rolls the toy car in one direction, ask her to push it in another direction.

2. Point out the different body parts on her large doll. Previously you showed these on your child but now she is able to learn them on a doll. Stick to the obvious parts, such as hair, head, eyes, feet, hands, mouth and ears.

3. Don't pressurize her. In your concern to improve her learning, you could have unrealistically high expectations of her achievements. By all means encourage her learning but make sure the challenges you give are reasonable for her age.

4. Practise, then break, then practise. When teaching your toddler a new skill, such as completing an inset board, let her do this for a couple of minutes, play with something else, then return to the inset board again after the break.

5. Let her struggle at times. Naturally you don't want your child to explode with frustration when the toy won't work the way she wants. But if you rush in with the solution every time, she won't learn the solution herself. Find a balance.

Q What size of jigsaw should my 15-month-old toddler be able to manage?

A Most toddlers can't manage a traditional jigsaw because it is a complex challenge, even if there are only two pieces. However, she will probably be able to place a flat wooden shape back into the correct space on an inset board, assuming there is only one space (or two spaces at the most).

Q How can I stop my toddler from being so impulsive? She is so quick when playing.

A Children vary in the way they approach a learning experience. Some – like your toddler – rush through it as quickly as they can, while others take their time. The next time your toddler plays with a toy, sit with her and chat to her; point to the toy, engage her interest in it and talk to her about it. This slows her down in her play, helping her be more reflective.

Toys: play dough, sand and water tray, plastic shapes, inset board, action toy, plastic tea set, duplo lego

Social and

Emotional Development

Social and Emotional Development

The moment your baby is born, her personality and emotions start to show through. She cries when she is unhappy, she's bright-eyed when she's enjoying herself, and she looks around the room when she is bored. You'll discover more and more of your baby's characteristics over the next 15 months, as you play with her, stimulate her and try to settle her into a stable feeding and sleeping routine. And her basic human need to mix with other people emerges during these first months as well, as she begins to become aware of other people and starts to seek attention from them.

Emotional Types

Every baby is different, with her own special and unique set of personal traits. However, psychologists have identified three main types of temperament in young children.

First, there is the easy child who copes happily with new experiences. She plays enthusiastically with new toys, sleeps and eats regularly, and adjusts easily to change. In contrast, the difficult child is the exact opposite. She resists any routine, cries a lot, takes a long time to finish her feeds and sleeps fitfully. And then there is the slow-to-warm-up child who is rather easy-going and passive. She doesn't get actively involved in anything and waits for the world to come to her. You can probably see aspects of all these types in your baby!

Nobody knows for sure where these emotional characteristics come from. Almost certainly, though, her personality and ability to relate to others is a combination of the characteristics she was born with and the way you raise her during childhood. There is also some evidence that emotional development begins during pregnancy. For example, studies have found that when a pregnant woman is angry, afraid or anxious, her emotional condition releases certain chemicals and hormones into her bloodstream which can affect the foetus, making the unborn baby restless and active.

Right: Your baby forms a close emotional bond with you.

Forming an Attachment

The biggest influence on your growing baby's social and emotional development during this early phase of her life, however, is bonding – that is, the two-way emotional attachment that she forms with you. This special relationship between you and your baby has a huge influence on her personality, emotional stability and friendliness.

Fortunately, your baby has an innate ability to form a close relationship with you. For instance, her hearing is tuned to pick up the sound of your voice, her vision enables her to focus clearly on your face during feeding, she can use her cries to express her feelings to you, and she is more responsive to the smell of your breast milk than she is to the breast milk of a stranger. These inborn social skills mean that bonding is a natural process, one that both you and your baby are ready for.

Here are some facts about bonding:

• **it doesn't have to happen at birth.** While there are some mums and dads who claim to love their

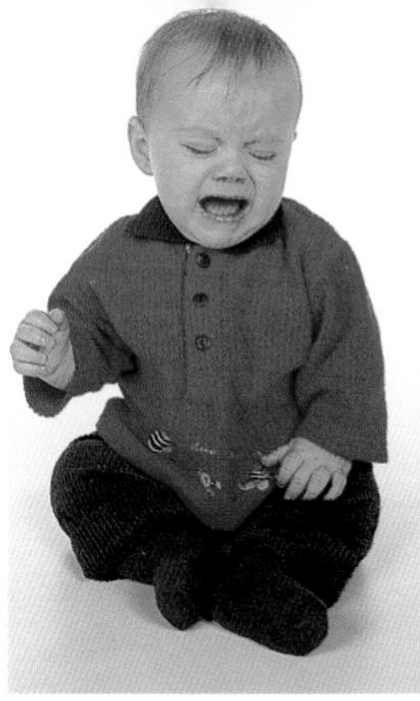

baby the second they set eyes on her, most parents take much longer to feel their baby is really theirs. At least 40 per cent of perfectly normal mothers take over a week – and sometimes months – to bond with their babies. So there is no reason to worry if it was not love at first sight for you.

• **it doesn't have to be all-or-none.** For most parents and babies, bonding is a gradual process. Like all your other relationships, the connection formed with your baby needs time. It is not a case that you have no bond with her one day and then suddenly the next day you have. The emotional attachment typically builds up day by day, month by month.

• **it doesn't only happen with one parent.** There is plenty of evidence that your baby is capable of forming an emotional attachment with more than one person at a time. She can have a psychological bond with you, and also with your partner, and with her grandparents. Each of these different relationships is very special to her and each contributes in its own way to her social and emotional development.

Get Involved

A strong connection between you and your baby brings her a sense of well-being, makes her feel safe and secure, provides a solid foundation for her to build future social relationships with others, and helps her learn to trust other people. And bonding is great for you, too, because it makes you feel good about yourself as a parent. It's a wonderful thought to know that your baby loves you and feels safe with you.

There's lots you can do to help this all-important psychological process along the way. Most importantly, try to relax when you are with your baby so that you can each enjoy the other's company. Of course, caring for her is demanding and you probably feel that you never have a minute to yourself; you may even have doubts about your own skills as a parent. Bear in mind, though, that your baby will be more comfortable with you when she senses you are at ease with her.

Physical love plays a large part in her social and emotional development, too. She just adores a cuddle from you, or from any other familiar person. There is something very special about being held firmly and gently in the arms of a loving adult. The closeness, the warmth, the body contact that are all part of a caring cuddle greatly increase her contentment and confidence.

Above: At 6 months some babies have developed the habit of thumb sucking which can act as a ready comforter in moments of distress.

Right: A close bond will enable you to understand and respond to your baby's needs more easily.

Stimulating Social and Emotional Development: Birth to 3 Months

During these first few months, you and your baby need time to get to know each other. You gradually learn the meaning of his cries, facial expressions and body movements and he steadily learns the meaning of your voice tones, manner and touch. The key to his satisfactory early emotional and social development is establishing a loving relationship with you.

Bottle-Feeding or Breast-Feeding

While scientific evidence proves that breast-feeding wins hands down when it comes to protecting your baby from infections during this early period, there is not one research study that suggests either bottle-feeding or breast-feeding has any particular benefit in helping you and your baby form a bond.

The style of feeding does have an effect, however. For instance, if you are tense and hurried when feeding him (whether using breast or bottle), he'll be tense, too; if you are irritable with him, he will sense this and have difficulty taking the feed. In other words, try to think positively during feeding.

Suitable Suggestions

The best help you can give your baby is to relax when you are with him. That's easier said than done, of course, because the stresses and strains of keeping up with his constant feeding, changing and bathing needs can seem overwhelming at times. And if things don't go entirely to plan because, for instance, he doesn't take his feed properly or because he cries for no apparent reason, you are likely to become anxious. Yet if you are tense and strained with your baby, he'll soon feel like that too. So it's worth making a special effort to be at ease in his company.

Another way to help you and your baby forge a strong emotional connection is to soothe him when he appears distressed. Your baby cries for any one of a large number of reasons, ranging from hunger to pain, from loneliness to tiredness, and it's hard for you to know the real explanation of his upset. The problem is that he can't speak to you to say what troubles him. But you can try to soothe him anyway.

You'll develop a repertoire of strategies for stopping his tears, including cuddling him, swaddling him, playing soft music to him, taking him for a run in the car, and playing with him. The success of these different techniques will vary from week to week, depending on his mood – the main thing is that you make a good attempt at finding a way to calm your baby.

Below: Close physical contact is reassuring to a new baby.

Above: Kissing, cuddling and talking to your new baby will help you learn to handle her in a calm and relaxed way.

Top Tips

1. Have confidence in yourself as a parent. Tell yourself that you will be a great parent. Act confidently and calmly when managing your new baby. Your self-belief will steadily increase as your experience grows.

2. Make lots of eye contact with your young baby. He loves it when you look deep into his eyes, because attention builds his confidence. It also teaches him the essential social skill of looking other people in the eyes when talking to them.

3. Let him know that you are interested in him. He needs to feel that he matters to you, and the best way of demonstrating this is by giving him lots of attention, by talking lovingly to him, and by smiling at him and giving him lots of cuddles.

4. Try to develop a stable feeding and sleeping routine. His nutritional and sleep needs change quickly during this period, and routines can be very difficult to establish. However, most babies are more settled in a steady routine.

5. Take him with you when you go out. It's good for him to see a range of faces and hear different voices, whether at the supermarket or in the street. This heightens his interest in other people and builds his social confidence.

You can also help his social development by letting him be held by other adults. True, he quickly gets used to your handling, warmth and smell, and he likes that. However, there is no harm in letting other caring relatives and friends give him a cuddle when they visit. This won't at all threaten the integrity of your emotional attachment with him, and it will strengthen his sociability. He'll enjoy a cuddle from his grandmother or from your best pal, even though he prefers you to hold him. This gets him used to being with other people from an early age, laying the foundation for future social relationships.

Below: If you enjoy it, feeding your baby can be a time when you feel very close to him.

Q If I go to my baby every time he cries, am I encouraging him to be attention-seeking?

A A baby left unattended while crying may feel lonely, isolated and insecure. After all, crying is your baby's main way of communicating with you. When he is a bit older, you might decide to wait a moment before responding, but at this young age he cries because he needs you.

Q By what age should my baby have formed an emotional bond with me?

A That depends entirely on you and your baby. There is no 'typical' time span. However, psychological research has found that a child who has not formed this form of secure psychological connection with a caring adult by the time he is around the age of 4 years is likely to have social difficulties throughout his life.

Toys: cuddly cot toy, rattles, gentle music box to play while feeding or cuddling him, floor multi-gym

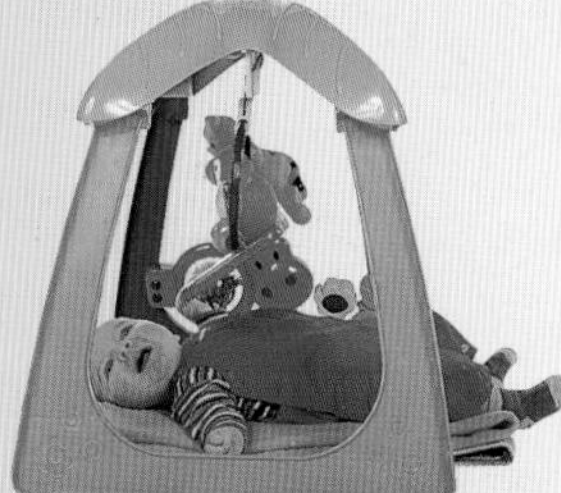

Stimulating Social and Emotional Development: 4 to 6 Months

Your infant's social skills increase as her need to mix with others intensifies. She starts to become more aware of other people around her and uses non-verbal communication to interact with them; she thrives on attention. But despite this enthusiasm to have company, her social confidence remains very fragile – the moment she sets eyes on a stranger she may well burst into tears.

Enduring Traits

Babies vary greatly in their sensitivity and moods. Maybe your baby is one of those who is very dramatic when it comes to expressing her emotions; perhaps she howls loudly the minute anything goes wrong and whines and moans most of the time. Or maybe she is an even-tempered infant, who happily goes with the flow and deals calmly with life's little challenges.

Whatever your baby's particular emotional characteristics, you will find that you adjust to them. Results from psychological research suggest that many of these important personality traits which are present during the early months are usually stable, in that they tend to stick with the baby for the rest of her life.

Suitable Suggestions

Respond eagerly when she communicates. Should she smile at you or make sounds to grab your attention, go over to her and play with her. Reciprocate her gestures, so that if she smiles, you smile back, if she passes you a toy, you pass her a toy, and so on. This reinforces her social skills. There will be times when she is happy to play on her own, especially as she nears the 6-month point, but for the time being she likes to have your attention whenever possible.

This doesn't mean, though, that you should be there with her for every second of the day. Part of social and emotional development involves your child establishing an element of independence, of managing on her own without you right beside her all the time. If you rush over to her whenever she calls for you out of boredom, your baby between the ages of 4 and 6 months will never learn how to amuse herself. During this period of her life, try to make sure there are times when she is left to play in the cot on her own. This strengthens her self-sufficiency.

Her innate desire to explore, coupled with her increased hand–eye coordination and movement skills, results in a whole new range of discovery opportunities opening up for her. The downside of this is that she might get herself into situations that prove difficult or frightening for her – for instance, when she crawls behind the sofa and ends up

Right: At around 6 months babies can begin to grasp basic reciprocal communication.

Above: At this age babies will show interest in other babies, though this is usually short-lived.

Top Tips

1. Let her play alongside other children her age. Although she will not play with them and might even just sit and stare at them, these other children will be of great interest to her. She watches and learns from their actions.

2. Talk to other people when she is with you. Your young baby needs to learn that language is a key part of most social interactions. Seeing you chat to people whom you meet provides a good model for her to copy.

3. Reassure her when she is shy with an unfamiliar adult. When she hides because a stranger talks to her, hold her hand, cuddle her and tell her not to be afraid. Your reassurance helps her overcome this dip in her confidence.

4. React to her sense of humour. The ability to laugh is an effective social skill. So laugh heartily when you hear her laugh, and try to make her smile when she has a serious expression on her face.

5. Don't pander to her grumpy moments. If your child is irritable at times, carry on talking to her and playing with her anyway. If you simply leave her alone when she is moody, her irritability will probably continue for longer.

jammed against the wall, or when she reaches for an ornament on the table and succeeds in bringing it crashing down on her head. Your child can be unnerved by these events, and might become timid and apprehensive.

Boost her confidence when you see this happening. Comfort her, calm her, wipe away her tears, and then encourage her to start exploring again. The great thing about your baby is that she will soon forget a bad experience if you are there to cheer her up. If her self-belief suffers a setback, help her regain her confidence through your support and encouragement.

Below: A 4-month-old baby is very dependent on you for his entertainment and will probably only play alone for short periods.

Q&A

Q Should I play with my 5-month-old when she wakes during the night?

A Of course you need to comfort her. Yet there is a danger that if you turn night waking into an enjoyable play episode, you may actually encourage her to wake up more frequently. A more effective strategy is to settle her, reassure her and then let her go back to sleep.

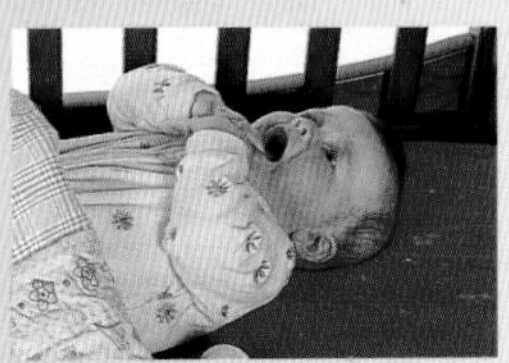

Q Is it true that as babies, boys tend to be more difficult to manage than girls?

A There is not a great deal of research evidence to support this idea. However, it is generally true that baby boys do tend to be more adventurous than baby girls, but this could be because parents let boys behave this way while they discourage their girls from displaying such high-spirited behaviour.

Toys: child-safe mirror with handles, small plastic blocks with a container, plastic or cloth books, small soft ball

Stimulating Social and Emotional Development: 7 to 9 Months

Your infant is less passive in the company of others. Now he is more out-going socially and makes active attempts to respond to other people. Although he hasn't any meaningful speech yet, he will babble loudly when someone talks to him – this is his form of sociable conversation. He has no difficulty letting you know when he is in a bad mood!

Comforters

Most infants become fond of a cuddly toy and like to have it with them. If yours does have a comforter (so-called because the object makes him feel contented), he adores the cuddly toy even though it is dirty, ragged and might even have bits missing. He loves the familiar feel and smell of the object.

Using a comforter does not mean your child is afraid or timid. In fact, there is no link between comforters in early childhood and emotional instability later on – if anything, evidence from studies shows that infants who become attached to a comforter are often more confident when they start attending school.

Suitable Suggestions

Increase your expectations of his sociability. Whereas when he was younger you might have chatted to him without expecting any reasonable response, it's time for you to give him an opportunity to react. So when you talk to him, leave a pause for him to babble back at you; when you ask him a question such as 'Do you want another drink?' look for an answer in his facial expression, body movements and sounds, instead of just giving him the drink anyway. Your encouragement will make him realize that he needs to get involved.

By now you should have begun to have clear ideas on discipline for use with your infant. Remember that discipline is not about controlling your child, rather it is about encouraging his awareness of others and his understanding that other people have feelings just like him. Rules about behaviour enhance his social awareness and help him establish self-control. Yet this doesn't mean he will happily do as you ask!

He knows the full meaning of the word 'no' and may be absolutely furious with you when

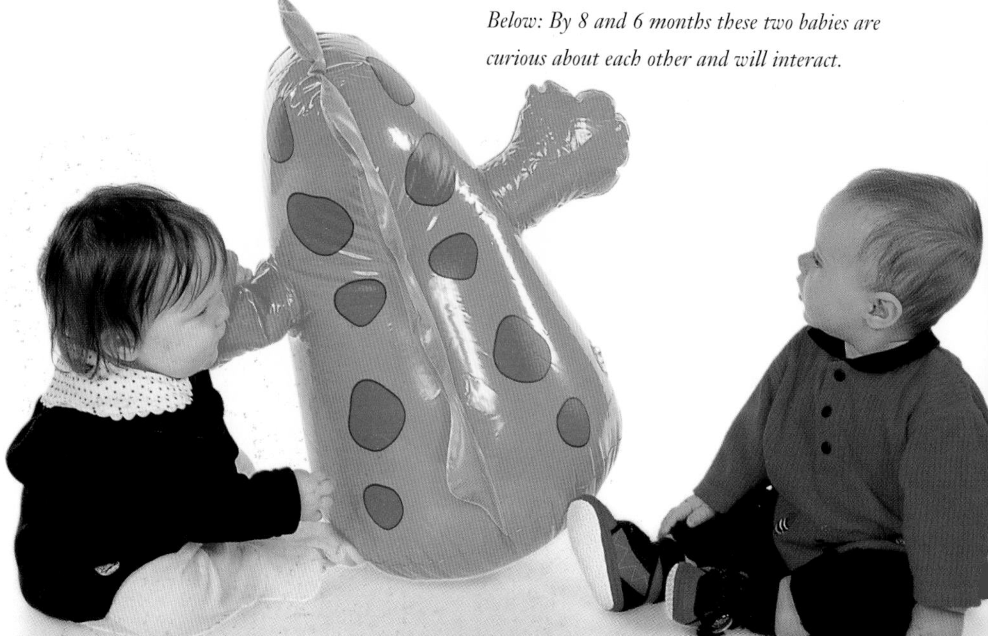

Below: By 8 and 6 months these two babies are curious about each other and will interact.

you stand in his way. That's a normal, healthy emotional reaction. However, you can help him gain control over his temper at this age by calming him, and by standing

Left: By 8 months babies enjoy their routine and will get excited when they know something they like is about to happen – like the daily bath.

your ground. Don't give in to his angry demands. Through this process, he learns how to modify his own behaviour and to develop sensitivity towards others.

A stable daily routine is helpful for your child's emotional development at this age. Meals at regular times and a reasonably fixed time for bed each night enable him to structure his day, and this structure contributes to his overall sense of security and well-being.

You'll find that he enjoys the familiarity of, for instance, his pre-bath and pre-bedtime routine because these actions signal what is about to come. He'll start to smile when he sees you bring his own bath towel from the cupboard or when he catches sight of you tidying his cot toys. Structure makes him feel safe. Of course you need to be flexible; in general, though, routine is emotionally beneficial for your child.

Below: At this age a baby still needs frequent reassurance and usually likes to know that you are near at hand.

Top Tips

1. Continue to show your child that you love him. Regular demonstrations that you love and value him increase his self-confidence. He soaks up every drop of parental love you put his way and he responds by acting lovingly towards you.

2. Make sure he achieves success in things he does. Success increases his 'feel-good' factor and confidence. For instance, completing a puzzle toy, or managing to bring a spoon to his mouth by himself, has a very positive effect on him.

3. Take him along to a parent-and-toddler group. He's still not ready to play cooperatively with other children (and won't be for a long time) but that doesn't stop him from enjoying being in their presence. This experience stimulates his social enthusiasm.

4. Give him plenty of praise. Your verbal praise and approval matters very much to your baby aged between 7 and 9 months. It acts as encouragement to persevere, while also boosting his self-esteem.

5. Use a baby-sitter so that you can go out without him. Aside from the benefits to you of going out on your own, it's also good for your baby to get used to someone else's care. He'll quickly adapt to this temporary arrangement.

Q My baby is 8 months old but still cries extremely easily. How can I make him more robust?

A He probably cries so much because this is an effective way of getting your attention. Start to ignore some of his crying episodes unless you are sure there is something seriously wrong. His tears may flow less frequently when he realizes they don't achieve the desired effect.

Q Should I let my 9-month-old baby continue to suck a dummy?

A It's entirely up to you. The biggest hazard facing a child who sucks a dummy at this age is that of poor hygiene. He probably throws it on to the ground, picks it up and puts it straight into his mouth, which makes him vulnerable to germs. So you should do your best to keep his dummy clean.

Toys: buggy rattle, plastic grab-ring, cuddly small animal, teething ring, Jack-in-the-box toy, single-picture cardboard book

Stimulating Social and Emotional Development: 10 to 12 Months

Her main emotional characteristics are clear and strong, and you can probably now predict how she will behave in most situations. However, your child's increased awareness of the world around her causes a temporary halt to the growth in her sociability; her attachment to you becomes more intense and her desire to mix with others slows down a little at this stage.

The Ambitious Toddler

Despite her clinging behaviour and fear of strangers, your toddler is very ambitious and has a tremendous belief in her own abilities. No challenge is too great for her once she has made up her mind to achieve it.

In reality, however, her ambitions outstrip her ability and this means you may find a sharp increase in episodes of tearfulness and frustration. For instance, she is extremely unhappy when the cushions of the sofa are impossibly high for her to reach, or when the door handle is too high for her to turn. She needs you to comfort her when these desired goals elude her.

Suitable Suggestions

The typical toddler feels very secure with her parents and also has an increased awareness of strangers. The ironic effect of these two trends is that you might find your child happy to play with you but more anxious with unfamiliar people, even though recently she was more socially adventurous. Don't be irritable with her when she clings tightly to you – this apparent increase in her emotional dependency on you will pass in a few months. She needs your patience and support at this time.

In the meantime, continue to encourage her to play in the presence of other children and continue to use other carers (for example a baby-sitter) when required. But do expect her to be a bit more clingy to you at this time. If she cries when you leave her with the baby-sitter – whereas before she didn't bother at all – give her bags of reassurance and then go out anyway. You can always call the baby-sitter a few minutes later to check that she has settled.

You'll find that when you take your 1-year-old to parent-and-toddler group, there may be times when she crawls over to another child and snatches a toy from her hands. Your toddler doesn't do this out of malice; it's just

Right: Approaching a year, it is easier for your baby to begin to share games and activities with other members of the family.

Left: Ironically, as your child becomes able to do more she may also become more clingy, as she identifies very strongly with her parents and is less accepting of strangers.

that she isn't mature enough to contemplate the emotional effect this has on the other child. And when her action causes the other child to burst out crying with shock, she stares with curiosity, unable to see the connection between her taking the toy and the other child's tears.

Respond calmly but firmly in these situations. Remember that part of your child's social and emotional development involves her increasing sensitivity to the wishes and feelings of others; she slowly learns that she doesn't live in a social vacuum, that her behaviour has an impact on those around her. So take the toy from her, telling her quietly but clearly that she shouldn't take things from another child like that, and return the toy to the original owner. Your toddler will howl in protest, and may try to reverse your decision, but return the toy anyway.

Above: Start to encourage good social behaviour. You can begin to explain things like taking turns in simple terms.

Top Tips

1. Use a familiar routine when leaving her with another carer. When you go out without her, follow the same format of saying goodbye, kissing her, then waving goodbye to her. Encourage her to reciprocate these actions to you.

2. Model good behaviour. You should avoid the trap of constantly correcting her when she misbehaves. She is more likely to learn appropriate behaviour if you tell her what she should do, instead of reprimanding her for what she shouldn't do.

3. Have fun with her. Toddlers can be very demanding to be with all day. But her confidence and social skills will improve when she knows that you are relaxed, laughing and smiling in her company. Her sense of security increases as a result.

4. Take pride in her achievements. Your child needs constant encouragement to progress, but you need to ensure that she knows you are pleased with her progress so far. Praise her current achievements before going on to the next stage.

5. Give her social reassurance. Reassure your socially anxious infant by speaking words of support to her, by hugging her when necessary, by giving her lots of opportunities to be with others, and by praising her when she copes without tears.

Q Should I let her hold the spoon at meals? She makes such a mess.

A She makes a mess because she can't do the job properly, but the only way she can learn is through practice. Try not to dampen her desire for independence, even though you could complete feeding quicker on your own. At least let her hold the spoon for part of the time.

Q My 11-month-old baby cries whenever I leave her with someone else. Would it be better for me to sneak out of the house quietly when she isn't looking?

A This may work at first, but your infant will quickly learn your strategy and become very anxious even when you have no intention of sneaking out. It's better for you to tell her goodbye, cuddle her, reassure her, and then just go.

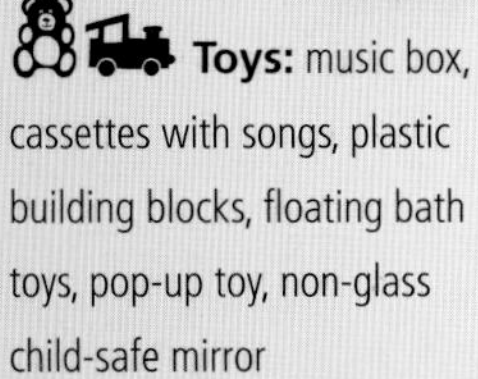

Toys: music box, cassettes with songs, plastic building blocks, floating bath toys, pop-up toy, non-glass child-safe mirror

Stimulating Social and Emotional Development: 13 to 15 Months

Your toddler can be more difficult to manage during this start to his second year. He wants to do more on his own and he is not at all pleased if you set limits on his behaviour. Tantrums may be frequent when he can't get his own way. He is curious about other people, and will stare uninhibitedly at anyone who attracts his attention.

FEARS

Toddlers this age are notoriously challenging and determined and can be remarkably confident with others. And yet this is also the time when small fears can develop. In fact, research confirms that most children have a least one fear from the age of 12 months onwards, such as a fear of cats, dogs, insects or spiders.

If your child does show fear of something, don't make a fuss as that will intensify his terror. Instead, remain calm, reassure him that he will be fine and just carry on with his normal routine. He will take his emotional lead from you – your relaxed, stable attitude will help him beat his fear.

Suitable Suggestions

Take him with you outside, when at all possible. People fascinate him and he loves watching them. If someone arouses his curiosity, he might toddle over to them and stick his face as close to theirs as he can; he is as likely to do this in the supermarket as he is at parent-and-toddler group. Bring him back to your side on these occasions and tell him not to stare (even though he doesn't fully understand what you mean) – he'll gradually learn that such social closeness is not welcome.

Right: Your child will now positively relish attention from other people she knows well – like grandparents.

Your 1-year-old has an increased sense of self, an increased awareness that he is an individual with his own likes and dislikes, his own strengths and weaknesses; and this is a key part of his emotional development.

One easy technique – used by psychologists to test the development of a child's self-image – is to let your toddler play with a mirror. When you are sure he has studied his own reflection in it, distract his attention with another activity for a few seconds.

Left: Children of this age need plenty of physical outlets for their energies and find it great fun if you join in sometimes.

Left: Make some basic decisions about what behaviour you will and will not tolerate and be consistent.

As you do this, discreetly put a red mark on his forehead (say, with a lipstick) but without making him aware that you have done this. Then get him involved in looking at the mirror once again.

If his self-image is sufficiently mature, he will touch his forehead in the approximate area of the red mark because he knows that this is his reflection and that therefore he must have that mark on his head. Approximately half of all children around the age of 15 months will try to touch the mark, compared with three-quarters of all 2-year-olds and virtually all 3-year-olds.

You can encourage your toddler's sense of self by making a special point of using his name when you talk to him. He knows this word is just for him and that when you look at him and say his name, you are referring to him alone. You can also help by starting to teach him the names of his body parts, such as hands, feet, eyes, ears and so on. He's much too young to say these words but he can start to understand them.

Top Tips

1. Give him advice on social skills. He needs you to point out to him, for instance, that he should pass the ball to the other child, and that he should say 'hello' when he meets another person. He learns these social skills gradually.

2. Praise appropriate social behaviour. When your child acts positively in a social setting (for instance, if he shares his toys, or smiles at another child) give him a cuddle to show him that you are delighted with his behaviour.

3. Don't pander to his fears. Your growing child won't learn to overcome a fear if you allow him to avoid the thing that frightens him. Keep to his normal daily routine despite his fear, rather than organizing his life around it.

4. Tackle jealousy when it arises. He may be resentful when you give attention to another toddler. This jealousy arises because he doesn't like sharing you. Talk to him until he calms down, then continue talking to his friend.

5. Have your evening meal with him, occasionally. Try to include your toddler at times when having the evening meal with the rest of your family. He loves the social nature of a family meal.

Below: Be prepared for tantrums when your child cannot get his own way and accept that they are part and parcel of your child becoming an individual.

Q My toddler screams the place down if I put the light out before he is asleep. What should I do?

A Fit a dimmer switch to his light. Without saying anything, each night gradually set the light a bit dimmer than it was the night before. You'll find that after a period of perhaps three or four weeks, he can sleep without any night light at all.

Q Our 14-month-old has insisted recently that he only plays with me, not my partner. Is that normal?

A Phases of attachment to one parent in particular happen occasionally, but are temporary. Arrange for your partner to play with your toddler, to bath him, feed him and so on, even though he prefers your company. This will help the attachment remain strong to both of you.

Toys: plastic book with pictures, puzzle boards, pull-along toy, child-safe mirror, crayon and paper, plastic construction blocks

toddler

16–36 months

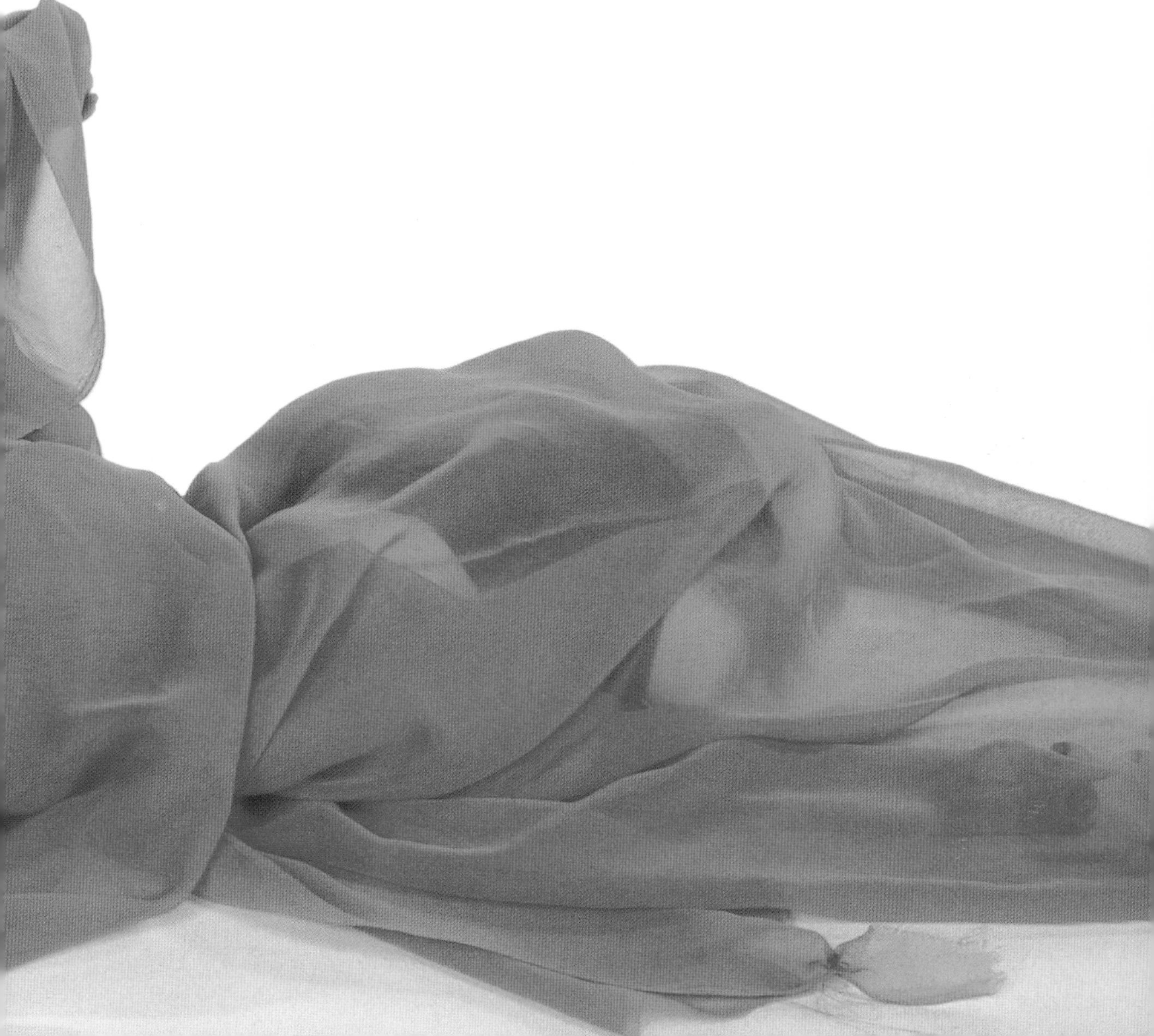

Tantrums

Temper tantrums are common between the ages of 16 months and 36 months – research confirms that this is the peak time for such uncontrolled outbursts. Your growing child suddenly becomes unable to wait for anything, tolerate any level of frustration or hear the word 'no' without exploding with rage or erupting in tears and/or shouts. Although this is a normal, if not universal, phase of development, he needs your help to gain control over his temper.

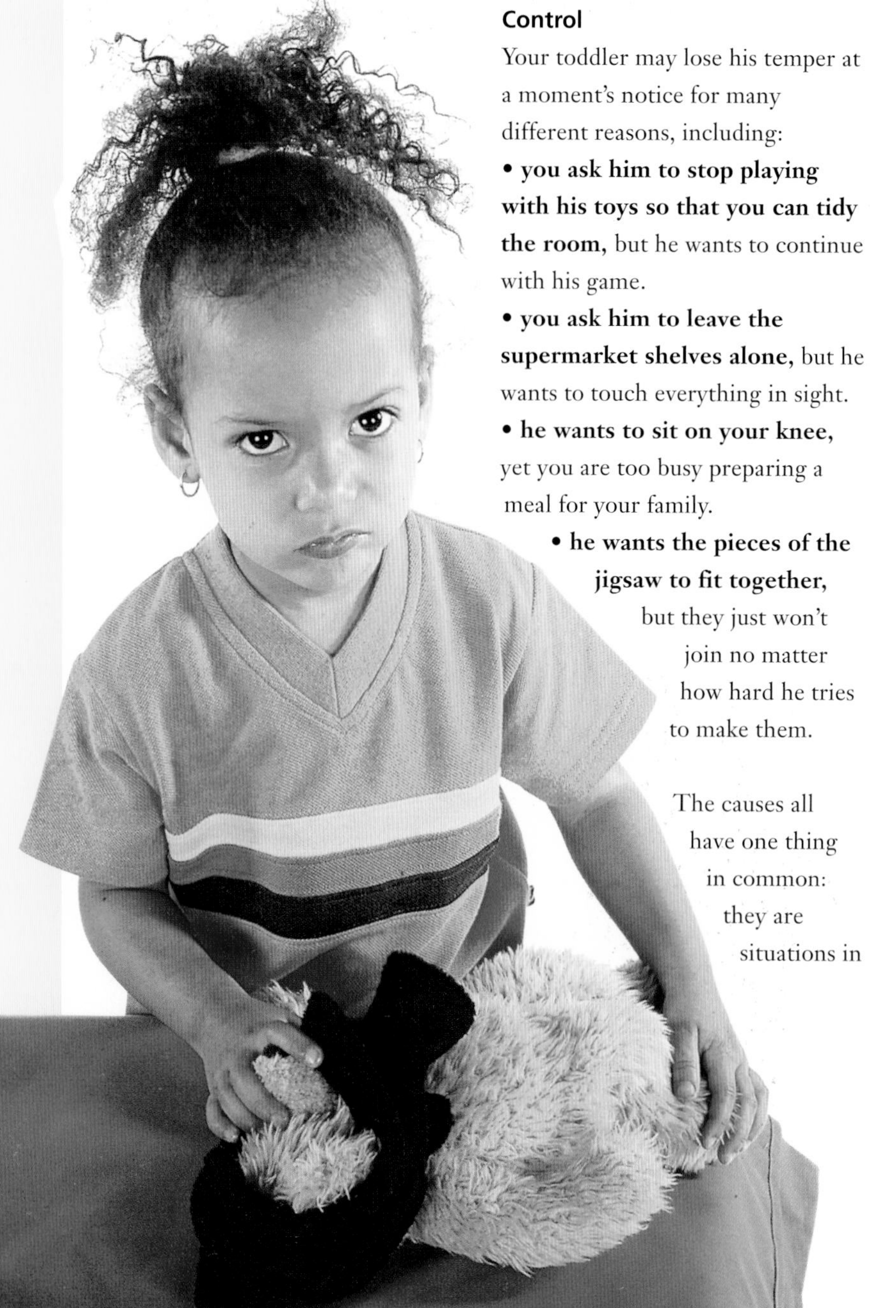

Control

Your toddler may lose his temper at a moment's notice for many different reasons, including:

- **you ask him to stop playing with his toys so that you can tidy the room,** but he wants to continue with his game.
- **you ask him to leave the supermarket shelves alone,** but he wants to touch everything in sight.
- **he wants to sit on your knee,** yet you are too busy preparing a meal for your family.
- **he wants the pieces of the jigsaw to fit together,** but they just won't join no matter how hard he tries to make them.

The causes all have one thing in common: they are situations in which your child can't get or do what he wants. It's not that he is naughty, rather his frequent tantrums reflect his strong desire to be independent and to be able to follow his own inclinations without any barriers put in his way and to achieve any target he sets himself. In addition, he sees the world only from his point of view and hasn't yet developed to the stage where he can understand why anyone should see things differently. Over the next few years most tantrum-prone toddlers gradually learn to control their temper and become more responsive to the needs of others.

Sometimes a child has a breath-holding tantrum, in which he becomes so enraged that he involuntarily holds his breath until he faints or until his parent forces him to breathe again. Your child won't harm himself during a breath-holding tantrum, although it is frightening for you to witness. But sometimes a child inadvertently

Left: Parents can often tell from their child's expression whether a tantrum is imminent; sometimes it is possible to diffuse the situation, sometimes not.

hurts himself during a temper tantrum, when out of sheer frustration he may throw himself on the floor or bang his head off a wall or table. Make sure you watch your toddler closely when he rages in order to prevent such injuries.

Set Limits

Ironically, the best help you can give your toddler when he pushes against the limits that you have set and rages in the hope of forcing you to change your mind, is to hold your ground. You can help him gain control of his angry emotions by sticking to your decision. He needs structure and consistency in his life and it's up to you to set this for him at home. If you say 'no' but then give in to him because of his tantrum, he'll learn that a 'no' can be changed to a 'yes', if he makes a big enough fuss. And before you know it you'll have to deal with even more outbursts.

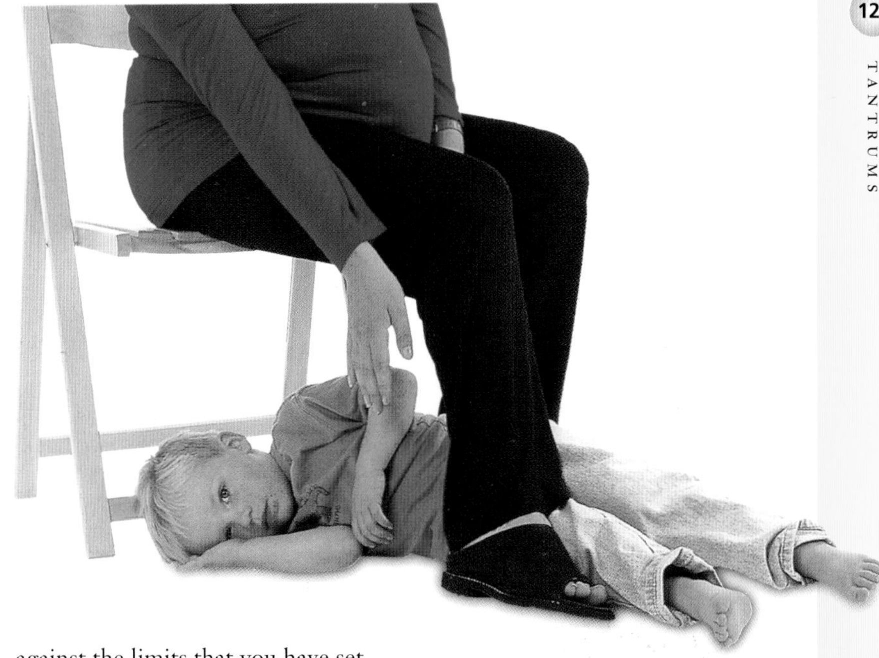

Above: While not giving in to him, if you stay close and reassure him he will regain control of himself more easily.

Try not to get angry with your child when he loses his temper or when he starts to show his frustration, as that will only make matters worse. Calm him down, and explain why he can't get his own way on this occasion (whether he actually listens to you or not). If he is annoyed because he cannot complete a game or puzzle, for example, show him how to achieve this by breaking the task down into small, manageable steps. This helps him learn how to deal more effectively with his emotions.

Left: At the age of 2 the smallest setback can be enough to cause frustration and, in some cases, tears.

Top Tips

1. **Prevent the tantrum,** if possible. You probably know your child well enough to spot the early warning signs, such as a reddening face, quiet moaning or irritability. If you see any indicators, distract his attention to another activity.
2. **Stay calm.** Your child is unlikely to regain control if you shout at him. Despite his fury – and he may even hit you during a tantrum – don't lose your own temper. By staying calm yourself, you'll help your child settle.
3. **Give him reassurance.** All the time that he rages, speak gently to him, telling him that everything will be all right. You may find that giving him a firm cuddle while he has a tantrum has a soothing effect on him.
4. **Talk to him afterwards.** Once the tantrum is over and tempers have cooled, discuss your child's behaviour with him. Explain why his actions are unacceptable and tell him that you won't give in when he behaves like that.
5. **Have confidence in yourself.** Remember that his tantrums are not your fault – they arise from his particular level of emotional development. Don't feel guilty, just do your best to deal with him calmly, firmly and consistently.

Eating Habits

Most toddlers pick at their food sometimes, much to the annoyance of parents. And the chances are that yours is no exception. Fussy eating might simply mean that your 16-month-old dislikes a particular food, or that your 2-year-old has a small appetite, or that your 2½-year-old just likes to push her food endlessly around her plate. In any case, she will probably assert her independence on food choices from the age of about 16 months onwards. Although fussy eating is often a passing phase in a young child's life, it can also develop into a long-term characteristic. Remember that sudden loss of appetite in a child who was previously a good eater may indicate a health problem, especially if she also has other symptoms. In such cases you should seek medical advice.

Managing your Fussy Eater

There is one key point to bear in mind when tackling your toddler's mealtime habits – you can't force her to eat. No matter how much pressure you put on her, she has to make the choice to eat. This is why confrontational methods of dealing with fussy eating won't work. You need to engage your child's cooperation.

Even before you consider strategies to encourage better eating habits, think about the meal from your child's point of view. Don't forget that when you sit down at the table to eat, you expect the meal to appear enticing, to smell good and to be at the right temperature – your toddler is no different. Consider the possibility that your child may be a fussy eater because:

- **the food is too greasy.** A meal that has a high grease content can make your child feel nauseated; other textures, such as chewy meat, can have the same effect.
- **the cutlery is the wrong size.** Small hands have a small grip, which means that cutlery suitable

Below: Sharing meals with the rest of the family is a social experience for a toddler and can help take the focus of attention away from what he does or does not eat.

for your hands will be too large for your child and will therefore make eating hard work.

• **the portion is too large.** Parents often increase the size of portion they give to their child when she has a poor appetite. Smaller portions are less intimidating.

• **she can't reach the food properly.** Her chair might be too low, or she might need a cushion on it. Make sure that your child is seated so that she can reach her food comfortably and easily.

• **the food is too hot.** Temperature affects the appeal of food. Your child may prefer her food to be neither hot nor cold, just a pleasant temperature in between.

• **she dislikes the taste.** She is perfectly entitled to dislike the taste of certain foods, and you may find that her preferences differ markedly from yours.

Avoid threatening your child when she won't finish a meal. Arguments make everybody tense and anxious and this reduces her appetite even further. Stay calm, be patient and allow plenty of time for meals. Many parents are concerned about their child's poor eating because of fear that she'll miss out on vital nutrients, but this rarely happens. A basic check from your family doctor will reassure you on this point.

Top Tips

1. Let your child choose. She will be more interested in eating her meal when she has been given some choice about it. If possible, let her select from a limited range of meal options so that her motivation to eat is high from the start.

2. Relax at mealtimes. Since tension is highly infectious, try to relax before serving a meal to your fussy eater. Even if you feel anxious and harassed, do your best to hide these negative feelings when your child is eating.

3. Involve her in making the meal. Although your toddler cannot cook meals herself, she could become involved in the preparation, such as bringing ingredients to you. The more she is involved, the more likely she is to eat.

4. Vary the presentation. If your child is fussy about meals served on a plate, she may be more positive about eating foods that she can pick up with her hands. Finger foods can be just as nutritious as a conventional meal and may be more appetizing to your child.

5. Praise her when she does eat. There will be times when she eats most of her meal, perhaps because she particularly liked the food. In such instances, give her lots of praise and even a small reward.

Eating with the Family

Remember that eating is a social experience – it's not just about your toddler satisfying her nutritional needs. The different schedules of those in your family might mean that it's more convenient for your toddler to eat on her own than to wait for everyone else. However, you may find that she enjoys eating together with the family. True, this might make the mealtime more hectic – and probably noisier as well – but your toddler learns from the eating habits of others and has more fun than when eating alone.

Another problem that can arise from your toddler eating her meal on her own is plain boredom. She is by nature sociable and she likes contact with others in the family. You can hardly blame her for, say, wanting to leave her meal and climb down from the table to play with her toys if she has no one else to talk to while eating. This is why you should try to sit with her while she eats, at least for some of the time. She is more likely to clear her plate when you are nearby.

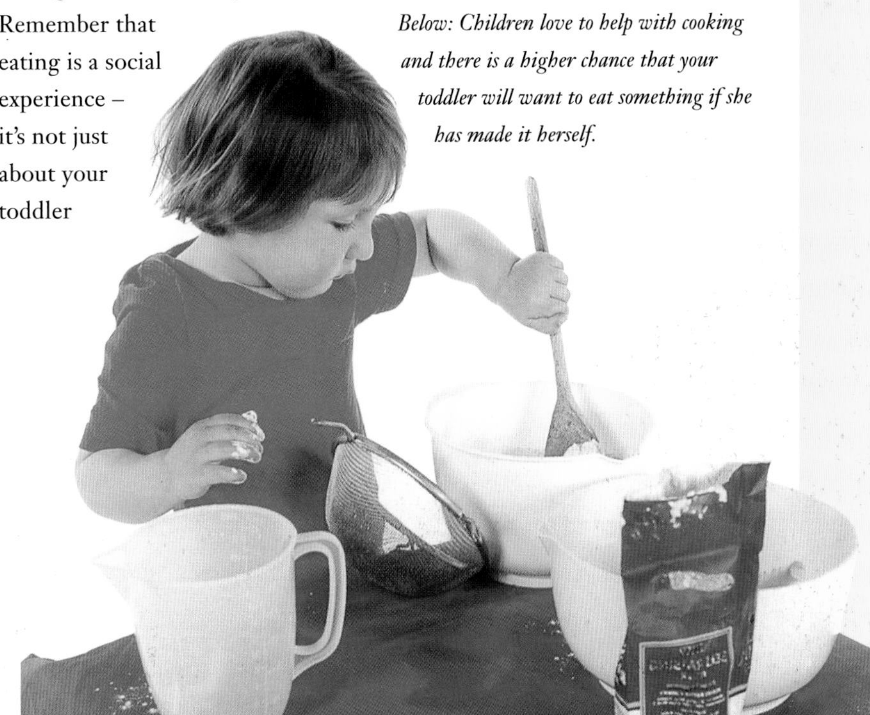

Below: Children love to help with cooking and there is a higher chance that your toddler will want to eat something if she has made it herself.

Potty Training

One of the most significant skills your child acquires between the ages of 16 and 36 months is the ability to control his bladder and bowels. Mastering potty training is a stage in his development that gives him independence and boosts his self-confidence. However, potty training itself doesn't always go according to plan, which can result in frustration and anger for both child and parent. When that happens, progress slows considerably or may stop altogether. If you maintain a relaxed approach and avoid battles, your child will steadily gain bladder and bowel control and you will be delighted with this new phase in his development.

Think about It

Resist any temptation to start potty training before your child is ready. The fact is that your child's muscle and nervous systems won't be sufficiently mature to control his bowel and bladder until he is at least aged 16 months, and it is usually best to wait until around 20 months before beginning training. Research confirms that boys are generally slower to acquire control than girls, although nobody is sure why this gender difference exists.

If you start potty training before your toddler's ready for it, you may end up in conflict with him; you'll feel frustrated by his lack of success and his self-esteem will drop for the same reason. Potty training is most effective when there is a positive partnership between you and your child.

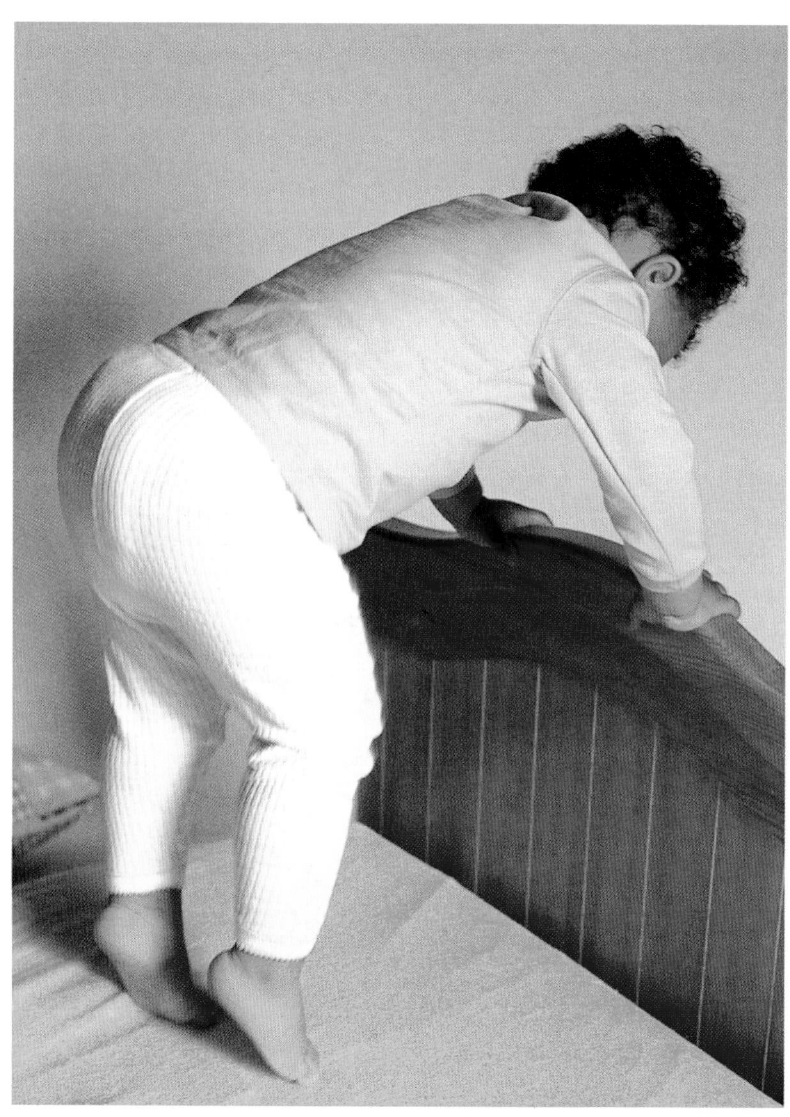

Right: There is no need to worry if your child is still in a nappy at night for quite a long while after he is potty trained during the day.

There are basic signs that let you know the time is right to introduce your child to the use of a potty. He may indicate to you he needs a clean nappy because he knows his nappy is wet or soiled, or he'll let you know the moment he starts to fill his nappy. Another possible sign of readiness is when you take off his nappy to change it after a few hours and you discover it is still dry. Any of these features suggest it's probably time for toilet training to begin. If you haven't spotted these signs by the time he's 2 years, start potty training anyway.

Top Tips

1. Be optimistic. Remind yourself that around 90 per cent of children manage to gain control over their bowel and bladder during the day by 36 months, and around 75 per cent have night-time control as well by that stage.

2. Choose the correct position. When using the potty, girls always take a seated position. Boys, however, have a choice when urinating – they can either sit on it or stand in front, facing it. Choose the position that you think is most suited to your child.

3. Make potty training fun. You could let your child read a book while he's perched on the potty or perhaps sing to him. If he stands up too soon, find something to attract his attention so that he continues to sit there.

4. Time the use of the potty carefully. Experience changing his used nappy has taught you when he is most likely to wet or soil. These are the best times to sit him on the potty, because success is more likely.

5. Buy trainer pants. Once your child has some bladder and bowel control, make the switch from nappies to trainer pants. Of course occasional toilet 'accidents' will continue to happen, but just clean up without a fuss.

Take your Time

Make up your mind to relax about the amount of time your child takes to become potty trained. True, there are some children who gain control within a week or so of potty training actually starting, but there are also others who require several months to acquire this skill. Assume that yours will need several weeks – and if his progress is quicker, consider that a bonus! Be prepared for a mess along the way. A child who is learning bowel and bladder control almost certainly wets and soils the carpet on occasions. This is part of the learning process, so make sure you are prepared.

The first stage is to let your toddler get familiar with the potty without pressure to use it. Let him play with it so that he becomes used to this new piece of equipment. Then you can begin to persuade him to sit on it without wearing a nappy, perhaps three or four times each day. He may find this difficult as he may feel vulnerable and exposed without a nappy. Reassure him and you'll find that he gradually grows accustomed to the habit.

If you do this regularly and often enough, he is bound to wet or soil into the potty eventually. And that's the time for a fanfare of praise from you! (Bear in mind, though, that some children initially dislike what they have deposited in the potty; they need to be reassured that what they have done is appropriate.) Let him see that you are delighted with his progress. It stands to reason that the more your child sits on the potty, the more successes he'll have with it. Once you've started potty training, calmly persevere no matter how long it takes. Your growing child will get there when he is ready, at his own pace. Remember that bladder control at night generally takes longer to achieve. Most children are not ready to do without a nappy at night before their third birthday.

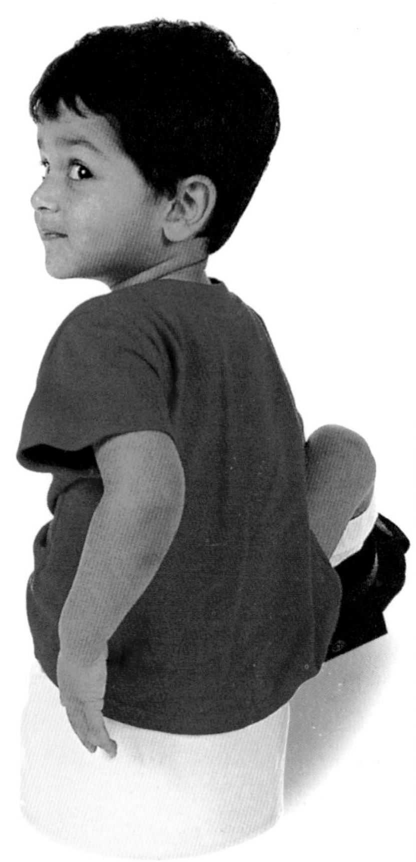

Above: If you wait until you think your child is ready and choose a time when you are relaxed, then potty training can often be achieved within a few weeks.

Bedtime and Sleep

Your toddler plays a much more active part in her bedtime routine now that she's older, more independent and more able to make choices. She has her own favourite toys to accompany her and her own set way of getting ready for bed. She enjoys choosing her pyjamas and maybe even the bed covers. Your child needs to have a stable sleeping pattern at this stage in her life – if she doesn't get a good night's sleep with regularity, she'll be tired, fractious, demanding and bad-tempered the next day. She may need help to establish good bedtime habits because she prefers to remain in your company.

Sleep Tight

Toddlers need on average about 10 hours' sleep a night, but there is considerable individual variation. You can help her settle before she goes to sleep by specifically involving her in calm, sedate activities at least 20 minutes before her bedtime routine normally begins. A predictable pre-bedtime ritual is advisable; this could be that she has a bath, puts on her pyjamas, brushes her teeth and then is read a story by you. Once this pattern becomes firmly set in her mind, she'll know that the first stage means bedtime is fast approaching.

If possible, stick to the same bedtime each night. This gets your toddler used to a fixed sleeping pattern, physically and psychologically. Of course, there will be evenings when this time varies, and that's fine. Once you

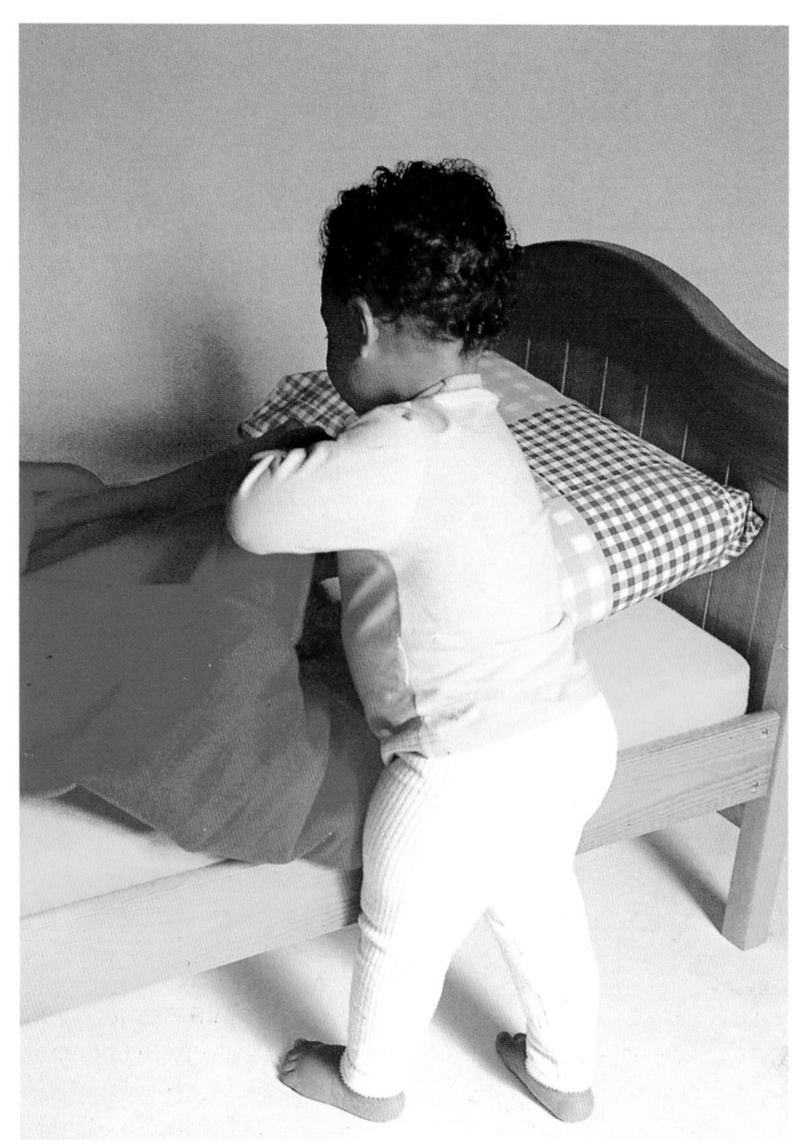

Right: If your child wakes at night, it is important to get him back to bed with the least amount of fuss; he will eventually learn that night time is for sleeping.

have tucked her in, read her a short story in a quiet voice to relax her. After that, give her a cuddle and a kiss and leave the room.

Waking Up

Research confirms that at least 15 per cent of all children around the age of 18 months still wake up regularly during the night. There are good reasons why your child might wake up and call for you during the night, perhaps because she had a bad dream, which may have been caused by a particular food or a scary story or video. When she wakes up crying, calm her and soothe her until she settles. You'll find that your reassurance helps her to get back to sleep quickly. Night terrors are different from nightmares. A child who is experiencing night terrors may have her eyes wide open as she sits up in bed screaming, totally convinced that the object of her fears is right there in front of her. Calm your child just as you would if she had a nightmare. Fortunately, night terrors are rare in toddlers.

Yet you may find that your toddler gradually develops the habit of night waking – and before you know it, she wakes two or three times a night without fail. To discourage this habit, keep your child in her bed when she wakes during the night. Naturally you should go to her when she cries or calls out, but try to prevent her from leaving her bedroom. If she insists on rising, say, to go to the toilet, take her back to bed as quickly as possible. Tell her that she'll soon fall asleep, and then leave the room once more. Don't go back in immediately if she calls out again – wait at least five minutes before responding to her.

There is no doubt that if your child continues to wake up and that if you then make the decision to take her downstairs for a drink or snack, or perhaps to play with her, she will probably wake up at the same time the following night, too. After all, as far as she is concerned waking up during the night is great fun – there's food, games and loads of attention from you! Of course, she may be angry with you for keeping her in the bedroom. But stick to your original plan of action. If you do, you'll discover that her waking at night soon becomes a thing of the past.

If your toddler wakes up early in the morning, encourage her to play on her own, rather than seeking your attention. Leave a pile of toys and books in the cot or by the bedside so that she can keep herself amused until you get up.

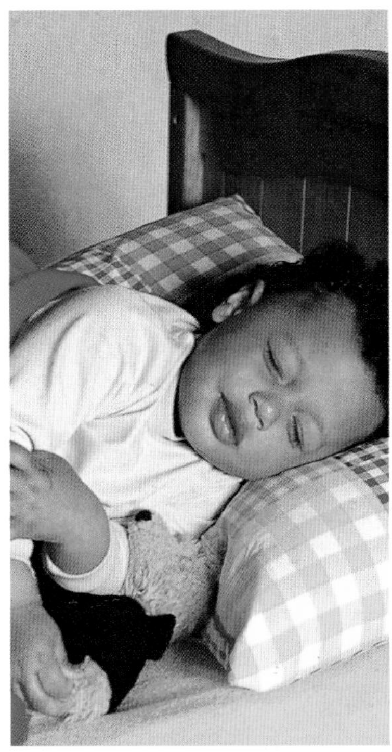

Above: If you adopt a calm and consistent approach, even a child who habitually wakes up will eventually learn to sleep through the night.

Top Tips

1. Avoid naps during the day. It stands to reason that a child who sleeps during the day is less likely to sleep at night. Do what you can to keep yours awake throughout the day, even if she has sleepy moments.

2. Always take her back to her room. Be sympathetic if you find her in your bedroom in the middle of the night. But once you have calmed her, take her gently but firmly back to her own bed.

3. Don't get angry. You'll feel drained when woken by your child regularly at night because you need sleep as much as she does, but stay calm. The more excited everyone becomes, the more elusive sleep becomes.

4. Make her bedroom pleasant. She will want to spend time in her room at night when she likes what she sees there. Involve her in choosing how it is decorated, and allow her to pick the toys she wants with her. Some toddlers go to sleep more easily when a night light is left on in their room.

5. Block out potential disturbance. Loud music or the sound of a television, for instance, may keep your child awake, as might noise from outside traffic. Do what you can to reduce any disturbing noises that might keep her awake at night.

Shyness

You may be surprised to see your normally outgoing toddler become shy when he meets an unfamiliar child or adult. Suddenly, he stops talking, his face reddens and he tries to bury himself against you. It's simply a lack of social confidence that brings on this shyness – the shock of seeing an unfamiliar face or of being the focus of unwanted attention. As soon as he leaves that situation, his shyness vanishes and he becomes his usual self. Boys tend to be more shy at this age than girls (though this trend reverses after starting school).

Shyness Changes

The way children experience shyness changes as they get older. When he's 16 months old, your toddler probably clings to you in the presence of someone he doesn't know. Even when within three or four months his confidence has improved and he charges about everywhere, full of his own importance and without a care in the world, he may still turn into a quivering, shy toddler if confronted by an unfamiliar face.

As his confidence gradually increases over the next six months or so, he is not so easily distressed by shyness. Of course, he may still be timid in the presence of people he doesn't know, but the panic reaction he experienced when he was slightly younger is no longer in evidence. He copes with shyness by giving a more neutral, controlled response than he did before – he is more likely to react with silence than by trying to hide. By 36 months, he's had so much experience of meeting other children and adults that he will respond to, and sometimes initiate, conversation and social interaction with strangers. Yet there will still be times when he reverts to the shy behaviour of a year or two earlier.

Be aware of the signs of shyness, because it may not be immediately obvious. When your child is feeling

Below: While the little girl on the right is happily absorbed in her drawing, the withdrawn expression of the child on the left shows that she is not at ease.

shy, he may suddenly become silent and have difficulty making eye contact with those around him – he may, for example, suddenly stare at his toes. He may be embarrassed and blush and may experience difficulty with swallowing. He may find himself rooted to the spot, unable to keep up with you, or he may struggle to get away from you. The way your child shows his shyness depends on his individual personality, and you will soon learn to recognize the signs in his case.

Top Tips

1. Don't let him avoid social situations. Your shy child might do his best to convince you, for instance, that he should not go to playgroup today because he can't face the other children. Persuade him to go along anyway.

2. Remind him of his strengths. A shy child is often convinced that the other children won't like him. So make a special point of telling him that the others will like him because, for example, he is fun to be with.

3. Give him something to do. He may not be able to think of anything to do or say when he meets other people. Suggest ideas for breaking the ice, such as telling the other child his name, or inviting the other child to play with him.

4. Teach him body language. Show your child ways to look as though he isn't shy, even though he might feel shy. Demonstrate how he should make eye contact, hold his head high and keep his hands from fidgeting nervously.

5. Provide social experience. The more your child mixes with others of his own age the greater his social confidence is likely to become and the less likely he is to feel shy when meeting new children and adults.

Causes of Shyness

Some psychologists claim that a tendency to shyness is inherited from parents and there is some evidence to support this view. For instance, the levels of shyness of identical twins (who have almost identical genetic structures) are closer than the levels of shyness of non-identical twins (whose genetic structures are no more similar than those of ordinary siblings).

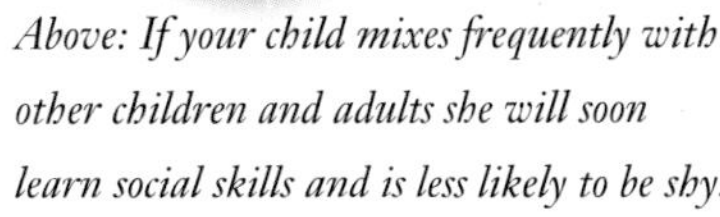

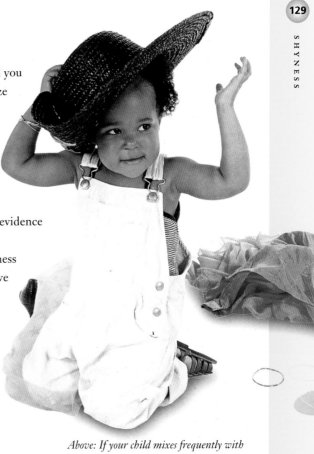

Above: If your child mixes frequently with other children and adults she will soon learn social skills and is less likely to be shy.

Other psychologists claim that shyness is affected by experience, upbringing and context. For instance, shy parents tend to have shy children, perhaps because the model of social behaviour experienced at home – which the children naturally copy – is one of shyness and so the children themselves are more likely to be shy. One study confirmed that children are more likely to be shy in an environment that values competitiveness and attainments, rather than valuing a child for his personal qualities, and this suggests the social context affects shyness. And children who live in homes where there are plenty of visitors may be less shy than those in homes where new faces are a rarity. Such findings challenge the suggestion that shyness behaviour is mainly genetic in origin.

Support

For a shy child, meeting new children and adults can be almost unbearable. Remember that his feelings are very real and that he does not behave in this way by choice. This is why it's important not to make fun of your child in the hope of cajoling him out of it; as far as he is concerned it is no laughing matter. And the thought that you might tease him makes him feel even worse. He needs your emotional support and reassurance. During an attack of shyness, a simple gesture of encouragement from you – such as a reassuring word or a calming cuddle – may be enough to lift his confidence to the point where he is able to overcome his feelings.

Development

Movement

- Walks unsteadily with support up and down stairs. Some toddlers may use different strategies such as crawling or going down on their bottom.
- Walks confidently about the home and outside.
- Picks up toys or other objects from the floor without toppling over.
- Trots towards you across the room, but may become unsteady if she starts to run.
- Starts to climb playground equipment, but will need constant supervision.
- May enjoy splashing and kicking in the swimming pool.

Hand–eye Coordination

- Sees a connection between her hand movements and the effect this causes. For example, she pulls at a string to make the attached toy move towards her.
- Enjoys making random marks on paper using crayons or paints.
- Starts to feed herself with her hands and a spoon.
- Holds two small items in each hand at the same time.
- May want to help dress herself.
- Hand preference may become apparent.
- Claps her hands together.
- Successfully completes a simple inset board activity.

Language

- Is able to follow and act on simple instructions.
- Consistently uses approximately six or seven words, but her understanding extends to many more words.
- Combines language and gestures to express her needs.
- Starts to learn the names of different parts of the body.
- Enjoys songs and nursery rhymes and will perhaps join in with some sounds and actions.

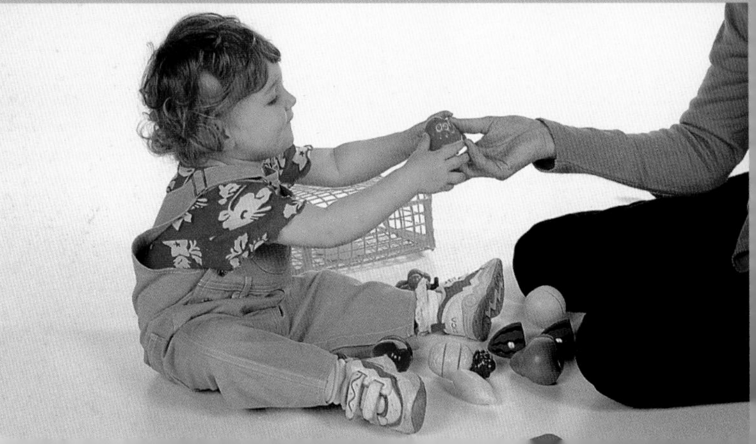

From 16 to18 Months

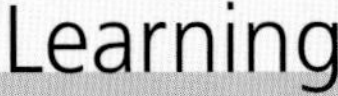

Learning

- Combines the use of different skills and capacities, such as concentration, memory, hand–eye control and understanding, to complete a complex task such as a simple inset board.
- Solves simple problems like removing the lid from a box to see inside.
- Learns the basic concepts of quantities and volume through water play.
- Improved attention span enables her to concentrate on and complete more demanding activities.
- Understands and follows stories that are read to her and responds to familiar characters.
- Remembers where she put an item that interests her, such as a favourite toy.

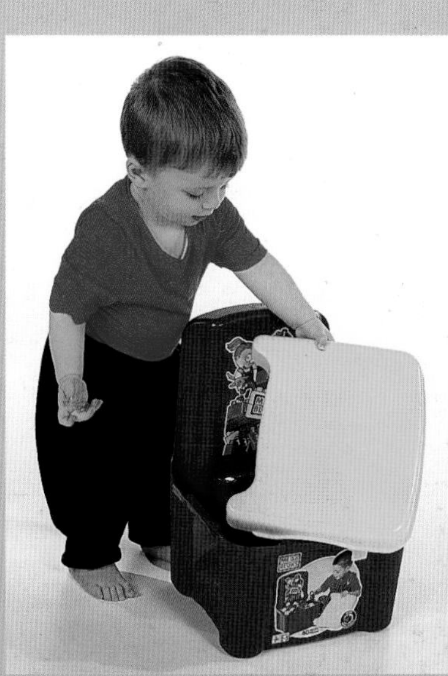

Social and Emotional

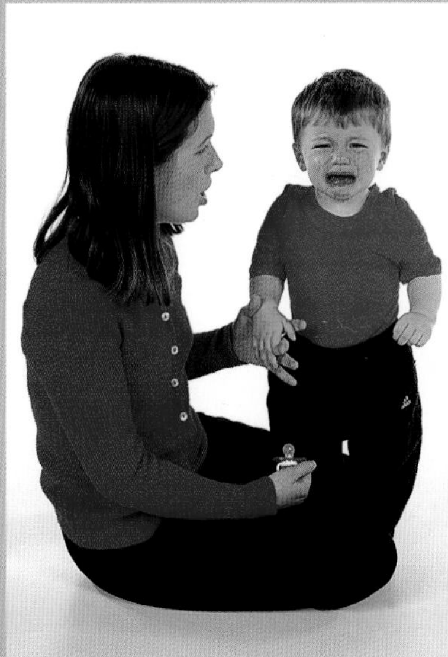

- May have a tantrum when she doesn't get her own way as she begins to assert her sense of independence.
- Wants to do more for herself, especially with feeding and dressing.
- Learns good eating habits by sharing mealtimes.
- Begins to learn basic social skills like passing a toy to another child.
- Plays alongside other children, watching them closely, and learns by taking in how they interact and play with toys.
- Expresses preferences for particular foods or for certain toys that she wants to play with.
- May become jealous when you pay attention to others.

Development

Movement

- Is able to undertake another activity while he is on the move. For example, he can trail a pull-along toy behind him as he walks.
- Likes to clamber over furniture.
- Climbs up and down from a chair.
- Improved balance and coordination leads to fewer instances of tripping over and unexpected falls when he is walking and running.
- Is able to use a wider range of playground equipment.
- Enjoys running freely in a park and in the garden.

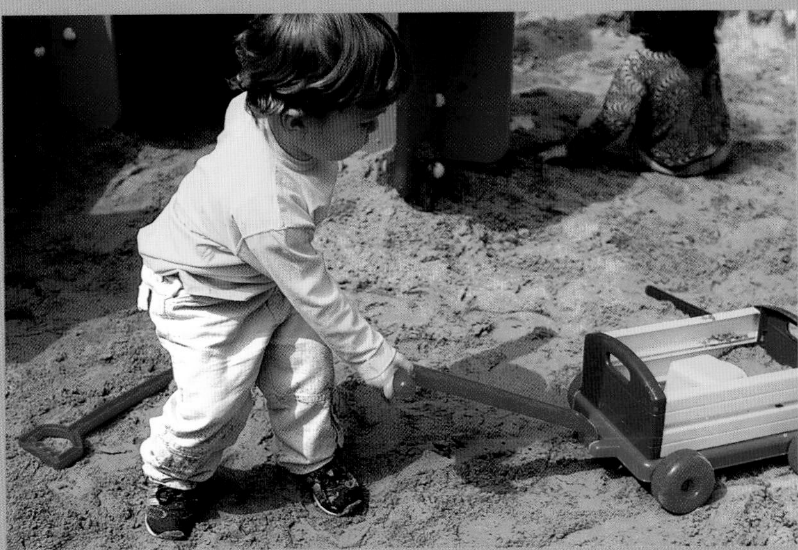

Hand–eye Coordination

- Enjoys playing with modelling materials like play dough or clay, and sand and water – making shapes and drawing 'pictures' into the surface.
- Likes rolling, throwing and perhaps even catching balls, both large and small, though he will find large ones easier to grasp.
- Stacks small wooden blocks on top of each other to make a tower of perhaps five bricks.
- Pours water accurately from one container into another one without too much splashing.
- Makes increasingly deliberate marks on paper with a crayon.

Language

- Has extended his vocabulary to dozens of words, mostly nouns that describe a general class of object such as 'car' for all vehicles or 'house' for all buildings.
- Tries to join in songs.
- Is interested in conversations and begins to learn conversational conventions, such as giving and waiting for answers.
- Puts words together to form two-word phrases.
- Develops an understanding that speech is about social contact as well as communicating basic needs.
- Spots familiar characters and objects in picture books and photographs and tries to name them.

From 19 to 21 Months

Learning

- Begins to use toys for imaginative play, as a result of his developing capacity for symbolic thought.
- His increasing problem-solving ability enables him to complete a simple inset board and these toys are now well within his capability.
- His developing curiosity makes him want to see what goes on outside and to explore closed cupboards.
- Uses all his senses, including sight, hearing and touch, to learn about the world in which he lives and becomes more confident in exploring new environments.
- Becomes more focused and determined and is more motivated to complete a challenging task.

Social and Emotional

- Appreciates your company and makes an effort to engage your attention through either talk or play.
- Can walk backwards a few steps.
- Shows that he is nearly ready to begin potty training, although full control is unlikely at this age.
- Persists in challenging decisions that he disagrees with.
- Begins to interact with other children but needs lots of basic social guidance.
- Is able to understand simple rules, although he may not always comply with them.
- Enjoys the security of a regular daily routine.

Development

Movement

- Pushes a pedal toy along with her feet, though probably cannot yet turn the pedals.
- Can stand on one foot while using the other to kick a ball.
- Runs confidently and rarely falls, although this activity still requires quite a lot of concentration.
- Moves fast as long as she goes in a straight line.
- Is able to throw and catch a ball from a sitting position.
- Dances to music.
- Can adjust her balance well on a swing.

Hand–eye Coordination

- Looks at books for several minutes studying each picture, pointing to images that catch her interest and turning the pages.
- Can participate increasingly in helping to dress and undress herself.
- Combines her index finger and thumb effectively in the pincer grip to pick up small objects.
- Receives and passes objects from your hand to hers and then back again.
- Makes increasingly rhythmic sounds with simple musical instruments such as drums and tambourines.

Language

- Accurately identifies everyday objects placed in front of her.
- Experiments with different (perhaps 'incorrect') word combinations.
- Tackles most sounds but often mixes up or mispronounces certain consonants such as 'c' or 's'.
- Names the main parts of her body.

- Listens with interest to other people talking to each other.
- Her vocabulary is at least 200 words, often combined in short sentences.

From 22 to 24 Months

Learning

- Understands that she can manipulate objects to learn more about them. For example, she twists objects to see inside them.
- Is enthusiastic about imaginative play, creating stories and scenes using toys, such as figures, to act them out.
- Watches you closely then copies you as a way of learning new skills.
- Has an unquenchable thirst for information and asks lots of questions about everything around her.
- Is increasingly able to understand explanations.
- Will be able to remember and recount some past events.

Social and Emotional

- Enjoys the company of other children, but has trouble sharing her toys and does not yet play cooperatively.
- Is able to feed herself with a spoon effectively.
- Potty training is probably underway but her bladder and bowel control may not yet be totally reliable.
- Wants to help wash herself at bathtime and clean her teeth.
- Enjoys the responsibility of carrying out small tasks.
- May cry when separated from you temporarily, although she soon stops when you are out of sight.
- May be shy with strangers.

Development

Movement

- Is able to jump a short distance off the ground from a standing position and with practice may be able to jump over a low obstacle.
- Successfully manoeuvres himself around obstacles while performing another task. For example, he can push a toy wheelbarrow around the room without crashing into the furniture.
- Is able to take short walks on foot rather than using the buggy.
- Walks up stairs in your house without your support.
- Stands on tiptoes for a couple of seconds.

Hand–eye Coordination

- Manages to thread large beads onto a lace.
- When painting and drawing grips the crayon or brush with his fingers and is able to make a controlled mark. For example, he may be able to copy a vertical line that you have drawn.
- Copes better with construction toys and games and puzzles that have pieces that fit together.
- Can do up and undo large buttons.
- Can start to learn how to use pieces of cutlery other than his spoon.
- Has firmly established hand preference.

Language

- Adores you reading stories to him just before he goes to sleep.
- Benefits from discussing his activities with you and will get more out of a television programme, for example, if you talk about it afterwards.
- Asks questions and listens attentively to the answers.
- Has a vocabulary of several hundred individual words.
- Enjoys simple conversations with familiar adults and other children.
- Uses language to extend the complexity of imaginative play, such as dressing up.
- Starts to use pronouns, such as 'he' or 'you' and prepositions, such as 'in' or 'on'.
- Recalls small amounts of personal information, such as his age and full name, and is able to relate that information.

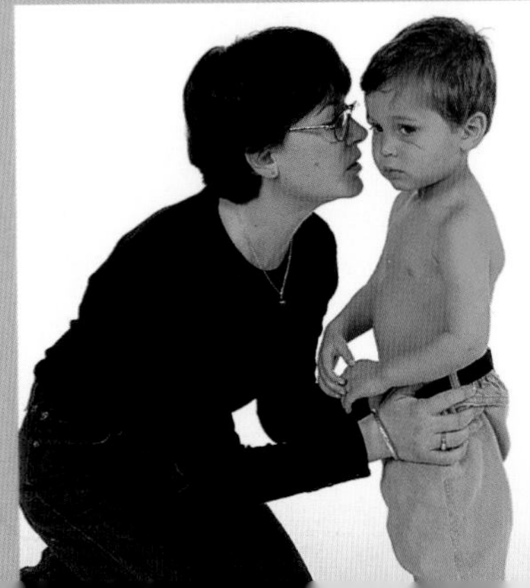

From 25 to 30 Months

Learning

- Begins to match colours, for example, by finding two bricks of the same colour.
- Understands that coins are 'money', but still has little concept of their value.
- Sorts objects according to specific characteristics. He is able, for example, to divide toys according to type – say, animals or cars.
- Begins to develop a broad sense of time. For example, he can probably distinguish between 'today' and 'tomorrow'.
- Identifies himself in a photograph shown to him.
- Is hungry for new experiences beyond the home and enjoys visits to new places such as the zoo.
- Ascribes human qualities to inanimate objects as an expression of his active imagination and perhaps as a means of understanding the world around him. For example, he may be worried that a favourite toy will be sad if he leaves it at home.

Social and Emotional

- May still be 'clingy' when you leave him in someone else's care.
- Starts to learn basic social skills, such as sharing, when playing with siblings and other children.
- Takes an increasingly active part in dressing and undressing. He may pull off his socks and jumper when getting ready for bed.
- Is more keen to play with other children at times, although arguments are still common.
- Insists on trying more things on his own but may become despondent when he experiences frustration and failure.
- Is prone to tantrums when things don't go his way.

Development

Movement

- Jumps from a small height, such as a single step, without losing her balance.
- Will attempt challenging balancing activities such as walking along a log or hopping, although she may not succeed.
- Balances for several seconds while standing on one foot only.
- Tiptoes across the floor without over-balancing.
- Is able to negotiate ladders and slides on large outdoor play equipment.
- Runs fast with great confidence.
- Can use the pedals of a pedal toy to propel herself along.
- Can accurately copy movements and participates fully in action songs.

Hand–eye Coordination

- Benefits from the wider range of play equipment and craft activities at a playgroup or nursery.
- Can build a tower of eight or more blocks.
- Begins to be able to cut paper with a pair of child-safe scissors, although she finds this difficult.
- Completes simple jigsaw puzzles.
- Due to improved control, her drawings are less random and their subject is often recognizable. She can copy simple shapes you draw.
- Carries out simple household tasks like putting cutlery on the table or toys in a box.

Language

- Issues instructions confidently to you.
- Frequently uses pronouns such as 'I', and 'me', although not always correctly.
- Has a vocabulary of at least a thousand words.
- Is ready for more complex stories with multiple characters.

- Asks frequent questions about the meaning of unfamiliar words that she has heard you or others use.
- Shows an understanding of grammatical rules, which she applies in her use of language.

From 31 to 36 Months

Learning

- Compares two objects in terms of size or height, albeit not always accurately.
- Makes up simple stories from her imagination.
- Remembers something you both did yesterday and may be able to recall exciting events in the more distant past.
- Anticipates the consequences of her actions. For example, she knows that if she knocks her cup over the drink will spill.
- Completes jigsaws with three or four large pieces.
- Is able to commit information, such as the name of an object, to memory by repeating it to herself.

Social and Emotional

- Has a distinct sense of self and is protective of her possessions and personal space.
- Is reliably clean and dry during the day.
- May form a special friendship with one child in particular.
- More aware of other people's feelings and makes efforts to offer help and comfort to another child who is distressed.
- Becomes more confident in new situations and in forming relationships outside the immediate family.
- Is more amenable to family rules and tantrums diminish in frequency.
- Enjoys exercising choice over what to eat or wear.

Movement

The Development of Movement

During the period from 16 to 36 months, your child's physical capabilities progress from being able to 'toddle' around unsteadily on her feet – having only recently taken her first few walking steps – into confident mastery of a broad range of complex physical skills, such as throwing, catching, running, balancing and kicking. Of course, her movement skills continue to develop in subsequent years but it is during this phase of her life that these advanced physical abilities begin to emerge.

Foundation for Change

The foundation for your growing child's better control over her arms, legs, body, balance and coordination stems from three sources. First, the seeds of these abilities have been sown in the previous 15 months, as your baby's coordination steadily improved from her original random arm and leg movements at birth into purposeful actions.

The second source is the stimulation you gave your baby as she steadily gained mastery over basic physical movements like rolling from her tummy onto her back and vice versa, using her arms and legs to crawl from one side of the room to the other, and eventually standing independently without support. She continues to need your encouragement in order to maintain her progress with coordination skills.

The third major source of her ever-improving movement skills is the physical changes that occur in her second and third years. Here are some of the changes that take place:

- **height and weight.** By around the age of 2 years, your child has probably attained half the height that she will be as an adult, and her weight has also increased. Her legs are longer and her muscles are stronger and firmer, enabling her to move in a more agile manner, at a greater speed, and with more purposeful actions.
- **brain.** At birth, your child's brain was approximately 25 per cent of its eventual adult weight, while at the age of 2 years her brain has grown to approximately 75 per cent of its full adult weight. And this increased brain size is accompanied by maturation in part of the lower brain (called the cerebellum), giving her more control over her balance and posture.
- **vision.** Another effect of the brain maturation that occurs in your child's second and third years is that her vision improves and she is able to focus her sight more accurately. To tackle effectively movement challenges such as climbing, running, throwing and balancing, your child must be able to use her vision continually to scan the area in front of her. She is much better able to do this by the time she is this age.

Right: By the age 2 of your toddler is likely to be walking confidently.

Left: He will be steady enough on his feet to carry bulky objects and manage steps without support.

Above: This 18-month-old boy has mastered throwing a ball. This kind of skill comes naturally to some children while others take longer to learn it.

My Child is Clumsy

There is huge variation in the rate at which children acquire coordination skills. You need only to watch a group of 2- or 3-year-olds to see that some are more agile than others. So there is no need to worry if yours is always the one who seems to trip most or who is last to manoeuvre himself onto the first step of the climbing frame – individual differences in the development of movement are perfectly normal.

Statistics reveal, however, that between five and seven per cent of young children are clumsy, in other words, they have difficulty with every activity involving arm, leg and body movements. Anything involving balance and coordination proves to be an overwhelming challenge for a clumsy child. The ratio of clumsy boys to clumsy girls is about 2:1.

The dividing line between a child who is slow to acquire new coordination abilities and a child who is clumsy is unclear. This lack of a clear definition doesn't really matter because every child – clumsy, average or agile – requires stimulation and encouragement to improve. Bear in mind that the root of clumsiness lies in the way the child perceives the world and in the way she is able to coordinate a number of processes – it is not due to any physical problem with her arms or legs.

The biggest hurdle facing a clumsy child – and in fact any child who struggles with a physical challenge – is that she may lose confidence in himself and may start to give up too easily when it comes to movement activities. A child with poor coordination often expects to fail and so doesn't try hard. She needs your support to overcome the difficulties she experiences so that she can maintain her self-confidence and continue to enjoy healthy physical play.

Safety

Now that your child is able to tackle a wider range of physical activities – either inside the home or outside, perhaps in the garden or in a park or playground – safety must remain a priority. As the coordination challenges she wants to tackle become more complex, the potential hazards she faces also begin to increase.

Aside from the obvious safeguard of keeping an eye on your roving child, carefully check all outdoor equipment. Buy climbing frames, slides and swings only from reputable toy suppliers, and make sure that the equipment is firmly assembled according to the manufacturers' instructions. Apply the same safety criteria to play apparatus in playgrounds and parks. Look at the equipment for potential hazards before you let your child play on it – if you are in any doubt, take her elsewhere to play.

Below: Children at this age have no real sense of danger and can get themselves into difficulties so make your child's safety a priority at all times.

Stimulating Movement: 16 to 18 Months

Your child becomes increasingly adventurous as his confidence in his ability to move grows. His natural curiosity, coupled with his new coordination skills, opens up a whole new range of play experiences for him. He realizes that he can move around much more easily without needing to seek help and struts about the house full of self-importance.

Changes In Walking Style

One of the things you'll notice is that your toddler's style of walking changes. And it's not just that he grows steadier on his feet as he approaches 18 months. When he walks his toes tend to point towards the front rather than inwards (which enables him to move at a quicker rate).

He also keeps his feet closer to the ground instead of lifting them as high as he did when he took his first steps (which helps him maintain balance) and he takes shorter steps. The combination of all these small changes results in improved stability and control while walking.

Suitable Suggestions

Toddlers have an amazing ability to improvise – for example, they go up and down stairs using a variety of different strategies, ranging from crawling on all fours to bottom-shuffling their way from stair to stair. There is no 'right' way to do this; your toddler will use the technique that best suits him and his level of physical development. The best help you can give is plenty of encouragement, because his enthusiasm can quickly be dampened by repeated failure, perhaps because he can't coordinate his feet well enough or because every time he bends down he falls over. When success eludes him, he may be tempted to give up trying completely.

That's why your presence can be extremely supportive, not just in giving your toddler verbal support but also in providing practical help. For example, you could hold his hand when he attempts to walk quickly – in this way you both know that there is no risk of him toppling over, and therefore he'll be prepared to try harder. Or you could form your hands into a protective cage around your child – without your hands actually touching him – as he does his best to climb up a set of steps.

Your presence gives him a feeling of safety as well as increasing his sense of delight in his achievements as he shares them with you. This boosts his self-confidence, motivating him to repeat the experience. Of course, your intention should be to reduce this level

Right: Give your child plenty of encouragement to take on challenges like climbing stairs. Keep your hands close to him to prevent a fall.

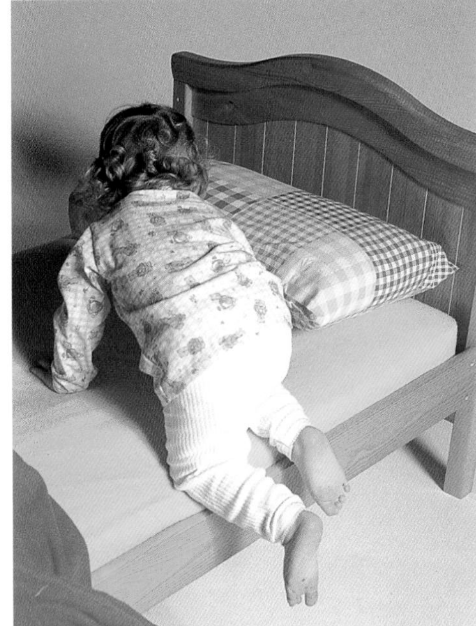

Left: Encourage your toddler to fulfil simple tasks for herself. It is good for her to learn to do things safely and she will enjoy following your instruction.

of direct involvement in his movement around the house gradually over the next few months as his coordination and movement skills mature. In the meantime, however, give him all the help he needs, without taking over completely.

He loves any game or activity involving movement and these let him get used to the sensations associated with changing posture and position. Your toddler squeals with delight when you and he recite action songs together and do the movements in synchrony. Try to learn a varied repertoire of these songs, for example, from other parents, books and videos.

Top Tips

1. Reassure him when he falls. The occasional tumble may upset him. All it takes to get him on his feet again is a cuddle from you, and reassurance that he is unlikely to fall again.

2. Demonstrate actions if necessary. Your toddler learns by experience and he may need you to show him, for instance, how to sit in a large chair. He watches you closely and then tries to do the same himself.

3. Calm his anxiety. He may become frustrated, for example, when the pull-along toy doesn't go in the exact direction he wants. Don't let him give up. Instead, calm him and then encourage him to continue pulling the toy as he walks.

4. Don't do everything for him. It's a lot easier and quicker when, for instance, you lift him into his chair. But he won't learn how to do this himself if that becomes your regular habit. He needs to try these manoeuvres on his own.

5. Make him aware of safety. Your toddler's new level of exploration skills potentially places him at higher risk. Remind him to take care and to watch what he does, but don't overdo the warnings or he may become unnecessarily fearful.

Above: At this age toddlers frequently fall and bump themselves as they are trying out new moves. Your comfort and encouragement will help your child through this phase.

Q&A

Q Do socks and shoes give my toddler confidence with walking?

A For outside the house, your toddler needs to wear socks and shoes to protect his feet. Inside the house, however, his movement skills will be helped by letting him toddle about in his bare feet. This gives his foot muscles maximum grip on the floor and allows him to use his toes more effectively for maintaining balance.

Q My toddler looks as though he has a fat tummy. Could this slow his progress with movement?

A At this age your child's liver is very large in proportion to his overall body size and also his bladder is still quite high in the abdomen. These physical characteristics may make you think he is overweight – even though he is not – and they have no negative effect at all on his movement.

Toys: pull-along toy, sit-and-ride toy, child-sized table and chair, inflatable soft balls, paddling pool

Stimulating Movement: 19 to 21 Months

The most significant change in your toddler's movement skills at this stage is her ability to move around while completing another activity at the same time. For instance, she can pull a toy behind her as she walks. Previously, the basic act of coordinating her arm, leg and body movements was so demanding that she required her full concentration for that activity alone.

Mastery Through Repetition

Don't be surprised to find your child going over the same movement experience again and again – this is her instinctive way of mastering a new skill. For example, you may discover your 21-month-old climbing up on to a chair so that she can sit at the table, then immediately climbing down again, followed by a further attempt to climb up again.

It's not that she is easily amused or that she can't think of anything else to do. She instinctively knows that repetition is the best way to improve her movement, balance and coordination, and she keeps going until she feels that she has got it right.

Left: Once your child is really steady on his feet he can master more playground equipment which in turn will help him improve his strength and coordination.

Suitable Suggestions

Although your growing child might be happy to sit herself down in front of the television or video for most of the day, for the benefit of her health and development make sure that there is plenty of physical activity in her daily routine. Encourage her to get involved with your own schedule, so that, for instance, she walks along the aisles of the supermarket with you or she follows you up and down stairs. The more movement activities she has, the better.

And you don't have to construct any specific physical exercises for her. Just following you around during the day will ensure that she gets all the practice she needs. She can climb on to the sofa alongside you while you read her a story in the morning or afternoon, she can scale the heights of a kitchen chair to watch you set out the table for the evening meal, and she can walk freely in the garden while you are out there, too. Utilizing everyday activities as they arise spontaneously ensures that she has ample opportunity to consolidate and enhance her coordination, balance and movement.

Below: At this age toddlers can complete more complex tasks like using a spade to fill a bucket with sand.

Left: Your toddler will love exploring new spaces like this playhouse. At home you can make a pretend house with a sheet draped over two chairs or from a couple of large cardboard boxes.

Begin to give her simple movement challenges that have more than one element in them. For instance, you could ask her to go over to the other side of the room, pick up the toy that is lying there and put it back into the toy box in the far corner. Or she can push her toy vacuum cleaner across the floor while you do the same with the real one. Any task that involves your toddler in moving her body from one place to the next, while simultaneously carrying out another physical activity, automatically benefits the development of her movement and coordination skills.

Your toddler loves showing off her new talents to you, whether it's climbing up stairs or running at a pace which she thinks is fast. This is why she asks you to watch her as she demonstrates each new achievement. Even though the task she is engaged in is perhaps beyond her, she is so proud of her newly acquired skills that she wants your approval. And when you smile at her effort, you are encouraging her to persevere until she achieves her goal.

Below: Your child will now be able to play independently on some moving toys and will gain an enormous sense of achievement from this.

Top Tips

1. Let her roam freely. Your toddler needs freedom to explore and to move around in the way she wants in order to test out her new skills. As long as you know that she is safe, allow her to venture around your house without restricting her too much.

2. Offer solutions. She may not be able immediately to spot the solution to the movement challenge facing her. If she struggles unsuccessfully at an activity, suggest ways that she could achieve her target – she will respond to your ideas.

3. Take your toddler to the park. Even if your local park has no play equipment for young children, she will adore playing on wide open, grassy areas. She knows that if she falls on the grass, she won't hurt herself.

4. Regularly rearrange her furniture. For instance, you might decide to put her chair at the opposite side of the table today. This means she has to use her movement skills in a slightly different way in order to climb into a sitting position.

5. Practise walking and stopping with her. You have great fun together as you teach her how to stop quickly. At first, she will need several steps before she can bring herself to a standstill from walking fast, but she soon gets better at this.

Q&A

Q Should she be able to walk backwards at this age?

A Most children can manage this by 21 months, though it can take time to learn. When your toddler faces you, she can probably take steps to go backwards, but if she half turns around to look over her shoulder as she moves in the reverse direction, she may tumble over. She should practise this on a carpeted floor.

Q Could a toddler climb up so high that she could open a latch on a window?

A Yes. You'd be amazed how skilful an active child can be in moving pieces of furniture together so that she can reach new heights – your child is very creative when it comes to problem-solving like this. Install child-proof locks on your windows, especially if you have rooms above ground-floor level.

Toys: tricycle with large pedals, child-sized furniture, plastic gardening tools, pull-along toy that makes a noise when moved

Stimulating Movement: 22 to 24 Months

Your child's improved balance and body movements, coupled with his increased chest, hips and leg strength, give him the ability and confidence to attempt physical tasks that he could previously observe only passively, such as running, jumping, kicking, throwing and catching. Naturally, he is still in the early stages of acquiring these particular skills, but he will make steady progress over the next few months.

Physical Maturation

There is wide variation in athletic ability among 2-year-olds. This is largely due to different rates of physical and neurological maturation. For your toddler to achieve complex movement skills, he must have developed the important underlying muscular and neurological structures. If his development hasn't reached this point, he won't be able to master skills like running, throwing and climbing, no matter how much he practises these actions. So be careful not to push your child too hard if he struggles physically – it's probably that his body just isn't ready. Try again in a few weeks.

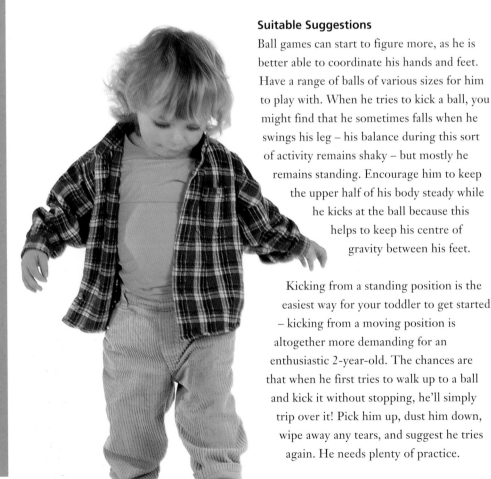

Suitable Suggestions

Ball games can start to figure more, as he is better able to coordinate his hands and feet. Have a range of balls of various sizes for him to play with. When he tries to kick a ball, you might find that he sometimes falls when he swings his leg – his balance during this sort of activity remains shaky – but mostly he remains standing. Encourage him to keep the upper half of his body steady while he kicks at the ball because this helps to keep his centre of gravity between his feet.

Kicking from a standing position is the easiest way for your toddler to get started – kicking from a moving position is altogether more demanding for an enthusiastic 2-year-old. The chances are that when he first tries to walk up to a ball and kick it without stopping, he'll simply trip over it! Pick him up, dust him down, wipe away any tears, and suggest he tries again. He needs plenty of practice.

Left: At around 2 years children will enjoy learning to kick a ball to you, though a fluid kicking action will generally take a while to master.

Gradually he will learn either to stop completely before he kicks the ball or to time his steps so that he can swing his leg at the ball without having to change stride. This is a complex skill that takes time to achieve. Make sure that your toddler has fun during these games; he'll lose interest if it becomes too serious.

The same applies to the actions of throwing and catching. The lower your child's bottom is to the ground, the easier it is for him to throw and catch a ball (because his centre of gravity is lower, which in turn increases his stability). Practise both throwing and catching while he sits on the ground and use a medium-sized ball that he can grasp easily. If you find that your child can manage these actions successfully from that position, he's ready to try catching and throwing while in a standing position. Be prepared for your toddler to fall a few times, as his attempts to catch and throw push him off balance. Again, regular practice is the key to mastering these skills.

Right: Toddlers love dancing and jumping around to music and it is a great way of expending excess energy on a rainy day.

Top Tips

1. Play with him on a swing. He enjoys the sensations of moving backwards and forwards on a swing, as long as he is securely fastened and cannot slip off. He learns to adjust his balance continually as the swing moves in each direction.

2. Listen to music with him. Your toddler will happily dance to the rhythm of the music of his favourite song. And he will try to imitate any dancer that he sees on television. His enthusiasm increases if you dance along with him.

3. Provide success. Have realistic expectations of your child's progress. He needs to experience success in activities involving movement or his motivation will soon diminish. When he does achieve something new, let him know how thrilled you are.

4. Expect occasional lulls in his progress. There will be temporary phases during which he makes almost no advance in his movement skills. This happens with most children. He will start to progress once again when he is ready for change.

5. Promote his independence. Your child is now at the age where he likes to do things for himself and you should encourage this. He doesn't need you to fetch and carry for him – he can cope with many physical activities on his own.

Below: Riding around on his tricycle will give your toddler a real sense of independence although at this age he may push himself along rather than using the pedals.

Q Will dancing improve my child's movement?

A There's nothing like dancing to music for getting a toddler to twist and turn his body. The dance won't be systematic or follow any set pattern, but it will require lots of movement, plenty of coordination, and loads of balance. This is a great way for your child to develop his agility while also having fun.

Q Is it true that 2-year-old boys are usually taller than 2-year-old girls and so are generally more athletic?

A It is true that by the age of 2, the rapid early growth rate has slowed down and that boys are generally taller than girls. But this height difference has both advantages and disadvantages when it comes to developing movement and balance. For instance, smaller children can often run faster than tall children.

Toys: ride-on toys with pedals, soft balls and bean bags for throwing and catching, outdoor garden play equipment

Stimulating Movement: 25 to 30 Months

Your child continues to increase in height and put on weight during her third year. And as a result of the continued process of physical, muscular and neurological maturation, she makes big progress in major movement skills such as jumping, running, climbing and balancing. Other children are of great interest to her now; when she sees them engaged in energetic, physical play she wants to get involved too.

I Can't Do It

Your child's increased social awareness can have a negative effect on her self-esteem, in that her confidence may drop when she realizes some other children are more agile than she is. If she comes to you in tears claiming 'I can't run like my friend' take her feelings seriously. It may be a small matter to you but it's extremely important to your sensitive 2½-year-old. Give her a reassuring cuddle, comfort her until she calms down, tell her that she will improve as long as she continues to try hard, and remind her of all the other movement skills that she has already acquired.

Left: Now that your child's balance and coordination are good you can allow him more freedom in the playground – but he still needs watching at all times.

Suitable Suggestions

You can encourage your toddler to become more active and more adventurous. You can show her how to move her body in ways that enhance her climbing and running skills. If you have a garden, some large outdoor play equipment is a great help. All of these strategies will sharpen her appetite for energetic play, but above all, make sure she spends plenty of time with other children her own age.

There is no bigger incentive to learn – for example, how to run faster – than the desire to keep up with a friend who races along at a furious pace. The same applies to all movement skills – watching others with different abilities boosts your child's determination to improve herself. It's not that her peers put direct pressure on her to do better – on the contrary, children this age rarely make comments about each others' physical ability. Rather, your child involuntarily compares herself with them,

Below: You can easily practise jumping with your child by holding his hands to help him balance as he pushes off the ground.

matching her skills against her friends' skills, and this fills her with a desire for self-improvement.

One of the best physical activities to improve your child's movement skills at this age is practice at jumping because this requires good balance, coordination of arm and leg movements, planning and muscular strength.

Above: When playing, toddlers are constantly on the move, fetching, carrying, putting away, taking out, all of which help to refine their motor skills.

It's also one of those games that fills your child with pride when she manages to propel herself further or higher than she did on previous attempts.

You'll have noticed that when she was younger and she tried to jump into the air, she literally couldn't get her feet off the ground. She stood rooted to the spot, despite strenuous efforts, and looked at you in amazement wondering how you could manage to do it when she couldn't. This changes, however, during her third year. It all seems to come together as she succeeds in launching herself into the air and coming down again on the same spot. Initially, the gap between the soles of her feet and the floor is minimal, but over time this distance gradually increases.

Don't Forget Safety

If you don't already have them, you'll certainly need stairgates now at the top and bottom of the stairs in your house. However, your child's increasing agility means that she soon may be able to climb over them, so you still need to supervise her.

Top Tips

1. Make a small hurdle to jump over. Place a line of small wooden bricks a few centimetres in front of her feet. Ask her to jump over them. Even if she can't and she just hits them, she is unlikely to stumble.

2. Walk with her rather than pushing her in the buggy. Your journeys are generally slower when your child walks with you instead of being pushed along in a buggy, but she'll be getting much more practice with her movement skills.

3. Play tickling games with her. She enjoys being tickled by you, and she'll roll around the floor as you do this or she may run away in order for you to chase her. This is a fun way to exercise her movement skills.

4. Ask her to put her toys into the toy box. As well as giving your child a little bit of personal responsibility and independence, this regular task involves her in whole body movements, including walking, bending, balancing and placing.

5. Run alongside your child, holding her hand. She's not very steady on her feet but she'll make an attempt to move quicker when she has the security of knowing you're beside her to support her if she falls.

Q&A

Q Why is it that most boys seem to prefer strenuous outdoor play, while girls generally prefer to engage in more sedate activities?

A Nobody knows for sure why this difference occurs; some claim it is biological, while others say it is due to social expectations. Whatever the explanation, your child, whether a girl or a boy, should be encouraged to join in play activities involving balance, movement and coordination. Every child benefits from these games, irrespective of gender.

Q My child is afraid of climbing. Should I just put her on the climbing frame anyway?

A This will probably just terrify her further. Far better to encourage climbing ability slowly by starting with a small obstacle to climb, such as a cushion lying on the floor. Next, make the obstacle two cushions, gradually building up her confidence with more challenging feats. She'll tackle the climbing frame when she's ready.

Toys: soft cushioned play-mat, medium-sized football, garden slide with small ladder, pedal toy, music tapes and dance videos

Stimulating Movement: 31 to 36 Months

As your child reaches the end of his third year, he is more agile, tackles any obstacle in the playground and loves joining in energetic activities with his friends. He still gets into difficulties from time to time, however – so don't be surprised to hear him screaming when he gets all the way to the top of the climbing frame and then suddenly freezes, unable to descend alone.

This Is Driving Me Mad

Your child is very determined. His imagination knows no limits and therefore he dreams about scaling barriers, throwing the ball high in the air and running very fast. And when he discovers his physical limitations, your child may explode with rage and frustration.

Don't get annoyed when he loses his temper like this. Instead, remove him from the activity that is the source of his anger and calm him. Point out that the more he cries, the less he'll be able to complete the activity. Explain that other children find this very difficult too and suggest that he tries to achieve an easier task.

Suitable Suggestions

Your child will have a go at anything involving movement now. Take running, for instance. Your youngster dashes about furiously whenever the opportunity presents itself. You can help improve his speed, balance and coordination by setting up mini tracks for him to race around. Go into the garden and set out three small chairs about 5 metres apart, in a triangular formation. Suggest that your child runs around the chairs, until he arrives back at the first one. He will manage to turn at the three corners without greatly slowing down his pace, as long as he concentrates on the task in hand.

When your child plays with a pedal toy, he can probably turn the pedals using his feet. Show your child how to place his soles on each pedal and then how to push so that the wheels turn. Initially, he will probably want to put his feet back on the ground, in order to propel himself along in the way that he's used to. But with your continued encouragement, and his perseverance, he'll eventually find that he can use pedal power to get the bike moving. And once he's made this discovery, there'll be no stopping him as he perfects the technique.

Try teaching him how to hop on one foot, though don't be surprised if this skill is beyond him at this stage. Hopping is a complex challenge, requiring good coordination between both sides of the brain, and your child may simply not have the neurological maturation yet to achieve this. But there's no harm in trying it – he may just over-balance when he tries. Outdoor play is crucial for the

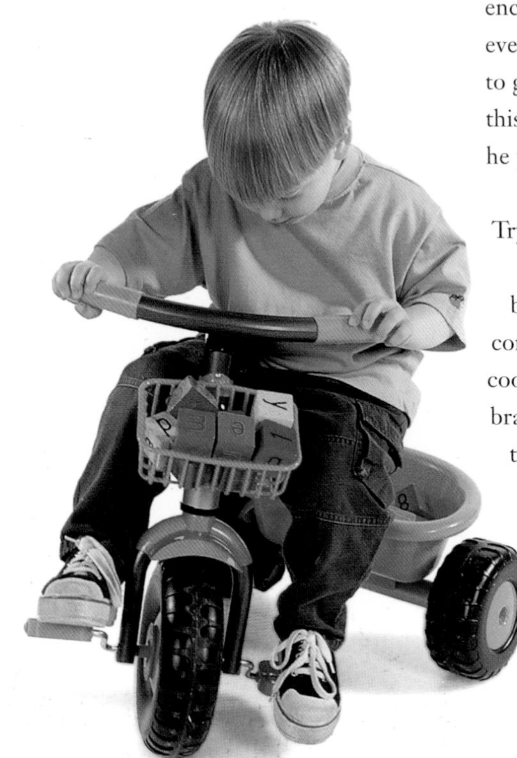

Left: Your child will feel very pleased with himself when he gets the hang of pedalling with his feet and steering at the same time.

Right: This little boy, at 34 months old, uses his outstretched arms to keep his balance as he stands on one leg.

development of your child's movement abilities. Of course there is plenty you can do with him indoors – there is no physical skill that can't be practised at home. Yet outdoor play on large, safe apparatus gives your child all the freedom he needs to experiment and to learn the extent of his agility. A small slide and ladder in the garden, along with perhaps a balancing log and a secure swing, provide endless hours of amusement for him. He'll have even more fun if you are able to take him to an adventure play area in the local park where he can also interact with other children.

Right: Your toddler will love being swung around by you. As long as you hold her firmly and make her feel secure, this sort of play can only enhance her physical skills.

Top Tips

1. **Play movement games.** Have him face you and ask him to do what you do. Then do actions such as bending, lifting your leg, waving your arm, and so on. He'll make a good attempt to copy you.
2. **Use positive reinforcement.** He is more likely to succeed in pedalling his tricycle, for instance, if he knows you are waiting for him further along the path. Although he has built-in motivation, incentives such as a cuddle also help.
3. **Do 'pretend' marching.** Put on appropriate music, and then tell your child to follow you around the room, moving his arms and legs like you. He'll chuckle as he tries to coordinate his movements to simulate your marching style.
4. **Let him walk along a log.** He'll probably fall over, so you will need to hold his hand as he walks along it. This is a very difficult activity for your child, but a good way to encourage his balance and movement skills.
5. **Have fun with your child.** No matter what you do to enhance your child's movement skills, make sure that the activities remain fun. If you push him too hard, or if the games become too serious, he won't learn anything new.

Below: A low wall, log or beam provides excellent balancing practice; if your child wants to tackle these by himself then let him, as long as it is very low.

Q&A

Q Should I discourage rough-and-tumble play because it is quite aggressive?

A Rough-and-tumble play may look aggressive and destructive, but is isn't. In fact, it's a very constructive form of play from a child's point of view because it develops his social and physical skills. If your child and his friends are happy playing this way – and it doesn't end in tears – leave them to get on with it.

Q I'm hopelessly uncoordinated and can't teach my child much in the way of movement. Will he lose out?

A Psychological research confirms that while parental interest in their child's movement skills has impact, children also learn about movement just from playing with others their own age. So do what you can to guide your child's physical activities and ensure that he has regular opportunities to spend time with his peers.

Toys: tricycle and other pedal toys, slide, climbing frame, see-saw, swingbouncer, balls for kicking and throwing

Hand–eye

Coordination

The Importance of Hand–eye Coordination

Although your toddler is more active, more mobile and more curious than ever before, he also needs to develop his hand–eye coordination to increase his learning and understanding. Between the ages of 15 and 36 months, your child's hand control increases, enabling him to manipulate small objects, to gain better control over the use of cutlery and to fetch and carry items by himself.

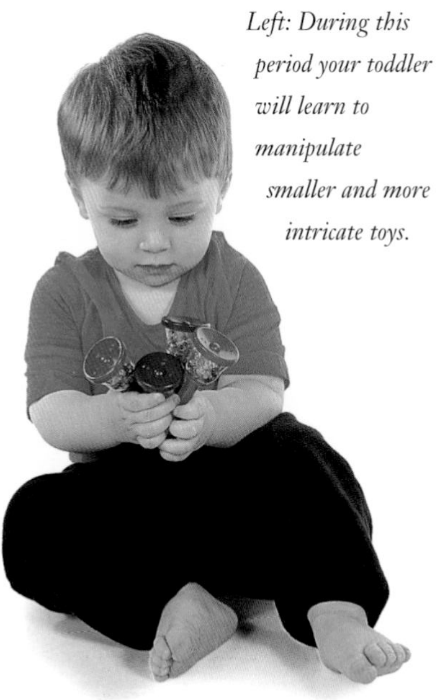

Left: During this period your toddler will learn to manipulate smaller and more intricate toys.

Remember, too, that hand–eye control involves vision as well as finger movements. Your growing toddler has matured to the point where his vision and hand control combine effectively to enable him to focus keenly on a small toy that attracts his attention and then put his hand out to grab hold of it. Games that previously were too demanding for him, such as jigsaws, now hold great interest. The challenge of applying this new hand–eye coordination to solve even more difficult puzzles entices your determined toddler.

Hand Preference

Your child's hand preference – that is, whether he prefers to use his left or his right hand – was not noticeable at birth, but it will start to become apparent between the ages of 15 months and 3 years. You'll notice that he generally uses the same hand for most tasks involving manipulation. Research indicates that approximately one boy in ten and one girl in 12 is left-handed; over 90 per cent of children are obviously left-handed or right-handed by the time they reach school age.

Psychologists don't know for sure whether handedness is inborn or learned. There is a suggestion that a child who is right-handed may have broader brain connections to the right side of his body, which give him greater control over that side as compared to the left. However, there is also evidence that parents who are concerned about their infant's possible left-handedness and who gently encourage him to use his right hand, may succeed in creating a preference for the right. But this strategy only works with some children and is ineffective if started after the first year.

We live in a right-handed world. The majority of children use their right hand for opening doors, for cutting with scissors, for drawing, for handling small objects, and so on. Life is more difficult for left-handers – for example, learning to write is more challenging because a left-handed child tends to drag his hand over his writing or drawing, often smudging it.

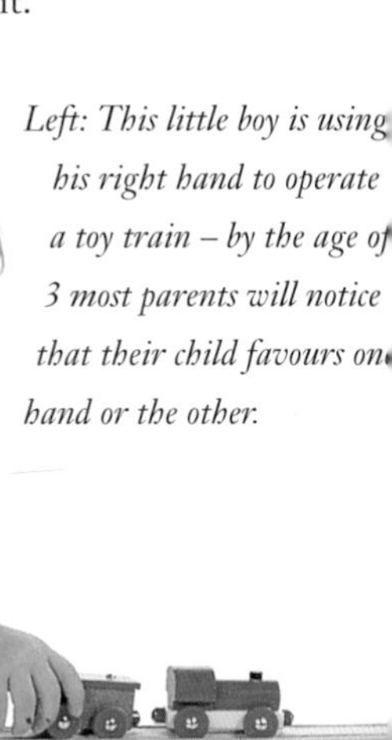

Left: This little boy is using his right hand to operate a toy train – by the age of 3 most parents will notice that their child favours one hand or the other.

Don't be tempted to force your toddler to use his right hand if his natural preference seems to be to use the left hand. This could cause difficulties in other areas of development. For instance, there is some evidence that since hand preference is controlled by the part of the brain that also controls speech, forcing a left-handed toddler to use his right hand could create language difficulties. In addition, pressuring your toddler to go against his natural preference will result in confrontation and frustration and could create a problem where none existed before.

Drawing Skills

New opportunities for drawing emerge at this stage in your toddler's life. Until now, he assumed paper was something to be crumpled up and that a crayon was something to be chewed. Improved hand–eye coordination combined with more mature learning and understanding allows your child to begin the early stages of drawing. It doesn't matter if all he manages is to make a mark on the paper. Drawing adds an extra dimension to his life and is something you should encourage whenever your child shows an interest.

Aside from helping increase his hand–eye coordination skills even further – and giving him lots of fun – drawing brings your toddler plenty of other benefits. For instance, by enabling him to practise making different shapes and patterns, it increases his pattern-recognition skills, which are extremely important later on when it comes to learning to read. It can also have a very positive effect on his self-esteem. When he sees his drawings pinned up on the wall of your home, he is full of pride at his own achievements.

Drawing is also a good way for your growing toddler to express his feelings. You only need to watch him scribbling furiously at a piece of paper to know that he is totally involved in this activity. He can draw what he wants, use the crayon in any way that he wants, and can become as excited during this activity as he wants. It's a great form of emotional release.

Dealing with Frustration

You'll know from your own experience of, say, trying to thread a needle or attempting to sew on a button, that activities involving hand–eye coordination can be very frustrating when they don't go according to plan. Your toddler feels the same way when that annoying last piece of the jigsaw won't fit or when the lid infuriatingly holds firmly on to the box despite all his efforts to dislodge it. Calm your frustrated toddler, and then show him how to complete the activity in a methodical, relaxed manner.

Above: At 2 years old this toddler knows how to remove the jar lid but does not yet have the coordination or strength to do it.

Below: This 18-month-old's inability to manoeuvre his blanket in the way he would like is leading to frustration. This can be a common emotion at this stage in a toddler's development.

Stimulating Hand–eye Coordination: 16 to 18 Months

Your toddler is able to do much more for herself. She can strut about, going wherever the mood takes her – and that means her little hands explore all those places you'd prefer to be left alone, such as electric sockets, flaps in video recorders, and inside cupboards. You'll need to keep a watchful eye on her at all times.

Right: Finger painting is a wonderful way to encourage your child to use her fingers and she will have great fun.

Balancing Safety With Challenge

Now that she feels more confident about her hand control, your toddler enjoys manipulating small objects. Therefore zips, tiny buttons, pins lying on the floor, small wooden beads, bits of dried food that she discovers, all fascinate her. She wants to pick them up and explore them, and perhaps even put them in her mouth.

She needs this sort of hands-on experience to develop her hand–eye coordination even further, but there is a risk of injury if she is unsupervised. You have to balance your safety concerns with her need for varied play opportunities. So keep all sharp items out of reach and watch over her very carefully when she plays with permitted small items.

Suitable Suggestions

Give her a wooden puzzle (called an inset board) that has different shapes cut out, which your child then has to fit back into the correct empty spaces on the board. She will enjoy spending time on these, but do remember that they are extremely difficult for her and she may become frustrated when the pieces don't fit the way she wants. Stick to inset boards that have basic, brightly coloured shapes, such as circles, triangles and squares. Those with irregular shapes are probably too demanding for her at this age.

Make sure she has plenty of paper and crayons close to hand. Drawing is one of those activities that she never tires of because she is able to create something new every time. Encourage your toddler to sit at a small table while drawing so that she is comfortable and relaxed. You won't be able to decipher her drawings at this stage, even though she may insist that she has drawn, for example, you or your house. Don't criticize her sketches, otherwise she will very quickly lose interest in drawing.

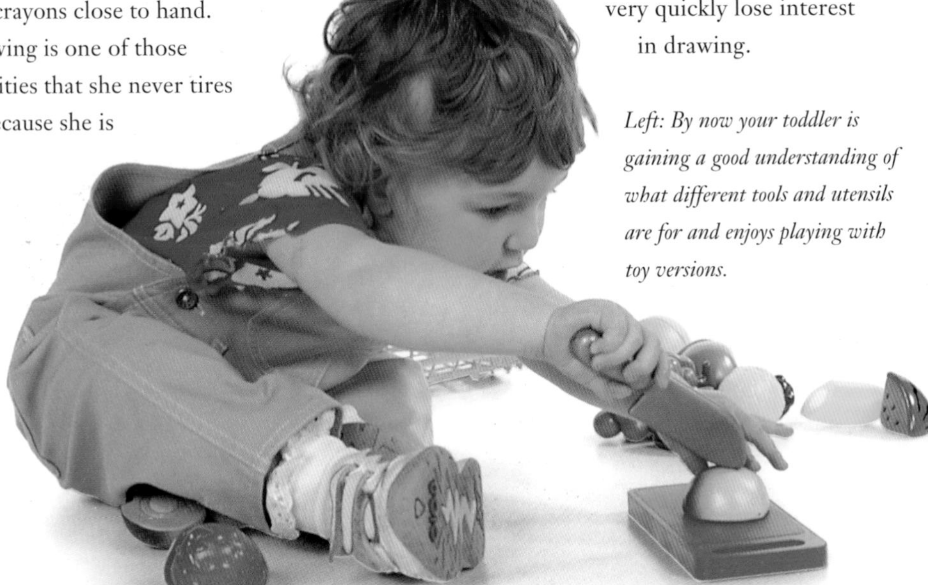

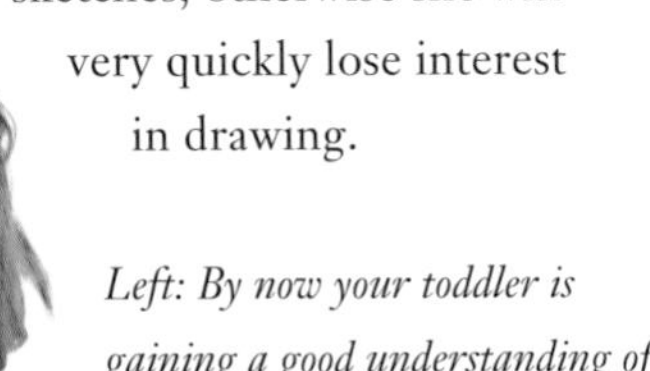

Left: By now your toddler is gaining a good understanding of what different tools and utensils are for and enjoys playing with toy versions.

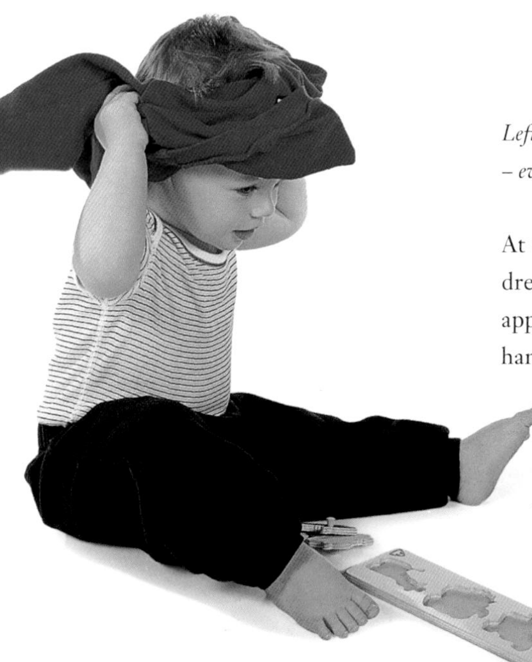

Left: Let your child help to dress and undress himself – even if he does need some assistance.

At this age, she may like to get involved with dressing and undressing. For instance, as you approach with her jumper, she may stick her hands and arms towards you in anticipation. Or she may try to pull her socks off her feet. Bear in mind that your toddler's ambitions outstrip her ability – so you may discover her in tears one day, with her jumper stuck half-way over her head, as she tries unsuccessfully to wrestle the item off completely. Show your approval when she does try to help in this way, but reassure and support her as necessary.

The same applies with feeding, whether snacks or meals. Her determination to do things by herself means that at mealtimes she insists on using the spoon to feed herself. Her hand control is not fully developed yet and therefore some of the food lands on the floor or on the table. Be prepared for a certain amount of mess and let her practise every day.

Above: Simple inset boards with pegged pieces are suitable for this age group though you may need to be on hand to help.

Top Tips

1. Keep her calm. If your child becomes tearful when, for instance, she can't lift the small piece of food from her plate, first calm her. Her hand–eye control diminishes when she's upset. When she is calm, encourage her to try again, but perhaps more slowly this time.

2. Make a special display area for her drawings. There is no better way to express your admiration of her drawing skills than by displaying her work prominently. You could set aside an area of the kitchen wall solely for this purpose.

3. Don't force hand preference. By now she probably prefers to use the same hand consistently for tasks involving hand–eye control. Let this aspect develop naturally. Certainly, never force a left-handed child to use her right hand instead.

4. Roll a ball back and forth. Sit a few metres away from your child, on the floor, and roll a ball towards her – when she has caught it firmly, ask her to roll it back to you. Although you find this easy, it's a challenge for her, so be patient.

5. Play clapping games. By now she is able to clap her hands together, but you can encourage her to clap less randomly. For instance, clap your hands together once and then again a second later. Ask her to copy you. Clapping along with music is also good practice.

Q&A

Q My toddler doesn't seem to understand how cause-and-effect toys work. What should I do to encourage her?

A It may be that her hand–eye coordination simply isn't good enough yet to operate the toys you give her. Check that they have been designed for her age group. If she doesn't understand how to make a toy work, then just show her what to do with it. You may need to do this a few times.

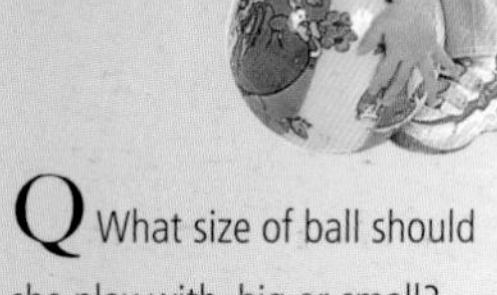

Q What size of ball should she play with, big or small?

A She needs a range of sizes. Different sizes require her to use different visual and manual skills. A small ball helps her strengthen her grip because she can hold it in one hand alone. A larger ball requires her to coordinate both hands in order to grasp the ball.

Toys: inset board with chunky handles, small soft balls of different sizes, building blocks that lock together

Stimulating Hand–eye Coordination: 19 to 21 Months

His improved attention span enables your child to cope with more complex hand–eye coordination challenges. At times he is totally preoccupied with, say, lifting something from a plate or fitting a toy together – his face is a picture of concentration as he persists in his attempt to complete the activity. Your toddler's increased confidence motivates him to try harder with more difficult games and puzzles.

Practice Makes Perfect

The typical toddler this age likes to get things right first time. And if he doesn't, temper and tears may follow. This often shows through with activities involving hand–eye coordination because they need concentration and patience to achieve steady hand movements. When the piece of the inset board doesn't immediately fit, he may end up hurling it across the room.

Encourage your toddler to practise again and again with any hand–eye coordination task that he finds particularly difficult. Explain to him that everyone learns gradually and that the more he tries, the easier it will become.

Left: By 18 months most children are able to build a small tower with bricks and will enjoy playing with building blocks.

Suitable Suggestions

He will naturally tend to play with toys that he can manage without too much difficulty. For instance, he'll play with inset boards he has already mastered, even though they are no longer a challenge. You may need to encourage him to persist with new toys and puzzles – he may prefer familiarity to novelty. Once you are aware of his level of hand–eye coordination, buy him an inset board that is difficult for him to complete but not too demanding. If he puts it to one side at first, sit with him and suggest that you do it together.

Your toddler finds it easier to concentrate on a hand–eye coordination activity when there are few other visual distractions. Suggest that he clears some of his other toys away before starting on something new. Having

Right: Your toddler will watch everything you do and can copy quite sophisticated actions.

only one toy at a time in his immediate visual field increases the likelihood that he'll complete the task. Give him lots of praise when he does persist until completion.

He does lots of reaching and touching, whether or not you give him permission. This is a sign of natural curiosity, not naughtiness, and is probably best dealt with in a firm but relaxed manner. Tell him what he can and cannot touch around the house, and explain why not. Your toddler is now at the age where he begins to understand explanations. The same applies when you visit someone else's house – tell him

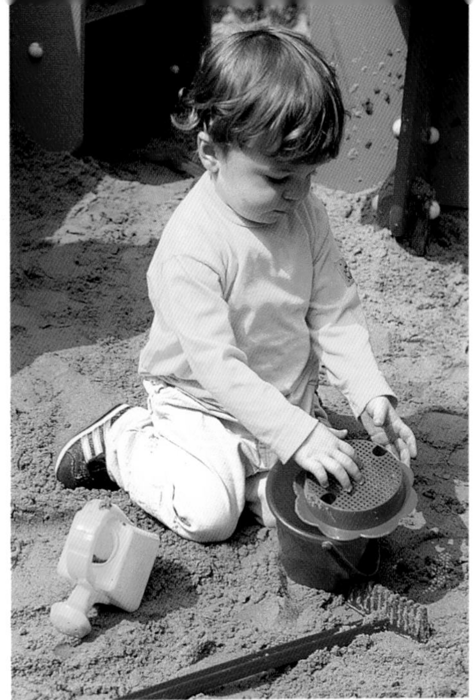

Above: Toddlers at this age are ready to start exploring different textures like sand and water.

beforehand that he mustn't touch objects in the house and remind him again as necessary when you are there. Be prepared for him to try to bend the rules, however. You will need to remain vigilant for potential hazards.

If you can, provide access to a sand-and-water tray. Mix the sand with just enough cold water to create a firm texture – if you make it too runny, there's not much he can do with it. Getting his hands messy in this play mixture is good for his hand–eye coordination. He can squeeze the sand mud between his fingers, build shapes with it or even draw pictures in its smooth surface.

Below: Play dough or clay will help develop good hand–eye coordination and engage your child's imagination.

Top Tips

1. Resist the temptation to compare your child. He will develop hand–eye coordination at his own rate. You may know other children his age who have better hand control than he does, but comparisons with them only make you anxious and dent his self-confidence.

2. Provide modelling materials. He can make any shape he wants from clay or play dough, and if he doesn't like what he has made, he can squash it and start again. As long as it doesn't dry out, clay or dough can be used again and again.

3. Wiggle his fingers. Demonstrate how you can stretch your hands wide open and wiggle your fingers in the air. Your toddler will try to imitate you, although he'll find that he can't move his fingers in such a coordinated fashion as you.

4. Play 'pointing' games. Name specific objects in the room and ask your child to point to them. He'll then scan the area, spot the object you have named and point his index finger towards it. This type of 'I spy' game is great fun.

5. Use household items. His hand–eye control benefits when he plays with everyday items. Dried pasta, for instance, can be arranged into many different patterns, and flour and water combine into a sticky mixture that he can manipulate.

Q&A

Q Why does my toddler's hand often tremble when he concentrates on putting shapes into the correct holes?

A This is a normal occurrence during an activity requiring great concentration. His desire to fit the shape in the hole is so strong that his hand and arm muscles start to tense up, and his whole hand begins to shake. It stops shaking when he relaxes.

Q My toddler won't let me help him when he struggles with undressing. What should I do?

A Although he won't let you give him a hand, you can still talk to him and can give helpful directions (for instance, 'Pull that sock off first, not both at once'). Once he starts to listen to your comments, he'll be more willing to let you give practical help.

Toys: set of stacking rings or beakers, doll with buttons and zips on its clothing, construction blocks of varying shapes and sizes

Stimulating Hand–eye Coordination: 22 to 24 Months

As she approaches the end of her second year, your toddler's fascination with other children her own age is strong. Although she does not yet play cooperatively, she watches her peers closely and will try to imitate their style of play. This can act as an incentive for her to play with toys and games that she was not particularly interested in before.

Step By Step

When faced with a challenge involving hand–eye coordination, your toddler might feel overwhelmed – she thinks it is simply too much for her. You can help her develop hand control by teaching her how to approach the activity in small steps. Suppose, for instance, she struggles to fit shapes into a shape-sorter. Show her a strategy. Explain that she should select one shape only, and that she should then take that shape to the first hole to see if it fits. If it doesn't, she should move the same shape to the next hole, and then repeat the process until she achieves success.

Suitable Suggestions

Whenever possible, arrange for your child to play with others her own age – she learns from and is motivated by their actions. For instance, if she sees another 2-year-old playing with construction blocks, she'll probably want to do the same herself, even if she isn't interested in these toys when she is on her own. The attraction of the example of her peers encourages her to develop new hand–eye coordination skills. Her social development, however, still has a long way to go and she may simply grab a toy from another child instead of asking for it.

Above: Passing an object to someone else and from hand to hand is something he can now achieve.

This is a good time to develop her ability to pass and receive objects from hand to hand. Her hand control is sufficiently established for her to be able to pick up an item, pass it to you and let go once you have taken hold of it. She can also do this action in reverse. Practise this with, say, a plastic cup or a small toy. Initially it might slip from her grasp at the change-over stage, but her skill will steadily improve.

Right: Children of this age don't often play cooperatively but will unconsciously absorb new skills by watching and copying each other.

Above: Your child's use of instruments will be less random and more controlled, though it may not sound it!

Your toddler is beginning to enjoy musical instruments. Whereas before she would have struggled to beat a plastic drumstick against a toy drum or to shake a tambourine in a coordinated way, her improved hand control allows her to make more planned use of toy musical instruments. Give her a range of these toys and let her play freely with them to discover their possibilities. Encourage her to use them as she listens to music. She will have great fun listening to the 'music' that she, in turn, creates.

Once she is comfortable with the instruments, ask her to beat the drum as you sing her a song. Show her how to grasp the stick at the end, holding it firmly in her hand, and start the song. Her beats on the drum will probably be random rather than rhythmical at first, but her skill will improve with practice. You could help her by moving your hand up and down every time she is to beat the drum. Be patient – moving her hand in time to music is difficult and she won't achieve mastery of this skill properly until much later.

Below: Giving your child some choice over what he wears will make him more enthusiastic about dressing himself.

Top Tips

1. Allow her to choose some of her clothes. She'll be more enthusiastic about trying to dress and undress herself if she has chosen the items to wear. Help her make the choice if she is unsure to start with.

2. Encourage her to clear up. For instance, once she has finished her meal, she can lift her plate and cutlery and carry it to the sink. Remind her that it's easier to carry only one item at a time.

3. Give her colouring books to play with. She won't be able to keep the crayon marks within the outlines yet, but this provides good early practice for writing skills. You'll find that at this stage she just scribbles in broad, sweeping movements.

4. Let her open doors. If she is tall enough to reach the door handle, show her how to turn it and then to pull the door open. Supervise her at first, as opening the door might knock her off-balance.

5. Give her a toy telephone with an old-fashioned dial. To turn the dial effectively, your toddler has to insert one finger in a hole and then rotate her whole hand slowly. This requires good hand–eye coordination and plenty of patience.

Q My child won't give up when she can't finish a jigsaw, even when she gets upset. What should I do?

A Suggest she temporarily leaves the challenge that upsets her and then returns to it later once she is calm. When you see her struggling, distract her with another activity – perhaps give her a drink of juice – and then let her go back to the activity.

Q Why does my toddler often fall over when she bends down to pick something up from the floor with her pincer grip?

A Picking something off the floor involves both hand–eye coordination and balance at the same time, and this may be too demanding for her. Putting all her concentration into coordinating her thumb and forefinger reduces her focus on balance – and hence she topples.

Toys: toy musical instruments, jigsaw puzzles, peg board with large pegs, nesting barrels that screw together

Stimulating Hand–eye Coordination: 25 to 30 Months

Your child is developing a more defined sense of self; in other words, he has a clearer understanding of his abilities, of what he can and cannot do, and he chooses to use his talents in ways that he sees fit. Improved hand–eye coordination, for example, enables him to be more independent, to pick up and manipulate objects without having to ask you for help. He thoroughly enjoys this increasing freedom.

The Unacceptable Side Of Hand Control

When roused to anger, your child is tempted to hit the source of his irritation – whether that is his brother, sister or parent. Without thinking through his action, he impulsively raises his hand and whacks the object of his wrath. Such misuse of his hand control skills is totally unacceptable and should always be discouraged.

Make sure your child understands that you are angry at his aggressive action, explain that he should express his displeasure verbally not physically, and ask him to consider what he would feel like if someone hit him in that way. You will probably have to repeat this process again and again until he gains better control of his impulses.

Suitable Suggestions

Your toddler occasionally tries to impose his ideas on other people within the family, whether they like it or not. For instance, if he wants you to read him a book, he looks for it, finds it, brings it over to you and puts it on your lap; if he thinks that it is time for something special to eat, then he goes to the cupboard, selects the item and brings it to you. However, his increased assertiveness stems from his developing skills, not from any underlying character trait. But you'll probably need to be assertive yourself, in order to ensure that he doesn't end up in charge!

Above: By now your child's manual skills will be improving all the time and you will notice how much better he is at puzzles and building towers.

Invite him to open packages for you. This could be a paper bag containing a food item, or a wrapped parcel, or a screw-top jar. His hand–eye coordination is developed enough for him to be able to cope with many of these manual challenges. Use events that arise in your daily routine, such as getting a slice of bread from the packet or opening the breakfast cereal box. If it proves too much for your child, half open the packet for him and leave him to complete the job.

Left: Children over 2 will have the dexterity to open boxes, wrapped parcels and containers that have screw-on lids.

Above: Drawing is now more controlled and your child will be able to copy simple shapes.

Top Tips

1. Teach him baking. He delights in mixing dough, rolling it out on the table and cutting it into small shapes. Watch his face when he sees his own 'biscuits' brought fully baked from the oven. He wants the whole family to taste them.

2. Show him how to use cutlery. He already uses a spoon but try to teach him how to use cutlery in each hand. Start with a fork in one hand and a spoon in the other. This takes time to master.

3. Give him varied drawing and painting equipment. Buy a range of coloured pencils, crayons and types of paper so that your child has choices when it comes to creative activities. Encourage him to vary the materials he selects.

4. Praise his independence. Each new stage of independence brings him pride and boosts his self-confidence, especially when he knows you are pleased with him. So, for example, give him a big cuddle when he manages to dress himself more or less properly.

5. Buy him a toy tool set. As well as developing imaginative play, he will improve his hand control by pretend-playing with plastic tools. Actions such as sawing, hammering and turning a screwdriver all provide excellent practice.

Practise fastening buttons with him. Instead of using his clothes, take a small square of cloth and sew three large buttons on to it, spaced at least 2 centimetres apart. Take another piece of cloth and cut three large buttonholes in it, matching them exactly to the spacing of the buttons on the other piece of cloth. Now you have all the equipment needed for your child to improve his buttoning skills. At first, he should try to complete only one button at a time, but once he has mastered this, suggest he fastens two buttons to the top cloth and then three.

Your child's maturing drawing skills mean that he is more able to copy shapes accurately. While he watches you, draw a vertical line on a piece of blank paper and tell him to 'draw one just like that'. His line will be shaky but it will be clear and in the correct orientation.

Below: Cooking is an opportunity for your child to practise a range of manual skills and making something will give her a great sense of achievement.

Q&A

Q My child is 30 months old and obsessed with dressing and undressing dolls. Is that normal?

A Yes. Children this age often become fixated with one toy in particular. Yours has turned his attention to playing with dolls like this because his hand control has developed to the point where he achieves success every time. Encourage him to play with other toys too.

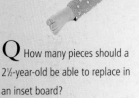

Q How many pieces should a 2½-year-old be able to replace in an inset board?

A As a rough guide, you could expect a child of this age to cope with a board that has five or six different pieces. The difficulty of an inset board is also affected by the shape of the inserts – irregular, large shapes are harder to fit than small regular shapes.

Toys: threading beads and laces, boxes with lids, construction bricks, jigsaws, toy cars, finger puppets

Stimulating Hand–eye Coordination: 31 to 36 Months

As she approaches the end of her third year, your child's hand control is becoming very sophisticated. So many of the activities that were previously beyond her are now well within her abilities. For instance, her cup-holding skill, her use of cutlery, her effectiveness at picking up and carrying objects, and her competence at dressing herself all help to make her much more self-reliant.

FROM INSET BOARDS TO JIGSAWS

Your child is ready to move from inset board puzzles to jigsaw puzzles at this age, though the transition is challenging. Unlike inset boards, jigsaw puzzles have no outer frame to guide your child. Pieces can fit anywhere in any orientation, so there are more possible combinations than for the pieces of an inset board.

Initially, buy your child a two-piece jigsaw only, one that has an easily identifiable picture. The picture, rather than the shapes of the pieces, will guide her. Once she has achieved a two-piece jigsaw, progress to a three-piece then a four-piece, and so on. Build up the degree of difficulty gradually.

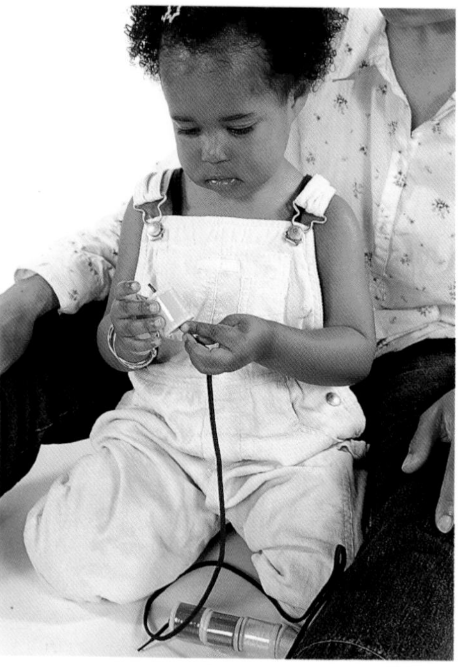

Left: This 32-month-old girl is completely absorbed as she threads bobbins on a piece of cord.

Suitable Suggestions

Your child's hand–eye coordination has reached the point where she is able to undertake ever more varied and interesting craft activities. She loves cutting up bits of paper with scissors – although this remains difficult for her – and then sticking these small pieces on to a larger sheet of paper in a random pattern. Use paper glue that is suitable for children (obtainable from toy shops) and be prepared for a bit of a mess.

You'll need to guide her until she becomes more skilled at using scissors. Cutting is a complex hand control task that takes a long time to achieve, so your child needs your encouragement. Never let her use ordinary scissors because they are not safe for small hands. Buy her safety scissors designed for children from a good toy shop.

Her drawings are also becoming more interesting. Your child has probably

Right: Cutting and sticking can still be quite a challenge but is great fun.

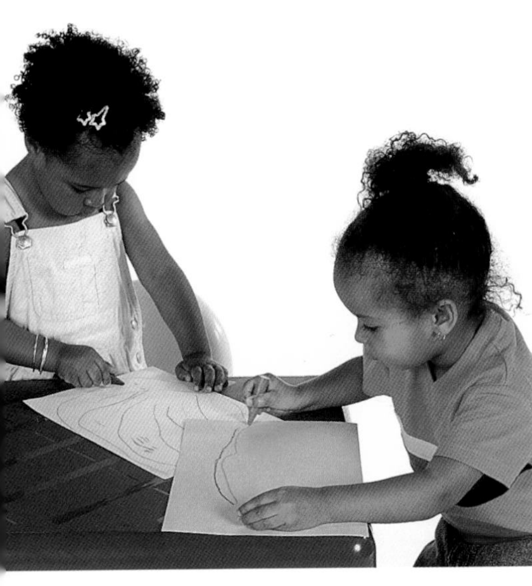

Left: At this age children begin to draw people or objects they see around them and elements of these drawings will start to be recognizable.

always enjoyed drawing pictures of people, but they have hardly been recognizable. They are becoming more accurate and you can tell the subject. You'll notice the head of the person in the drawing is disproportionately large, and the legs are like little sticks jutting out from the underside; children this age generally miss out the body altogether. There are usually no other details, except perhaps a couple of pencil points to represent the eyes.

Motivate your child to use her hand–eye coordination purposefully to improve her daily life. For instance, she is probably reliably clean and dry during the day. With her level of hand control, she should be able to dress and undress herself for the toilet – she's thrilled when you point out to her that she is like 'a big girl' now. This is also a good time to teach her how to wash her hands after using the toilet. The taps may be too difficult for her to turn but encourage her to try anyway. Show her how to rub her hands together under the running water and dry them on the towel.

Below: Nearing 3 years old, your child will get great stimulation from meeting other children and playing with different toys at playgroup or nursery.

Top Tips

1. Give her time. Now that she attempts more complex hand–eye coordination games and activities, she needs lots of time to relax and concentrate on them. Let her continue until she achieves her goal, and resist the temptation to hurry her along.

2. Plan outings. It takes longer for your child to use the toilet without help from you than with your help. This can be frustrating for you when you are in a rush to go out. Don't undermine her confidence by hurrying her, but ask her to use the toilet well before you intend to leave on your trip.

3. Encourage more accurate colouring. Point out to your child how her crayon marks go over the black outlines. Suggest that she tries a little bit harder to keep the crayons closer to the lines themselves, by making slower hand movements.

4. Allocate responsibility. She'll love involvement in your household routine, such as being responsible for dusting a table top, or for sweeping a rug with a small brush. Her hand control means that she can complete these jobs if she tries.

5. Take her to nursery or playgroup. She will benefit from mixing with other children, from playing with them in novel ways, and from having access to a new range of toys.

Q&A

Q My 36-month-old has good hand control but prefers me to fetch and carry for her. How can I change this?

A Resist carrying out tasks you know she is capable of doing. Eventually her desire for the toy or the piece of food will become so strong that she will get it herself. And when she does, reinforce her behaviour by telling her how delighted you are that she did this all by herself.

Q How many wooden blocks should a child of this age be able to stack to make a tower?

A Most will be able to build a tower of nine or ten blocks. Yet an uneven table leg or a slippery table top can easily make the tower fall before it reaches that height. Don't worry if she only manages, say, seven or eight blocks in the tower.

Toys: plastic tea set, art and craft materials, toy farm animals, toy figures, plastic or wooden train set with tracks

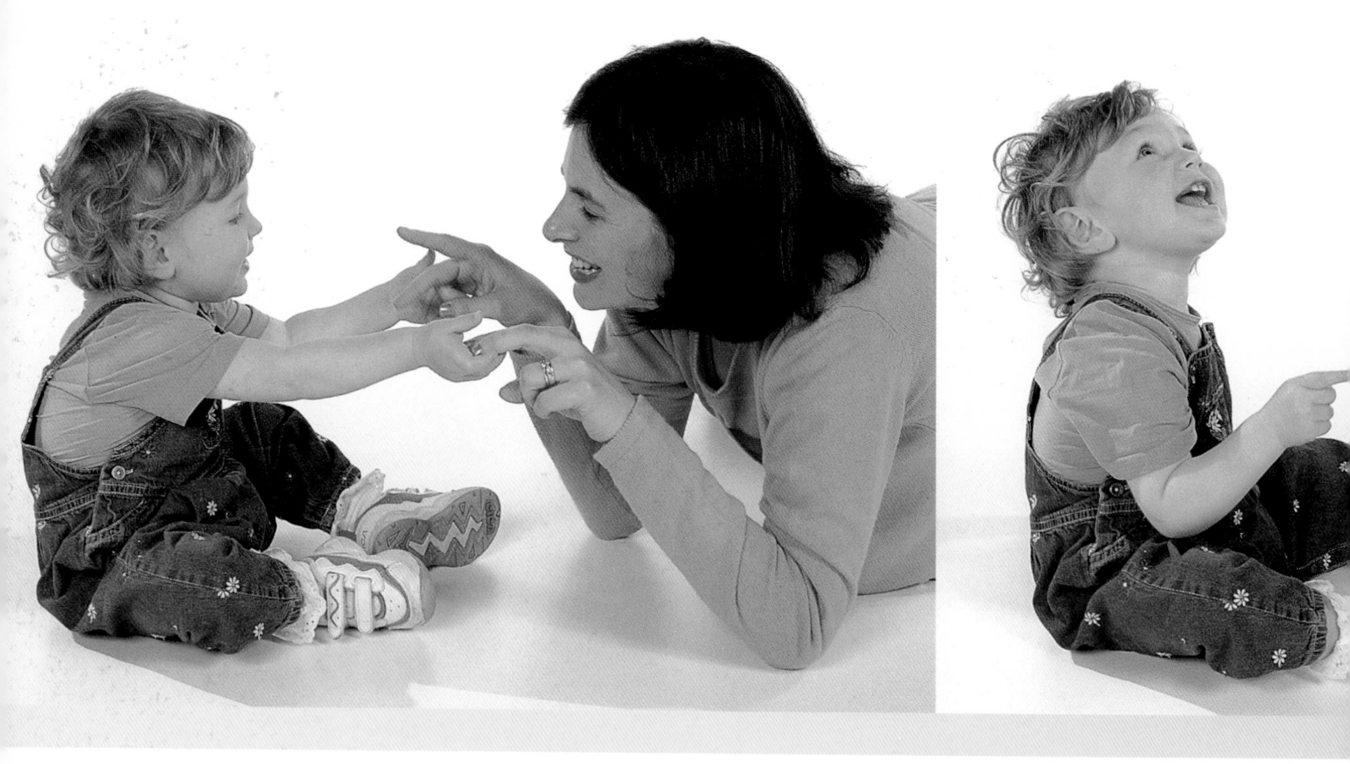

Language

The Progress of Language

If you gasped in amazement at your baby's language development during the first year – when she changed from a baby who could only cry into someone who could say her first clear word – then you will be stunned by the language explosion that occurs when she is a toddler! In her second and third years, her language takes a tremendous surge forward, enabling her to take part in conversations, to relate her experiences and to voice her feelings.

Here are some of the main changes to look for:

- **vocabulary.** At the age of 16 months, she can probably use about six clear words, most of which are names of people in the family or familiar objects. Estimates vary but it is safe to assume that by the time she is 36-months-old, she can use more than a thousand words, and of course she understands a lot more. Her vocabulary is very varied by this stage, and she is able to use words in an appropriate context in order to communicate effectively.
- **structure.** Her ability to combine words together to form phrases and short sentences develops. Initially, she could say only one word at a time, each word representing a complete thought. But around the age of 18 months, she starts to combine two words together to form a meaningful phrase, such as 'me teddy', meaning 'I want my teddy', and by 36 months she talks in short structured sentences, with at least three or four words in them.
- **grammar.** The typical 36-month-old uses different types of words, not just nouns as she did when she first began to speak, but also adjectives, verbs and pronouns. For instance, she might say 'I want my teddy', clearing indicating her wishes in a grammatically correct sentence. She starts using words such as 'in' and 'on', and she is able to add 's' on to a word sometimes to make it plural. (In some cases she may do this incorrectly, for example, saying 'mouses' instead of 'mice'.) However, it's not until much later that she learns to use present, past and future tenses.
- **pronunciation.** Your toddler uses most consonants and vowels, although at times she becomes confused. Word beginnings in particular often get mixed (for example, 'lellow' instead of 'yellow'). You may be tempted to laugh when she makes these normal mistakes but do your best not to. In any case, her speech is clear enough for most other children and adults to understand.

Listening Skills

Your child becomes a better listener during her second and third years, which aids her language development because it is through listening that she hears language spoken, and this enables her to interpret instructions and take part in conversations. Remember, however, that she remains egocentric – she

Below: At 30 months old this little boy's vocabulary is wide and he is able to name the different parts of the body.

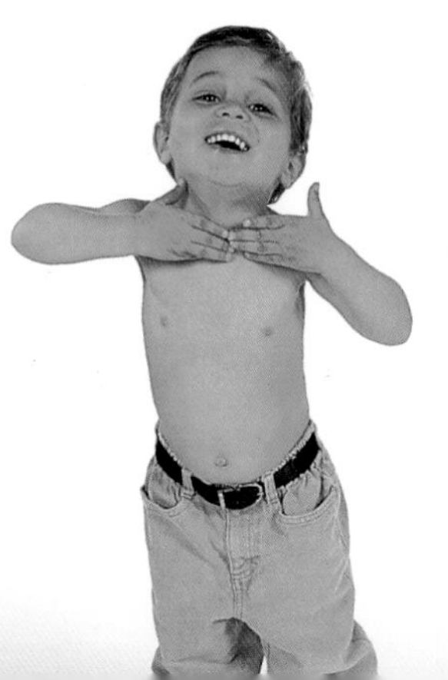
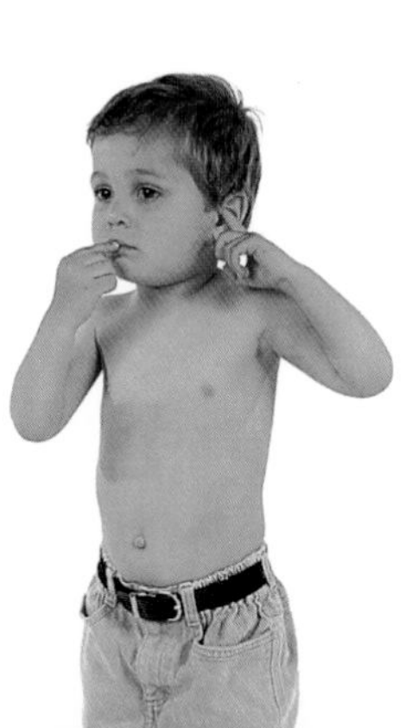
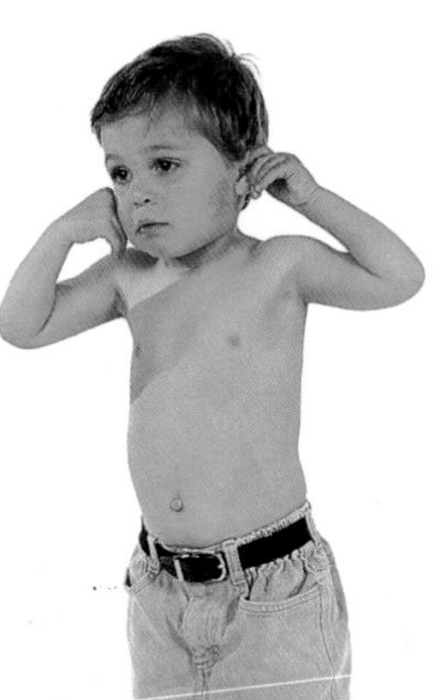
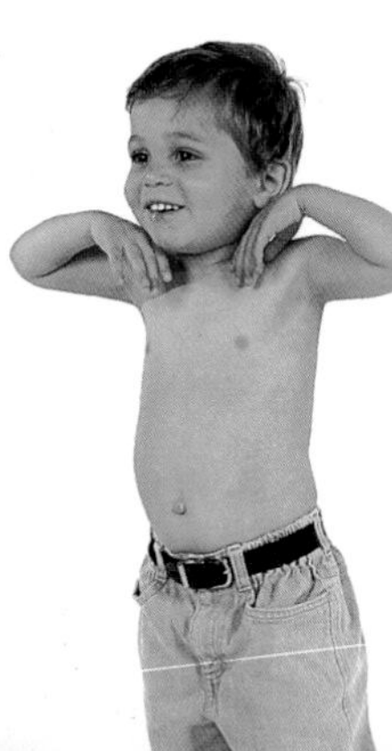

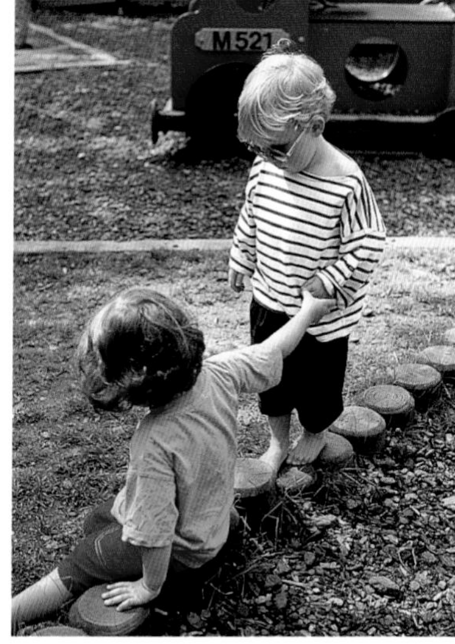

Above: At 36 months your child will be able to make himself understood to other children and adults, most of the time.

still expects the world to revolve around her and therefore she will often not feel any need to listen to you when you talk to her.

When you find that, for instance, your 36-month-old continues to watch television after you have asked her to come to the dining table for her evening meal, the chances are that she heard you but deliberately chose to ignore your message. At this age, she's good at exercising 'selective attention'! On the other hand, a child who consistently fails to respond to comments directed at her may have a hearing problem.

If you're not sure whether your child ignores you by choice or because she simply doesn't hear properly, look for other possible indications of hearing impairment. For instance, she might study your face and mouth closely when you speak, she might ask you to repeat questions over and over, or she might mix up certain sounds in her speech (such as 't' and 'k'). None of these findings definitely signify a hearing loss, but if you are at all concerned, have her hearing checked by your family doctor.

Why Speak?

Your child's ability to talk not only enables her to express herself easily and accurately, but also allows her to gather information – it's a great means of satisfying her endless curiosity. That's why your 2-year-old starts to ask questions, and once she starts, she doesn't stop!

Prepare yourself for an onslaught of 'why', 'who', 'how', and 'what' questions. She doesn't ask these questions in order to confront you or to challenge your views; she has a genuine interest in the replies. You'll discover that she has an amazing ability to ask about things that leave you at a loss for any easy answer. For instance, 'Why is the car that colour?' or 'Why do you have hair?'

She is also likely to repeat questions, even though you thought you had answered them already. The fact is that your child may not have understood your initial explanation and so she wants you to tell her again. This can be exceedingly frustrating for you, but her question stems from a genuine desire to use her improved language skills to enhance her understanding of the world around her. She may use endless questions as a way of gaining and keeping your attention, which she loves. She'll have already learned that when you are talking to her, no matter what the subject matter, you are focused on her – and she wants to keep it that way.

Above: From the age of 2 onwards children ask increasing numbers of questions as they try to understand the world around them.

Left: As she comprehends more, she will become more attentive and conversations will be less simplistic.

Stimulating Language: 16 to 18 Months

Your toddler's vocabulary starts to build steadily as he listens to conversations around him. Typically he uses several different words a day – and understands the meaning of literally hundreds more – and he begins to form meaningful two-word phrases. You quickly discover that there is one word that he likes to use himself and yet hates anyone else to use, and that's 'no'!

Read To Your Toddler

Reading to your toddler is one of the great contributions you can make to his speech development. Even though he may seem to listen passively as you go through the story, studies have found that young children who listen to stories read to them by their parent for just 10 or 15 minutes each day usually have more advanced language development than those children who miss out on this valuable experience.

Of course, your toddler can also improve his speech skills by listening to other sources of stimulation, such as television and video tapes, but there is something very special about you reading to him, something that harnesses his imagination and enthusiasm more than most other forms of language stimulation.

Suitable Suggestions

It's important to make good eye contact when chatting to your child. As well as grabbing his attention and improving his listening skills, encouraging him to maintain eye contact while someone talks to him is a good social skill that will help him mix more effectively with others in the future. You may find that he doesn't appear to listen to you unless he is facing you, so position yourself in a way that ensures you are able to look at each other.

His imagination is developing fast and you can use this to stimulate his use of language. For instance, you can talk to his toy animals and pretend that they reply to you – tell your child what they say and ask him to speak to them, too. He'll very quickly join in this type of imaginative play; soon he will be able to tell you their names and all sorts of things that have happened to them. A toy telephone serves the same purpose at this age. He'll

Below: Use moments when you have your child's full attention to point out and name familiar objects – like the parts of the body.

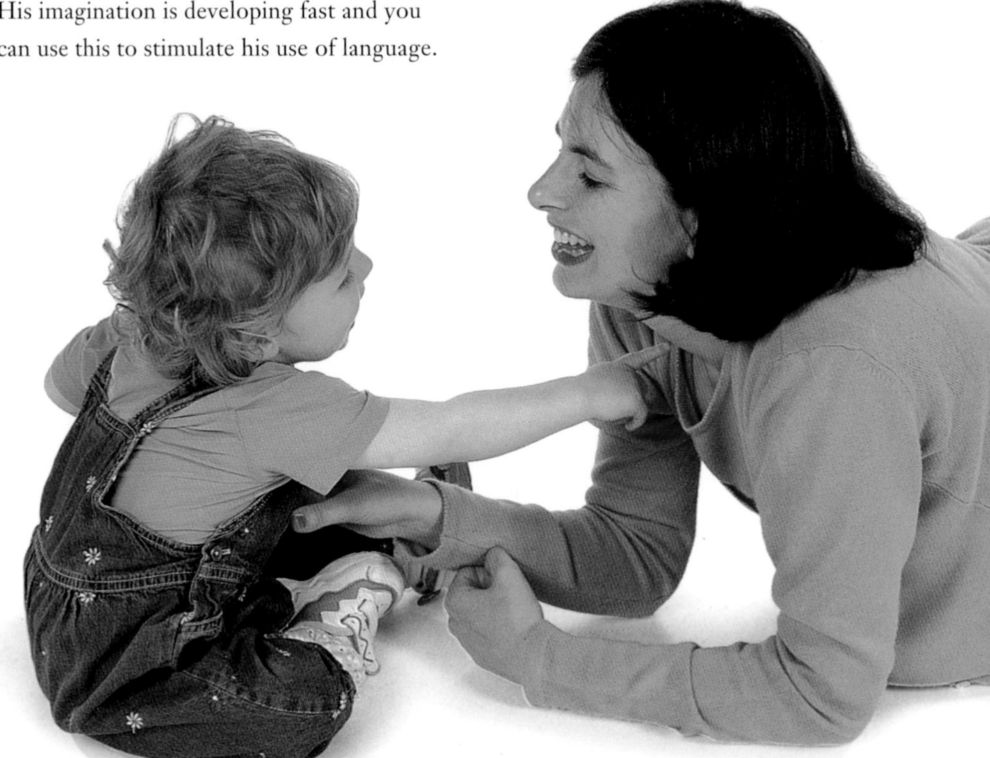

have great fun prattling away on the phone as he has an imaginary conversation with one of his friends or perhaps with a grandparent or another member of the family.

Although your toddler usually has quite a lot to say for himself, there may be times when he is frustratingly slow in communicating his ideas and feelings to you. Try not to rush him or he will just give up the idea altogether. Relax and let him take his time. He probably simply needs another few moments to find the words that he wants to use. Be as patient with him as you can.

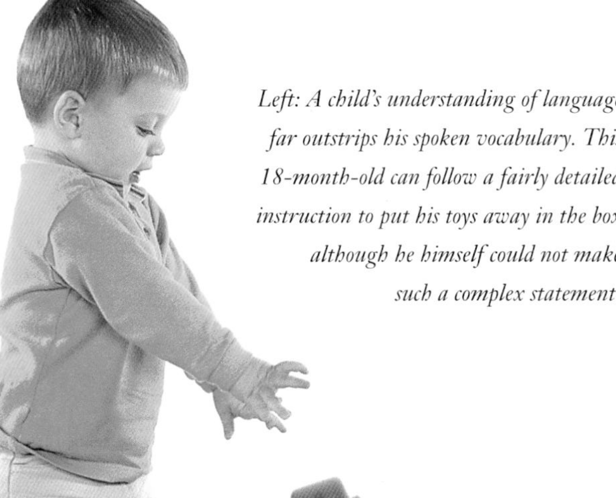

Left: A child's understanding of language far outstrips his spoken vocabulary. This 18-month-old can follow a fairly detailed instruction to put his toys away in the box although he himself could not make such a complex statement.

At this age he starts to learn the names of the various parts of the body. A good time for teaching these words to him is at bathtime or when he undresses for bed. Make this activity informal and enjoyable, perhaps by stroking the palm of his hand when you tell him 'This is your hand' or gently touching his ear when you explain that 'This is your ear'. The same applies to names of familiar household objects. Instead of saying to your toddler 'Put these away', you could say 'Put these toys in the big box'. You will help to expand his range of vocabulary through your own use of language when you speak to him.

Top Tips

1. Point out the names of the primary colours to him. While he is too young to learn the names of colours, your naming them can help him become aware of the differences between them.

2. Remove distractions when trying to attract his attention. There is absolutely no point in speaking to your toddler when he is totally engrossed in a television programme. Switch the set off for a moment while you talk to him.

3. Make a tape of familiar sounds. Tape record everyday sounds, such as a car driving past, a cup filling with water, and so on. Watch your child's face to see if he recognizes any of them – go through the tape again explaining each sound.

4. Miss out the last word of his favourite song. Sing all the song until you approach the very last word, and then stop. Look at your child with an expression of anticipation on your face – he'll try to say the missing word.

5. Look closely at your child when he speaks to you. Your toddler speaks because he has something important to say to you. Listen carefully and respond positively, even if much of what he said was unclear.

Q&A

Q How can I get my toddler to speak instead of pointing at what he wants?

A You can't force your child to speak but you can encourage his language development by not reacting to his non-verbal gestures. There is a greater incentive for him to speak when he finds that body language alone doesn't get the desired result. And when he does use words instead of pointing, always react quickly and praise his use of language.

Q My child talks to himself. Is this normal?

A Yes. One of the best ways for him to improve his language skills is through regular practice and what better way to practise free from interruption than by talking to himself? You won't understand most of what he says during these self-directed monologues, but remember that his words are not intended for you to hear.

Toys: dolls and cuddly toys, toy telephone, plastic cups and saucers, story books, bath toys

Stimulating Language: 19 to 21 Months

Progress in language continues and your child realizes that speech is not just for the purpose of communicating her ideas and feelings – it's also a good way to make social contact. She is increasingly interested in two-way conversation. Her broadening vocabulary and use of more complex sentence structures enable her to make more sophisticated contributions when you engage her in discussion.

Early Words

Psychologists studying the types of words that children first acquire when they start to speak have found that over 50 per cent of these early words are general in nature, referring to objects within a general class, such as 'ball', 'car' and 'house'. And a word such as 'dog' may be used for all animals. Less than 15 per cent are specific, referring to particular people or objects, such as 'Mummy' and 'teddy'.

Another finding from this area of research is that many of a child's first words are connected with things she can actually use in some way or another, for instance, words like 'spoon', 'juice' and 'cup'. This is further proof that your child's language growth reflects closely her everyday experience.

Suitable Suggestions

Encourage your child to talk to you about events as they occur – don't wait until the end of the day to recap as she may have forgotten about the incident. Bear in mind that she is fascinated by everything going on around her, and has an inherent desire to speak to you about her experiences. Whether it is putting on her vest and pants in the morning or going out for a walk in the afternoon, your talkative toddler is delighted to chat to you about it and needs you to respond. Use clear language, with words that she can easily understand.

Above: Your child will initiate more conversations by commenting on what he is doing or something he sees.

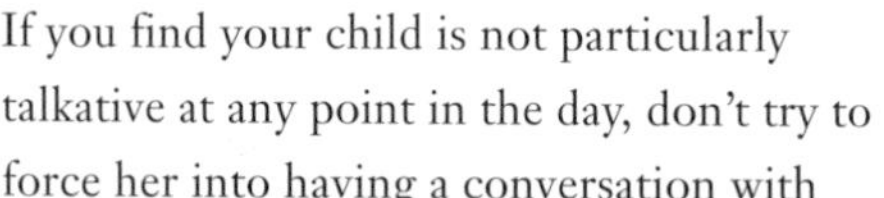

If you find your child is not particularly talkative at any point in the day, don't try to force her into having a conversation with you. Maybe she's tired or perhaps she is in a bad mood. Whatever the reason, let her have quiet times. You'll probably find that she becomes more communicative again later in the day.

Left: Talking to your child during everyday activities will help increase his vocabulary and understanding.

You can also further your child's understanding of both receptive language (the language she understands when it is spoken to her) and expressive language (the

Above: At this age your child may prefer to watch others than to talk to them.

Top Tips

1. Ask her to name objects. Point to an object she knows and ask her what it is called. Gradually extend this to new objects that you haven't heard her name before – if she's not sure, tell her the word she is looking for.

2. Respond when she talks to you. Whether or not you fully understand what your 21-month-old toddler says to you, give her a positive response, such as a smile or a nod. She needs this sort of encouraging feedback from you.

3. Expect her to 'clam up' in company. Despite her instinctive desire for attention, your child may suddenly lose her confidence to speak when she is confronted by a sea of faces. She'll speak once she is alone with you again.

4. Use doll play. Give your toddler instructions for her doll. For instance, 'Put your doll over there' or 'Give your doll a drink'. This helps develop her ability to listen, to think, to interpret and then to act on what she has heard.

5. Sing songs together. Her increased speech and language skills mean that she can join in more easily when you sing songs to her. If you pick her favourites, you'll find that she tries to sing along too.

language she uses to voice her own ideas and feelings) by demonstrating the meanings of new words with which she is not fully familiar. For instance, if you want to say to her 'That man is very tall', raise your hands high at the same time so that she sees a visual interpretation of your comment. Words accompanied by a physical demonstration of their content enhance her grasp of their meaning.

Make up listening games to play with her. For instance, you can ask her to shut her eyes and to listen very carefully and tell you when she hears a car go past your house – if she doesn't get it right first time, let her try again. Or you could read her a story, substituting her name for the name of the central character, and ask her to let you know whenever she hears her name mentioned as you read. Any game at all that involves your child in focusing on listening closely for information will benefit her language development and provide lots of fun along the way.

Q&A

Q My 21-month-old child has a stilted way of talking, as though abbreviating what she is saying. Is that typical for a child this age?

A Her language sounds abbreviated because it contains only the key words, such as 'want milk' or 'me sleep'. Over the next year she starts to add in other types of words such as prepositions and adjectives. This is the way in which language development normally progresses over the months.

Q My toddler speaks so hurriedly I can't make out what she says. What should I do?

A She is just impatient to express herself. Over the next few months she naturally slows down her speech and it will become easier to understand what she is saying. In the meantime, if she is over-excited when she speaks to you, try to encourage her to speak more slowly. But there is absolutely no cause for concern.

Toys: story books, tapes or CDs of children's songs, animals and farm buildings, toy cars, children's video tapes

Stimulating Language: 22 to 24 Months

Speech is very much part of his life now. By the time he reaches his second birthday your child is much more communicative, has a better grasp of vocabulary, grammar and sentence structure, and likes talking to other people. In particular, he enjoys mixing with other children of his own age, even though they can't always make themselves understood to each other.

He Stammers

Stammering (also known as stuttering) is common in children as young as 2 years; a child of this age often starts to say a word, doesn't complete the whole word, starts to say it again, and so on. Repetitions and uncertainty like this occur frequently when a child's language development is beginning to accelerate. Fortunately, most 2-year-olds pass through their stammering phase without any help as their confidence grows.

If your young child stutters, make sure that nobody (including older siblings) makes fun of him, tries to mimic him, or attempts to hurry him along. He needs your time, patience and support to get through this temporary phase.

Suitable Suggestions

You continue to have a huge influence on your toddler's language development. You will find that he picks up the style of words and sentences you use. Try to make the language you use with your child basic but varied. Instead of using the same words each time, offer alternatives that have the same meaning. For instance, the word 'big' could sometimes be replaced by 'huge' or 'large', the word 'nice' could be replaced by 'good' or 'great' – your child takes his cue from you and when he hears you use different words he'll start to do the same as well. This gradually broadens his vocabulary.

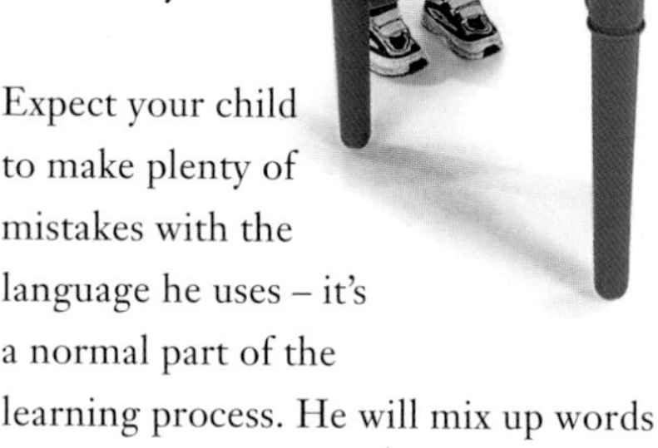

Right: At around 2 children begin to talk to each other more.

Expect your child to make plenty of mistakes with the language he uses – it's a normal part of the learning process. He will mix up words

Below: Meals are a good time to introduce language concepts: naming different foods and their colours, whether things are tasty or nice, hot or cold and so on.

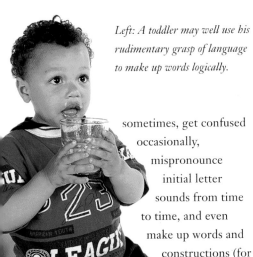

Left: A toddler may well use his rudimentary grasp of language to make up words logically.

sometimes, get confused occasionally, mispronounce initial letter sounds from time to time, and even make up words and constructions (for instance, when he finishes a glass of juice, he might say 'juice gonded', thereby creating an entirely new word for himself).

Don't correct him when he makes language mistakes or he may become anxious. A more effective strategy is to reiterate what he has tried to say, using the correct words or construction, as if you were agreeing with him rather than pointing out his mistake. If he watches a dog walk away from him and says, for instance, 'Doddy gone away' you could say 'Yes, that's right. The dog has gone away.' Modelling language in this way shows him how to say the words correctly, without weakening his self-confidence.

Your child expects everybody to understand him – he knows what he is trying to say and so he assumes you do as well. And he may explode with frustration when he suddenly thinks that you don't grasp his meaning. The more you ask him to repeat himself, the angrier he becomes. In this situation, use a variety of strategies. You might decide to distract his attention on to something else altogether, or you could just nod your head as though you have understand exactly what he has said.

Top Tips

1. Let him speak at mealtimes. Whether eating on his own or with the rest of the family, encourage him to chat as he eats. The relaxed atmosphere, coupled with the pleasure of eating, is likely to make him particularly conversational.

2. Play tongue and lip exercises. Place him in front of a mirror and show him how to wiggle his tongue about, blow through his closed lips, and make 'p', 'b' and 'd' noises. This improves tongue and lip control.

3. Ask him to make up songs. Play a simple tune without words and suggest that he makes up his own words to accompany it. He may look at you in amazement at first, but once he gets the idea he will have great fun creating his own songs.

4. Show him recent family photographs. He studies photographs very closely when he recognizes people in them, and he loves to see pictures of himself. Use this as a stimulus to talk about the family events and holidays in the pictures, which he may partly remember.

5. Make occasional 'mistakes' when reading stories. To sharpen his listening skills, read a familiar story to him but change it in one small way (for instance, the name of the family pet) and wait for him to spot your error.

Below: Encourage your child to make up simple songs – it's a great way for him to play around with words.

Q Why is it that my child says 'f' for 's' and also says 't' for 'c'?

A Say these sounds slowly yourself – you'll discover that 'f' and 't' involve your teeth, lips and the tip of your tongue, while 'c' and 's' involve the back of your mouth. Your child finds front-of-mouth sounds much easier at this age and hence makes these substitutions. He will gradually master the whole range of sounds.

Q Is it true that some stories meant for children can actually frighten them?

A Some stories have the potential to frighten your child. That's why it is important to choose carefully the books that you want to read to him, to ensure the content is appropriate for his age and understanding. He is unlikely to feel very positively about books and pictures if he experiences some that disturb him and make him afraid.

Toys: story books, picture cards of familiar objects, finger puppets, cuddly toys, craft and drawing materials

Stimulating Language: 25 to 30 Months

The sophistication of her language shows through in your child's everyday speech, as she starts to use pronouns (I, you, he/she) and descriptive words more consistently. She is able to hold conversations with other children of her own age, and she enjoys talking to adults as well. The minute details of family life fascinate her and she constantly asks questions.

Playgroup And Nursery

At this age, your child's language development can be enhanced by mixing with other children as much as it can by stimulation from you. Of course, she bickers sometimes with her peers when they play together, but for most of the time they prattle away happily to each other, sharing stories and experiences.

The incentive of communicating with a friend in order to play together is strong enough to prompt better speech and more mature listening skills. That's why it is so important for you to arrange regular contact with others her own age, at either a playgroup or nursery, or even during visits at home.

Suitable Suggestions

Show interest in the endless tales that she brings to you, about this friend or about that toy. She is excited about everything that goes on around her and she wants to share this with you. You'll find that your child likes to sit beside you, cuddling up to you as she gives an account of her latest exploits. It's important that you respond with questions when she talks to you to let her know you are listening and are interested, and also to force her to think more deeply about the subject.

You can also use these conversations to help your child clarify her speech. For instance, when she starts to tell you about an incident involving another child at nursery or about an older sibling, she probably does so without actually mentioning the name of the child. Point out that she should name who she is talking about at the beginning. Of course she won't remember this immediately, but at least you are beginning to encourage her to plan her conversation and to think about the needs of the listener.

Above: Conversation with your child is now a two-way thing. She will enjoy telling you things but rely on your questions to draw her out further.

Now that her imagination is more advanced, try to involve her in pretend play, for example, dressing-up games. Your child thrives on this sort of activity and it provides an opportunity for her to develop her language skills because she can pretend to be a completely different person. Observe her during this type of play – the chances are that when she dresses up as an adult, her voice tone changes and she uses different

Right: Stimulate her imagination by using dressing-up clothes and by talking about characters that appear in stories and nursery rhymes.

words. She has great fun marching about the place using new forms of language as she pretends to be someone else.

When you don't let her do what she wants, she might try to shout you down – her instinctive reaction on hearing something she doesn't like is to tell you to be quiet. Calm her, then continue to say what you wanted to say anyway. She eventually learns that you have as much right to speak as she has, even though she is unhappy with the message you convey to her. Once you've had your say, listen attentively to her response.

Top Tips

1. Make music together. Play along with her as she tries to get sounds out of her toy musical instruments. She likes blowing the trumpet and harmonica, and bashing the drum. Encourage her to sing as you make music together.

2. Talk to your child about the programmes she watches. When she has finished watching a television programme or a video, chat to her about the programme. Ask her basic questions such as the name of the central character.

3. Emphasize prepositions in your speech. You can help her understand the meaning of words like 'in', 'on' and 'under' by demonstrating them. For instance, show her how the food goes 'in' the cupboard, and how her plate goes 'on' the table.

4. Cuddle up together when reading a story. Physical contact is very soothing for both of you. Snuggling together during story time relaxes your child and settles her into a positive mood so that she is ready for listening and talking.

5. Play sorting games with your child. Take some familiar toys such as teddies, building blocks or books, and put them in a pile in front of her. Then ask her to give you all the teddies, for instance. She will demonstrate that she can group some objects.

Below: Television programmes are much more valuable if you watch them with your child and then talk to him about them afterwards.

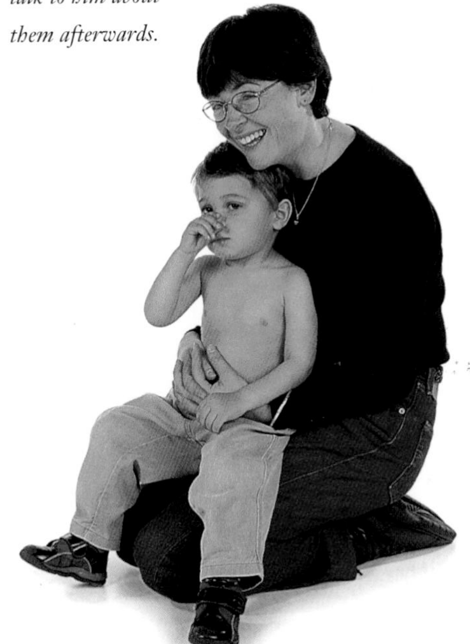

Q&A

Q What should we do about our child's lisp?

A Many children develop a temporary lisp while they acquire speech (in other words, they substitute 'th' for 's', 'f' for 'th' and so on). In most instances this speech pattern disappears spontaneously as they grow older. Therefore at this stage you should do nothing in particular, except provide appropriate speech patterns for her to copy.

Q Is it true that boys are somewhat slower in learning to speak than girls?

A Evidence from psychological studies confirms that, in general, girls acquire spoken language at an earlier age than boys and they also develop more complex language structures before boys. This is only a trend, though; it doesn't mean that every boy says his first word later than every girl. Much depends on the individual child.

Toys: plastic human figures, clothes for dressing up, toy zoo with animals, story books, music tapes or CDs, cuddly toys

Stimulating Language: 31 to 36 Months

By now your child has grasped all the basic language skills and the foundations are set for further advances in vocabulary and grammar – a process that will continue throughout the remainder of his childhood and into adulthood. He still has a lot to learn, but he is a fully fledged 'talker' by 36 months.

Nursery Rhymes

Many of the traditional nursery rhymes date back hundreds of years. For instance, 'Ring-a-Ring-o-Roses' refers to the Great Plague of London – the 'ring' is the red rash indicating the disease has started and the 'all fall down' line at the end is self-explanatory. And this is one childhood tradition that you really should endeavour to maintain.

Nursery rhymes promote your child's language through repetition, through developing his awareness of rhyme, through demonstrating the poetic quality of language and through showing him that language has a fun element. Some nursery rhymes are tongue-twisters (such as 'Peter Piper') and are great for improving his mastery of different sounds and varied pronunciations.

Suitable Suggestions

There are lots of ways you can help develop your child's ability to use language for the purpose of interpreting and explaining his experiences. For example, talk to him about the television programme he just watched; ask him questions about the story line, about the characters in it, and about his opinion of the programme. Questions like these make him use language in ways other than just telling you what he wants or doesn't want. You can do the same about his friends, by asking about them and why he likes them. You might be surprised at the thoughtfulness of explanations he gives.

You'll also find that his interest in words themselves intensifies. He starts to ask you questions about the meanings of different words, perhaps ones that he has heard you use or that he heard at nursery. The meaning of these words may be obvious to you, but not to him. So be patient, give him your attention, and answer appropriately. Particular words may fascinate your child for no apparent reason. One day he hears someone say something and the actual sound

Below: At around 36 months children begin to hold lengthier and more fluent conversations with each other as they interact more and more in play.

Right: There are lots of opportunities to introduce your child to the names of colours – especially when you are painting, drawing or using play doh.

combination of the word amuses him – before you know it he uses that word constantly, probably not accurately. Make sure he knows its real meaning.

Around this time, the focus of your child's language moves away from himself to include other people. It's no longer all about what he wants, or what happened to him, or what he thinks – his increasing social awareness turns his attention towards the feelings and reactions of others. This is a positive step forward, and you can enhance this aspect of his language by providing lots of opportunities to mix with other children and adults. Apart from the obvious social experiences of playgroup or nursery, he benefits from mixing with siblings and with other family members of all ages. You might also consider enrolling him in a leisure activity class such as swimming or dancing, or whatever interests him. The speech and language he uses and hears in these varied contexts extend his own language skills even further.

Top Tips

1. Start to teach individual colours. Although he may not be able to name individual colours, he is probably able to sort them. Give him a pile of coloured bricks, hold up a red one, for example, and say to him 'Find another one like this'.

2. Give factual replies to his questions. Investigations reveal that children in this age range mainly ask questions about facts rather than about feelings – it is a way of enhancing their knowledge. So give brief and accurate answers as required.

3. Choose stories that are more demanding. He is ready to listen to stories with more complex plots and multiple characters. Pick books that are interesting and at the level of your child's understanding – these will grab his interest.

4. Provide explanations. He is now at the age where he begins to understand explanations about why he should behave in a certain way. He is more likely to follow rules about behaviour when they are explained to him.

5. Talk about his drawings and modelling. When your child shows you his latest creative production – in paints, pencil or modelling material – chat to him about it. Listen appreciatively as he explains it to you in great detail.

Below: Talk to your child about what she is drawing – at this age she is likely to have a particular image in mind though you may not recognize it on paper.

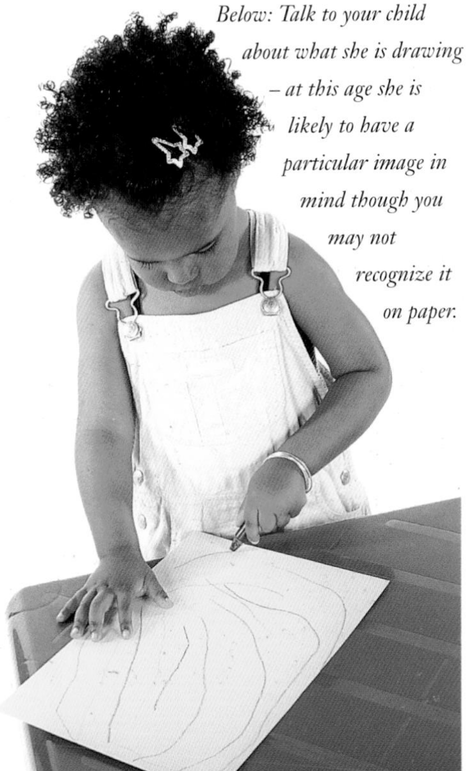

Q&A

Q My child still only uses single words, without forming short sentences. Is this normal at this age?

A The rate at which children acquire speech varies greatly. However, most children are further ahead with their language at this stage. The chances are your child's speech will develop normally and that there is nothing to worry about. But you may find it reassuring to have a chat with your family doctor about this.

Q At what age do children start understanding jokes?

A Humour develops from birth – your child probably first smiled at around six weeks. The use of language as a means of stimulating laughter starts around the age of 2. Although your child's jokes may not strike you as funny – perhaps because they simply involve words in an unusual order – they make him giggle.

Toys: soft toys and dolls for imaginative play, sing-along tapes or CDs, story books, child-sized kitchen

Learning

The Development of Learning Skills

Your child's learning ability continues to grow rapidly during this phase of his life. A good way to define learning ability (also called 'learning skills', 'thinking skills' and 'cognition') is your child's ability to learn new skills and concepts, his ability to make sense of events that happen around him, his ability to use her memory accurately and his ability to solve small problems.

Every day you'll notice examples of how your child's reasoning skills, his understanding of new concepts and his problem-solving skills are developing throughout his second and third years. He becomes altogether better at both thinking and learning.

Here are some of the main changes to look for:

• **symbolism.** Until he reached 18 months or so, your growing child was unable to use symbols – in other words, he could only think in terms of here-and-now, and if an object was not physically in front of him he had difficulty thinking about it. But this changes mid-way through the second year, when he starts to think in images. The emergence of symbolism vastly increases the possibilities for learning.

• **attention.** Part of learning involves focusing on a piece of information long enough to extract meaning from it. Babies have a random attention span, but as your child nears the end of his second year he begins to exercise control over the attention he gives to an object or activity, and when something grabs his interest, he focuses on it until he has satisfied his curiosity.

• **memory.** The ability to recall previously learned information is an essential part of learning and this capacity increases in the second and third years. Both his short- and long-term memories become more effective. This allows him to remember recent experiences (something that happened perhaps a minute ago) and distant experiences (something that happened several months ago).

• **language.** Learning and language development are closely connected.

Your toddler's language explosion improves not only his communication skills but also his ability to learn. He uses language to ask questions, to test out his ideas, to reason, and to improve his understanding of the world.

Remember, however, that he continues to learn principally through explorative and discovery play and through listening, talking and discussing. It doesn't matter whether he plays with an empty box, with a bath toy, with his cutlery during meals, with a jigsaw, or in fact with anything at all – when he interacts playfully with

Right: Your child learns incidentally from her everyday experiences. So relax and have fun with her whenever you can.

anything in his environment he learns new things. The same applies to language – he learns something new in every conversation he has. Look on him as a dynamic scientist, who soaks up information like a sponge and is then eager to put this new knowledge into practice.

Of course, there are specific things you can do to stimulate and promote your child's learning skills, but do keep in mind that a substantial amount of learning takes place every day just through your child following his normal routine. For example, getting dressed in the morning is a complex task involving sorting, matching, coordination, memory and concentration. Bit-by-bit, each day he learns more about dressing until he achieves a level of mastery at the age of 36 months that seems light years ahead of his competence at the same task when he was only 16 months old.

His View of the World

It's important not to make assumptions about your child's thought processes – despite his remarkable progress in learning as a young child, there are still two distinctive characteristics of his learning skills that are different from yours.

First, he doesn't fully understand cause and effect, and may identify a connection between two events where no such connection exists. This is partly due to his immature reasoning and partly due to his lack of experience. For instance, if a light goes out – perhaps because the bulb has broken – at the exact moment that he sneezes, your child may think that his sneeze has caused the lights to go off. Then in future you could find that every time he sneezes, he looks around anxiously waiting for something to happen to the lights!

When your child makes a comment about a cause-and-effect connection (for instance, when he tells you that he made the rain appear because it started when he put his coat on), you should explain clearly why the connection doesn't really exist. He might not believe you at first, so you will probably need to repeat your explanation later.

A second major difference in his thinking is that he still tends to see things only from his own point of view. That's why your 2-year-old looks blankly at you when you reprimand him, for example, for playing with his older brother's toys when he was previously warned off. The rebuke 'How do you think your brother feels when you mess up his toys?' goes right over his head, because he isn't yet at the stage when he can easily see things from another person's perspective. He begins to be able to appreciate other points of view by the end of his third year.

Above: Getting dressed and dressing-up involve many learning opportunities including coordination and concentration.

Above: Much learning takes place through self-motivated exploratory play – often with everyday objects.

Stimulating Learning: 16 to 18 Months

Your child's increased learning skills enable her to take more control over her daily life. She begins to think for herself, tackling challenges with great enthusiasm. Her improved memory allows her to recall where she has previously placed items, for example. Concentration also improves and she plays with toys for longer, leaving her less dependent on constant stimulation from you.

Listen Please

You probably find that your toddler occasionally fails to respond when you speak to her. The problem is that you compete against many other sources of stimulation. There's so much to attract your toddler's attention that it is hardly surprising that she doesn't always listen to you.

You can help develop her listening skills by putting a 'name' prompt into the sentence. For instance, if you want her to follow an instruction, start off by saying her name, and only deliver the instruction when she turns around and makes eye contact with you. The more she listens, the more she learns.

Suitable Suggestions

Your toddler likes to experiment with toys and she won't need much encouragement from you to do this, but be ready to offer suggestions anyway. Now is a good time for her to become more creative in the way she explores. She has the determination and self-confidence to be more varied in her responses; all she needs is a little guidance and prompting from you.

For instance, when she struggles to place a particularly awkward shape in the shape-sorter box, remind her that she can turn the shape around or that she could try alternative shapes for that hole. She may be unwilling at first to follow your advice because she'd rather achieve success without your help, but she'll give it a try eventually. The specific advice you offer her isn't so important – what matters is that you have helped your toddler to think more creatively, approaching challenges from different perspectives.

Right: With some gentle guidance you can often help your child with something she finds tricky – turning potential frustration into achievement.

Left: By now your child will enjoy following a simple story and will respond to familiar characters.

Continue to develop her imaginative play even though her imagination is still limited. For instance, read her stories in a lively way, using different voices and varying the loudness depending on the action. You'll find that her facial expressions match yours as she listens to every word, synchronizing her mood with the mood you express. Do not make story-telling too dramatic, though, as toddlers may become so engrossed that they are upset by the emotions aroused.

Gradually improve your child's attention span, as this will help her general learning ability. One strategy is simply to sit by your toddler as she plays with her toys. There is evidence from psychological research that a child is likely to play for longer in the presence of a parent. Another strategy is to observe her at an activity, and when you see that she is ready to move on to something else, suggest that she continues with it for a little longer. Don't expect too much from her at this stage, though.

Below: Water play will enthral children of this age group and gives them a basic idea of volume and quantity.

Top Tips

1. Broaden her play interests. She'll learn best when she plays with a range of toys instead of focusing on just one or two. If you notice that she continually plays with the same few toys every day, try to engage her interest in other items.

2. Provide opportunities for water play. Whether at the time she has a bath or at some other point in the day, let your toddler play with cups and water. She'll learn about quantities and volume through the experience of filling and emptying containers of different sizes.

3. Look for gradual changes. Naturally you hope that she will progress rapidly with learning. Try to avoid placing too much pressure on her to learn new skills all the time or she may become anxious, intimidated and unable to learn. From time to time allow her to relax by undertaking an activity that she's already thoroughly mastered.

4. Practise new learning in short bursts. She learns best for short periods of time. For instance, several five-minute episodes of learning separated by 15-minute breaks is a better way to learn than one continuous session lasting an hour.

5. Give her time. Your stomach may churn with frustration as you watch your toddler try every solution to the puzzle except the right one. But don't rush in too early; she needs time to test out different strategies for herself.

Q What type of jigsaw should my 18-month-old toddler be able to manage?

A Although her learning and coordination skills have improved, she still finds jigsaws and similar puzzles very challenging. The typical child of this age successfully tackles inset boards with around three or four wooden pieces. However, she'll probably need practice before she is able to place all the pieces in the right place.

Q My toddler is impatient with learning. If she can't solve the puzzle, she has a tantrum. What should I do?

A Her desire to learn is so strong that she can't wait, and hence her rage when the solution isn't immediately available. Calm her first and then sit with her and teach her how to solve the problem. Finally, ask her to complete the activity under your supervision.

Toys: inset boards, story books, plastic shapes, construction bricks, sand and water tray, nesting cubes

Stimulating Learning: 19 to 21 Months

The principal change in your child's learning at this stage is that he becomes more outward-looking. Of course he has always been curious to learn, but now he looks further afield for stimulation. His confidence has grown, leaving him emotionally ready to tackle new learning challenges. He becomes more focused and determined – you'll discover that he becomes ever more motivated to finish what he starts.

Object Permanence

You know that when you put, say, a pullover into a drawer and then close the drawer, the pullover is still there even though you can't see it – that's what psychologists call 'object permanence'. It's not until your toddler is older than 18 months that he fully grasps this concept.

Before this stage, he would stop looking for an object that was out of his line of vision. It was a case of out of sight, out of mind. Now, however, he fully understands object permanence – so he looks for an object even though he didn't actually see where it was placed.

Suitable Suggestions

Feed his unquenchable thirst for new facts and new information. For several months he has been keen to explore all the hidden spaces of your house. Now is the time to broaden his sphere of interest. When you take your child shopping or to a friend's house – or anywhere at all – encourage him to look around, to pay attention to whatever is going on around him. The activity of a busy urban street, the hustle-and-bustle of life in the aisles of a typical supermarket, all contain new stimuli to enhance his learning. Talk to him about his surroundings, point out the different people and objects as you move along, and respond to his questions.

He loves play that involves getting his hands messy, such as painting, modelling, and sand and water play. Perhaps it's the tactile sensations he derives from immersing his hands in these substances that make these activities so pleasurable, or maybe it's just the chance to mess around without worrying about tidiness. Either way, he learns about

Below: Your child becomes more curious about the world around him and loves to watch others playing.

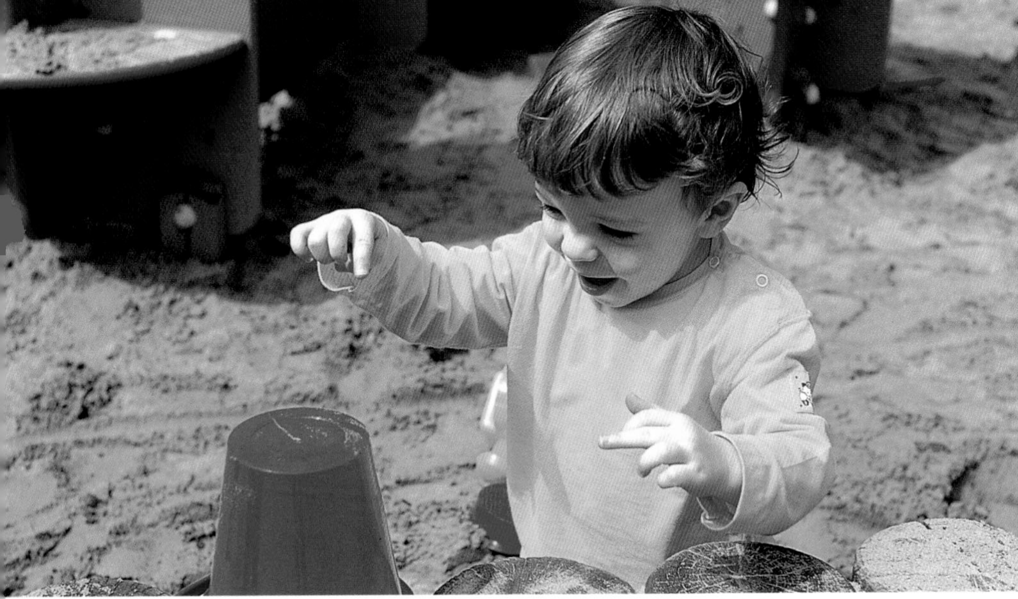

Above: Your child will love the texture of sand: running it through his fingers, raking, digging and moulding it.

Top Tips

1. **Engage him in conversation whenever possible.** Talking with you stimulates his mind, helps him consider things that he might otherwise ignore and allows you to direct his thoughts on to specific topics. This is a good boost for his learning.
2. **Reduce distractions.** You can strengthen your child's ability to concentrate by reducing distractions while he plays. For instance, turn off the television while he plays with his toys, and perhaps remove some of the toys he isn't playing with.
3. **Encourage him to explore.** If your child is timid at times and is reluctant to investigate and explore on his own, say to him, for instance, 'Let's look and see what this is.' Your support gives him the confidence to be more adventurous.
4. **Provide emotional support.** His trial-and-error method of learning is effective, but results in some experiences of failure and frustration. Always be ready with a comforting cuddle when he doesn't achieve success in the way he had hoped.
5. **Give him items to stimulate his use of symbolism.** Toy vehicles, toy people or toy animals encourage him to play imaginatively, as he acts out scenes he makes up himself. Suggest he tries this, if he hasn't already thought of it himself.

shape, size and patterns while engaged in that form of play. Try to build this type of activity into his regular schedule.

Give him specific tasks to strengthen his memory. For instance, you could ask him 'Can you find your ball?' or you could say 'Bring me the cup from the kitchen.' He won't always carry out these instructions – in fact, you may find he doesn't return for ages, having completely forgotten what it was you asked him! Yet basic requests like these improve his short- and long-term memories.

At this age he needs to explore both to learn and to satisfy his curiosity. Yet you need to ensure he remains safe. So be prepared to declare boundaries or even no-go areas if you think your exploring toddler may be at risk of injury.

Below: Getting upset when things don't work out is very common at this age and your reassurance is extremely important.

Q Do children of this age understand about colours?

A Colour awareness is present at birth, and develops from that moment on. At this age, though, your child won't be able to name colours or even to sort different colours into groups. Yet he appreciates the different visual characteristics of different colours. Help this process along by naming the colour of his clothes as you dress him.

Q Is there an optimum amount of time my child should spend watching television daily?

A There's no 'ideal' amount of television because much depends on the type of programme he watches. Whatever the amount of time your growing child spends watching television, make sure the programmes are suitable for that age group, that he doesn't just watch the same programme over and over again, and that television doesn't crowd out other activities. You can use television programmes to enhance language and understanding by talking to him about what he has watched.

Toys: modelling clay or play dough, soft toys, shape puzzles, inset boards, toy figures, picture books, boxes with lids

Stimulating Learning: 22 to 24 Months

As she approaches the end of her second year, your child is more independent in all areas, including her thinking skills. She understands that she has some control over what happens around her and this increases her willingness to explore. Through imaginative play, she tests out new ideas, and you'll find that this is a favourite form of activity.

Intelligence Tests

An intelligence test is a series of small tasks that some psychologists use to assess a child's learning skills. This form of assessment looks at learning abilities including memory, pattern recognition, reasoning, language and understanding. Intelligence tests are standardized, which means that an individual child's score is compared against the typical score for a child of her age.

Although these tests were once extremely popular, many psychologists don't use them nowadays because there are serious questions concerning the reliability and validity of such assessments. In addition, they are thought by some professionals to be too narrow, resulting in an inaccurate picture of the child's true learning potential.

Suitable Suggestions

Let her follow you around the house as you tidy up, make meals, watch television, make a phone call, or do any other routine activity. Your child learns by watching you closely, by asking you questions and by imitating your actions. So you should be prepared to have your 'shadow' trail you wherever you go and to explain things to her as you go along. For instance, tell her the reasons why you need to wash the vegetables you are preparing for the family's meal. Your child listens to these explanations attentively.

Encourage her to play with a range of puzzles. Try to find ones that are challenging but not so difficult that she gives up without trying. She is already familiar with inset

Below: Approaching 2, he will have a better idea of how to put things together. But don't be afraid to help if something is too complex for him to tackle alone.

boards and therefore feels confident enough to attempt unfamiliar ones with a greater number of pieces. You could give your child her first jigsaw – this should consist of only two pieces, which easily fit together and which are a good size for small hands to manipulate. She thrives on your praise when she shows you her completed solution.

You can improve her memory by asking her to find a familiar object. She enjoys helping you and likes the challenge. Make this into a game. For example, let her see you place the newspaper on the kitchen table. A few minutes later, when you are both in another room, pretend that you can't remember where you left it and ask her 'Where is the newspaper?' She thinks for a moment, hurriedly makes her way into the kitchen and returns proudly a few moments later.

Top Tips

1. Let her sit at a table. Your child is more likely to spend longer playing with her toys when she is seated comfortably at a table with her toys laid out in front of her but within easy reach.

2. Ask her to explain her actions before she carries them out. This encourages her to think ahead. For example, when you see she is about to build something with her construction bricks, ask her to tell you what she plans to make.

3. Chat about yesterday's routine. She enjoys your attention and will be happy to chat away to you about the previous day's activities. Pretend that you can't remember some of the things you did together, in order to prompt her recollection.

4. Start to talk about categories. You can help your child develop the ability to group items by emphasizing common groupings in your everyday conversation – she begins to understand there are categories of things called, for example, 'toys', 'clothes' and 'drinks'.

5. Have a settled time each day. Make a specific point of having a quiet time every day when you and your child sit in the same room, each engaged on your own leisure activity without any other distraction. This boosts her concentration span.

Above: Start to teach him how things fit into groups like animals, birds, flowers, food and so on.

Remind her to think about a puzzle and its possible solutions before trying to solve it. Of course she still needs to use trial-and-error techniques as part of her learning, but she has a greater ability to think before she acts. Encourage her to look at the puzzle before handling it and once she has spent a few seconds thinking about it, tell her to test her idea. If it doesn't work, she should think again and then try once more.

Below: Your child is learning the rudiments of planning: if you ask him what he is going to do next when playing with blocks he may well tell you that he is going to make a tower, for example.

Q&A

Q Why is it that my 2-year-old remembers some things from months ago but not others?

A Memories are easier to retrieve when they are vivid, meaningful and exciting. That's why your child remembers her friend's party that she went to several months ago and yet can't recall what she watched on television yesterday. The more stimulating the experience, the more likely it is that her memory of it will endure.

Q Is it true that humour and intelligence are connected?

A Every child is capable of humour and laughter, irrespective of her learning skills. The fact that one child laughs more than another is due to personality differences, not intellectual differences. However, some verbal jokes involve a sophisticated understanding of language and therefore a child has to have achieved that level of development in order to appreciate the humour.

Toys: inset boards, jigsaws, shape boxes, floor puzzles, crayons and paper, set of toy tools or gardening implements

Stimulating Learning: 25 to 30 Months

What a transformation in your child's understanding of the world around him! As well as spending time with you, he loves the company of others his own age. Through playing together and talking with his peers, your child learns a whole range of skills more rapidly than he could do on his own. You may be surprised at the new ideas he acquires from other children.

Animism

Psychologists use the term 'animism' to refer to a child's tendency to ascribe human qualities to non-human objects. At the age of 2½ years, for instance, your child might tell you that the moon smiles at him every night. Or if he sees that your car has a dent in it, he may try to cuddle it in order to make it feel better.

This is a further sign of his increased imagination and ability to use symbolism, and it also makes him feel more secure. His tendency towards animism lasts for several years, and some adults retain this thought pattern (for instance, calling a ship 'her').

Suitable Suggestions

Your child is as interested in the details as he is in the broad picture, which is why he seems so curious about every little thing. Foster this inquisitiveness by providing new sources of stimulation, such as visits to the zoo – or even just to a pet shop. Be ready to answer all his questions about why birds have feathers and he doesn't have any, why a tiger has stripes, and so on. And be ready to break the news to him that he can't have a giraffe at home!

If you do buy him a small domestic pet such as a goldfish, he will sit quietly watching it swim round and round the bowl. The actions of the fish totally mesmerize him. This is a sign of his desire to learn. Suggest to him

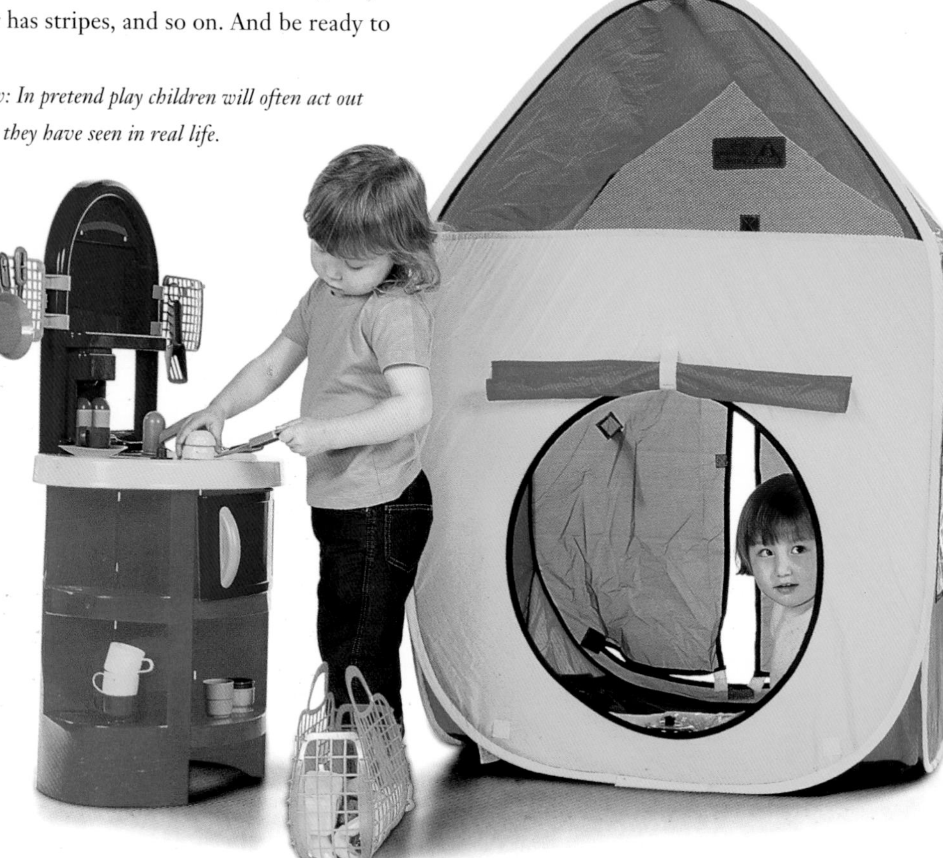

Below: In pretend play children will often act out what they have seen in real life.

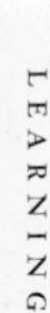

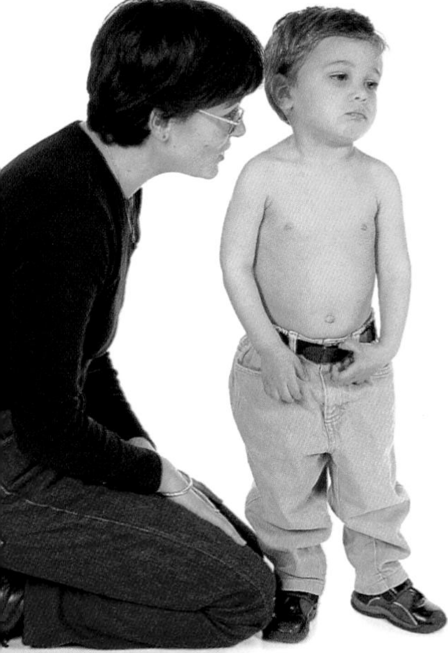

Above: Be understanding with difficult behaviour. It may be hard for him to understand the reasons for some rules.

Top Tips

1. Don't restrict him too much. Allow your child to explore freely while under your supervision. However, safety must always remain your first priority. If he does aim for potentially dangerous territory, gently redirect him on to safer ground.

2. Name an object and ask your child to remember it. When he is settled at an activity, tell him something to remember, perhaps a type of food or a piece of clothing. After several minutes, ask him to recall the item you mentioned.

3. Read lots of stories to him. You'll find that he not only listens attentively but he now asks you a lot more questions about the events in the story as you read to him. Every so often, ask him what he thinks will happen next.

4. Show him recent family photographs. Ask him to identify the people in the snapshots, and then ask if he knows where the picture was taken. If necessary, give him prompts to jog his memory. He thoroughly enjoys this activity.

5. Practise colour matching. When you dress your child in the morning, set out three garments of different colours. Hold up a red item and say to your child 'Bring a pullover the same colour as this.' He may get it right!

that he draws a picture of the fish. Explain why the fish needs to be fed regularly and to have the water changed each week. Every detail matters to him.

You'll find his fascination with detail given full expression when he looks at picture books. He spots aspects of the picture that would previously have gone unnoticed simply because he wasn't mature enough to appreciate these elements. Now he misses nothing. Spend more time on each page, allowing him the opportunity to study it in detail. Only go on to the next page when you feel he has extracted all the information he wants.

He loves pretend-playing situations that mimic real life, such as being in the kitchen or in a shop, and this boosts his learning. If possible, set up a play kitchen with as many toy implements as possible. Ask him to make a cake – he'll be only too pleased to mix up flour and water, to play with the mixture in his hands, and to pour it on to a plate for you to 'eat'. Similarly, he will enjoy playing in his own 'shop'. He will play with his friend, and act out buying things and getting change with toy coins and paper money.

Above: A safe outdoor environment where you can watch your child while allowing him the freedom to explore independently is great for his self-confidence.

Q&A

Q Is it true that the youngest child in a family usually possesses more creative thought processes than the oldest?

A There is evidence that second-born children and youngest children are often more creative thinkers than their first-born sibling. Whatever the explanation for this, you may find that your youngest thinks more flexibly and develops more innovative solutions to problems than his older brother or sister.

Q Does the fact that my child needs regular reminders about behaviour mean that he doesn't understand the rules or that he chooses to ignore them?

A He certainly knows the meaning of 'no' and probably understands more rules than you think. But his ability to use the information he has learned is affected by many factors, including his level of excitement and attention span. He easily forgets what he has learned if he becomes overwhelmed by other distractions.

Toys: toy household utensils and appliances, art and craft materials, large-piece jigsaw puzzles, construction kits

Stimulating Learning: 31 to 36 Months

Your child's learning skills become more advanced over these six months. Her memory has improved, she has an increasing ability to interpret the meaning of her experiences, and she has a vivid imagination, sound use of language and higher level of concentration. By the time she is 36 months, your child is ready to learn a whole range of new concepts.

Self-Fulfilling Prophecy

You have probably formed your own opinion of your child's abilities by now, and you may have already unconsciously decided whether she's bright, average, or even a slow learner. But this can create what psychologist's call 'a self-fulfilling prophecy'.

For instance, suppose you think your child is not very clever. You'll expect less of her, and you'll accept lower achievements from her; this will probably de-motivate her, and sure enough your child's progress slows down. Your prediction becomes self-fulfilling. That's why it's vital to expect the most of your child's learning potential, and to continually provide a high level of stimulation for her.

Suitable Suggestions

Bear in mind that your child continues to learn from her everyday experiences with you and with other children, from her daily routine, and from her play activities. These remain key sources of natural stimulation. And now that she is more mature, she can happily sit quietly and focus her attention for longer periods, which increases her capacity to learn.

If your child is particularly restless during situations requiring concentration, help improve her attention span by sitting with her. Whenever you see her attention beginning to turn away, gentle reminders will help her focus on the activity in hand.

Play games specifically to extend and improve her memory. For instance, place approximately six household objects on a tray in front of your child. Ask her to look at the tray and try to remember all the objects. Explain that you'll take the tray away, so she has to remember all the items she can. Remove the tray. You'll find that she probably recalls at least two or three objects, and quite possibly more. Once she has made her guess, let her look at the tray again.

Left: Your child's lively imagination will become increasingly obvious in her play.

You can improve your child's performance of this activity by teaching her the strategy of rehearsal. When she tries to memorize the objects on the tray, suggest to her that she says the names of the objects out loud, over and over again. This technique – which you probably use yourself when memorizing, say, a new telephone number – will increase her recall of the objects. She'll be pleased with the results. Likewise, when you give her a simple instruction to carry out, ask her to repeat the instruction back to you. This increases the

Above: At 36 months this little girl constantly absorbs ideas and information from her older sister.

amount of information stored in her short-term memory.

As well as reading stories to your child, suggest that she makes up a story to tell you. This encourages her to use symbolic thought, to draw on previous experiences and long-term memories, to blend concepts, and to try out new language structures. Her make-believe story may be hard to follow but it is an active use of her existing learning skills.

Top Tips

1. Teach early number concepts. Hand your child one toy brick and say 'That's one for you', then hand another and say 'That's two for you'. Your child may understand numbers up to three or four, even at this young age.

2. Give her sorting activities. For instance, ask your child to put her toy animals in one place and her toy people in another. You'll find that she can achieve this as long as she thinks carefully.

3. Continue to take an interest in her learning. She may be older and more mature but she still needs you to be proud of her attainments, and to praise her when she learns something new. Your child wants your approval.

4. Help her form classifications. For instance, say 'Tell me what you like to eat' and when she has named a few items, ask her to tell you more. If she includes a non-food product, say 'No, you don't eat that.'

5. Teach her to recognize her name in writing. Initially, she won't be able to tell the difference between her name and other written words. Point it out to her, and encourage her to find the same word elsewhere on the piece of paper.

Above: At this age your child will still particularly enjoy sharing activities and books with his parents.

Q Does progress in learning slow down as she approaches 36 months?

A No. Your child's rate of learning actually increases because she can think about concepts that were meaningless to her before. For instance, she starts to grasp the meaning of numbers and the significance of size and time. She may also recognize that letters and words have shapes, which is an early stage of learning to read.

Q When my child saw me pour exactly the same amount of water into a tall, thin glass and a small, fat glass, she insisted that the tall one contained more. Why does she think in this way?

A Your child doesn't understand that the amount of water can be the same no matter what vessel it is in. She notices that the thin glass is taller, however, and mistakenly concludes that it must therefore have more water in it.

Toys: toy figures and vehicles, colour- and shape-matching games, eight-piece inset boards, larger jigsaws, dressing-up clothes

Social and

Emotional Development

The Importance of Social and Emotional Development

By the age of 16 months your child's personality characteristics are showing through clearly and you are able to anticipate how she will react when she, say, meets strangers or can't find a toy she looks for, or when things don't go according to plan. Her social and emotional development enters a new phase at this time as her own identity begins to develop. She wants to make choices, to do things by herself, and she can be very assertive.

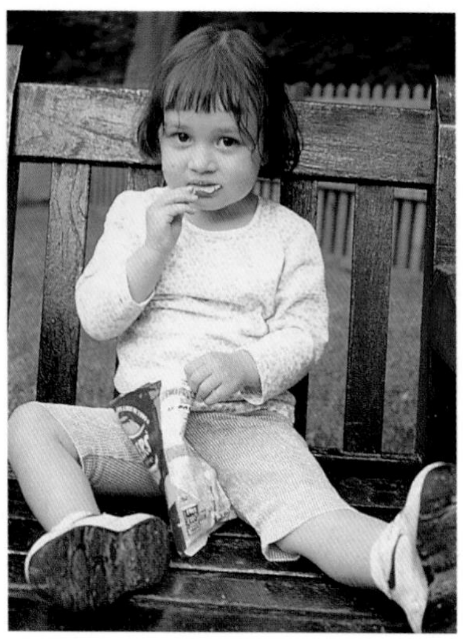

Left: Toddlers are by nature egocentric and are therefore often self-focused.

As you will quickly discover, your toddler likes to get her own way. From the age of about 15 months onwards, she becomes very self-absorbed. When she wants something, she expects to get it right away and she isn't bothered by the fact that you are worn out or that she's been nagging at you all day. As far as your growing child is concerned, she comes first and your thoughts and feelings don't exist.

And it's not just that she would prefer to be in charge – she insists on it. If you don't let her do what she wants she may explode with temper. It's almost as if your child is outraged by your impertinence at not doing what she wants you to do at the exact moment she wants you to do it. The dogged determination of your furious toddler knows absolutely no limits.

Toddler Egocentricity

Although this type of behaviour in an adult would be described as selfishness, that description doesn't apply when it comes to a child of this age. Her behaviour is 'egocentric' in the true sense of the word, rather than 'selfish'. She is egocentric because she literally cannot understand anybody else's point of view. There have been many psychological investigations that confirm that children of this age struggle to consider how other people think and feel.

This stage of egocentricity – which may last until around the age of 3 or 4 years – affects your child's social and emotional development in a number of ways:

- **low tolerance of frustration.** Her egocentricity means that she is totally shocked the moment her wishes are blocked, whether by you or because she simply can't achieve her target. She may experience a sudden surge of frustration that overwhelms her – she just can't believe that she can't get what she wants, when she wants it.
- **social indifference.** When you observe your 16-month-old toddler playing in the company of other children of the same age, you'll

Above: Before the age of 36 months your child spends much of his time on his own activities rather than playing with others.

notice how unaware they are of each other's feelings. Egocentricity means that one child will thoughtlessly snatch a toy from another child's hand without asking simply because she wants to have it.

• **frequent anger.** When you have to draw the line with your child aged 2-plus, she'll probably be furious with you. She can't accept that you have set rules for her to follow; from her perspective, her feelings come first and it doesn't matter to her that you are the parent and she is the child.

Remember, though, that your toddler is still a wonderful, loving child who gives much love to you and to others in her family. Despite an increase in tantrums and other frustrations, there are plenty of times when she is settled and when you have great fun just enjoying her company. Enjoy these frequent moments, and do your best to avoid them becoming overshadowed by the more challenging episodes.

Vulnerability

Despite this surge of determination and independence, your toddler remains vulnerable socially and emotionally. This same child, who only a few minutes ago howled at you angrily because you had the nerve to ask her to stop playing with her toys in order to prepare for her bath, now clings to you sobbing because she can't find her favourite cuddly toy. Self-confidence is easily rocked at this stage, turning happiness into distress, laughter into tears, in the flicker of an eye.

And the same applies to your child's sociability. You will have noticed that she enjoys the company of other children, although she doesn't yet have the social skills necessary to play cooperatively with them. When she is with her peers, she stares at them curiously and appears comfortable and contented in their company. But all it takes is another toddler to approach her unexpectedly, and before you know it she rushes over to you for protection because she is afraid.

Support and Sensitivity

This contrast between the assertiveness and determination of your growing child and her obvious emotional vulnerability means that you need to handle her changing moods sensitively. On the one hand, her temper tantrums will push you to the absolute limits of your tolerance and you will need plenty of resolve to withstand her demands. On the other hand, she needs your affection and support when she is upset.

Above: A 36-month-old can seem very self-confident, but this is easily dented if he comes across something he is unsure about.

You can help your child by teaching her what is acceptable behaviour and what is not, by giving her lots of love to increase her sense of security, by offering her help and advice when she faces challenges that are too demanding, and by suggesting ways that she can learn to mix better with other children.

Below: Remember that however trying your toddler can be at times, your love and attention is central to her happiness and her progress.

Stimulating Social and Emotional Development: 16 to 18 Months

Your toddler becomes more assertive during this period. He wants to do more on his own and he may become annoyed when you set limits on his behaviour. Tantrums may be frequent when he can't get his own way. He is getting more interested in other children, and will play alongside others his own age, although he won't actually interact with them.

Comforters

Some children form an attachment to a cuddly toy or an item such as a blanket, or continue to suck a dummy long after they have stopped bottle- or breast-feeding, or develop the habit of sucking their thumb or twiddling their hair. This is a normal pattern of behaviour, and is nothing to worry about.

Psychologists believe that comforters of this sort give your child extra security at times when he particularly needs it, perhaps when he's tired, in unfamiliar surroundings or when going to bed. Most children grow out of this behaviour by the time they are 3 or 4.

Suitable Suggestions

The best strategy to enhance your toddler's social development is to provide opportunities for him to mix with others of his own age. The fact that he plays alone in social situations like this doesn't reduce the importance of this contact – he learns from watching other children's behaviour and from studying the different ways in which they play with toys.

Below: Although these toddlers are happy to play in proximity to each other they are all involved in their own separate activities.

One of the most popular ways to provide social contact is by taking him to a local parent-and-toddler group. As you are with him throughout his time in the group, your presence will give him enough confidence to attend without tears. Going regularly gets him used to being in larger groups of people, which in turn builds his social confidence. If there isn't a local group, invite parents of children the same age to your house so that all the toddlers can play together. And, of course, accept social invitations on your child's behalf. These social contacts are great for parents, too, providing opportunities to share experiences and talk through problems.

Left: At this age your child will begin to show preferences for particular toys and have a clearer idea of what he wants.

His identity builds more firmly now. This shows in a number of ways. For instance, he starts to pick the toys he wants to play with himself, instead of waiting to be guided by your choice; he takes more initiative in aspects of personal independence, such as feeding and dressing; and he probably asks for specific foods at mealtimes.

When your toddler expresses his own preferences, he isn't being deliberately awkward – it's just that he is beginning to think for himself. His drive for independence can be difficult for you, especially when he starts to make choices that clash with your own plans, but the development of his individual identity is an essential part of the growing process and is something to be encouraged. Naturally your child can't have everything he wants. Yet you can help him in his drive for self-reliance by giving him the chance to make small choices.

Top Tips

1. Improve his social skills. Suggest that when he is with other children he should move towards them instead of staying beside you all the time. Tell him to pass a toy to another child when they are together in the same room.

2. Praise appropriate social behaviour. When your child acts positively in a social setting (for instance, if he shares a toy, or smiles at another child) give him a cuddle to show him that you are pleased with his behaviour.

3. Let him try new challenges. If he insists that he can do something by himself, stand back and let him make the attempt (as long as he is not in danger). He learns a lot about himself and his abilities through direct experience.

4. Deal calmly with jealousy. You may find that he becomes annoyed when he sees you talk to another child, because he likes to keep you all to himself. Calm his agitation, give him a big hug and reassure him that his special place in your affections is not threatened.

5. Include your toddler at family meals. Whenever possible, have your child sit at the family table for meals. Although he may be demanding, he will learn more quickly from example how to behave at the table than if he eats alone.

Right: This toddler's growing sense of independence is clear from her purposeful and confident body language.

Q My toddler insists on having a night light. Should I discourage this?

A There's no harm in having a night light, although you can gradually reduce his reliance on it by fitting a dimmer switch. Make the light slightly dimmer each night, in such small stages that he doesn't realize you are doing this. You'll soon reach a point when he falls asleep without any light.

Q What can I do about my 16-month-old who refuses to leave my side at toddler group?

A Be patient with him, despite your embarrassment at his behaviour. He's obviously not ready yet to venture into the playroom alone. In the meantime, let him stay at your side. Almost certainly his natural curiosity will eventually take over and he'll soon start to drift slowly away from your side towards the exciting activities on offer elsewhere.

Toys: cuddly toys, toy musical instruments, inset boards, toy telephone with receiver, books with pictures

Stimulating Social and Emotional Development: 19 to 21 Months

Your child's developing sense of self makes her increasingly determined to challenge the rules and structures that you set for her at home. She is willing to push further than before, despite your insistence that she should follow what you say. Yet this apparent self-confidence can crumble very quickly indeed – all it takes is a small disappointment to send her rushing to you for a reassuring cuddle.

Discipline

It's a mistake to think that discipline is principally about punishment of misbehaviour. You should aim to create a system of rules at home that enables your child to learn how to behave appropriately.

Rote learning of rules, however, is not the most effective way of teaching your child good discipline. If your child knows a rule without having any understanding of why there is such a rule in the first place, then she'll probably break it the moment your back is turned. Always try to explain in simple terms the purpose of the rules you lay down for your child.

Suitable Suggestions

The irony about this phase is that the more your child tries to break the rules you set for her (for instance, by continuing when you ask her to stop, by demanding more sweets when you have told her that she's had enough, by touching that fragile ornament when you have said to leave it alone), the more she needs you to stick to the rules. A child raised in an environment where she determines the rules may become insecure and unhappy because of the lack of structure and consistency.

Above: The playground is a good place for children to mix – ownership of toys is not such an issue and there are always exciting distractions.

This means that you should be prepared to meet your toddler's assertiveness head-on, without losing your temper. Remind yourself that it is in her long-term interests to follow rules of behaviour. After all, other children will not want to play with her later on if she thinks only of herself.

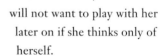

Left: If you can encourage your child to share toys at this early stage, it will make things easier for both of you in the long run.

Above: You may find that your child begins to put more physical distance between you and him as he goes off to explore in the park or playgroup.

Top Tips

1. Believe in your parenting skills. Tell yourself that you are an effective parent, especially when your demanding toddler gets you down. Do your best to keep a high level of self-confidence so that you feel able to manage her competently.

2. Enjoy her company. She loves spending time with you. Listen to her as she tries to tell you her latest exciting piece of news, and play games with her. She needs to know that you care for her as much as ever.

3. Structure her day. Your child likes to have some predictability in her day. For instance, you might have meals within a set time range each day, or you may allow her to watch a video tape each morning. Routine makes her feel secure.

4. Comfort her when she is distressed. You may be surprised to hear her crying when you saw her playing contentedly only a minute before. She may quickly become upset by something that seems trivial to you but seems huge to her.

5. Keep explanations of rules basic. Your toddler at this age understands simple explanations such as 'Don't hit me because it hurts me and makes me cry'. Offer explanations that spell out the implications of her actions in terms she understands.

Be ready to offer advice in social situations because the solution that is obvious to you may not be obvious to her. It may not occur to her that, for example, she should say 'hello' to a child who approaches her. So give her plenty of basic social guidance.

The same applies to play. She might not realize that to let another child play with her toys is an effective social skill. The chances are that she isn't ready to follow all your advice, but starting to give her pointers about social interaction at least gets her thinking about these matters.

She expresses her ever-growing desire for independence in many ways. For example, she might hit your hand away when you try to help with feeding. Now is a good time to look for signs that she is ready for toilet training. Remember, though, that every child is different and that although many children start toilet training at around 21 months, there are some who are not really ready to start until later.

Q Why does my 19-month-old toddler still wake up several times each night, calling for a drink?

A She probably wakes up so often because she enjoys your attention. When you go to her during the night, make sure that you don't lift her out of bed or give her a drink; instead calm her, without taking her from her bed. Her habit of night waking will gradually diminish if you use this strategy.

Q I feel as though I'm in constant confrontation with my toddler every day. What can I do?

A Try to take a more positive approach. Start to use more praise for good behaviour instead of reprimands for misbehaviour; make a point of spending time together just having fun; and do your best to keep any disagreements short so that anger between you and your toddler doesn't carry on for hours.

Toys: song tapes and CDs, modelling clay or play dough, toy versions of household tools, pull-along toys on wheels, shape-sorters

Stimulating Social and Emotional Development: 22 to 24 Months

Your child becomes much more sociable as he approaches his second birthday, although many of his contacts with other children still end up in tears – usually due to squabbles over toys. He may be shy with strangers and may greet relatives he hasn't seen for a while with a blank silence. He is more adept at feeding himself (although he still makes a mess) and he will be gaining better control of his bladder and bowel.

CRITICISM

Regularly criticizing your child for his misbehaviour reduces his self-confidence and creates a bad atmosphere for everyone at home. When you want him to change his behaviour, merge your negative observation with a more positive comment.

For instance, instead of saying 'You're naughty for leaving such a mess' you could say 'I'm surprised at this mess because you normally tidy your toys away'. Avoid criticizing your 2-year-old as a person ('You're horrible for doing that'), which may make him feel unloved. Instead focus on your disapproval of his behaviour ('I love you but I don't like what you did').

Suitable Suggestions

People talk of the 'terrible twos' when referring to this stage of development because it is associated with difficult and challenging behaviour. And there's no doubt that there is an element of truth in this observation. For example, dealing with your child's tantrum in the middle of a supermarket checkout queue (because he demands a bar of chocolate that is temptingly stacked where he can see it) is extremely embarrassing. He can appear completely unreasonable at times. Living with a tempestuous 2-year-old tests the patience of the calmest parent. But try to maintain a positive perspective no matter how despairing you may feel at times with his behaviour.

Reassure yourself that this behaviour – albeit infuriating – is normal and that it does not mean you are an inadequate parent or that you are doing anything wrong. Of course, cultivating this attitude won't have any direct effect on your 2-year-old's behaviour, but it may help you feel better about yourself. Make an effort to look for the more endearing qualities of your growing child, such as his sense of humour, his caring personality and his never-ending curiosity. This helps you maintain a balanced outlook on parenthood.

Right: Your 2-year-old is now likely to be developing a more sophisticated sense of humour, so you can share more jokes with him.

Left: Turn the tables sometimes and let your child brush your hair or help you get dressed by fetching your shoes – he will relish the responsibility.

By now your child may have good bowel and bladder control during the day, and he is pleased that he now wears pants 'like a big boy'. He continues to need lots of praise and encouragement for his successes with the potty, however; give plenty of reassurance when he occasionally wets himself accidentally. His bowel and bladder control will improve as long as his self-confidence remains high.

Friendships start to play a more important role in his life now. He enjoys being with other children and you may find that he becomes bored, fractious and moody when he spends too much time on his own. On the other hand, don't be surprised to find that he and his friends bicker frequently, though do your best to sort out any squabbles. At this age, children don't bear grudges and quickly forget earlier disagreements. Try to make arrangements so that he has someone of his own age to play with most days.

Top Tips

1. Let your child see that you value his achievements. His self-confidence depends greatly on how he thinks you view him – he needs to feel valued by you. He feels good about himself when you praise him and give him your attention.

2. Encourage him to think of others. He will become more sensitive to the feelings of other people if you specifically suggest this to him. Ask your child to think about the children he mixes with and to think of the games they could play.

3. Give him small tasks of responsibility. Even at this age, you can tell him that he's in charge of putting his toys into the toy box. Small amounts of responsibility like this increase his maturity and level of independence.

4. Teach him how to take turns. This very important social skill is one that you can practise with him at home. Give him experience of waiting to have a drink until you have had one, or letting his sister speak before him.

5. Make time for yourself each day. You need time just for you alone. You will feel more able to deal with your 2-year-old's fluctuating behaviour when you also have time for yourself, just to put your feet up.

Above: Never let potty training be something you get cross about. It will upset your child and success in this area depends very much on his level of confidence.

Q Why does my toddler refuse to apologize when he does something wrong?

A You expect too much of your child by insisting on an apology. You can't force him to speak the words you want to hear. Instead, make sure that he knows you are unhappy with his actions and that you will be furious if he does the same thing again.

Q How can I make my child less timid when he is with other children?

A There are some techniques to consider. Do not allow him to avoid social interactions; reassure him that the other children will like him and will want to play with him; and arrange for him to play with only one child at a time instead of a group. These strategies may help to reduce his timidity.

Toys: dressing-up clothes, books with pictures, large play-mat, construction toys, stacking toys, inset boards, picture cards

Stimulating Social and Emotional Development: 25 to 30 Months

Your child's social development advances as she becomes more able to get on with other children. She is keen to play with her friends and they interact together more effectively. You'll probably notice that she is more caring towards another child who is upset. However, alongside her increasing independence, during her third year you may also find that she becomes anxious about situations with which she previously dealt confidently.

Fears

Evidence from studies suggests that most children develop at least one fear during the pre-school years, though girls tend to have more fears than boys. Fears develop at this age as a result of a combination of the child's very active imagination and her fluctuating confidence.

Typical fears of a child aged around 30 months include fear of small animals that move quickly, and fear of darkness. These fears tend to appear very quickly and also vanish very quickly. You can help your child get over a fear by supporting her, by encouraging her to face it, and by not making fun of her.

Left: If your child goes through a clingy period and doesn't want you to leave, give him as much comfort and reassurance as you can.

Suitable Suggestions

At this age your child may exhibit increased anxiety when temporarily separated from you, perhaps when you go out and leave her in the care of a baby-sitter or relative. It's surprising to see her become tearful at the prospect of parting from you for a short time – especially when you did not see this sort of behaviour from her when she was younger. This new anxiety may be because she is so attached to you and now has the imagination to worry about coping without you.

If your child does seem likely to become tearful when she realizes you are off somewhere without her, then try to calm her at the moment of departure. Reprimanding or making fun of her for what appears to be immature behaviour only makes matters worse. Instead, give her a firm cuddle, tell her that you will be back soon and that you will hear about all the games she played while you were away, and then leave whether or not she cries. Lingering with your child until she settles completely might actually make the situation more stressful for her – a brief,

Right: Introduce 'sharing' by encouraging your child to offer food to others – if she also has a biscuit she'll be happy to do this.

Above: Sharing toys and equipment with other children is always likely to cause tension – but persevere with the idea of taking turns.

Top Tips

1. Help her achieve success. There is nothing like success to make her feel confident. So guide her when she tries to complete a puzzle toy or when she does something to increase her independence – she loves the taste of success and it will spur her to continue with that activity.

2. Have loving physical contact with her. She's not too old to enjoy a loving, warm cuddle while you read a story to her. Close contact makes the activity much more enjoyable for both of you.

3. Comment on her strengths, not her weaknesses. Your child is likely to feel sorry for herself when she can't achieve her goal. When she is feeling negative, tell her the reasons why you think she's fabulous. You won't 'spoil' her with praise.

4. Listen when she talks to you. Once she has finished playing with other children her own age, she will want to tell you all about what happened. Listen attentively to her observations, nodding and frowning in all the right places.

5. Discourage rude behaviour. Your child might not know that it's rude to push to the front of a queue or to point at a spot on someone's face. She depends on you to teach her 'manners' at this age.

affectionate separation is more likely to build confidence in the long run.

She is better at sharing but still finds this social skill hard to put into practice. While she happily takes sweets and toys from her friend, the chances are that she clings tightly to her own possessions. She may not grasp that sharing should be reciprocal! Talk to her about this and encourage her to share under your supervision. For instance, watch as she shares some sweets with her brother and sister or friends. In general, petty bickering with her peers diminishes.

If she isn't already assisting with dressing and undressing, now is the time to get her interested in this activity. It really doesn't matter how much she does – whether she tries to put on her vest and pants by herself or barely pulls her socks off her feet – just as long as she shares the responsibility for this activity. Don't do everything for her simply because it's easier and quicker for you.

Below: Succeeding in an endeavour – like learning to use a slide – will encourage a child to take on other new challenges.

Q Is it true that girls are generally more caring towards others than boys at this age?

A Psychologists researching this question have indeed found this difference is present between boys and girls. The most likely explanation is that girls are encouraged to be caring and nurturing by their parents right from birth, and conversely, that aggressive behaviour is more tolerated from boys than from girls.

Q Is it normal for a child of this age to feel jealousy?

A Yes – jealousy is a normal human emotion. You'll see it in your child, for example, when you show interest in another child instead of her. When your child exhibits jealousy, reassure her and settle her. She learns to control her jealousy through experience.

Toys: sand and water tray, modelling clay, crayons and paper, soft ball, toy car

Stimulating Social and Emotional Development: 31 to 36 Months

He is an altogether more caring, sociable and sensitive child as he reaches his third birthday. Friendships are regarded as important and he looks forward to seeing his friends each day, whether at home or at playgroup or nursery. Tantrums are less frequent and less intense, as he gains a better understanding that the world does not always revolve around him.

When He's Unhappy

Every child of this age has moments of temporary unhappiness, but these negative feelings soon pass. If he appears continually unhappy, do you best to find out what's troubling him.

Your child can be upset for a number of reasons, even though these may seem trivial to you. For instance, not being able to draw well, being unable to climb the ladder up to the slide, or a comment from another child about his speed of running, could make your child feel unhappy. Talk to him when he seems down and try to offer a solution to his difficulty. Above all, reassure him that you think he is terrific.

Left: Somewhere around 36 months children become more sensitive in their relationships with others and start to develop firmer friendships.

Suitable Suggestions

By now he plays more cooperatively with his friends – they don't always share and take turns without arguing, but minor disagreements are becoming less frequent. His social skills are generally more mature. Make a special point of praising your child when he does play well with others, because this praise reinforces appropriate social behaviour. There's also no harm in reminding him, for example, before you take him for a visit to a friend's house that he should behave properly and share toys and games with his friend.

Right: At this age children begin to cooperate far more with each other during play and enjoy being part of shared games and activities.

Your child gradually becomes more amenable to your family rules and the frequency of challenges to the limits you set decreases. His thinking and language skills are more advanced, too, so now is a good time to spend more time explaining to him why you have rules. Don't make your discussion too long or complicated. Keep it basic. Once you have explained to him the reasons why, for instance, he shouldn't hit

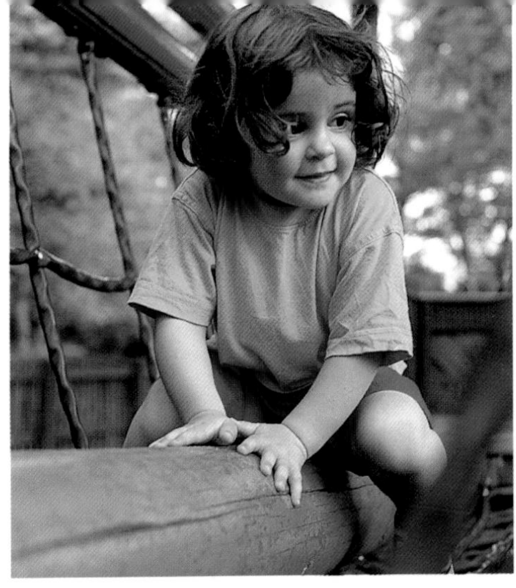

Above: Your child will be far more confident in new situations and when you are not there.

Top Tips

1. Help him overcome any episodes of shyness. If he suddenly seems unwilling to attend his new playgroup or to go to a friend's house because of shyness, encourage him to go anyway. Tell him that there will plenty of exciting activities that he will miss if he doesn't go.

2. Model good social behaviour. One of the ways your child learns basic social skills is through imitation of you and others in your family at home. Let him see you cooperate and share with each other, without bickering.

3. Discourage aggressive behaviour. Some youngsters go through a phase of slapping other children when they don't get their own way. Make sure yours understands that hitting anyone else is wrong – don't tolerate physical violence.

4. Buy him a small domestic pet to care for. Keeping a goldfish or hamster, for instance, is a good way to develop his concern for others, and is relatively trouble free. Suggest to your child that he should always feed the pet before he has his own meal and let him help with other aspects of its care.

5. Be there for him. As far as your child is concerned, every single thing that worries him is urgent – he isn't mature enough to wait for reassurance. Attend to his anxieties the moment you spot them, before they assume a greater importance in his mind.

someone, ask your child to explain the rule to you. As well as being a good way of testing his understanding, it also reinforces the message.

By this age your child is capable of undertaking basic tasks in the house, such as putting waste paper into the bin or putting his toys back in the cupboard. You may need to explain to him how to carry out such a task, but it will be within his capabilities and he will glow with pride when you then praise his helpfulness.

By now, his sense of self is more clearly defined. He is more aware of who he is, of his own distinctive strengths and weakness, of his likes and dislikes, and of the way other people react towards him as an individual. You'll find that he becomes indignant when he discovers that his personal space or possessions have been used by someone else. This is a very positive sign of his maturity, though you may find his pleas that things should be done his way rather tiresome! Involve him in minor decisions about clothes and food choices, where possible. Engage him in discussions about paint and wallpaper for his room when it's time to re-decorate.

Below: Your child will love exercising simple choices – like what ice cream to have!

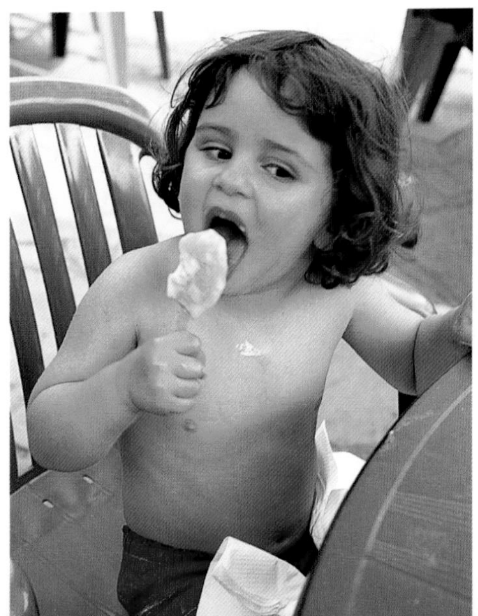

Q How can I stop my child trying to do things that I know are much too difficult for him to achieve?

A He does this because he has such confidence in himself, and there is not much you can do to encourage him to be more realistic. However, when he does aim high and fails to reach his target, help him to avoid disappointment by reminding him of all his successes.

Q My child loves watching adult television programmes. Could this be harmful to him?

A Psychological studies confirm that a child is influenced by the content of the programmes he watches, and there is no doubt that watching aggressive programmes can increase a child's aggressiveness. While many adult programmes have no harmful content, it is probably best to direct him towards those designed specifically for children.

Toys: child-sized furniture, soft ball, jigsaw puzzles, construction toys, dressing-up outfits, pedal toy, creative art materials

child

3–5 years

Night Training

Now that she is 3 years old, your child's independence takes a huge surge forward. In particular, she becomes ready to gain bowel and bladder control at night. This is because she now has a higher level of self-confidence, is able to move from the bed to the toilet easily without requiring any help from you, already has experience of learning to become dry during the day, and is motivated to achieve this skill because she wants to be like a 'big girl'. Night training, however, rarely goes according to plan, so be prepared for occasional disappointments along the way.

Left: Setbacks may upset your child but if you are patient and approach the situation calmly she will overcome them.

Choosing the Right Time

By the time she reaches her third birthday, your child has probably been reliably dry during the day for a number of months. Memories of changing her nappy several times during the waking hours are in the past. Of course she still has occasional 'accidents', perhaps when she becomes so engrossed in a piece of play that she leaves it too late to reach the toilet in time. These occasional episodes of wetting during the daytime are perfectly normal and become less frequent with each passing month.

Now is a good time to extend your child's bowel and bladder control to night-time, too. Many parents start night training between around the age of 3 years, although some leave it even later than that. Choose a time that suits you and your child. Remember that she isn't going to achieve night dryness instantly, so be prepared for mounds of extra washing, particularly when you begin the process.

The best time to begin night training is when your child is ready – there is little point in starting until your child is interested and ready to cooperate with you. There are various signs of readiness that you should look out for. For instance, your child might ask to go without a nappy at night – positive motivation is a great foundation. Or she may take off her nappy in the morning and proudly show you that it is bone dry.

When you have decided to begin toilet training at night, take your child with you to buy trainer pants to wear instead of a night nappy. This gets her involved right from the start. Also buy a plastic mat to go under her sheet, just in case she has any accidents. Explain to her that you hope she'll have a dry bed in the morning when she wakes up but that she shouldn't get upset if the bed is not dry. Make sure she can find her own way to the toilet during the night if she wakes in darkness; you could leave a light on in the hall or on the landing in case this should happen. You could also have a potty in her bedroom, rather than leave her to negotiate the stairs alone in the dark during the night. It makes sense for her to use the toilet just before bedtime.

Top Tips

1. Establish sensible drinking habits. Although your child's bladder fills when she is asleep whether or not she has a drink just before she climbs into bed, common sense tells you to restrict her fluid intake as bedtime approaches.

2. Talk positively. Always take an upbeat approach, in which you anticipate success rather than failure. Use the terms 'dry' and 'not dry' instead of 'wet', and give your child lots of reassurance that she will be dry tomorrow.

3. Don't wake her during the night. Some parents wake their child before they go to bed themselves, then take her to the toilet. However, this strategy simply means that the parents take responsibility for bladder control, rather than handing it to their child.

4. Persist. It can be demoralizing to be faced with one wet bed after another, morning after morning. But don't put her back into nappies. Once you have made the decision to start night-time training – and assuming she is ready to begin – follow it through until she succeeds.

5. Be philosophical. She'll get there eventually. If your child struggles to achieve bladder control at night, it does not mean there is anything wrong with her or with your training techniques. She is just not ready to master this skill yet.

Some children – even those who became daytime potty trained very quickly – take several months to achieve dryness at night, too. Look on the process as a partnership between you and your child. Statistics suggest that boys take longer than girls to acquire night-time control; around 75 per cent of children achieve this goal at around 3 years.

Patience, Patience, Patience

Night training needs a calm atmosphere to work effectively. No child can be coerced into achieving dryness at night: coaxing and support is more appropriate. If you find that your child is wet during the night, calmly put her sheets and pyjamas into the washing machine and tell her that you're sure she'll have a dry bed tomorrow morning. There is no point in showing irritation with her. Be patient – remember that she is just as keen as you that she wakes up dry.

When she does achieve success – which she will eventually do one morning – give her a big hug and tell her how proud you are of her. It's common for a child to be dry for a couple of nights, then wet, then dry again. Although the unpredictable nature of night training in the first few weeks can be daunting for both parent and child, the pattern will probably stabilize after a month or so.

Below: Some children initially feel insecure with no nappy at night. Reassure and encourage her to see the process as positive.

Encouraging Kindness

Your child has a natural tendency to be kind and caring towards others – you'll already have seen him comfort his tearful friend, perhaps by giving him a cuddly toy to ease his unhappiness. Acts of this sort occur spontaneously during childhood, suggesting that a child has a caring instinct. However, he has other instincts that compete with this, such as the need to satisfy his hunger, and so your 4-year-old might push another child out of the way in order to grab the last biscuit. You can help your child to develop and enhance his caring attitude so that his sensitivity and kindness dominate.

Aspects of Kindness

There are three main aspects to kindness in childhood:

• **cooperation.** This occurs when your child works with another child in order to complete a common activity, such as building a model with construction blocks. Cooperation requires your growing child to think about the other child, to take that child's point of view into account, and to play in synchrony with him – all key characteristics that underlie kindness.

• **sharing.** In the true sense of the word, sharing involves your child giving up something of his own without any guarantee of anything in return. Genuine sharing means that your child is willing to put his personal happiness at risk in order to please someone else. So when your 4-year-old decides to let his best friend play with his favourite jigsaw, he is demonstrating his caring nature.

• **empathy**. Your child shows empathy when he experiences the feelings of someone else. It's quite different from sympathy, which is the feeling of sorrow on seeing another person in distress. For your child to be empathetic, he has to understand the other child's point of view and to feel what that other child feels – for instance, you may find that he cries when he sees his friend cry.

Do your best to encourage these particular attributes in your growing child. He is strongly influenced by the behaviour of those around him. If you

Below: This 5-year-old is mending a skipping rope for a younger child. Praising kindness will encourage further instances.

demonstrate kindness towards him, and if others in your family show that they care about each other, your child is likely to adopt such an attitude as well. Research has also shown that a child who feels loved and valued, and who has a strong emotional connection with his parents, tends to be more caring towards his peers.

Above: Sharing is hard for young children because they are naturally self-centred and still learning to control this instinct.

Top Tips

1. Provide opportunities for sharing. When your child is with his friend, make a specific point of giving him a small snack that he has to share (under your supervision). The more opportunities he has to share, the better he becomes at this.

2. Explain consequences. Your child may not fully grasp the consequences of his behaviour: for instance, that kindness makes people happy or that selfishness upsets them. Point out the effects his actions have on those around him.

3. Play board games. Board games that have more than one player can only be played properly if all the players cooperate, take turns and follow the rules. This is good practice for your child, though it may take him some time to learn these skills.

4. Acknowledge kindness. When you do observe your growing child making a spontaneous caring gesture, perhaps towards his friend or sibling, let him know you are delighted with his behaviour. He warms to your praise.

Toys and Books

There is evidence that the toys your child plays with can have a direct influence on the way he relates to others his own age. Studies have found, for example, that a child who plays with an aggressive-type toy (such as a toy weapon or soldiers) has a higher level of aggression in his play with others for several hours after he has stopped playing with those toys. Likewise, it has been shown that a child is likely to be more caring towards his peers in the hours following play with non-aggressive toys (such as a bat and ball or paramedic toy figures).

Your child's toys, therefore, do make a difference. It's up to you to decide on the extent to which you let this influence your selection of activities, but common sense tells you that a child who is excited and caught up in a fantasy world of aggressive play may be rougher with friends when he is in that frame of mind. An unvaried diet of aggressive toys and games may suppress his innate caring instinct.

You can also encourage your child's kindness by choosing books for him that involve stories with a caring theme. There are plenty of great books for children that tell a story in which the central character helps others who are weaker or unwell. Your impressionable child is affected by these fictitious role models, and it's better for him to want to be like a caring story character than like a selfish one. Read the book first before deciding whether or not it is suitable for your child.

Left: Teaching a child to look after a pet can help her to understand the wider importance of a caring attitude to others.

Shyness

Your child faces many new social experiences between the ages of 3 and 5 years, such as starting nursery or playgroup, meeting the other children her childminder also looks after, or starting the infant class itself. Each time she meets a set of unfamiliar children and adults, her social confidence is challenged – it's hardly surprising, then, that your child has episodes of temporary shyness during this phase of her life. Fortunately, she draws on the lessons learned from previous social encounters and is able to consolidate and extend her existing social skills to overcome shyness when it arises.

More Confident

Compared to her shy behaviour when she was a toddler, your 3-year-old is much more composed in company. Those earlier moments of sheer social panic when she saw an unfamiliar relative or friend approach are less frequent now. Experience has already taught your child that nothing dreadful is likely to happen in the company of others, and she also has higher self-esteem. This means that when she starts nursery or playgroup (and similarly when she starts school) she actually looks forward to it. Of course her shyness may return as she approaches the nursery door for the first time, but these feelings will quickly pass. One of the terrific advantages that young children have over adults is that they can make social contact without having to exchange any words at all – they can play together silently, letting conversation come later.

Below: New situations – like starting at a nursery or school – can be daunting but support will help overcome initial unease.

Shyness becomes even less frequent as your child approaches 5 years old. She mixes with other children her own age every day, and this reduces any feelings of shyness she might have. However, her social confidence remains vulnerable. All it takes is a sudden thought that her shirt isn't the right colour, or the unexpected fear that she won't know what to say to the others, to trigger a wave of shyness. But at this age she recovers quickly, with your help, and continues with her social plans.

Psychological research has revealed some other facts about shyness at this age:

- around four out of every five adults can remember episodes of shyness when they themselves were pre-schoolers.
- around one-third of all parents describe their 4-year-old as shy, depending on the social circumstances.
- there are huge differences in the degree of shyness experienced. For one child, shyness is momentary; for another, it lasts much longer.
- shyness is more common when children know they have to compete with one another than in situations where cooperation and free play is the norm.
- typically, boys are more shy than girls when they are between the ages of 3 and 5 years. However, the start of school signals a reversal of this trend.

Top Tips

1. Give her plenty of opportunities to mix. This is an important age for making friends and for developing social skills. She should be allowed to play with other children on most days, whether at home, playgroup or nursery.

2. Accept that shyness is normal. Almost every child is shy sometimes, so an occasional loss of social confidence is nothing to worry about. It is not a sign of any underlying emotional problem and it will probably pass very quickly.

3. Arrange for structured activities. Your child may be shy at times when the social situation is not structured, and/or when there is no adult supervision. That's why she might prefer organized leisure classes with an instructor and a clear purpose to her activities.

4. Don't draw attention to shyness. If you see that your child is shy, try to distract her attention from it, perhaps by pointing out something or by introducing a completely new topic of conversation. This might help.

5. Never force shyness away. By all means insist she goes to the party despite her shyness – as long as you also provide advice on how to overcome it – but do this gently and firmly, not harshly.

Take Her Seriously

Never belittle your child when she's shy. On the surface, her behaviour may seem silly and irrational – after all, you know she is a wonderful, popular child and that all the others will like her. Your child, though, isn't so sure of herself at that precise moment (hence her shyness). She needs your support, not ridicule.

Watch her closely as she approaches social encounters. You do not want to make her self-conscious, but do look subtly for the tell-tale signs of shyness, such as drooping shoulders, embarrassment, fidgeting hands, physical closeness to you, complaints of feeling unwell, lack of eye contact or gentle sobbing. Much depends on your child's individual personality. You are probably aware of the indicators of her shyness, so watch out for them.

At these times, simply reassure your child that she'll be fine. Avoid long discussions that delay the moment when she meets the other children. Instead, emphasize how much fun she'll have when she gets there, explain the sorts of activities she will participate in, and keep her moving. Give some practical help, too. For instance, you could help her join a group of other children by going over to them yourself and then gently drawing her in; or you could encourage the other children to come over to you while she stands at your side. She needs you to be strong and supportive when her shyness appears.

Below: Encourage your child to join in group activities that will help boost his confidence.

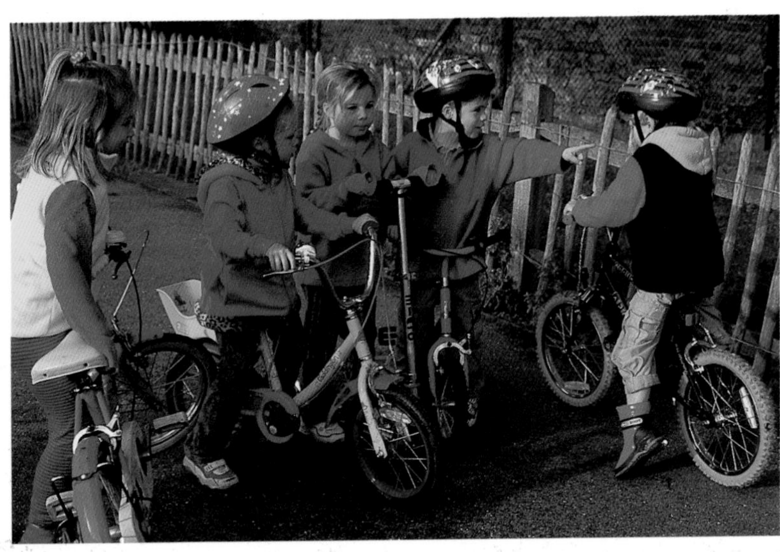

Making Friends

Friendships matter to your child. Through social relationships, he shares ideas, exchanges information, learns about himself and others, keeps busy, and – perhaps most important of all – has fun. But making friends isn't always easy. Establishing and maintaining relationships with others his own age can be challenging for your child, as it involves lots of social and personal skills, and often hard work. Friendships rarely run smoothly, making it necessary for your child to be able to resolve disagreements with his friends. Spend time helping your child with his friendships – in general, a sociable child is a happy child.

Chop and Change

Your child's friendships change from week to week, and even from day to day. At this age children form friendships for many reasons, most commonly because they like the other child but sometimes because they simply want to play with another child's toy for a few minutes and so become pals with them just for that purpose. Don't be surprised, therefore, when your child tells you that he has a new best friend.

Girls tend to be friends with girls and boys with boys – same-gender friendships generally dominate during the pre-school years, although girls are typically more tolerant of boys than vice versa. Research also shows that a child is usually friendly with someone who is like him in terms of personality, humour and intellect.

Some of the key social skills that help your child to make friends are:

• **pleasant appearance.** Although it's not fair, children do make

Below: At 5 and under friendships are quickly established but may be transitory.

judgements based on first impressions, and this initial assessment can have a long-lasting effect. Your 4-year-old is much more likely to be approached by his peers if he has a smile on his face, looks relaxed, is clean and tidy, and appears contented. A happy appearance makes others feel that he is approachable.

Above: Sharing a joke is an important part of childhood friendships – children will find things hilarious that are lost on adults.

Top Tips

1. Teach him to use social skills. Your child probably demonstrates many of these basic social skills spontaneously, without any encouragement from you. If not, give him lots of suggestions and then practise these social skills using role play at home.

2. Explain about compromise. Relationships change quickly at this age, often because neither child is ready to give way. Tell your child about compromise, so that he understands that it's possible to reach an agreement that suits both of them.

3. Give him a 'caring' job. He's more likely to form friendships when he has a caring attitude. One way to develop this is by giving him a task at home that benefits others, such as setting the cutlery on the dinner table for everyone.

4. Talk to him about friendships. Chat to your child about his pals, and encourage him to think about why he likes his best friend. This helps him to identify the characteristics he looks for in a friend and makes him more aware.

5. Encourage particular friendships. It's difficult to influence his choice of friends – he'll make his own decisions. However, if there is a child you think would make a good friend for yours, suggest that they play together.

• **self-confidence.** Body language helps to create an air of confidence and friendliness. For instance, encourage your child to look at the other children, stand beside them and hold his head up when alongside them. You'll also boost his confidence by telling him how much the other children will want to play with him and to talk to him.

• **manners.** Of course children aren't bothered about the finer points of social etiquette, but they won't be keen to play beside another child who constantly makes rude noises, pushes his way in front of others, refuses to share his toys and makes insensitive remarks about other children. Good personal hygiene also matters.

Social Language

Friendships are mainly formed – and kept – through spoken language. By the time children are 3 or 4 years old, they chat constantly to each other when playing. Your child will get on better with others when he is prepared to make 'small talk' (by asking, for instance, 'What is your favourite game?') rather than sitting in total silence. And once the introductory stage of friendship is over, it is through words that emotions are expressed, ideas are exchanged and fights are resolved.

Encourage your child to be chatty, to talk to the other children instead of sitting quietly without saying a word to anyone. He doesn't need to be the funniest child ever, or the most adept with words – he just needs to make a remark every now and then to the others. Spoken language oils the wheels of children's social relationships.

Many childhood friendships break up simply because the children are unable to resolve petty bickering. Rather than say what he feels, a child in this age group is more likely to act on his feelings – that's why he snatches the toy from the other child instead of asking for it. Encourage your child to voice his thoughts, and to resist the temptation to act without explaining himself first. In addition, explain that he needs to be a good listener in order to give his friend a chance to say what he feels, as this cements a friendship and makes it less likely to break up.

Starting Nursery

When your child reaches the age of 3 years – or possibly even sooner – you'll probably consider a placement in nursery for her. As well as giving you more time for yourself, a nursery placement provides an array of activities and experiences that supplement the stimulation you provide for your child at home. In addition, she meets new children and learns how to mix with others. Despite all these advantages for promoting her development, starting nursery is a huge step in her life (and also in yours). She needs your help to ensure that she gets off on the right footing.

Choosing the Nursery

There will probably be several nurseries in your area, all meeting the needs of children under the age of 5 in their own way. Find out as much as you can about these by reading their brochures and by asking other parents. Listening to parents whose children actually attend these nurseries is perhaps the best source of external advice. Then visit each one yourself.

Below: A good nursery should have a wide range of stimulating activities tailored to the different age groups it caters for.

Contact the head of the nursery and arrange a time when the place is full of children, not when they have all gone home. Don't take your child with you on these visits, as she'll distract you and she may like a nursery that you don't. Consider the following points when choosing a nursery for your child:

- **practical arrangements.** There is no point in selecting a nursery whose hours don't suit your own timetable, or that is too difficult to get to, or that does not offer the children lunch when you work at that time. Make sure the organization of the nursery suits you.
- **staffing quality.** Ask about the qualifications of the nursery staff and their experience. You can also enquire about the regularity of staff training. Since your child will spend a considerable amount of time under the care and supervision of these adults, you should be satisfied with their professional standards.
- **nursery building.** A clean, new, freshly painted building doesn't guarantee that the children in it are happy. Yet there is plenty of evidence that children respond best when their immediate surroundings are bright, fresh and well maintained. Have a good look around the entire nursery, including the toilets and playground.
- **nursery activities.** There should be clear programmes for the different age groups. Get an outline of the typical week your child

would have at the nursery, in order to find out about the range of activities. Watch how the staff and children interact, and look at the children's work on the walls. The noticeboards carry useful information, too.

Once all your visits are over, and you have considered all the pros and cons, make your choice. Tell your child about the selected nursery, without telling her about the others you also considered. Speak positively about it and mention the names of any children there whom she already knows.

Top Tips

1. Stay relaxed. You'll probably be tense at the thought of leaving your child to cope on her own without you at the nursery. Hide any negative feelings you may have from her, however, or she'll become upset too. Be positive with her.

2. Expect tears. Many children cry when their parent leaves them at nursery for the first time, through a combination of excitement, anxiety and lack of experience. Tears on parting at nursery are common, but she will settle soon after you leave.

3. Keep the separation brief. If your child is upset as you are about to leave, don't stretch out the moment of leaving – that would only make her more upset. Instead, cuddle her, reassure her and then depart from the nursery.

4. Chat to him about his nursery day. On the way home after collecting your child, chat to her about the other children there, the friends she made and the range of activities she enjoyed. Your interest sharpens her enthusiasm.

5. Get progress reports from staff. Talk to the staff regularly, especially in the early weeks, to find out about your child's progress and any minor problems that she experiences. (Do this when she starts school, too.)

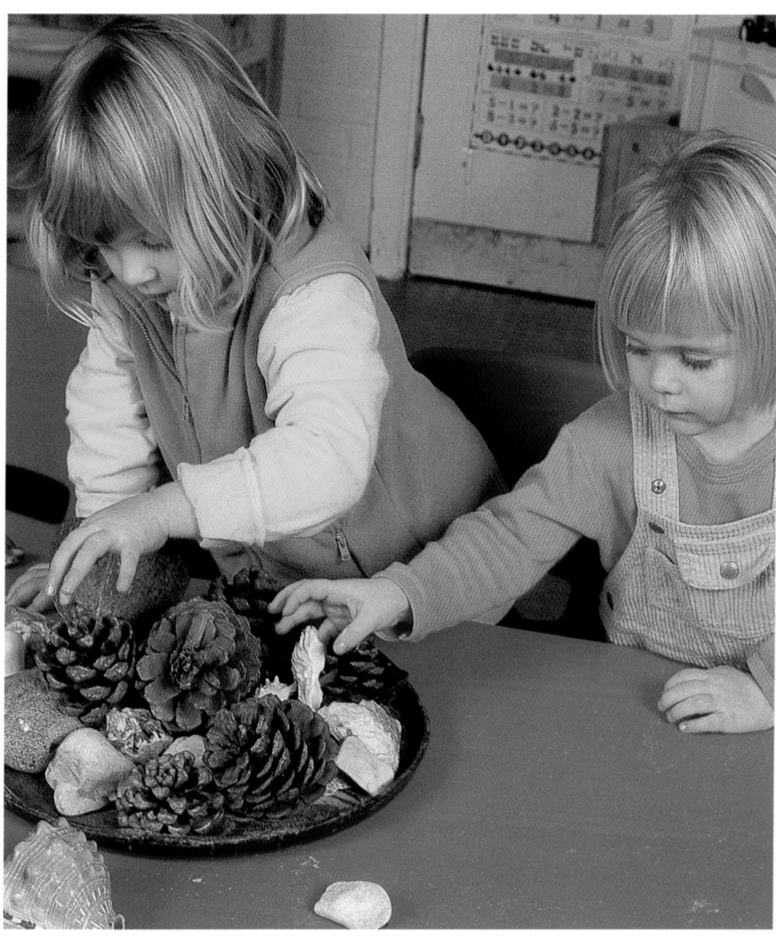

Above: Talking to your child about what she has done at nursery will give her a sense of pride in her day's achievements.

Making a Start

Arrange for you and your child to visit the nursery together for an hour, preferably a week before she actually starts there. Stay in the nursery room with her during that visit. When it's over, talk to her about all the marvellous things she saw and did there. This helps foster her enthusiasm for the first day.

When that day arrives, stay calm even though you may feel a little upset yourself. Explain to your child that you will settle her in (and probably stay in the nursery for part of that session) to ensure that she is comfortable there, and then you'll leave her and collect her later. Emphasize that she will thoroughly enjoy herself, that the other children will like her, that the staff are terrific, and that you'll see her very soon. When the time comes for you to leave her there for the first time, give her a quick cuddle, a word of reassurance and then leave. Rest assured, she'll be fine.

Getting Ready for School

The first day of school approaches very quickly, and before you know it your child is about to wave goodbye to you and enter the infant classroom for the first time. This is a big moment for him (as he starts on this exciting new venture) and for you (as you watch your child take a leap forward in his independence). If your child is well prepared for becoming a pupil, he'll have a great start to school – if he's not, then he may have difficulty settling in. That's why it's important to think ahead about this major transition in your child's life.

Personality, not Intellect

Your child's success in the early days of starting school does not depend on how good he is at reading, counting, writing and spelling – teachers expect to teach children these skills. It's personal traits that really matter. Some of the key attributes to encourage in your child long before he actually starts school are:

- **strong motivation.** A teacher can't force your child to learn – he must want to learn. Ensure that his innate thirst for knowledge remains strong, for instance by taking him to the library, being enthusiastic yourself when you see him learn new things and stimulating his learning skills.

Below: If your child has already developed basic social skills he will find it easier to mix with other children in the playground.

• **self-belief.** He'll learn more in the classroom, and at a faster pace, when he believes in himself as a learner. In other words, his self-confidence affects his school progress. Give him lots of stimulation to develop his learning skills (as outlined in this book) and praise him when he has successes.

Top Tips

1. Meet some of his future classmates. You probably know some of the children who will be in your child's class at school – he may even play with them at nursery already. Having this social contact helps to reduce his potential anxiety.

2. Involve him in school-related purchases. His enthusiasm for school remains high when he is allowed to express his view about the choice of school bag, pencil case and crayons. He likes to make these choices for himself.

3. Talk positively about school. Whether or not you have pleasant memories of your own school days, talk positively about school to your child. Your bright outlook rubs off on him – discourage doom and gloom tales from older siblings.

4. Visit the school. Take advantage of the school pre-entrance visiting days for prospective pupils. This allows your child to meet his teacher and the rest of the staff, plus the other pupils, and also gives him a chance to look around the entire school building.

5. Allow plenty of time. Avoid rushing your child in the morning – if you are stressed he will be, too. Instead, make sure you know what is needed each day (for instance, PE equipment) and prepare it the night before.

• **listening skills.** For much of the time in the classroom your child listens, sometimes to information and instructions for the whole class, sometimes to instructions just for his group or even for him alone. He also needs to listen to other pupils who share their ideas with him when they work cooperatively.

• **friendliness.** Getting on with his classmates in the classroom and in the playground is extremely important for your child. Aside from playing with his peers every day, he also learns with them in small and large groups. He is required to mix with others, to avoid unnecessary arguments and to share ideas with them.

Independence

Another key quality that affects your child's start to school is his level of independence. Of course he is under supervision at all times from the school staff, but there are lots of everyday challenges he is expected to manage on his own, and you can help him to develop these skills before he becomes a school pupil by practising them with him at home:

• **dressing.** When he starts school, your child should be able to take his jacket on and off, hang it on a designated peg, and take his shoes on and off without any help. Make it easier for him by choosing items that have simple fastenings. For instance, avoid shoes with traditional shoelaces until he's at least 6 or 7 years old.

Right: Make sure your child can take her coat and shoes off and put them on before she starts school – practise this if necessary.

• **toilet.** He'll use the school toilets several times each day, so he needs to be able to attend to his toileting needs independently. These include knowing when to use the toilet, managing to pull his pants and trousers down and back up again tidily, and washing and drying his hands afterwards.

• **eating.** When lunching at school, your child has to be able to make a reasonable choice from the foods available, to place this along with cutlery on his tray, and to carry it to a seat at a table. Good eating habits help him retain popularity with his classmates – nobody wants to sit beside a messy eater.

• **structure.** He'll settle into school if he can adapt to the structure of the typical school day. For instance, he should separate easily from you each morning, be able to find his way around the school building, and be tuned in to the classroom routine so that he knows what to do.

Problems at School

Every parent wants their child to do well at school, to fulfil her potential, to enjoy attending and to like the other pupils and the teachers. And in most instances, that's exactly what happens – the majority of young pupils love school. For some children, however, minor problems occur in the first few months of school which upset them and interfere with their potential progress. Remember that school staff are there not just to teach subjects to your child but also to help her settle in. With the combined efforts of everyone involved, most small challenges facing your child can be resolved quickly.

Minor Hurdles

There are lots of reasons why your child might not feel comfortable in school, ranging from learning difficulties to uncertainty about the location of the school toilet – you'd be surprised at the minor challenges that can completely preoccupy the mind of your child. Often you have no idea that something troubles her until perhaps she comes home from school in tears, or maybe one day she tells you that she doesn't want to go to school again.

Always take these complaints seriously: if your child works up the courage to tell you, then it must be important to her. See what you can do to help – if you don't support her through this, the chances are that nobody else will. Your child depends on your help at this stage. Typical problems that occur early on in a child's schooling include:

- **school-based difficulties.** Your child might not be able to find her way around the school building for instance, or she may not like the smell in the dining area. She might be reluctant to use the toilet because there's not enough privacy.
- **class-based difficulties.** The noise in the classroom unsettles some children at first. If the teacher speaks in a loud voice and is sharp with the pupils, your child may become anxious. Changes in class routine can also unsettle her.
- **friendship-based difficulties.** She wants to have lots of friends. Small arguments with her new pals, or even feeling left out by others, can cause distress. She likes to feel she is part of the crowd.
- **learning-based difficulties.** Coping with the educational demands of school can be overwhelming for some children. Classroom activities require a level of concentration, effort and understanding that she may not be used to.
- **home-based difficulties.** A child can become unsettled at school if she thinks, for example, that her

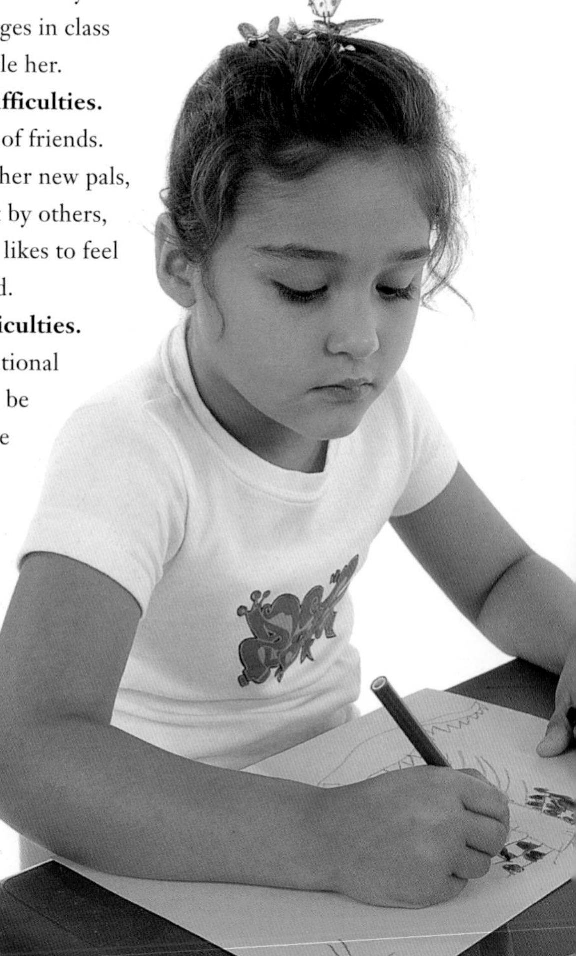

Right: At school your child will need to concentrate hard and for longer than before which may take getting used to.

parents are at home giving attention to the new baby. Fights between parents in the house can also make a child feel insecure at school.

You'll probably realize that your child is unhappy at school without having to wait for her to tell you herself. Monitor her progress carefully, especially in the early stages, and talk to her each day about what happened at school. It is important to keep a close dialogue going between the two of you so that you can help her to overcome any problems before they become magnified.

Look out for any signs of distress, such as lack of interest in school, loss of appetite, a poor sleeping pattern, tears when she comes home, reluctance to talk about classroom activities when previously she was very enthusiastic and communicative, and lack of friends. Sometimes an emotional difficulty manifests itself as a physical problem. True, if your child tells you she has a sore tummy, this could be a genuine physical complaint. Should it persist, however, and your family doctor cannot find anything medically wrong with her, the chances are that her discomfort is psychological in nature.

Deal with any concerns as soon as they arise – the sooner the better. Check out all possible reasons for your child's unhappiness at school. There has to be some explanation for her anxiety. Make an appointment with the class teacher and then discuss it fully with him or her. Any problem facing your child is more likely to be resolved when you and the teacher work together in partnership.

Below: If your child is unhappy at school try to find the cause and help to resolve it as quickly as possible.

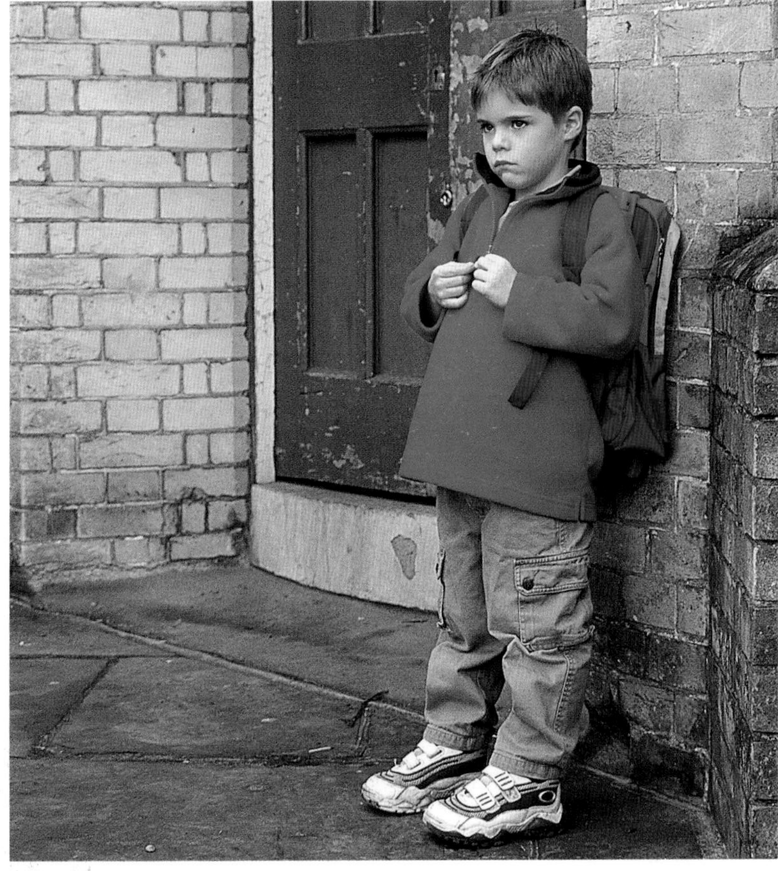

Top Tips

1. Be optimistic. Most difficulties that trouble your child at the start will be minor and won't take much to be solved. Your bright, cheery approach – even if you are inwardly anxious – fills her with confidence and this helps her as well.

2. Reassure your child. Let your child know that you recognize that she is worried. Then reassure her that the problem can be solved. Tell her what you intend to do so that she is aware of your plan of action.

3. Maintain good attendance. She should attend school every single day, no matter how troubled she is about going there (assuming she is not ill, of course). Talk to her teacher about your worries and agree a strategy for dealing with her difficulty.

4. Check it out. Whatever practical solution you reach – for instance, to change her grouping in class or to let her take her own lunch instead of buying school food – implement it. Then evaluate it every few days to see whether or not this works.

5. Talk to other parents. It's likely that your child is not the first pupil to have faced this particular difficulty. You may benefit from listening to advice from other parents whose children have had a similar experience.

Development

Movement

- Can propel a pedal toy such as a tricycle slowly along an even surface.
- Balance and coordination are more mature, giving him more confidence when it comes to walking fast and running.
- Copes with walking up small slopes.
- Can jump from the second stair to the ground, with both feet together, when he has seen you do this.
- Stands on his tiptoes for several seconds without putting his heels on the ground, and also walks forward on his tiptoes.
- Enjoys dancing to music, twisting his body and shaking his arms and legs more or less in time to the beat.
- Climbs into his chair at mealtimes and twists his body to get comfortable.

Hand–eye Coordination

- Holds small objects with a steady hand and moves them without dropping them from his grasp.
- Uses a pile of wooden blocks to build a mini-tower of eight or nine blocks before it eventually topples over.
- Manages to grip scissors firmly in his hand so that he can cut through a large piece of paper.
- Uses a small rolling pin to roll modelling clay, then mashes it up to start again.
- Can unfasten large buttons (the larger, the better) by using his fingers to open the buttonholes.
- Can hold his toothbrush correctly if you show him how, and clean his teeth after a fashion.

Language

- Loves listening to stories and becomes more involved, perhaps discussing it with you as you read to him, trying to turn the pages and pointing to the pictures.
- No longer uses the minimum amount of words to convey meaning but instead uses a string of four or five words.
- Begins to use prepositions.
- Uses adjectives to describe everyday objects or people in his life; at this stage he only uses two or three regularly.
- Can understand and carry out verbal instructions that contain up to three pieces of information.
- Enjoys songs even more now that he is able to learn and remember the words.

From 3 to 3½ Years

Learning

- Develops an elementary understanding of numbers because he hears and sees other people using them.
- Demonstrates his increased intellectual maturity through drawing, though his picture of you shows the head extremely large, with no body attached to it and legs sticking straight out from underneath.
- Short-term memory advances to the extent that he may be able to hold new information for a few seconds and then report it accurately back to you.
- May be able to recite the first few numbers in the correct order, though can easily become confused.
- Understands rules of behaviour and the reasons behind them if these are explained clearly to him.
- May confuse coincidence with cause and effect, linking two events that are not in fact connected.

Social and Emotional

- Feels more confident in social situations as a result of mixing with other children and adults, and is more at ease in company.
- Is still emotionally vulnerable, and cries easily over minor upsets.
- Finds it easier to make new friendships; likes to chat to you about his friends and wants you to like them, too.
- Understands the social dimension of eating and wants to be independent at the table, just like the others in his family.
- May have achieved bowel and bladder control at night.
- Enjoys having a small pet, such as a hamster, to care for (with your help and supervision).

Development

Movement

- Has enough confidence to try out all the items in the outdoor play area, including climbing onto a swing and reaching much closer to the top of the climbing frame.
- Enjoys bouncing on a trampoline or bouncy castle.
- Can walk upstairs and downstairs putting one foot on each step at a time, using the banister or wall for support.
- Likes to kick a ball along the ground or pick it up and throw it; catching remains more of a challenge for her.
- Copies you to hop for one or two paces if she concentrates and doesn't go too high.
- Combines physical tasks that each require concentration, such as carrying an object while negotiating the stairs.

Hand–eye Coordination

- Is able to copy accurately many of the lines that make up written letters, but can't yet form complete letters.
- Can hold a piece of cutlery in each hand, and can drink from a cup.
- Enjoys mixing ingredients with a wooden spoon, rolling the mixture flat, cutting out shapes and putting these into the oven.
- Loves challenging activities that involve hand–eye coordination, such as small jigsaws, and tries hard to achieve success.
- Can find and collect specific items from supermarket shelves by combining her visual skills and hand–eye coordination.
- Threads wooden beads or bobbins (that have a hole drilled through them) onto a thick lace that has a metal tip.

Language

- Humour emerges, much of it revolving around language, reflecting her ability to go beyond a literal understanding of the spoken word.
- Realizes that language can be used to improve her learning and starts to ask 'How?' and 'Why?' questions.
- Increases the length of sentences by using 'and' as a link, but often makes sentences uncomfortably long for the listener.
- May be able to match words of only two or three letters that are printed clearly on individual cards.
- Grasps basic language rules, such as plurals and verb tenses, and uses them in her everyday speech.

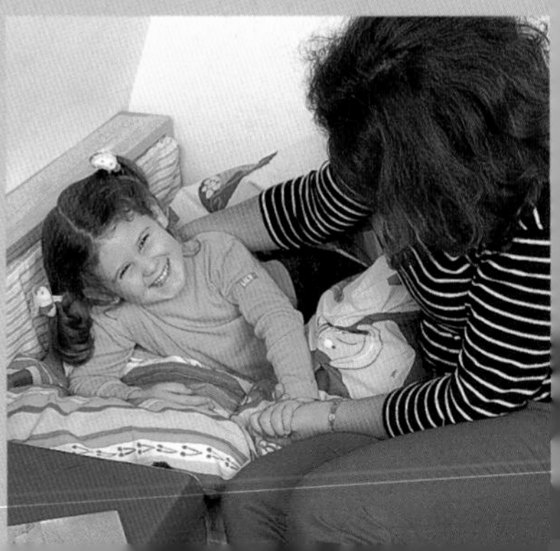

From 3½ to 4 Years

Learning

- Improved short-term memory allows her to memorize a short poem or telephone number through repetition.
- Concentration increases, so that she plays at one activity or watches a television programme for several minutes before her attention wanders.
- Her organizational skills improve, enabling her to make a more systematic search for something for which she is looking.
- Uses her imagination to create an image that isn't actually in front of her, and is able to tell you details about what she sees.
- Learns discovery strategies and problem-solving skills by watching other children.
- Reaches the first stage of genuine counting – for example, she counts a row of small blocks up to the second or third block and makes an attempt to count on her fingers.

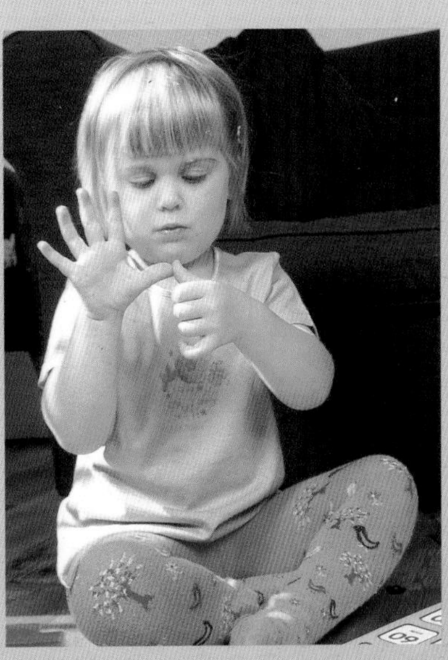

Social and Emotional

- Knows that it is wrong to tell a lie, although she still probably denies her misbehaviour even when you catch her red-handed.
- Becomes upset when she sees one of her friends cry, and tries to comfort the distressed child and cheer her up.
- May react aggressively (physically or verbally) when conflict arises with a friend or family member.
- Dressing skills have improved to the extent that she makes a good attempt to put on her clothes in the morning without help, although she sometimes gets things mixed up.
- May still show extreme shyness when faced with a daunting social situation, such as a party.
- Has a better understanding of the social rules when playing with her friends – for example, she is more able to share her toys, take turns in a game and follow rules.

Development

Movement

- Tries hard to do his best when taking part in simple team games, such as relay races.
- Begins to be able to propel the garden swing himself.
- Hops perhaps three or four paces while still retaining balance, before putting both feet back on the ground.
- Can walk several paces accurately along a straight chalk line, as long as he maintains good concentration.
- Makes an attempt at using a skipping rope, but finds this very challenging.
- May succeed at hitting a soft ball with a large bat or racket.
- Maintains a good steady running speed while still managing to swerve in order to avoid obstacles in his path.

Hand–eye Coordination

- Likes to wash his hands and face, dress and feed himself independently, though he still needs your help and supervision.
- Can hold a pencil properly if shown how, and makes a good attempt at writing his name, as long as he has a written example to copy.
- Enjoys activities involving hand–eye coordination, such as clearing up dishes after a meal or picking up small items from the floor when tidying up.
- Can stack his toys and games neatly in the cupboard after tidying up, which helps to develop his organizational skills.
- Manipulates modelling clay into many different shapes, using his fingers to mould it instead of simply shaping it with pressure from his hands.
- Still enjoys water play, and can now pour from one container to another without spilling anything.

Language

- Chats freely to other children at every opportunity and likes to voice his opinion.
- Gives you a reasonably accurate account of a recent experience, perhaps something that happened to him in nursery earlier that day or a video or television programme he watched.
- Uses language to talk to you in some detail about his friends; he tells you why he likes playing with them.
- Probably knows the names of the primary colours and is able to identify them accurately, either as a matching activity or in response to a question.
- Likes to recite familiar rhymes and poems to you, and joins in with songs whenever possible.
- May be able to play 'I spy' using the sounds rather than the names of the first letters to identify objects.

From 4 to 4½ Years

Learning

- Makes clear comparisons between two objects using one characteristic at a time, such as 'fatter' and 'thinner', 'heavier' and 'lighter'.
- Understands the difference between right and wrong but judges the morality of an action in terms of its consequences, not in terms of the intent.
- Offers his own solutions to everyday and hypothetical problems.
- Has an awareness of time, that the day is split into sequences which predictably follow each other and that certain events always occur at certain times of the day.
- Starts to show interest in the way that plants and animals grow, and asks you questions about life and death.
- Enjoys practical experiments involving weighing, measuring, mixing, dissolving and so on.

Social and Emotional

- Is more comfortable in the presence of familiar and unfamiliar adults, and can answer enquiries about himself appropriately.
- Has better communication skills, making good eye contact with the person speaking to him and replying in a clear voice.
- Boys tend to play with boys and girls with girls; gender stereotypes have formed – he has different expectations of the way boys and girls dress, behave and play.
- Friendships are more stable, and petty arguments during play with others are on the decline.
- Judges the merits of his own abilities by comparing himself to others he plays with; self-esteem is influenced by peer comparisons.
- Is able to take some responsibility for washing his hands and face regularly, brushing his teeth morning and night, and wearing fresh clothes (though you will need to check on these things).

Development

Movement

- Walks longer distances with you, especially if you make the journey more interesting by pointing out the sights.
- Engages in virtually all energetic play activities including climbing, sliding, balancing, throwing and catching.
- Skips from foot to foot and gives a hard kick to a large ball.
- Runs quickly upstairs – but don't let her do this in the opposite direction.
- Learns to use roller skates, but needs your support and encouragement until she is confident with them.
- Begins to master the difficult skill of using a skipping rope.
- May be able to ride a two-wheeled bicycle with stabilizers.

Hand–eye Coordination

- Cuts more accurately with scissors, and can cut a large piece of paper into two pieces that are approximately the same size.
- Makes a good attempt at writing (not copying) her own first name, though the letters differ in size, the word goes up and down, and it's not very neat.
- Colouring-in is neater and closer to the border lines, with less of the colour outside the edge of the shape.
- Her drawings of people have much more detail than before; her picture of a house contains windows, a door and even a letter box.
- Uses a planned strategy to complete jigsaws instead of relying on luck to fit the pieces together.
- Once shown how, she can wash and dry her hands properly without supervision.
- Makes a good attempt at eating with a knife and fork.

Language

- Can use several thousand different words.
- Uses a broad range of words and sentences to convey her feelings to you; speech can become unclear if she is excited.
- Can give accurate biographical details to an adult who asks appropriate questions.
- In many ways, her speech and language patterns resemble more closely those of an adult than those of a younger child.
- Cannot yet distinguish between a 'white lie' (told to protect another person's feelings) and an unacceptable lie (told to conceal the truth).
- Has clear views, expects you to listen carefully and to discuss things with her.

From 4½ to 5 Years

Learning

- Realizes that when counting a row of objects, one number goes with one item, in sequence – she doesn't miss one out at this stage.
- May already be able to recognize and name written numbers up to five, and recite numbers up to ten.
- Improved concentration means she persists at an activity, without needing a break, until she is satisfied that it is finished.
- Enjoys learning the very basics of using a computer.
- Increased memory and stronger ability to organize herself allow her to plan ahead, perhaps to make preparations for an activity tomorrow.
- Sorts objects using two characteristics, such as colour and shape, at the same time.
- Is able to participate in board games involving a die – she can count the number of spots on the die and move the appropriate number of spaces on the board.

Social and Emotional

- Her natural instinct to be kind flourishes with your interest and approval, and she is more caring and sensitive towards others.
- Separates well from you when you drop her off at her childminder, nursery or playgroup.
- Values her friendships very much, and specifies particular children with whom she likes to play.
- Can cooperate with others to achieve an aim or complete a task.
- Is better able to deal with disagreements with other children assertively but not aggressively, if this is explained to her.
- Takes much more responsibility for herself, but still needs prompts and reminders from you.

Movement

The Development of Movement

Your pre-school child consolidates and advances the physical skills he developed in earlier years. Coordination challenges that eluded him before – such as hopping, skipping and balancing – are now accessible to him and he can attempt many of these activities. Of course he has a long way to go before he achieves total competence in these areas, but he is significantly more agile and athletic than before – the difference in movement ability between a toddler and a pre-school child is very noticeable. He loves practising these new physical skills, whether at home, at nursery or in the park.

Physical Transformation

The main reason for this maturation of movement skills is the underlying physical change that occurs between the ages of 3 and 5 years. Your child becomes taller, with an accompanying increase in size – he probably grows around 8 centimetres in height each year and puts on about 3 kilograms in weight. His head size becomes smaller in proportion to the rest of his body, and his face broadens in preparation for the second set of teeth which will come through in a couple of years. Neurological changes take place in the brain, spine and nervous system as well.

The combined effect of all these normal physical changes is that your child becomes leaner and more agile. His body is in better shape and is stronger, with less fat to slow him down, and he can take part in energetic physical activity for longer without tiring. You'll also notice that during this period the size of his toddler's tummy decreases – this, too, adds to the increased agility of his arm and leg movements.

Many parents worry that their child doesn't eat enough to keep pace with this physical transformation. Such concerns are usually unnecessary. Your growing child almost certainly has an adequate daily intake of food and drink, but a routine check with your family doctor should allay any anxieties.

The Daredevil

Your child's improved physical skills mean that he wants to run and climb around every potential play area (and it doesn't matter whether it's an 'official' play area, such as his bedroom or a park, or an 'unofficial' play area, such as your kitchen or the other side of the street). At this age, he delights in using his improved motor skills, even when the activity is potentially hazardous.

Right: If your child is naturally adventurous, safe outdoor play equipment will provide the perfect opportunity for him to explore, although do keep a close watch.

Many parents find that their child becomes a bit of a daredevil at this stage, as a result of typical pre-school enthusiasm.

Make sure he has plenty of opportunities to explore safely, so that he doesn't need to put himself at risk in order to achieve adventure and excitement. Well-structured outdoor play areas with swings and roundabouts, climbing frames and balancing logs are great fun and help to keep his curiosity stimulated – and the beauty is that they are designed with safety in mind.

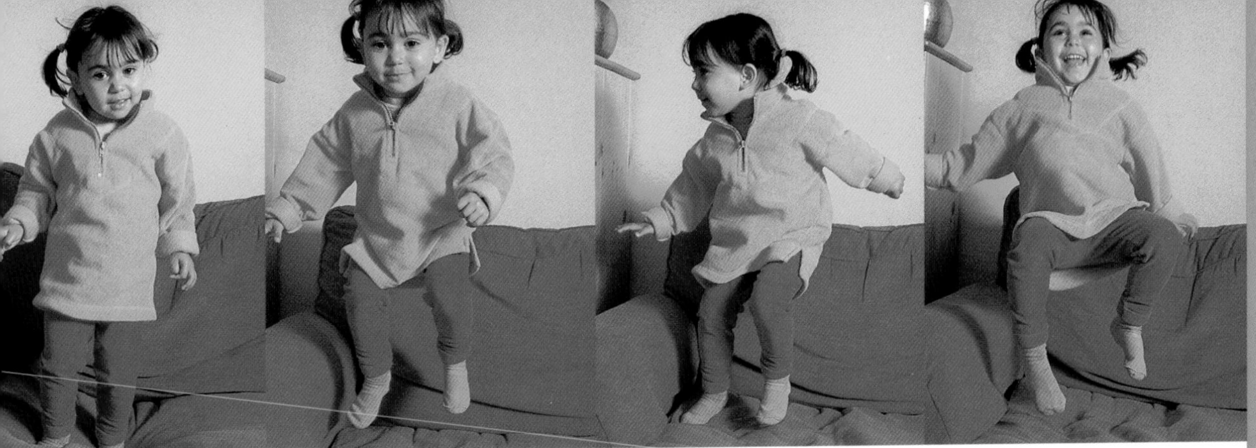

Above: At 3 years and above, children are inclined to try out their physical skills anywhere, so be aware of danger areas.

Take him along to a leisure class, such as swimming, gymnastics or any other type of sport. Choose a well-supervised class that offers a safe, secure environment. Energy and enthusiasm are encouraged in these activities, not frowned upon. Although your child might be reluctant to go along at first, he'll soon settle in once he realizes the fun that awaits him.

Give your child lots of praise when you see him play energetically but safely – when you see him setting his own limits. Point out, for instance, how pleased you are that he only went half-way up the climbing frame because he wasn't sure how he would get down. Give him a cuddle when he remembers to walk along the street, instead of running wildly.

It is not easy to strike a balance between protecting your child so much that he becomes afraid to take part in energetic play, and letting him go until he reaches a point where he is at risk. A combination of sensible guidelines about keeping safe, coupled with positive directions about how to have adventures without danger, is the most effective strategy.

Timid

Some children are by nature timid and are afraid to explore wide open spaces in the park or adventure playground. You know the excitement that awaits your anxious child if he would only be bold enough to venture on to the climbing frame or kick the ball against the wall. But if your child is timid, he misses out on a wide range of stimulating activities.

Resist the temptation to push him too hard, too quickly. If he is genuinely afraid of hurting himself or of falling over, then he will freeze if pressurized to be more adventurous. Far better to use gentle, sensitive persuasion – sarcasm or ridicule about his timid behaviour will only make matters worse. He needs to feel that you are on his side, ready to guide him instead of laughing at him. Bear in mind that your timid child will be more willing to extend the limits of his physical skills when there is adult supervision. For example, he will be less afraid to learn to swim in a pool that has attendants and when you (or an instructor) are in the pool beside him.

Below: As your child gets more agile he will become more creative in his play, which may make some playground equipment hazardous even for a 5-year-old.

Stimulating Movement: 3 to 3½ Years

Your child's movement skills become more sophisticated and controlled and her learning ability also increases. She combines these two areas of development so that she can take part in a varied range of activities. Instead of trying to acquire a new physical skill come what may, she is more able to listen to your advice and to plan a strategy for reaching her goal.

Rough And Tumble

Evidence from psychological research confirms that parents tend to accept rough-and-tumble play in boys and are less likely to intervene, whereas they discourage it more actively in girls. This gender difference in parental attitudes towards rough-and-tumble play may be one of the reasons why the energetic play of 3-year-old boys often ends up in tears, while girls are more likely to cooperate with each other.

Think about your own attitudes to this. If you consider that boys are naturally more aggressive during physical play – and vice versa for girls – then your own child may conform to this expectation.

Suitable Suggestions

At this age, you should try to establish the idea in your child's mind that exercise is part of her daily routine. She doesn't need to go in the car from place to place, or be driven up to the front door of the nursery each session. Walking every day should be normal practice. If she gets used to taking part in physical movement at the age of 3, she is less likely to become a couch potato later on.

Use music to make movement activities more fun. For instance, dance along with your child to her favourite music. Her lack of inhibition means that she willingly twists and turns her body and shakes her arms and legs in time to the beat; she's not at all bothered

Below: Dancing is a wonderful way to encourage children to use their bodies in different ways, perhaps pretending to be an animal or a plane.

about what others might think of her. Every so often, ask her to copy a particular dance movement that you make. This is simply another form of energetic play that stimulates her arm, leg and body movements.

Be prepared to teach new movement skills if she struggles to learn them spontaneously. Take walking on tiptoes, for instance. Your child's initial reaction to this challenge might be to rush at it, the end result being that she falls over and loses her confidence. Break the activity down into small stages. First, she should stand steady with both feet firmly on the ground and then raise her heels slightly. Once she is comfortable she can raise them higher, and so on, each time getting closer and closer to standing on her tiptoes. Eventually she will be confident about standing independently on her tiptoes.

The next stage is to teach her how to walk in that position. Encourage her to move one foot forward a few centimetres only, while the other is stationary. Then the forward step can become longer, and then she can start to move her back foot a few centimetres. In other words, gradually lead her towards mastering the movement skill. Be patient with your child. You'll find that she learns at her own natural pace.

Below: By 3½ most children have sufficient strength and coordination to kick a ball quite forcefully and some can even master this while they or the ball are on the move.

Top Tips

1. Encourage planning. If your child faces an activity or challenge involving movement, suggest that she thinks what to do instead of rushing headlong into it. A few seconds' planning could be all that is needed in order to ensure success.

2. Play on a see-saw with her. Moving gently up and down on a see-saw uses her leg muscles (as she pushes off), her arm muscles (as she holds on) and builds her confidence. Keep the movements steady and even.

3. Roll a ball towards her. Face your child, with 3–4 metres between you, and softly roll a football towards her. Ask her to kick the ball as it reaches her, without stopping it first – she may manage this with some practice.

4. Let her seat herself. She is now capable of climbing into her own chair at mealtimes and twisting her body until she achieves a comfortable position for eating. Resist the temptation to place her in the chair yourself.

5. Walk on slopes. Make sure that you and your child don't only walk on perfectly flat areas. Strolling up a slight incline strengthens her leg muscles and builds up her stamina for movement. She copes with a small slope.

Q My child is 3½ years old and she insists on climbing all over the furniture. What should I do?

A Make it clear that climbing over the furniture is not acceptable. Point out to her the risk of possible injury to herself and the damage she could do to the furniture. At the same time, suggest a play area in which she can exercise her climbing skills freely.

Q Should I expect a growth spurt in my child at this age?

A No. A growth spurt – a rapid period of growth in your child's height, weight and body volume – occurs at two points during childhood. The first takes place approximately between birth and 2 years, and the second during adolescence. Her growth rate is steady between the ages of 3 and 5.

Toys: tricycle, other pedal toys, plastic bowling pins and ball, balls, toy cars, plastic playhouse

Stimulating Movement: 3½ to 4 Years

Your child is much more confident with activities involving movement skills. He knows that his balance, coordination and muscle strength is greater and he eagerly takes part in kicking, throwing and catching games. This same enthusiasm is extended to outdoor play, where he becomes more adventurous with the play equipment. Stairs are no longer a major hurdle for your 4-year-old.

The Others Are Better

Once your child attends playgroup or nursery, it's only natural that he compares himself to others – and that includes comparing his movement skills. His self-esteem may dip if he realizes that some of his peers are more agile and athletic than him. Reassure him in these circumstances.

Encourage him to continue to join in to the best of his ability. Explain that he will get better with practice and that he's great even though a couple of the others can do things he can't. He will gradually learn to accept that individual differences exist, and that he has his own level of skills.

Suitable Suggestions

Your child wants to use the whole range of movement skills in his repertoire, but probably needs suggestions from you. Show him the wide variety of energetic play activities now available to him, as he may not think of them himself.

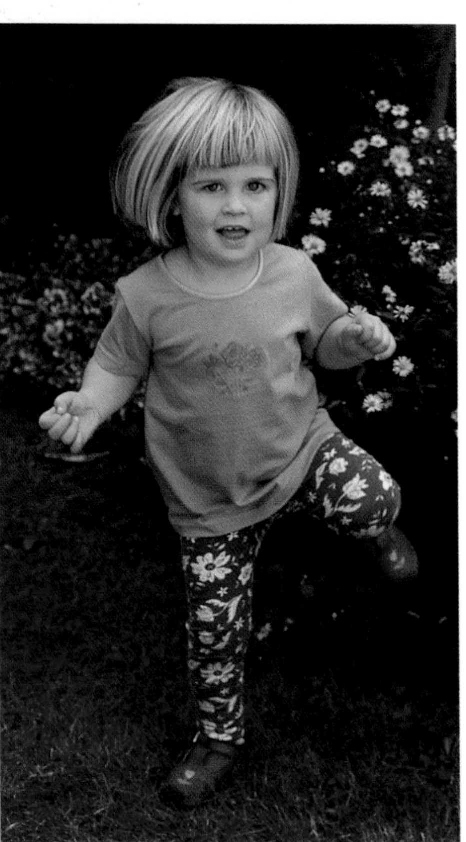

For instance, he can hop alongside you, though don't jump too high or he may fall over as he tries to imitate you. Your child finds hopping easier when wearing outdoor shoes because the soles provide a more stable landing area. However, he should also hop on a carpeted surface without wearing socks or shoes as this involves more of his foot muscles. You could also place a small object on the floor and invite him to walk up to it quickly, then pick it up and hand it to you.

Ask your child to fetch you an item from upstairs, and remind him to concentrate as he brings it to you. Just to be on the safe side, stand at the bottom of the stairs as he is about to descend with the object in his hand. Tell him to use either the banister or the wall as support while moving downwards, and add that he should move slowly. This is a challenging task for your 4-year-old because both parts of your request – the carrying and the descending – require his full attention. But he will achieve it as long as he takes his time and concentrates all the way through.

Left: Hopping requires a good sense of balance and by 3½ your child may be ready to try this, although some children may still find it beyond them at first.

Left: Take advantage of any opportunity to improve your child's movement skills. Running alongside you will give her the confidence to run faster.

If possible, arrange for him to play on a 'bouncy castle' at a play centre. This air-inflated piece of apparatus allows him to practise jumping and falling without any risk of injury to himself. Encourage him to watch out for others, though. You'll notice that although he may be timid to start with, he becomes much more energetic with his jumps as his confidence builds. This will improve his jumping ability when he is on the ground. Likewise, try to get him access to a trampoline. A child this age loves jumping up and down on it – he can also bounce up and down while on his knees.

Top Tips

1. Play throwing and catching. Stand a metre or so away from your child, facing him. Gently throw a medium-sized soft ball to him. He may be able to catch it with both hands – once he has the ball in his hands, he should throw it towards you.

2. Run in time to music. Pick a song that he likes (one with a steady beat) and suggest that he runs beside you as you keep up with the beat. Sing as you run. He'll keep going until he is breathless.

3. Establish good nutrition. Your child likes to eat lots of snacks, especially after energetic play. Provide him with milk and fruit juice instead of fizzy drinks to quench his thirst. Encourage him to avoid sweets and foods with additives.

4. Build a small obstacle course. In good weather, use the garden whenever possible. Construct an obstacle course with objects for him to run around, climb over and duck under. Time him as he progresses through it.

5. Enrol him in a swimming class. Your child may have already learned to swim, but whether he has or not, he'll benefit from instruction by a qualified swimming trainer. His confidence in the water grows steadily.

Below: Learning to swim at an early age has many benefits for a child – as well as being confident in the water, she is safer, too.

Q&A

Q I've heard that children who grow faster are smarter. Is that true?

A Some studies have found that children who have very quick growth patterns in early childhood do tend to score slightly higher in school tests than children with a slower growth rate. Yet there are plenty of small children who are brighter than their larger peers. Growth rate is only one small factor.

Q Why is it that when my 4-year-old tries to throw the ball to me it ends up going behind him?

A When he throws a ball, he has to decide on the moment of release from his hand. Like many others this age, he is so intent on getting force behind his throw that he mistimes the release – hence the ball goes in the wrong direction.

Toys: climbing frame, plastic stepping stones, toy digging tools, play tunnel to crawl through, ride-on toy

Stimulating Movement: 4 to 4½ Years

Your child is on the go all the time – no matter how much she runs around, she never tires. And she doesn't need any more sleep. You'll probably find that your child spends more time in energetic movement play than she does on games that involve her sitting still. The feeling of achievement she gets from using her movement skills adds to her enjoyment.

IT'S THEM, NOT ME

Research shows that when a boy has an injury during physical play, his first reaction is to blame someone else – he is unwilling to admit a connection between his movements and the accident. In contrast, a girl is more likely to blame herself; she recognizes that what she did was a crucial factor.

This means that boys rarely learn how to manage their energetic play even after they have hurt themselves. That's why you need to spend more time explaining the consequences of exuberant actions to a boy than to a girl, otherwise he'll just do the same again the next time.

Suitable Suggestions

Now is a good time to begin playing bat-and-ball games with your child. Buy her a large bat or racket and a very soft ball. When she turns the racket flat and horizontal with the ground, place the ball on top so that when she moves the racket up in the air the ball flies from it. Do the same again, only this time drop the ball onto the racket from a few centimetres above it. Then throw the ball, underarm style, on to the racket from about a metre away, while encouraging your child to

Below: Once your child has got the hang of hitting a ball with a bat, a whole new range of play opportunities open up for him.

swipe at it. This is a complex task, which she probably finds difficult.

Think about gentle jogging together in the park. She'll thoroughly enjoy this activity with you, and will be able to keep up if your pace is slow enough for her little legs. Tell her how pleased you are to be running with her. Or just go for a brisk walk together. Take her to the local swimming baths if she enjoys that activity.

At infant school, she'll play team games. Introduce her to these now. Organize two teams (even if there are only two members in each) and set up a simple challenge, such as to run up to a chair, clutch one of the plastic blocks sitting on it and return to the team so that the next person can do this. Team games make winning or losing dependent on the overall performance of all the members. She'll try her hardest to do well. Comfort her if she gets upset because her team didn't win.

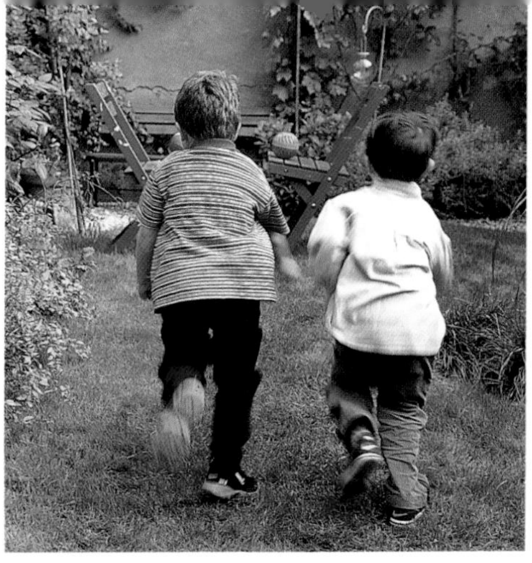

Above: Team games are simple to organize and great fun – as well as stimulating physical activity they also encourage a sense of cooperation.

During free play with her friends, she'll spontaneously play at football, climbing, running, crawling, rolling or skipping. She enjoys playing in the playground of the local park at every opportunity, though she has plenty of this type of play in nursery. If you are at all concerned that she doesn't get enough exercise, take her out yourself at weekends.

Below: At this age, your child's movement and coordination skills have reached quite an advanced level and she is able to manoeuvre a swing by herself.

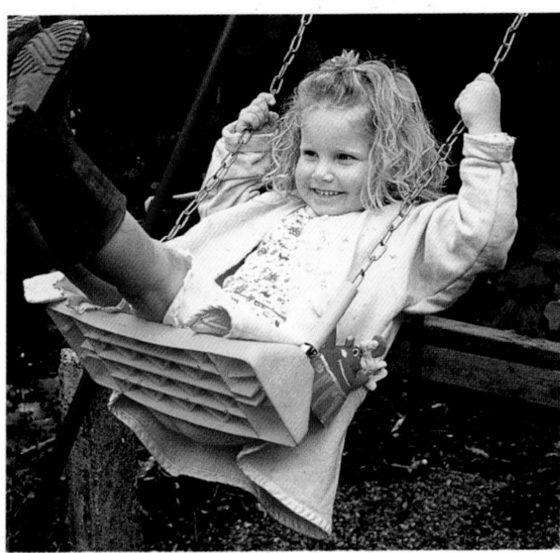

Top Tips

1. Make a hurdle to jump over. Tie a piece of elastic between two chairs, a few centimetres from the ground. Once she has successfully jumped over that, increase the height of the elastic each time. If she hits the elastic, it will simply stretch.

2. Ask your child to push the supermarket trolley, under your supervision. Pick one that has smooth-running wheels. Position your child so that she grips the handle firmly with both hands, then invite her to push. Help her steer it accurately.

3. Let her propel the swing herself. This isn't easy, but she might manage. Explain to her that she should keep her body still as she bends it slightly forwards and then backwards. With luck, the swing will gently gather momentum.

4. Play movement games. Make up games involving hopping, running, skipping and walking. You can even do this in time to music. The main thing is that she has fun using her movement skills.

5. Praise her for success and effort. When you see her try hard at a physical activity – whether she is successful or not – give her a big hug so that she knows you are delighted with her.

Q&A

Q Is it better to concentrate on one movement skill at a time or to encourage lots of different ones simultaneously?

A Too much focus on one skill can put your child under unnecessary pressure. And anyway, she'll learn a new skill best when she practises it for a few minutes, has a long break and then practises again. Those rest periods in between have a positive effect.

Q My child trips a lot when she runs. Could there be a problem?

A The reason she falls is more likely to be lack of concentration than any difficulty with balance and coordination. She's so busy looking excitedly at everything around her that she doesn't keep an eye on minor obstacles. Encourage her to scan below eye level as well when she runs.

Toys: bat and ball, skipping rope, small plastic hoops to throw and catch, football, plastic roller skates

Stimulating Movement: 4½ to 5 Years

Your child is ready to take part in all the physical activities of the infant school. His movement skills are sufficient for him to walk around the school building comfortably, negotiate any flights of stairs, walk while carrying objects (for instance, in the classroom or in the dining room) and enjoy the wide open spaces of the infant playground.

ACTIVITY AND REST

As your child approaches – and then reaches – school age, he spends more time sitting down than ever before. Concentration is an important factor influencing progress, and he needs to learn to sit calmly while giving his full attention to the activity in front of him.

But he still needs time to run around energetically. Of course you will do your best to get him into a good frame of mind for school and to prepare him for listening intently to the teacher's instructions. Make sure, however, you build time into his daily routine for periods of high activity, too.

Suitable Suggestions

This is a good time to sharpen your child's existing movement skills. Give him plenty of opportunities to practise basic skills such as throwing and catching, kicking a ball, running, walking and any other physical activity he enjoys, such as swimming, gymnastics or dancing. Do this at home, out in the street or in the local park. If there are any movement skills that are not as strong as you would like them to be, give a few minutes' extra attention to them each day.

Below: As she gets older your child will be able to use a much wider variety of play equipment and will be spurred on by watching other children.

Playing with other children is very important either at home, at nursery or in a supervised activity class. As well as learning from social interactions, your child is also able to measure his own level of physical agility against his peers, and this provides him with reassurance.

Try to improve a couple of his more sophisticated movement skills, such as using a skipping rope or moving himself on roller skates. He'll have played with these pieces of equipment before, but as he approaches his fifth birthday he should be able to develop a better mastery of them. Don't let him give up just because the rope keeps catching on his

Left: At 5 these girls are able to use roller skates. Your child will still need your help when attempting something like this for the first time.

feet or because the roller skates seem to stick in every small crevice in the ground. Gently persuade him to persist until he notices the improvement himself. He'll have to acquire new movement skills during physical education lessons in school, and working at these challenges now teaches him a strategy for learning more complicated physical tasks later on.

Don't forget static activities involving arm, leg and body movements, because these also enhance your child's sense of self and help him to understand both the limits and potential of his own physical development. Ask your child to stand upright with his arms by his sides and then touch his toes with the tips of his fingers, without bending his knees as he does so. He might over-balance at first, or perhaps try to bend his knees. Other examples of useful static exercises include balancing on one leg – and then while in that position, swaying gently in a circle.

Below: At this age children are more likely to persevere with a toy like a skipping rope, trying the actions repeatedly until they master it.

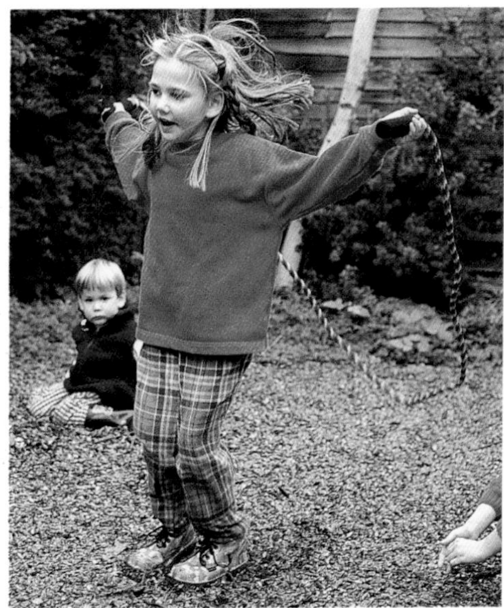

Top Tips

1. Keep it fun. Although you need to prepare your child physically for starting school, these activities and exercises should be fun. He could become anxious if he thinks the expectations at school will be too great for him to meet.

2. Walk longer distances. This is a good way to build up his physical stamina. Instead of the usual amount of time you and your child spend walking together, gradually add on an extra couple of minutes before you turn round for the return journey.

3. Teach movement skills in small steps. New movement skills don't appear from nowhere – they develop gradually over time. So don't expect your child suddenly to be able to do something he couldn't do before. Show him step by step.

4. Combine balance and movement. Give him more demanding movement challenges. For instance, draw a thick, zigzag chalk line on the ground and ask him to walk along this while carrying a nearly full glass of water.

5. Consider a two-wheeler. Your child may be willing to try pedalling a two-wheeled bicycle, assuming it has smaller stabilizing wheels attached to it. Stand right beside him as he starts to push with his feet just in case the bike topples over.

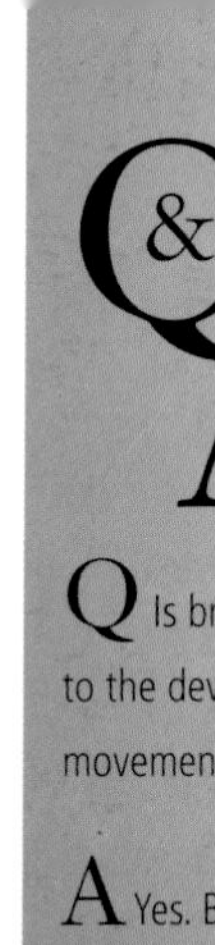

Q Is brain growth connected to the development of movement skills?

A Yes. By the time your child is 2 years old his brain is around two-thirds of its eventual adult size, and by the time he is 5 his brain is almost 90 per cent of its adult size. This additional brain growth between 2 and 5 years makes many of these physical skills possible.

Q My child refuses to walk any distance with me. What should I do?

A Try to make walks more interesting – for instance, by pointing out interesting objects, animals and colours along the way. Also, do your best to pick a time when he is fresh and not feeling tired. Chatting to him as you walk will also harness his enthusiasm.

Toys: outdoor play equipment, ride-on toys, hoola hoop, garden games: net and bats, quoits, basketball ring

Hand–eye

Coordination

The Importance of Hand–eye Coordination

As your growing child progresses through the pre-school years, hand control becomes increasingly important, not just because it helps her become more independent (for instance, she can undo large buttons without asking for your help) but also because it is linked to problem-solving (she can manipulate jigsaw pieces in order to complete the puzzle) and to learning (her ability to hold a pencil correctly and to draw patterns on paper gradually transforms into basic writing skills).

Maturation

Don't forget that your child's progress with hand–eye coordination depends on the interaction between the stimulation and encouragement she receives daily, her physical and neurological development, and her motivation. These three different dimensions need to be carefully balanced before she can move from one stage to the next.

In particular, she will not be able to write like a 5-year-old when she is only 3 years old, no matter how hard she tries, because she simply does not have the muscular and neurological maturity to make such fine hand movements. If you put your child under pressure, for example, to 'write neatly like your big sister', you run the risk of turning off her interest in writing altogether. Instead of setting a target that is based on an older child's drawing and writing achievements, look carefully at your child's ability and then encourage her to develop it a little bit further.

Right: Even in general play you will notice improvements in hand–eye coordination.

Paints or Crayons?

You may also find that she prefers using paints to crayons, and so doesn't draw fine lines the way you'd like her to. Paint brushes are often more interesting than pencils or crayons to a child, for a number of reasons. First, it's easier to make a large, colourful picture with sweeping brush strokes than it is with a crayon – pictures are created more quickly with paints. Second, a chunky paint brush is easier to grip and doesn't require such fine finger control. And third, painting has a wonderful messy side to it that pre-school children generally adore.

Your child needs experience of painting as well as drawing and writing; each activity develops skills that help the other, so let her choose between a selection of paints, crayons and pencils. As long as she dabbles in each of these, her hand–eye coordination will progress at a satisfactory rate.

Left or Right?

Your child's hand preference – that is, whether she prefers to use her left hand or her right hand – will probably be fully established by the time she starts school (though approximately 10 per cent of children who start the infant class still switch between their left and their right hand).

Although psychologists don't know for sure whether handedness is inborn or learned, there is some evidence that it is linked to the two

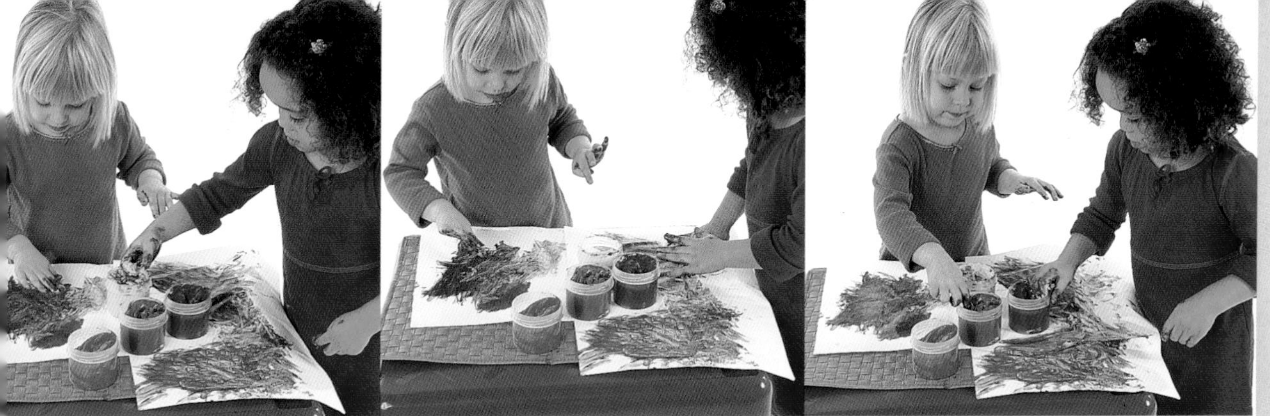

Above: Nearly all children love finger painting – even those who do not show much interest in drawing or colouring.

halves of the brain. For instance, in right-handed children, the left side of the brain may have a stronger relationship with the entire right side of the body. Whatever the true explanation, however, you'll already have noticed her established hand preference from around the age of 2 years onwards, perhaps even before then. Resist any urge you may feel to transform your 'leftie' into a 'rightie' before she starts school. That would be a mistake.

Below: Although being right-handed is the norm, you should never discourage your child from using her left hand if that comes more naturally to her.

True, we live in a right-handed world. True, learning to write is more challenging for a left-handed child because she tends to drag her hand over her writing or drawing, often smudging it. Yet there is some evidence that forcing your left-handed child to use her right hand – either when she is with you at home or at nursery – could create speech problems. And aside from that, battling with her to go against her natural preference will damage your relationship and will make her feel there is something wrong with her. All in all, it's best to leave the matter of hand preference entirely to your child.

Comparison

Now that your child mixes more with other children – whether it's friends who come over to her house to play or joining in with others at nursery – she compares herself to her peers. She judges the worth of her own paintings and drawings by the extent to which they measure up against those of the other children with whom she plays. This can have a positive or negative effect – positive if she considers her creative efforts to be at least as good as the others', negative if she believes that her own drawing ability is inferior to her friends' creative talents.

A 4-year-old's enthusiasm for challenges involving hand–eye coordination will rapidly evaporate in the face of apparently better efforts by her pal standing next to her. And when she loses belief in her own abilities, she'll be very reluctant to paint, draw or write the next time an opportunity arises.

That's why she needs bags of encouragement from you to continue with activities involving hand control, whether it's threading small wooden beads onto a lace, cutting paper into small pieces with scissors, copying her name onto a piece of paper, colouring in a shape or line drawing, or completing dot-to-dot puzzles. Your positive comments boost her motivation.

Improvements in hand–eye coordination typically occur steadily but slowly between the ages of 3 and 5 years, making them difficult to detect. Your child might need you to point out that she is now much more adept at cutting her food with a knife than she was, say, a couple of months ago. She needs you to draw her attention to these small steps forward.

Stimulating Hand–eye Coordination: 3 to 3½ Years

The wide range of toys and games available to your child now that he has started attending nursery stimulates his hand control even further. He wants to try everything he sees, even though many of the items there are too challenging for him. His desire to keep up with the other children he plays with is a further incentive to improve his hand–eye coordination.

Teaching Patience

In the same way that you feel frustrated when that annoying piece of thread refuses to pass through the eye of the needle, your 3-year-old experiences inner tension when a hand-control challenge proves too difficult. Tears and temper may ensue when the small objects won't go where he wants.

Calm your child at these moments, reassure him that he has the ability to complete the task if he remains calm, and then encourage him to start again slowly. You could also suggest he leaves that particular activity for a few moments in order to compose himself – allow him to return to it later.

Suitable Suggestions

Your child's innate drive to become independent strengthens as he realizes that there are more things he can do by himself. You can help him by giving him small tasks that combine personal responsibility and hand control. When he tidies his toys encourage him to put them away neatly. Show him how to hold his toothbrush so that he can clean his teeth properly. Of course he still has a long way to go, but he will try hard to achieve targets you set for him.

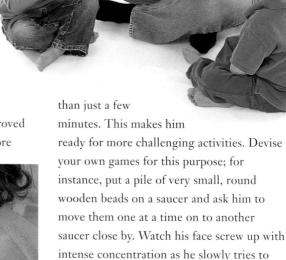

Below: Clapping games and action songs all help to improve a child's repertoire of hand movements.

At this age, his concentration has improved and he can persist at an activity for more than just a few minutes. This makes him ready for more challenging activities. Devise your own games for this purpose; for instance, put a pile of very small, round wooden beads on a saucer and ask him to move them one at a time on to another saucer close by. Watch his face screw up with intense concentration as he slowly tries to complete the task.

If he does manage to move the beads from one saucer to the other, you could repeat the

Left: When she is 3 or so you can encourage your child to brush her teeth more accurately, targeting top and bottom and back and front teeth.

Above: At this age your child may have the patience and skill to move on to more complex puzzles with more and smaller pieces.

challenge, but on this occasion time him using a watch. Maybe he can do it a little faster the next time. It's important, however, to keep this play session fun, otherwise what should be a pleasant game could turn into an episode of frustration and anger. Let him know how delighted you are with his attempts at this activity. Make sure he doesn't take it all too seriously.

Jigsaws remain an effective way of improving hand control. Speak to the playgroup leaders or nursery staff to find out the level of jigsaw he plays with there. You may find that the ones he has at home are now too easy for him and that he requires puzzles with a greater number of pieces. If so, quietly remove the smaller jigsaws from his toy box and replace them with more advanced ones. He'll be delighted with any new puzzles you give him, especially if the picture grabs his interest.

Top Tips

1. Reassure him. He may be upset to discover he has made a mess of something even though he tried to be neat. Tell him you are pleased with his effort, and that he'll make less of a mess the next time.

2. Play finger games. Make up games involving finger and hand movements. For instance, his hands could be two spiders crawling their way along the table. He can clap his hands to copy you, each time making a different sound.

3. Roll modelling clay. His hand–eye coordination benefits from practice making clay shapes, or rolling lumps of clay with a small rolling pin. Once they are made, he can mash them up and start over again.

4. Ask him to bring items to you. He loves helping you, so use this to boost his hand control. For instance, he can unscrew a jar to bring you a biscuit or open a box to bring you a button.

5. Stack bricks in different patterns. Provide construction examples for him to copy, such as a number of bricks in the shape of a small train with a funnel, or in the shape of an house. He tries to imitate your design.

Q My child's hand strength doesn't seem to be very good. How can I improve it?

A The power in his muscles will increase spontaneously as he matures, so you don't need to do anything special at all at the moment. However, you could play a game in which he grips a small soft ball in his hand and then squeezes it repeatedly. You can also encourage him to play with construction toys.

Q Is my son too old for finger painting now that he can hold a brush?

A Finger painting uses different parts of his hands and fingers compared to painting with a brush, so he should have an opportunity to take part in both activities (as long as you are prepared for the mess). It's also great fun, no matter how old he is.

Toys: jigsaws with more pieces, colouring-in books, small wooden beads, play figures and furniture

Stimulating Hand–eye Coordination: 3½ to 4 Years

The most remarkable change in your child's hand–eye coordination during this six-month period is her increased expectations of her own ability and performance. For instance, she plays more intricately with small doll's house furniture because she knows she can move the very small pieces more accurately, and she spends more time on her drawings because she delights in adding finer details.

Dot-To-Dot

Joining dots together provides terrific practice in hand control, but most dot-to-dot books rely on a child's ability to recognize numbers and to know the number sequence. This means they are probably unsuitable for your child at 3½ years old, so make up your own patterns for her to complete.

Draw shapes such as a circle, square or triangle. Instead of drawing full lines, put a dot for each corner and several dots in between to give a rough outline. Explain to your child that she should join all the dots together in order to reveal the shape. If she is uncertain, show her what to do at first.

Suitable Suggestions

Achievement with hand control is more likely when your child has a good sitting position. Many of the activities she now enjoys using hand–eye coordination need her to be in a chair, to adopt a stable position and to lean over the toy or game so that she achieves maximum vision. But your child is used to rushing through things quickly, moving from one activity to another without organizing herself appropriately. You can help her achieve more success with her hand–eye

Below: This girl is able to play successfully with her toy drill but the expression on her face shows that she is having to concentrate hard on her hand movements.

Below: Give your 4-year-old plenty of different drawing materials. Sand can be used to practise writing or drawing skills and is also great fun.

coordination skills by encouraging her to sit properly and comfortably in a suitably sized chair while completing the task.

Explain to her that, for instance, moving small items of furniture from one room to another in her doll's house is easier when she sits in a chair facing it. Naturally she prefers to play this game standing up because she feels less constrained, but direct her towards a seated position anyway. She needs you to point this out to her at this stage. The same applies when she is drawing or colouring-in: suggest that she works at a table or desk, with her chair pulled close to it so that she is right over the toys she plays with or the paper she is using.

Top Tips

1. Practise copying. She can now copy more complicated patterns and shapes. Draw some ordinary shapes and a couple of irregular ones on paper, then ask her to copy them underneath on the same piece of paper.

2. Sand and water play. Mix up sand and water in a basin so that the mixture is thick and sticky. She enjoys rubbing her hands in this, squeezing the 'mud' out between her fingers; she may also do this in the nursery.

3. Play pointing games. Stand on one side of the room with your child. Tell her to select an object on the opposite side and to point to it without saying anything. You have to guess first time what she is pointing at.

4. Bake together. A child this age loves mixing ingredients together in a big bowl using a huge wooden spoon, rolling out the mixture flat, cutting it into shapes and then putting these into the oven to cook.

5. Develop her visual memory. Put five objects on a tray, such as a spoon, a cup, a small toy, a pencil and a hairbrush. Let her study them for a minute, cover them with a towel, and see how many items she remembers.

Lighting is also an important factor – she'd happily sit in a slowly darkening room rather than make the effort either to ask you to switch the light on for her or to switch it on herself. Remind her that she is able to see her toys more clearly when there is good lighting. And if one area of the room is brighter than another, tell her to sit there when playing.

Hand–eye coordination involves vision too, of course, and she's now at the age when she can play challenging visual games. For instance, when you are out together, ask her to look for cars that are the same as yours or to tell you every time she sees a baby being pushed in a buggy. The object you choose for her to identify is unimportant, just as long as she has to use her vision to locate it. You can also practise this type of activity whilst in the supermarket by asking your child to find a particular item for you.

Below: You will find that with some direction from you and practice your 4-year-old will be able to point accurately at small objects within the room.

Q Why does my child make such strange faces when she concentrates hard while playing with very small toys?

A The chances are that you do the same when, for instance, you try to thread a needle. Her twisted facial expression simply helps her focus her attention more on the job in hand, that's all. As she gets older, she will do this less and less.

Q Although my child is under 4, she insists on trying to button her coat by herself. This ends in tears. What should I do?

A Work in partnership with her, not in opposition. For instance, you can pull each button most of the way through, leaving her to tug the last section into place. This way she will be delighted with her success, and confrontation is avoided.

Toys: crayons, paints, pencils and paper, jigsaws, people play figures and toy buildings, construction bricks that join together

Stimulating Hand–eye Coordination: 4 to 4½ Years

Your child's handwriting skills consolidate and develop further. He probably realizes that the infant class is not too far away and his pretend play may reflect this – he plays 'schools' with his pals or with his play figures. This sharpens his enthusiasm for writing and drawing. He wants to be like 'the older ones', so he tries hard to be independent with manual tasks.

Getting Dressed

Despite your child's best efforts, getting himself dressed may be too difficult. Help him become independent by making this job easier. There are several ways you can do this. Advise him to lay out his clothes the night before in a neatly ordered pile, with the first item at the top.

If he can't tell the front from the back of, say, his jumper, put a small white sticker on the front. Once he has put it on properly, he can remove the sticker. Show him how to put one item of clothing on completely before turning to the next one.

Suitable Suggestions

Look closely at the way your child holds a pencil. You may discover that he has an unusual grip or that he holds it too far from the lead-exposed end, making the challenge of writing more difficult than it need be.

The most effective and efficient way he can grip a pencil for writing purposes is to hold it firmly between his thumb and forefinger (using his normal pincer grip), and then to place his middle finger so that it supports the pencil from underneath – the thumb and two fingers beside it form a tripod with the pencil in the centre. The three digits should meet at a distance from the pencil tip of about 1–2 centimetres.

If your child has been used to holding the pencil in a different way, he may find this grip uncomfortable at first. Don't worry, he'll very quickly get used to it. Explain why this way of holding the pencil is best (for instance, because it's held firmly in position,

Below: This little boy is demonstrating the best way to hold a pen – between thumb and forefinger with the middle finger supporting the pen.

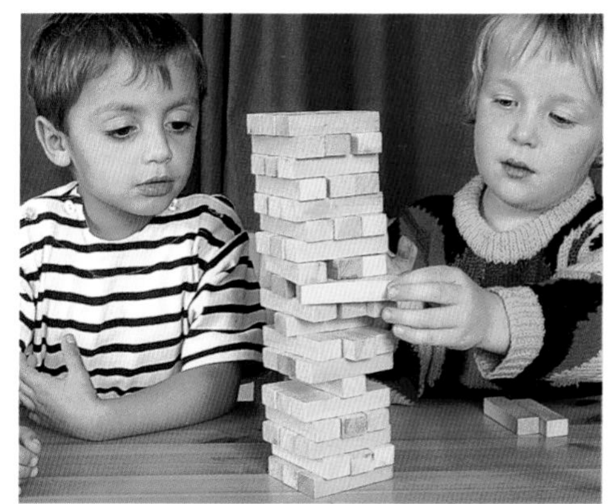

Left: At 4 children can master games with simple rules like this block game – delicate movements are needed to remove bricks without the tower collapsing.

and because he makes a mark on the paper more easily), encourage him to persist, and check that he doesn't resort to his old style. Within a few minutes, he'll be delighted with the results, whether he copies letters, traces over shapes, colours in pictures or just doodles on a sketch pad.

Top Tips

1. Let him play on a toy piano. True, this guarantees you'll have a noisy afternoon. However, striking the keys is good for his hands and fingers. He'll be pleased with the tune, even if you're not.

2. Expect him to be a tidier eater. You can reasonably expect him to use his cutlery neatly at mealtimes. Assuming your child takes his time while eating, most of the food should arrive in his mouth with less on the table.

3. Make his own book. Tell your child to cut up some sheets of paper, and then let him see you staple these together to make his own special book. He wants to fill the pages with drawing and writing.

4. Refine his personal hygiene. Supervise him when he cleans his teeth or brushes his hair. These challenging activities should be easier for him now, but be prepared to guide him if you discover he doesn't do them properly.

5. Allow lots of water play. Fill a bowl with water and drop in two measuring jugs, one smaller than the other. Ask your child to fill the small one and then to pour it into the larger one without spilling a drop.

A lot depends on the size and width of his fingers. Some children struggle to hold a pencil properly because it is so thin compared to the spacing that naturally forms between their fingers – in that instance, grip is enhanced by attaching a small rubber triangular grip close to the top of the pencil.

Help him develop his organizational skills, too. For instance, suggest that he keeps the play desk in his bedroom neat and tidy, with all the items put away at the end of each day before he goes to bed. He should also stack his toys and games neatly in the bedroom cupboard. Basic tidying and sorting tasks that involve hand–eye coordination also teach him to organize himself and his workspace, a skill that will be extremely useful once he joins the infant class.

Below: Children of this age group love the responsibility of helping in the kitchen – and pouring, mixing, stirring and measuring all help with their motor skills.

Q My child insists on gripping the crayon with his palm, not his fingers. How can I change this?

A He does this because a palmar grip enables him to make a firm mark on the paper, whereas the proper finger grip is more challenging – gentle persuasion is therefore required. Demonstrate how the finger grip gives more control, softly encourage him to try this occasionally and point out how much better his drawings are when he holds the crayon in the proper way.

Q What can I do to improve my child's cutting skills with scissors?

A Give him a variety of cutting exercises, such as cutting a piece of paper into any number of pieces, cutting the corners off an oblong, cutting paper from one side through to the other, or cutting around a shape drawn on paper. He benefits from regular practice of this sort.

Toys: multiple-piece jigsaw puzzles, small construction bricks, colouring books and crayons, finger puppets, toy tool kit, peg board

Stimulating Hand–eye Coordination: 4½ to 5 Years

In these final few months before your child starts school, her hand–eye coordination has reached the stage where she can probably write her first name without needing to copy it. Her hand control and pencil control still have a long way to go and you will continue to notice improvement over the next few years, yet the foundation of writing skills is firmly established.

Writing Skills Take Time

The rapid growth in all other areas of her development leads you to expect that her writing will progress rapidly too, but often that doesn't happen. Writing is a very complex combination of manual dexterity, hand–eye coordination, muscular and neurological maturity, and visual perception skills.

In addition, your child has to understand that writing goes in one direction only (from left to right), that words contain lots of individual letters instead of one large pattern, and that a slightly different combination of the same shapes forms a completely different letter. No wonder, then, that few 5-year-olds write clearly!

Suitable Suggestions

Remember not to focus exclusively on encouraging your child to write, or she will soon get bored – and this could de-motivate her by the time she starts the infant class. There are many other ways to boost hand–eye coordination, all of which indirectly improve her writing potential. For instance, make up (or buy) a little book of mazes: each maze should consist of two parallel zigzagging lines roughly a centimetre apart, and the requirement is for your child to draw a line while keeping the tip of the pencil inside the lines of the maze. This isn't easy for a child aged 5 years whose hand is perspiring and trembling with excitement. If she tries to progress through the maze too slowly or too quickly, the line she draws will be erratic. Don't expect her to keep the pencil within the lines all the time. Playing this game makes her concentrate hard on her hand and eye movements.

Right: By now your child will be able to visualize and construct more complicated structures like buildings and bridges.

Drawing shapes and lines in sand is another suitable activity. Fill a flat plastic basin, or a tea tray that has raised edges, with silvery sand. Keep water away from it so that it remains dry all the time. Ask your child to use her index finger to draw, say, a circle in the sand. Once she has drawn various shapes and smooths the sand again each time, she can start to draw the letters of her name.

She continues to enjoy jigsaws, though she is now able to use a planned strategy instead of relying on luck to get a match between the pieces. Give her advice on this. For instance,

Above: Children of this age group are able to approach jigsaws in a less random way, identifying which areas they want to complete first.

Top Tips

1. Involve her in cooking. She will thoroughly enjoy helping you by stirring various food mixtures with a spoon, or smoothing out a piece of pastry with a rolling pin. Even adding seasoning to food involves controlled hand–eye coordination skills.

2. Expect better use of cutlery. By the time she is 5 years old, your child can make a good attempt at eating with a fork and knife (although she probably prefers just to use a fork in her dominant hand). Give her encouragement.

3. Suggest more complex constructions. Now when she plays with construction blocks that link to each other, ask her to build a larger structure such as a small building, a car or a bridge. She is ready to tackle more demanding challenges.

4. Teach her to stack her clothes neatly. She might do this already, but if not, show her how to pile her clothes carefully so that they don't get crushed. Your child can't always fold them neatly but ask her to make an effort.

5. Show her how to wash her hands properly. Demonstrate that effective hand washing involves both hands rubbed together and that the fingers should also interlock while covered in water. She should also be able to dry her hands.

you could suggest that she finds the four corners first of all, followed by all the straight-edged pieces. Once she joins these bits together properly, she can fill the inside area. Or she could select the main object in the picture and identify all the pieces of that. The actual strategy doesn't matter so much as the fact that she uses her hand control in a planned way in order to achieve her target. This ability is extremely useful for all assignments in the infant class.

Below: This type of electronic maze will provide your child with a real challenge and he will need all his concentration to complete it successfully.

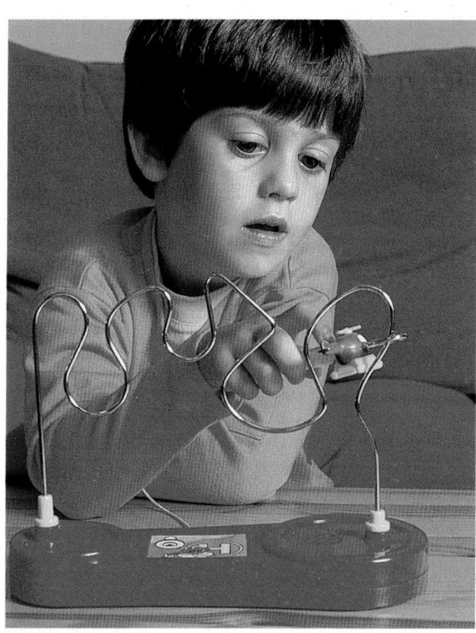

Q How can I help my 5-year-old form letters of the alphabet?

A Encourage her to make lots of writing patterns involving circles, wavy lines and straight lines. Start each pattern yourself and then ask her to complete the line. In addition, you could write her name in large letters at the top of a blank piece of paper and ask her to copy them underneath (or to trace them). Eventually, she will be able to write her name from scratch without copying.

Q Which letters should my child learn to write first?

A This varies from child to child. However, you will probably find that those letters involving either curves only (for example, 'c' and 'o') or straight lines only (for example, 't' and 'l') are rather easier for your child to learn than letters that involve combinations of lines and curves (for instance, 'b' and 'q').

Toys: pencils, crayons, colouring books, dot-to-dot books, child-sized scissors, jigsaws, plastic tool set, chalk and board, plastic utensils

Language

The Progress of Language

Your child uses language in ever more sophisticated ways during this phase of his life. This occurs partly through a better grasp of the rules of language, partly through his increased vocabulary and partly through his better learning skills. He starts to use language not just to communicate his own needs, but also to listen to the feelings and views of others. His sentences become longer, with a more complicated grammatical structure, and they carry more meaning, too. The typical 5-year-old can make a good contribution to any conversation with other children and adults.

Listening Skills

Now that he has a grasp of the fundamental elements of language, he builds on this by listening attentively to others – he learns a great deal about language just by focusing on what others say. But these skills vary from child to child.

You can help your child to sharpen his ability to tune in to what others say. Bear in mind that young children are frequently impulsive, preferring to spend more time doing exactly what they want to do instead of listening to someone else. That's why he may need additional help to develop listening skills. One of the most effective ways to achieve this is by reducing distractions. For example, he won't listen to what you say if you shout your message across the room while the television is blaring loudly beside him. Turn off the television before you speak to him, and remove other distractions if possible.

You may find that by the time he gives you his full attention he has missed the first part of your comments. To avoid this, say your child's name at the start of your sentence and only speak to him again when you are sure he is listening to you. Encourage him to make eye contact while you speak to him. If you think your child hasn't listened properly to you, ask him to repeat your instruction. Do this gently, not as a form of confrontation, but as a way to help him acquire good listening skills by the time he starts attending the infant class.

Reading

Some children aged 4 and 5 years spontaneously learn to read without any instruction from anyone. Just by looking and listening, they pick up the basic elements. Others need to be taught reading skills, however, and this is given full prominence in every infant class curriculum. But you don't need to wait until your child sets foot in school before he begins to learn to read – there is lots you can do to start the process.

You know that there is a direct connection between spoken language and written language: that what is written on paper is simply somebody's thoughts. Your growing child doesn't necessarily see the connection, so point it out to him. Use the written words that are all around him, those words that are part of his vocabulary already. For instance, he knows the name of his local supermarket – the next time you go there, show him the sign above the entrance and read the name to him.

Right: Reading books with your child is one of the most effective ways to stimulate language and an enthusiasm for words.

Above: At 5 years of age this girl has the vocabulary to carry out a detailed pretend shop transaction – from naming her purchases to asking for change.

Do the same with the wrappers that bear the name of his favourite sweets, or the carton that contains the name of his favourite video. Basic activities like these help him to see that reading is connected to everyday language, that it isn't something special just for school. He'll love cutting out the words from labels of products with which he is familiar.

And give him plenty of books to look at, even though he hasn't a clue about the individual words themselves. At the age of 3 years, your child can begin to understand that a book's title appears on the front page, that it is written by the author, that it needs to be held in a specific orientation for reading purposes, and that it starts at the front and finishes at the back. These facts are obvious to you, but not to your child. Understanding the nature of books is a fundamental pre-reading skill and it will also fire his enthusiasm.

Looking at comic books with your child is yet another source of language stimulation. He also loves those books that hide words and pictures under flaps.

The Art of Conversation

Your child is now more familiar with the concept of conversation – with the idea that he speaks, then the other person speaks, then he speaks again, and so forth. It is through this form of language interaction that he consolidates and improves his verbal skills, and therefore it is important that he is given plenty of opportunities for a two-way dialogue.

Make sure that you chat to him every day. Ask him simple questions about himself, his ideas and his feelings. Of course, he may not have much to say and would rather continue playing than talk to you at that particular moment. But chat to him anyway. Listen to what he has to say, even though it might appear trivial and repetitive. Your interest in his spoken words encourages him greatly.

Family life is often hectic, and at the end of a hard day a child aged 3, 4 or 5 years may not be able to get a word in because all those older than him – and therefore more fluent in spoken language – speak first and talk louder! Give your growing child space and time to speak.

Above: When you pick your child up from school or nursery, ask her about her day. Your interest encourages her to speak and she will enjoy telling you what she has done.

Below: This little girl is chattering happily to herself as she plays.

Stimulating Language: 3 to 3½ Years

Progress in language continues as your child is more animated in her use of words, phrases and sentences. She enjoys talking – even when you would rather have some peace and quiet – and is happy to tell you all her news. She combines words, gestures and facial expressions to make her accounts vivid and interesting. Her words flow more easily, with less effort.

Body Language

Although your child's spoken language skills improve, she still uses body language to convey meaning. Pay attention to her facial expressions, hand and arm gestures, breathing and posture, all of which tell you something about her feelings. By now you are probably skilled in interpreting these indicators.

One of the useful aspects of non-verbal communication is that it is harder to control than spoken words because most of it is involuntary, without any underlying planning – as a result, it can give you a more accurate impression of your child's feelings. This is particularly helpful when she won't express her emotions verbally.

Suitable Suggestions

There may be times when you collect your child from nursery or playgroup, or perhaps a friend's house, only to discover that she is quiet and reflective. She simply doesn't feel like chatting to you. That's fine and should not become a source of confrontation between you. It could be that she is tired from her long day, or maybe she has fallen out with a friend and is in a bad mood. Whatever the cause of her reluctance to chat, give her space. She'll return to her usual talkative self within the next hour or so if you just leave her alone.

Below: As children play together they will often describe to each other what they are doing in their game.

Use people and animal play figures to stimulate her language. Suggest to your child that she makes a farm scene using these figures, toy farm buildings and fences. Once she has done that, ask her to give you a 'guided tour' of the farm, explaining who the people are and what they do on the farm.

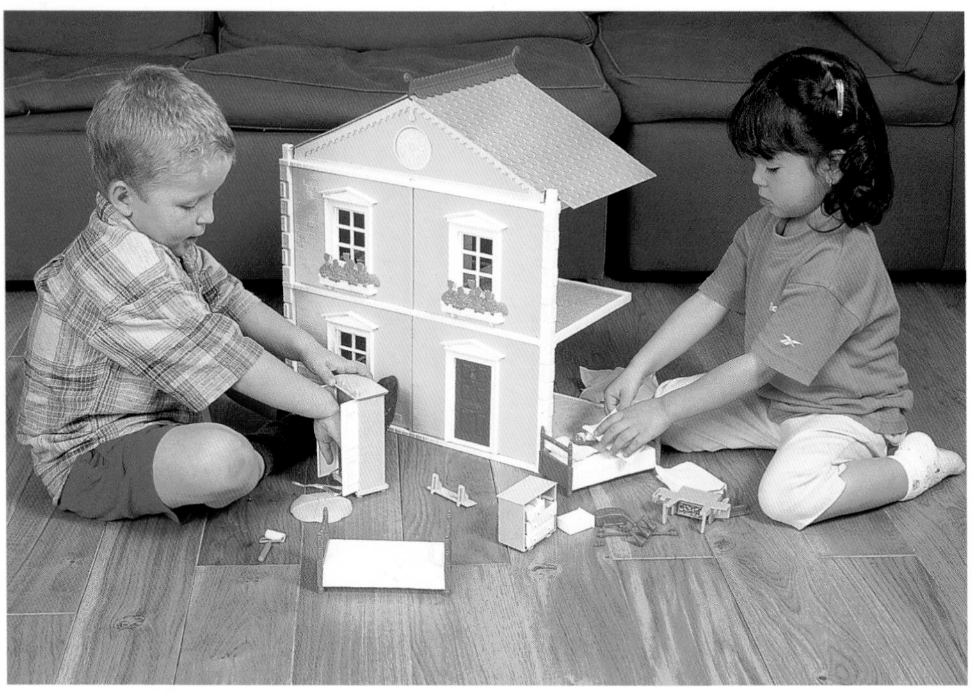

You'll be surprised at the extent of her imagination and the sorts of information she gives you about her pretend play sequence. Look interested, make positive remarks and pose questions to her on the basis of comments she makes.

When you take her with you on a shopping trip to your local supermarket, as you reach the door point to the name of the store in the sign above and let her stare at it for a few moments. When you get home, cut out the store logo and name from the plastic carrier bag and paste it into a little book of blank pages for her. You could also do this with the logo of her favourite breakfast cereal, putting one on each of the blank pages.

The next time you return to the store, tell your child to bring the book with her. She has to let you know when she sees the name logo anywhere throughout the supermarket – put a tick in her book as a reward. This game uses print images in her environment to build her basic word recognition skills even though she can't read individual letters yet.

Above: By the age of 3 your child will be able to follow an instruction that you give her involving two or three consecutive actions.

Top Tips

1. Give more complicated instructions. Make a request that contains two or three pieces of information, for example: 'Go into the kitchen and bring me the blue cloth.' If she concentrates on what you say, she is able to complete the task.

2. Sing songs together. Your child enjoys singing even more now that she is able to learn and remember the words. Take a musical tape or CD with you for car journeys. This relieves the boredom and improves her language skills.

3. Play puppet games. Encourage her to play imaginatively with her finger puppets so that they talk to each other or to you. Some children use more language in this play format than they usually do in everyday life.

4. List 'sounds like' words. This isn't easy, but she might manage. Say a couple of words that rhyme (such as 'cat' and 'mat'), making sure that you stress the end sound. Then ask her to suggest other words that sound like these. Most children find this harder than finding words with the same starting sound.

5. Play listening games. With her eyes closed while listening to a video or television programme with which she is familiar, ask her to identify the different voices she hears. The chances are that her guesses are accurate.

Below: Make-believe games with toy characters encourage your child to use language in a creative and imaginative way.

Q My 3½-year-old has trouble saying some sounds, such as 'th' and 'sm'. What should I do?

A This is a common occurrence, which you don't need to do anything about. Many children this age experience temporary difficulty with double-letter blends like these – for instance, substituting 'f' for 'th'. However, this self-corrects over the next few months as her pronunciation in general improves.

Q Why is my 3½-year-old so quiet at nursery? She prattles away non-stop at home.

A You know from her talkative nature at home that she can speak fluently and appropriately. Her silence at nursery probably arises because she is not yet fully at ease with the other children and adults. Her use of language there will steadily increase as she begins to feel more comfortable.

Toys: finger puppets, dressing-up clothes, doll's house and furniture, story books, magazines and newspapers to cut up

Stimulating Language: 3½ to 4 Years

As he approaches his fourth birthday, your child starts to use language more creatively and more purposefully. His questions are more penetrating as he seeks more detailed information. He also applies the rules of grammar himself, though he doesn't always do this correctly – that's why you might hear him tell you that his friend 'gonded' instead of 'went'. His sentences are longer.

Hearing Difficulties

Hearing loss is the most common reason for a child's slow progress with speech and language development. Although problems with hearing are usually picked up in the first couple of years, there are some children whose difficulty isn't identified until later.

Signs of possible hearing loss in a child this age include his slower than expected progress with speech, a lack of response to questions, his habit of watching the speaker's face and mouth closely, and a high level of frustration. These signs by themselves don't necessarily mean he has hearing loss, but if you have any doubts, check this out.

Suitable Suggestions

As well as generally chatting to your child, ask him questions that require him to think about a topic and then respond to you. For instance, you could ask him to tell you what it is about his favourite cuddly toy that he likes so much, or why he prefers playing with one child rather than another. He is ready to cope with this level of discussion, but may need your prodding to get him going. When you have had a good chat, tell him how much you enjoyed talking to him.

You'll also find that his humour shows through, although he'll burst out laughing at something that doesn't even make you smile! At this age, much of his humour revolves around language. Your child might say a word out of context, then roll around on the floor with laughter – you may not see what is so funny, but he thinks he has made a hilarious joke. Just go along with his verbal humour: don't ask him to explain it to you. He'll also like stories involving characters with funny names who say strange things to others in the story. This is a sign of his ability to go beyond a literal understanding of the spoken word.

It's important that your child feels that you listen to him. If possible, stop what you are doing and give him your full attention. If you can't do this because you are particularly busy, tell him this and explain that you'll listen to him in a few minutes when you have some time. And make sure you do seek his views later on or he'll soon stop making the effort to talk to you.

Above: At this age your child will love the novelty of a walkie-talkie toy – this is likely to enthral even the most reluctant talker.

Above: Magnetic letters on a board or the fridge are a great means of familiarizing your child with the alphabet.

Top Tips

1. Talk about holiday photographs. Get out the pictures you took during your previous family holiday and chat about them with your child. Let him look at them, ask him to point out the various details and tell you what he recalls about the trip.

2. Use magnetic letters. Initially, use these for letter-matching games. Draw a letter on paper, hand it to your child and ask him to find the magnetic letter that is the same. Vary the complexity of this.

3. Play word lotto. The chances are that he can't read any of the words on the lotto board, but he may be able to match the cards with them if given enough time to compare them. Pick cards with words containing only two or three letters.

4. Teach him poetry. Encourage him to learn a poem containing only, say, two lines. Rehearse this with him until he is reasonably confident. The next time relatives visit, suggest he recites the poem to them.

5. Ask him to describe flavours. Give your child four different items to taste and ask him to describe their flavours. Tell him you don't know which one he has tasted so he needs to try hard to give you a clear description, such as 'nice' or 'horrible'.

Some children this age start to stammer when they speak while excited. It's as if they are so desperate to get the words out quickly that they jumble them up. Encourage him to talk more slowly. Speak to him in a quiet, steady voice, reminding him to slow down and to take a breath at the end of each sentence. With your advice and support, this temporary speech mannerism will pass.

Below: Children love looking through photo albums and talking about the pictures, particularly those of events that they remember.

Q I don't read fairy tales to my 4-year-old because I think they are frightening. Am I right?

A Fairy tales can be scary for young children, but it depends on the way you read them. If you use a voice tone that makes him nervous, he will be frightened. But if you use a pleasant voice, filled with excitement, then he'll probably enjoy listening to these tales.

Q Why has my child started to develop a lisp? He says 'th' instead of 's'.

A This type of sound substitution is normal, and often happens around the age of 3 or 4 years. In virtually all instances, the lisp disappears as the child matures, usually before he sets foot in the infant class. He may feel self-conscious, so don't draw attention to it.

Toys: reading books, picture cards with lots of details, magazines, magnetic letters and board, nursery rhyme books

Stimulating Language: 4 to 4½ Years

Your child's better use of language enables her to deal with more complex thoughts. Many of the pre-school language skills emerge now, such as identifying and naming colours and shapes. This boosts her confidence, curiosity and desire to know more – so her questions increase, too. She chats freely to other children at every opportunity, and likes to voice her opinions.

Repetitive Reading

Most children this age love to hear the same story over and over again. To you this may appear to be a dreadfully boring and pointless exercise, but to your 4½-year-old it is fascinating. She loves the familiarity and predictability of the story because it is reassuring and comforting.

Repetition of stories like this also improves her language development – you'll find that she starts to mouth the words as you read, or maybe even says the next line of the story before you do. Of course, as well as reading familiar stories to your child, you should gradually introduce new ones, too.

Suitable Suggestions

Listening is an essential part of communication. Your 4-year-old, however, may be more intent on expressing her own point of view (loudly) – especially when she is driven by righteous indignation – than she is on listening. When she feels hard done by, she is determined to let you know. It's best to let her have her say (whether you agree with her or not), while you listen calmly. When she has finished, take your turn. Tell her that you have listened to what she said and ask

Below: Your child will now sing confidently and can accompany himself on instruments; get him to make up words for a familiar tune or invent new songs.

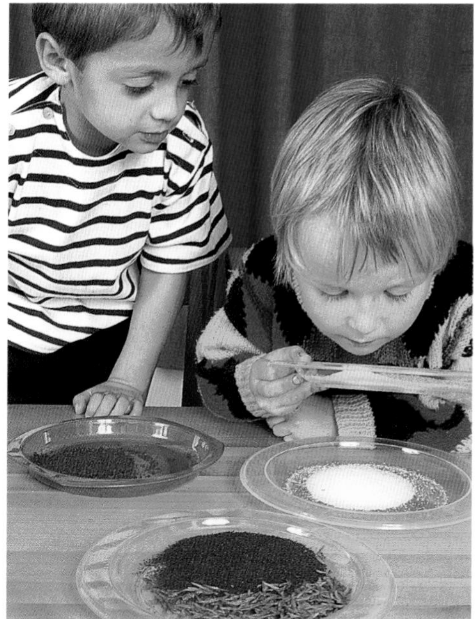

Left: These two boys are trying to identify different smells – this is an excellent way to get them to stretch their descriptive vocabulary.

her to listen to you now. Then say what you think about the matter.

You may find that your child simply repeats what she said the first time, as if in the hope that repetition will ensure she wins the argument. Each time she does this, repeat the point you made and ask her to reply to that specific comment. Slowly but surely, you'll help her transform from a determined 4-year-old who aims to win an argument by verbal force into a sensitive child who listens to the other person.

This is also a good time to explain to her about the power of language, that words can cheer up another person or can make them unhappy: in other words, that her speech and language have an emotional impact on others. She probably makes hurtful comments completely unintentionally – she simply says what enters her mind at this age, without giving a thought to the potential consequences to those she's talking to.

For instance, when she sees another child who looks different from her, she may say 'You look funny', perhaps because of that child's haircut or the clothes he wears. She doesn't realize that her remark could cause upset. You can broaden her perspective by asking her to tell you how she would feel if someone made that comment to her. Point out that others feel the same way as well.

Books should occupy part of her daily routine now. She probably points to some of the words as she sits beside you while you read to her, and she may pick out letters that are included in her name. Playing with magnetic letters and a board builds her emerging reading skills.

Top Tips

1. Discuss recent experiences. No matter what she has done that day, make sure that you ask her about it. Get her into the habit of giving you a good account of her experiences, whether she was at nursery or played at home.

2. Select her television viewing carefully. Since her language is influenced by what she sees on television, do your best to ensure that she watches quality children's programmes that are made specifically for young viewers.

3. Encourage letter recognition. Instead of asking her to pick out her name from, say, six names that you write on paper, just write the first letters of the names. Ask her to pick out the letter that starts her own name.

4. Use verbal humour with her. She begins to see that there are additional humorous aspects to language, such as gentle sarcasm. For instance, when she spills something, smile as you say 'That's good, isn't it'. Your child understands the joke.

5. Play 'I spy'. Ask her to identify objects starting with a specific sound, such as 'p' or 'm'. Vary this by making the starting sounds a two-letter combination, such as 'st' or 'tr'. Help your child if she struggles to do this.

Q Which should come first, naming shapes or identifying them?

A Your child will be able to pick out specific shapes when requested long before she can actually tell you the name of each shape. In most instances, a child's receptive language (the words she can understand) is ahead of her expressive language (the words she can say), and so shape and colour identification emerges before naming does.

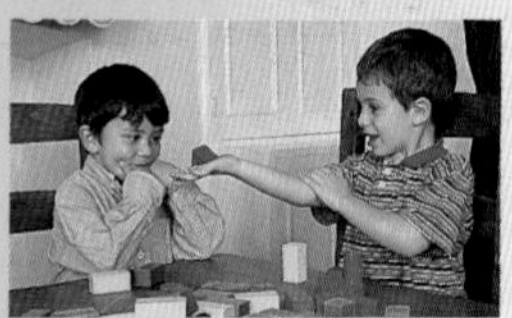

Q Whenever my child hears a new word, she says it over and over again. Why?

A Put simply, she finds words fascinating. To you, word repetition is boring, but to your child, this is a great game. Just leave her to it. Once she has integrated the word into her vocabulary, she won't need to use it so often.

Toys: people and animal play figures, lots of books, magnetic letters and numbers, coloured shapes, dressing-up hats

Stimulating Language: 4½ to 5 years

Language has become your child's elementary tool for learning – he understands the importance of books and looks at factual books, not just fiction. He also uses language as a key social skill. When he was younger, he acted first and then asked permission; now it's usually the other way around. Your child is confident talking to an adult and can answer personal questions.

Verbal Politeness

Politeness with words does matter, to both children and adults. A child who is able to say, for example, 'please' and 'thank you' is far more likely to keep his friends than a child who just grabs at what he wants without saying a word. Although most children this age act on impulse, it's best if he can learn basic verbal politeness before starting the infant class.

Set a good example at home. Gently but firmly insist that he asks appropriately for a sweet, toy or game instead of barging his way through, and don't give him what he wants unless he asks nicely. This use of language makes life easier for him.

Suitable Suggestions

You can enhance your child's social use of language by teaching him opening gambits to use when meeting new children for the first time, as he will do when he starts the infant class. Children are often shy when mixing with others they don't know well, and this results in their not knowing what to say.

To help your child have an easier social start to school, suggest to him that he says, for example, 'Would you like to play with my toy?' or 'I like jumping. Would you like to play with me?' or 'That's a nice jumper you're wearing.' He may feel silly practising these sentences at home with you, but he'll understand their social purpose.

Encourage him to be confident when asking questions. This is crucial for the infant school, not just to acquire knowledge in the classroom but also for personal issues as well. For instance, there are some children who fail to use the infant toilet in the first few weeks of starting school simply because they don't have the courage to ask the teacher where it is located. And you don't want your child to fall into that trap about any question he needs to ask.

Get him used to asking you for things, instead of anticipating his requests. He could also, for instance, ask the local shopkeeper for an item (in your presence, of course). The more he does this, the more confident he becomes with questions. Remind him that he should only ask when he genuinely needs to know something, not to

Right: This little girl is taking the lead in a shopping game. Getting your child used to asking questions will help her at school.

Above: If you teach your child some basic ways to open a conversation he will feel more confident when meeting new people.

Top Tips

1. Use print in his surroundings. Draw his attention to road and shop signs, all of which carry important information. Explain what each sign tells you and encourage him to identify the starting letter.

2. Give him blank paper and pencils for writing. It's important for your child to realize that he can write the words that he says. Help him note down a short sentence that he has spoken to you, and then read it back to him.

3. Put up labels. You could put labels on key objects around your house, such as the table, chair, door and television. Don't do this for everything – just for, say, half a dozen basic items. He'll soon be able to read these labels out of context.

4. Include him in conversations. If your child is quiet by nature, he may prefer to take a backseat role when others talk. Make a point of including him in your conversations, irrespective of his possible reluctance to speak.

5. Use lettering of different sizes, type style and case (capital and small letters). Instead of looking for reading books with the same size and style of print, give your child a variety. That's better than uniformity because it gets him used to a broad range of print.

make himself the centre of attention. With your guidance, he'll strike a balance.

By now he should be immersed in reading books, magazines, newspapers and comics, as well as his own made-up books. Take him to your local library each week. Make a point of reading together each day, and ask him lots of questions about the characters and the plot, about what he thinks will happen next and about his enjoyment. You could even suggest that he writes a letter (with your help) to the story's central character.

Below: Once your child can read she will enjoy reading alone although many books she likes will still be too complex for her to read unaided.

Q Does a child this age understand the concept of a 'white lie'?

A A white lie (a lie whose purpose is to protect another person's feelings) can confuse a 5-year-old. He may not realize the difference between this type of lie and an unacceptable lie to conceal the truth. If he hears you tell a white lie, he may take this as a sign that lying is permissible.

Q What is phonological awareness?

A This is an important language skill, and is your child's ability to understand that a whole word such as 'cat' can be broken into the segments 'c' and 'at'. There is evidence that a child who grasps this idea by the age of 4 or 5 years is likely to make good progress with reading in the infant class.

Toys: puppets and dolls, musical tapes, books, newspapers, clothes for imaginative play, word lotto, board games

Learning

The Development of Learning Skills

Your child's learning ability (also called 'intelligence', 'learning skills', 'thinking skills' and 'cognition') continues to grow rapidly during these remaining pre-school years. Her ability to learn new skills and concepts, to make sense of events that happen around her, to use her memory accurately and to solve problems steadily improves.

An Active Thinker

By the time she reaches her fifth birthday, your child is a much more active thinker, with a great deal more knowledge and grasp of concepts than she had a few years earlier. Look for changes in the following areas:

- **concentration.** She is now able to focus her attention more accurately and is less influenced by distractions; she blocks out irrelevant information in order to concentrate on the item or object that catches her interest. This skill is particularly important in the infant classroom, where she will need to concentrate on one activity only while a lot goes on around her.
- **inquisitiveness.** Your child has an innate curiosity that drives her to learn more and more. There is so much she wants to understand, and the intensity of her questioning increases. She also learns by hands-on discovery herself – physical exploration remains a key strategy for enhancing her learning, though she approaches such activities in a more organized way now.
- **number concepts.** Genuine understanding of the significance of numbers begins to emerge around the third and fourth year. Initially, she tries to count in imitation – without understanding the meaning of numbers – but then she starts to match small groups with the same number of objects in them. This is a huge step forward in her ability to deal with abstract concepts.
- **memory.** Her increasing memory skills underpin much of her learning – if her memory was weak, she wouldn't recall what she had learned the previous day and would have to re-learn it all over again. Now she can hold two or three pieces of information in her memory while she acts on them. Her short- and long-term memories both show signs of increased capacity.
- **symbolic thought.** She starts to use imagery as part of her thinking. She is more able to discuss people,

Below: By the time your child is 3½ her concentration increases, allowing her to complete tasks like a dot-to-dot puzzle.

objects and toys that aren't actually there in front of her at the time, so she is no longer tied to what she can see. This opens up a whole new range of learning opportunities. Imagery also enables her to generalize what she has learned from one situation to another.

Learning Style

By now, you'll have a good idea of the way in which your child approaches learning activities and her attitude towards them. Psychologists call this her 'learning style', and it is important because it affects her progress at school. Spend a moment or two observing your child play with a brand new toy. Perhaps she grabs at it, hurriedly takes it out of the box and then immediately tries to operate it. Or maybe she looks at the box and the toy first, as she tries to make sense of it before playing with it, and then slowly begins to play.

These two different approaches to acquiring information are known as:

- **impulsive.** With this learning style, a child acts before thinking the problem through properly. She is driven by impulse and instinct, heading for a solution that she guesses might be effective or that has worked in the past with a different problem. The impulsive child doesn't wait to evaluate, but instead tries to solve the problem before weighing up all the possibilities.
- **reflective.** With this learning style, a child tends to think before she acts. She gathers as much information as she can about the challenge facing her before searching for a solution. When she thinks she is ready, she starts to apply some of that newly acquired data in a problem-solving strategy. Time is of no consequence to a child with a reflective learning style – she acts only when she feels ready.

You'll probably see elements of both learning styles in your child, and there is a place for each of these approaches when it comes to learning during the pre-school years. For instance, if your child takes too long to reach a decision about, say, the best biscuits to eat, other children may have finished them all by the time she makes up her mind. On the other hand, she is likely to have a safer childhood if, for instance, she studies the traffic pattern very carefully before crossing the road. Each style has merit, depending on the learning context.

Above: Inquisitiveness, prior knowledge and logic enable these children to work out how to get biscuits from a high cupboard.

Right: At 3 this little boy has his binoculars the wrong way round but he will soon realize this and try them the other way.

Confidence with Learning

As your child's thinking skills increase, she inevitably tries more challenging learning activities. In some instances she will fail to achieve her learning target, whether that's completing a large jigsaw puzzle or learning the sequence of the first five numbers. This can depress her self-confidence, thus reducing her willingness to learn new information in the future. Do your best to keep her confidence as a learner high so that she maintains an upbeat, positive outlook about her learning skills.

Stimulating Learning: 3 to 3½ Years

The main change in your child's learning at this age is that he concentrates more efficiently on every activity, enabling him to glean as much new information as possible. He is also more confident with learning, which makes him ready and keen to acquire new concepts. Elementary counting attracts his interest, and he considers concepts such as shape and colour in more detail than before.

Suitable Suggestions

Young children this age are typically egocentric, in that they see the world only from their own point of view. That's why, for example, your 3-year-old demands your attention even though you are tired and have a headache – he doesn't recognize that you have needs, too. This perspective is normal for a young child, and indicates his lack of

Above: Making different shapes with modelling clay is an excellent way to get your child to think about relative size and volume.

Below: With her toy tea set your child can practise laying out the right number of place settings for her friends or toys.

Cause And Effect

Your child is still at the age where he believes that there are connections between two events that occur one after the other, even though they are not linked. For instance, he may conclude that your car doesn't start because he is in a bad mood with you. You know the two are totally unconnected, but your child's lack of experience allows him to establish a cause-and-effect link in his own mind.

When you see your child make this sort of mistaken relationship between two episodes, point out to him that they are not connected but occurred one after the other by chance. Advise him that things can happen together by coincidence.

maturity, not his insensitivity. But his egocentric outlook affects his learning, too.

Try this. Shape two pieces of play dough or modelling clay into two round balls that are the same size. Place them in front of your child and ask him to agree that they are both the same size. Talk about them being the same size, for a couple of minutes. Next, in full view of your child, roll out one ball so that it is long and thin, and the other so that it is short and fat. Make sure that your child watches you do this.

Put the two new shapes side by side and ask him which one has more in it now. The chances are that he will immediately point to the long, thin shape. He does this because his perspective on the world is limited and he can only fixate on one dimension at a time. Try to explain that they are both the same size. Follow this procedure with other materials, such as containers with water. These activities lead him to take a broader approach to learning.

To help improve his concentration, take him shopping with you at the supermarket. Hold up a particular food can and ask your child to find one exactly like it. Do this at the top of the aisle which contains the product. Encourage him to scan each row systematically as he walks along. If you see that he rushes down the aisle, missing items as he passes, suggest he slows down. Do this three or four times during any shopping trip – it's good practice for focusing his attention. You can also ask him to identify, say, red cars when you next go out driving with him.

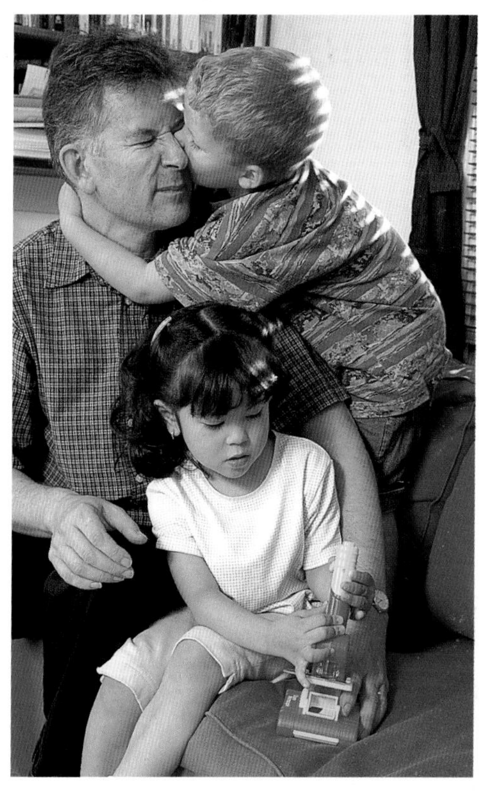

Above: At this age your child's learning depends very much on your input and he will demand a great deal of your attention.

Top Tips

1. Show by example. Remember that your growing child learns a great deal from watching you and the way you manage situations. Explain to him why you completed something in the way you did so that he learns this strategy.

2. Counter his frustration. In his search for new learning skills, he is bound to experience frustration. In that situation, calm your child, reassure him until he is more settled, then stay with him as he tries the same activity again.

3. Play sorting games. Ask him to tell you all the things he likes to drink. If he mentions foods, not drinks, remind him that foods are not included in this group. Do the same for several other categories of objects.

4. Help him set the table. Explain to your child that he should put one knife, fork and spoon on the table for each person. He needs to think about how many people there are, and then match each set of cutlery to each individual.

5. Clap rhythms. Clap out a simple rhythm and ask your child to repeat it – for example, two quick claps followed by two slow ones. Once he is able to do this, repeat the activity using a slightly more complicated sequence.

Q Do children this age understand about rules of behaviour?

A Yes. Your child may not like the rules that set limits on what he is allowed to do, and he may even try to break them, but he understands rules about his behaviour. Always explain a rule to your child, especially the reasoning underlying it. He learns rules quicker when they are applied consistently.

Q Now my child is older, how much television should he be allowed to watch?

A Your child can learn a lot from short, quality television programmes that present new information in exciting and challenging ways. The danger, however, is that he may spend too much time staring aimlessly at poor quality viewing just because the television set is there in front of him. Monitor what he is viewing and the amount of time he spends in front of the television so that you are aware of his viewing patterns.

Toys: toy telephone, imitation household utensils, alphabet jigsaw, letter puzzles, soft toys, construction blocks, doll's house

Stimulating Learning: 3½ to 4 Years

As she approaches the end of her fourth year, your child begins to use her memory more efficiently in order to locate objects and to recall information that is important to her. A genuine understanding of numbers develops. Other pre-school skills emerge too, such as colour and shape identification; she may recognize her own name. Your child learns from playing with other children.

Measuring Learning Ability

Psychologists have devised a series of tests to measure a child's progress with learning. Called 'intelligence tests', these assessment tools claim to provide an IQ score (intelligence quotient) for a child. A score of 100 is average, while a score over 140 is exceptionally high.

Yet critics of these tests claim they are artificial and have no relevance to everyday learning situations. The best way to know if your child is learning at a satisfactory pace, say critics of intelligence tests, is to watch her playing with a wide variety of toys. You'll be able to tell from these observations whether or not she plays appropriately.

Suitable Suggestions

By now, she'll have had lots of experience mixing with other children, probably at nursery and at home. These social interactions boost her learning skills because she observes other children's actions and imitates some of their discovery strategies. Children also talk to one another about challenges they face – when it comes to problem-solving, they may be more creative as a group than as individuals. Your child is likely to be more enthusiastic about learning when she is in the presence of others.

You'll find that her imaginative play starts to utilize her newly acquired concepts, and this should be encouraged. For instance, she pretend-plays shops, selling goods to customers and giving them change from her toy cash register. Provide toys that stimulate this sort of imaginative play. Your child may also start to play 'schools' with her friends. She isn't sure what really goes on there, but has an idea from older siblings and television programmes.

A useful strategy for helping your child's memory is to encourage the use of rehearsal (repetition). Teach her a short poem and explain that she should learn this one bit at a time. For every few words suggest that she recites it out loud, over and over again. You intuitively use this technique when trying to commit something to memory, but your child doesn't – she needs you to suggest it.

Below: You can fire your child's imagination by providing some simple dressing-up items; enthusiasm for this will be greater when he plays with his friends.

Right: More complex toys come into play at this age. This little girl is able to record her own voice and then play it back.

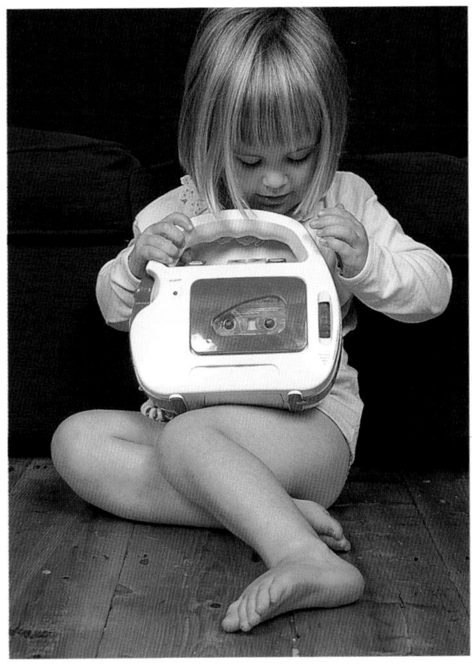

Let her walk up and down the house saying the information over and over again. She'll be surprised to discover that she can easily recall it the next day, too.

There might be times when she is convinced she is right about something even though you know she is wrong. A child this age has an amazing capacity to deny reality in the face of conflicting evidence. If you find yourself trying to persuade your 4-year-old that, for example, her new jumper is red not blue, calmly bring the jumper out to show her, patiently point out its real colour, and then change the conversation. The next time she talks about the jumper, she'll refer to the colour of it as red.

Top Tips

1. Encourage her to use a desk. She'll soon discover that she feels more comfortable when trying to complete a puzzle or draw a picture if she sits at a desk, with the activity placed firmly in front of her.

2. Ask her to help you solve problems. Pose everyday problems to your child. For instance, ask her to think of the best way to store all the tin cans from the supermarket in the cupboard. Encourage her to think of alternatives.

3. Allow time gaps. When your child tries to learn something new, don't allow her to persevere for hours. Instead, let her practise for a couple of minutes, then make sure she takes a long break before returning to it.

4. Increase her awareness of numbers. Point out to your child that numbers appear all around her – in shop windows, on price tags and on street signs. Ask her to identify numbers between one and nine when she sees them.

5. Make memory games more challenging. Now, when you ask her to remember the items on a tray covered with a large towel, increase the number of objects from six to a dozen (though she won't get them all right).

Below: By the age of 4, children are more likely to work together to solve problems – in this case a jigsaw puzzle.

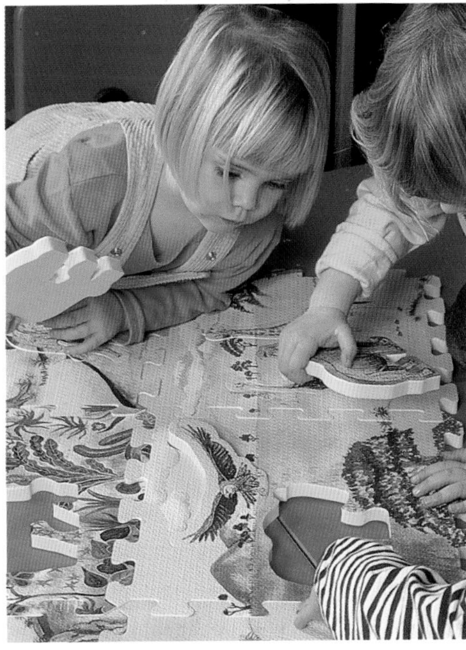

Q&A

Q Are some children naturally gifted and talented?

A There is no doubt that some children possess exceptional abilities in some areas of development. For example, musical ability is thought to be innate, and musically talented infants show this skill very early on, perhaps by playing tunefully with toy instruments. Yet virtually all children – including yours – can learn new skills at every age, whether they are innately talented or not.

Q Why does my 4-year-old keep asking for more toys, even though we tell her they are too expensive?

A She does this for two reasons. First, she wants more toys. Second, she assumes you are able to buy them. She hasn't yet learned that there are limits on your resources. In time she develops a more realistic outlook, but in the meantime she persists with her requests.

Toys: toy microscope or magnifying glass, notebook and pencil, dressing-up clothes, face masks, construction set, magnetic numbers

Stimulating Learning: 4 to 4½ Years

Your child shows many of the learning characteristics that will soon help him thrive in the infant class. His awareness and understanding of numbers, shapes, sizes and time all increase, and he deals with other abstract thoughts such as comparisons. Concentration and memory also improve – he plays for longer with one toy and completes more activities instead of leaving them unfinished.

Making Him Think

Learning is not just about acquiring information but also about developing problem-solving strategies. You can extend your child's thinking skills by posing simple problems for him to solve, such as asking him what you should do if you are out in the car and it breaks down, or if you go to a shop and then discover you have no money.

As he offers his own solutions, discuss each one in detail, looking at the advantages and disadvantages. Be positive about his suggestions, even if they seem inappropriate. What matters is that your child develops strategies for reaching solutions.

Suitable Suggestions

Encourage him to take a more organized approach to learning situations: if your child chooses to draw or make a model or complete a puzzle, suggest to him that before he starts he should think about everything he could need. This might include pencils and paper, a tray or desk to lean on, a small snack, a comfortable cushion, proper lighting and the toy itself. Once he has identified the key items, tell him to arrange them in a way that suits him. Having organized himself like that, your child is now ready to begin, without having to get up unnecessarily. He concentrates better as a result, and therefore learns much more effectively.

Play lots of memory games with him. These are good fun, while also benefiting his recall skills. You could play 'When I went to the supermarket I bought a....' – each time the next person repeats what the previous players have bought and then adds a new item to the end of the list. Another suitable game is to cut out several squares each from blue, yellow and red cards, then show your child a short sequence of, say, a red, a blue and a yellow square, take it away and ask him to make the same sequence with his own cards. Vary the sequence of cards each time. Your child will probably manage to remember three or four items accurately before becoming confused.

Below: By getting your child to predict the results of experiments like deciding what will float or sink you will help to develop his powers of reasoning.

Above: By this age your child will be intrigued by basic scientific concepts – like the fact that certain things dissolve in liquid – and will love to perform simple experiments.

Top Tips

1. Give him number activities. Ask him to set the table for five people. He should count out five knives and five forks, and then set them out on the table. This type of activity relates number calculations to everyday life.

2. Explain about encyclopedias and dictionaries. When your child asks you a factual question, whether or not you know the answer, let him see you look up the information in a reference book. Tell him where to find these in your house.

3. Discuss time phases. Chat with your child about the different events that occur during his day, using time-related words such as 'morning', 'lunch' and 'afternoon' in your discussion. This reinforces his underlying concept of time.

4. Play sequence games. Draw a sequence of three actions on separate cards – for instance, a child with a full plate of food, with a half-empty plate, and with a totally clean plate. Ask your child to put these pictures in the right order.

5. Talk about similarities. To help your child's classification skills, name two or three items and ask him to say how they are the same. For instance, say 'horse', 'dog' and 'elephant' – he'll guess accurately that they are all animals.

To improve his performance at these games, suggest that he uses imagery. For instance, if the first colour in the sequence is red, he could imagine the front door of his house is red; and if the second colour is yellow he could imagine his hall carpet is yellow, and so on. This type of imagery helps improve his recall of the colour sequence.

Practise counting with your child, too. He can probably count to ten by rote, without missing out any of the numbers. He may also be able to count objects up to ten, perhaps counting each step as he walks slowly upstairs or counting a row of blocks in front of him, although he may miss out some. Give him number-sorting and matching activities. For instance, make a pile of four wooden blocks and ask him to make a similar pile. Vary the numbers involved each time. As well as consolidating his grasp of numbers, these games boost his confidence with learning.

You can also use learning activity books – covering topics such as numeracy and literacy – available from most quality bookshops. Do some practical science experiments with your child, such as weighing different amounts when cooking, dissolving sugar in warm water, measuring lengths of objects, using magnets – each time, ask him to predict what will happen. Explaining about growing plants in the garden also fascinates him.

Q Is there a difference between creativity and learning ability?

A Yes. Creativity is best described as the ability to think in new and innovative ways about old problems. A genuinely creative idea is unusual, relevant, and offers a completely new perspective. To encourage your child's creativity, let him use his imagination, show interest in his questions and give plenty of praise when he offers unusual suggestions.

Q How much detail should I give in my replies to my 4-year-old's questions? He asks lots about science.

A Reply to any questions about science in a way that is suitable for his level of understanding. Although your 4-year-old might ask what appears to be a deep question, he needs a reply that is pitched at his stage of development and understanding, without too much detail.

Toys: balancing scales, magnetic numbers and letters, plastic binoculars, toy medical kit, child's desk, alphabet wall chart

Stimulating Learning: 4½ to 5 years

In this six-month period which leads up to – and perhaps includes – your child's start in the infant class, she consolidates her existing learning skills, leaving her ready to take on the key educational challenges of reading, writing and counting. Although she is perhaps both apprehensive and excited about the prospect of the classroom, she has a positive attitude to learning.

Birth Order

Research studies reveal that children who are first-born in the family tend to learn quicker and better throughout life and to achieve more (compared to their younger siblings), probably because they have their parents' attention and stimulation all to themselves for at least a couple of years. Second-born children have to share parental attention, and so miss out on this 'head start'.

So, make a specific point of regarding each of your children as special, if possible giving your youngest as much learning stimulation as you gave your first-born child. Each child is an individual, with her own learning needs.

Suitable Suggestions

Now is the time to have a long think about the main characteristics needed for your child to thrive educationally once she starts school, and then, having identified them, to boost them. Take listening skills, for instance, which are important for learning in the classroom. Tell her to listen while you read a short story and add that you will ask her some questions about it afterwards. Practise this type of activity with her, gradually making both the story itself and the subsequent questions more difficult.

Above: Board games involving a die and simple counting will entertain your child and help his counting to become more automatic.

She is ready to play board games that involve rolling a die. Encourage her to study the die closely so that she can count the correct number of spots, then to move her piece on the board the appropriate number of squares. Be patient with her when she becomes confused, and encourage her to count again if necessary.

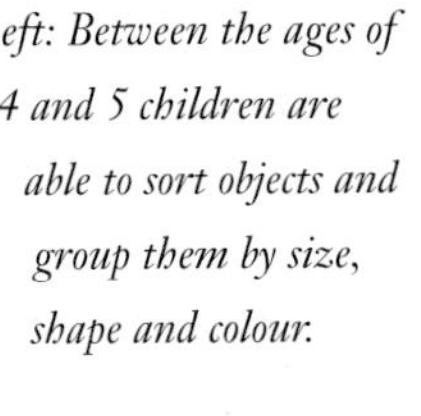

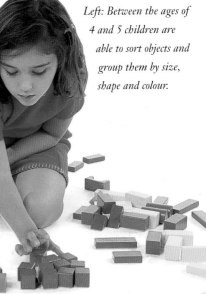

Left: Between the ages of 4 and 5 children are able to sort objects and group them by size, shape and colour.

Above: A garden or park offers a wealth of opportunity for your child to observe different plants and the way they change throughout the year.

Top Tips

1. Talk positively about school. An anxious child doesn't learn as quickly as a relaxed child. Do your best to put her at ease, take her on any pre-entry visits, and tell her how much she will enjoy learning in the infant class.

2. Teach coin recognition. Pick one low-value coin and tell your child its name and how much it is worth. When she is ready, let her pick out coins of this value from a bundle you hand to her.

3. Get her familiar with computers. You may have one at home; if so, encourage your 5-year-old to become generally comfortable with the very basic uses of a computer. There are lots of child-centred CD Roms available and she'll enjoy playing with these.

4. Play matching and sorting games. Give her items which she can sort by various characteristics such as colour, shape, big and small, hot and cold, rough and smooth, loud and quiet. Then get her to sort using two characteristics – for example, putting the smooth, blue blocks together.

5. Encourage persistence. Do what you can to persuade your child to persist with a learning challenge until she achieves success. Suggest that she keeps trying for a few minutes more even though the solution eludes her at the moment.

Help her to be aware of her surroundings, and to scan around her as she walks along. For instance, she should notice traffic and take suitable safety precautions, she should observe the road crossing lights and she should memorize the shops along her regular route. Processing information from her everyday world sharpens her information-processing skills in general. Talk to her about the way in which weather and plants change with the seasons, and about the different people and places she sees when out walking.

She won't yet have realized that she can structure areas of her memory, just as she can, for instance, structure areas in her bedroom. Teach her this strategy as an aid to her memory. For instance, show your child a collection of nine objects – three to do with writing (pen, pencil, paper), three to do with eating (fork, cup, biscuit) and three to do with crafts (scissors, adhesive tape, glue) – mixed together. Once she has looked at them for a few seconds, ask her to remember as many as she can. Then ask her to remember the ones to do with eating. She'll find that her recall is better when she uses an orderly system to access her memory.

Below: Although your child can't yet tell the time, she is aware that her day is made up of different phases: that she has breakfast in the morning, has lunch at midday and goes to bed at night.

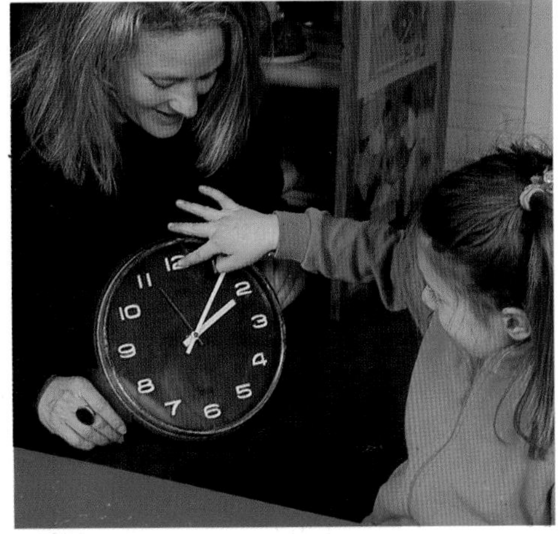

Q My 5-year-old won't sit still. What should I do?

A Tell her gently that you expect her to sit for longer periods. Give her an interesting activity (such as colouring-in) and ask her to work at it until you tell her to stop. Finish after a minute. Give her praise for sitting there. Gradually extend the time by 15 seconds each session.

Q How can I teach my child basic number skills?

A The most effective way at this age is to teach number concepts using practical objects, such as a row of blocks spread in front of her, or her fingers. Show her that numbers correspond to objects. Then there are number songs too, such as '10 green bottles' or '5 little speckled frogs'. Make all learning activities about numbers informal, relaxed and fun.

Toys: pencils and sharpener, child's desk, jigsaws, board games, word lotto, flashcards, toy money and cash register

Social and

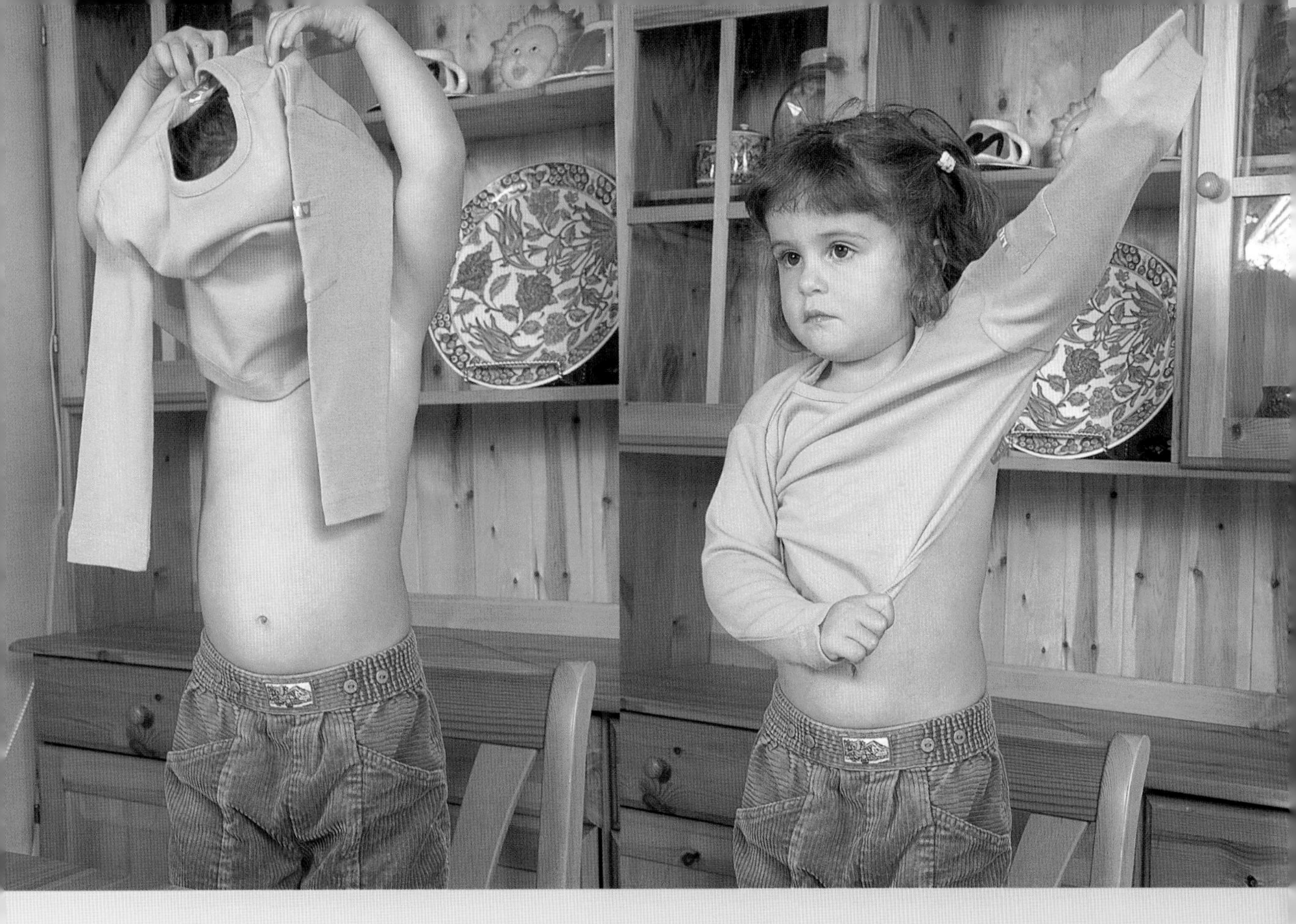

Emotional Development

The Importance of Social and Emotional Development

The change in your child's emotional and social development during this phase of his life is remarkable. His individuality shows through in all areas, and he becomes his own person with his own characteristics, his own strengths and weaknesses, and his own relationships. No longer so dependent on you for everything, your growing child strives to manage things by himself.

Your Changing Child

Of course, these changes render him vulnerable. One minute he is very buoyant and confident in the company of other children his own age, the next he bursts into tears and then clings tightly to you; one minute he insists he doesn't need any help putting on his vest, the next he screams hysterically because his arms are entangled in the garment.

Some of the major areas of emotional and social change that your growing child experiences between the ages of 3 and 5 years are:

- **friendships.** Your child's awareness of his peers – and his innate need to form connections with them – assumes considerable importance in his young life. He wants to be liked and to have plenty of other children with whom he can play. As he discovers, however, friendships function within a system of rules concerning sharing, supporting and turn-taking – many of these essential social skills don't come naturally to a pre-school child. He has to learn them.
- **independence.** Not only does he want to do more for himself, he becomes increasingly capable of achieving that target. For instance, he is reliably clean and dry during the day and he wants to achieve this control at night, too; he handles cutlery more effectively, preferring to eat alongside his family than to have meals on his own. As before, though, you may find that his aspirations outstrip his ability, and that he simply can't always manage independently.
- **gender.** His sense of 'boyness' and 'girlness' – in other words, his understanding of what makes a boy a boy and a girl a girl – strengthens. Children this age begin to drift towards same-sex friends and same-sex toys and games. Boys and girls begin to express different preferences for clothes as their gender identity develops, and they form clear ideas about appropriate behaviour for boys and girls. Gender stereotypes show through.
- **sociability.** Social situations are less challenging now as his confidence when mixing with others increases. Much of this stems from experience of

Left: Although your child increases in confidence all the time, he will need your reassurance when a situation becomes too much for him.

Above: Play fighting – and real fighting – between siblings is normal but this is a crucial age at which to establish what is acceptable behaviour and what is not.

mixing with other children and adults, whether at playgroup, nursery, in the street, out shopping with you or at family gatherings. There are continued episodes of shyness, especially when he is confronted by strangers, but he is generally more at ease in his relationships with others. He is fun to be with.

- **morality.** Your child's grasp of right and wrong goes through a noticeable transformation. He understands about lying and why he shouldn't do it (though he still resorts to this strategy at times), and he is also more aware that swearing and stealing are not acceptable. By the time he is 4 or 5 years old, your child may have very rigorous, inflexible moral principles which he expects everyone to follow. His sense of justice is also rigid. When he thinks an injustice has taken place he may be extremely upset, convinced that it needs to be righted – and he might be inconsolable until this happens.

Accepting Him

His key characteristics are evident at this age, and you'll see his nature and personality type showing through. In many ways, the challenge facing you is not to change your child's individual traits but to encourage and channel those that you admire and discourage those you do not value so highly. For instance, determination is a great asset for any child, but not when this creates distress for everyone. A child with that personal characteristic needs to be shown how to manage his determination so that it works in his favour, not against him.

This means that you should accept your child for who he is, with his own unique blend of features that make him so special. The fact is that changing his personality is extremely difficult, but helping him to develop particular strengths is easier. He needs your support and guidance at this stage – not criticisms or objections – to fulfil his full social and emotional potential. His basic need to be loved and valued by you remains strong; he wants your approval.

Below: Whatever your child's personality she needs your encouragement to help her gain self-confidence and self-esteem so that she can cope with the world outside.

Self-Esteem

The knowledge that you think he's marvellous is one of the foundation stones on which his self-esteem and self-confidence rest. But they also depend on the reactions that he receives from other people. That's why an innocent remark from another child about his inability to run fast or his poor drawing skills throws him into emotional turmoil. He cares that others think highly of him or poorly of him; he wants to be valued.

His feeling of competence is also very important as the start of school approaches. A child who has a confident, capable frame of mind, full of self-belief about his abilities, looks forward to the infant class with great excitement. Self-doubts create the opposite effect in a child, leaving him in fear at the prospect of the classroom. Help him develop a positive attitude towards school.

Stimulating Social and Emotional Development: 3 to 3½ Years

Making new friends is the name of the game now. Your child loves mixing with others and her social skills improve significantly. These relationships with her peers boost her social confidence, making her less shy with unfamiliar children and adults. Her independence surges, especially with night-time bowel and bladder control, but also with other areas of self-care such as dressing and eating.

Comforters

There are plenty of children this age who use a comforter (typically, a favourite cuddly toy) when they are tired, unwell or even just watching television quietly. The comforter helps the child relax, bringing feelings of security and contentment, and is a normal part of childhood.

Do your best to discourage her from taking the comforter with her to nursery, however, as she may be the only child there with one. If she does ask to take it, tell her to leave it behind in a safe place and that she can have it when she comes back home.

Suitable Suggestions

There is lots you can do to encourage your child's natural kindness towards others, especially now that she spends more time in the company of her peers. Point out to her that her caring actions have direct effects on others. For example, when she brings you a biscuit from the kitchen instead of just taking

Below: Remember that simply by spending time having fun with your child you are making him feel that you value and enjoy his company.

one for herself, tell her how good that made you feel. She is more likely to act kindly towards others when she realizes the impact of her caring acts. Make a big fuss of your child when you see her help her friends – your praise for that behaviour reinforces it.

This is also a good time to develop her self-help skills further. Not long ago, she presented signs that she was ready for night toilet training (by waking in the morning with a dry nappy, by complaining during the night that her nappy needs to be changed, or even by asking you outright if she can try sleeping without a nappy). Even at this stage you may still be letting her go to bed wearing padded pants. Don't expect completely dry nights now, although you may not have to change the sheets every morning as you used to. Remember to keep telling your child that you hope she will have a dry night, and add that she mustn't worry if the bed isn't dry when she wakes in the morning. Accidents will happen less and less often at this stage.

Make sure that you find time every day to spend alone with your child. Her basic need to feel valued and loved by you remains as strong as ever. Of course, relationships with peers are vital, but her basic emotional connection with you remains the cornerstone of her development.

Top Tips

1. Don't let her barge into conversations. Your child slowly learns that chatting to someone involves listening as well as talking. If she does break in while you are in mid-sentence, continue talking until you have finished and then let her speak.

2. Comfort her when she cries. Despite her apparent surge in confidence, she remains fragile and emotionally vulnerable. When you see her upset over what appears to be something minor, give her a big reassuring hug to cheer her up.

3. Use non-physical forms of punishment. Smacking your child for her misbehaviour will only make matters worse. Far better to find a non-violent way of punishing her, perhaps using a verbal reprimand or sending her to her room.

Below: Your child will relish the sense of independence she gets from doing things for herself – like choosing her own breakfast and pouring out her own milk.

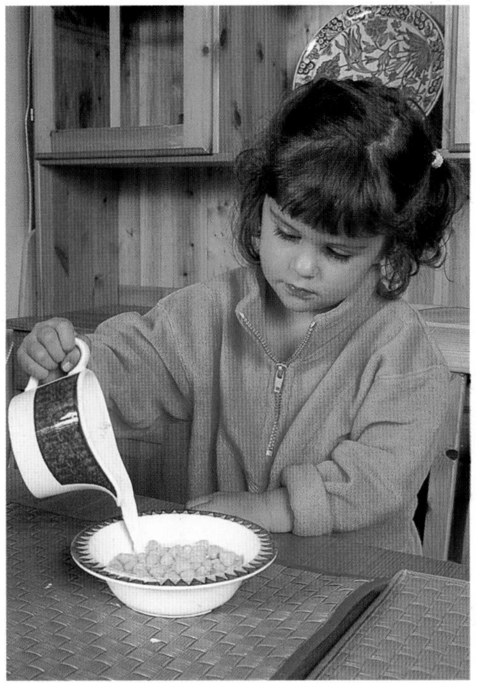

Q&A

Q My child still wakes up too early in the morning. What can we do?

A Tell her the night before that if she does wake up early, she should stay in her room and play quietly with her toys. Certainly, she should not come into your room at that time. Leave a pile of books and toys by her bedside so that she can reach them easily in the morning.

Q My 3-year-old talks to an imaginary friend. Does this mean she is lonely?

A No, it doesn't. Many popular children this age have an imaginary friend. Most psychologists agree that the appearance of a fantasy playmate is simply an extension of the child's imaginative ability. You'll find that her imaginary friend disappears one day, just as suddenly as it first appeared.

Toys: dressing-up clothes, animal and people play figures, toy cars, pretend cutlery and crockery, elementary board games

Stimulating Social and Emotional Development: 3½ to 4 Years

Aside from improving his social skills during this period, your child begins to understand the difference between the truth and a lie. He knows that it is wrong to lie – but he'll tell a lie at times if he thinks that is the best way to get himself out of trouble. You may find that an element of competitiveness creeps into his relationships.

Telling Lies

Psychological research has shown that almost every child is capable of lying, if the threat of punishment for admitting the truth is very extreme. Four-year-olds do occasionally tell lies because they think this will get them out of trouble. They also tell lies for other reasons, such as to make life more interesting, to express their vivid imagination and to exaggerate their achievements. While you should deal with lies immediately they arise, don't be too harsh or your child will simply make a bigger effort to conceal the truth the next time.

Explain to your child why he should not lie (for instance, because others won't want to play with him, or because you'll be sad), and make any punishment for lying small, quick and appropriate.

Suitable Suggestions

Arguments are common among young children, and it's important for your child to learn how to handle them without resorting to aggression. His first reaction when in disagreement with one of his pals might be to become physically abusive (hitting, punching or biting) or to become verbally abusive (swearing, screaming or name-calling). Help him manage his aggression so that he resolves conflict in a less confrontational manner. Most importantly, explain to him that you disapprove strongly of acting aggressively towards others, that this upsets them and that other children will not play with him if they think he is aggressive.

In addition, suggest to him that he voices his feelings instead of acting on them, so that when another child snatches a toy from his hands, he might say 'I'm playing with that toy, you can have it when I've finished', instead of lashing out in anger. If that doesn't work, he should tell the nearest adult what has happened.

When you do offer guidance to your growing child, try to phrase your advice positively. A

Below: Whatever you want to say to your child, word it positively, even if you are telling her not to do something – criticism undermines her self-esteem.

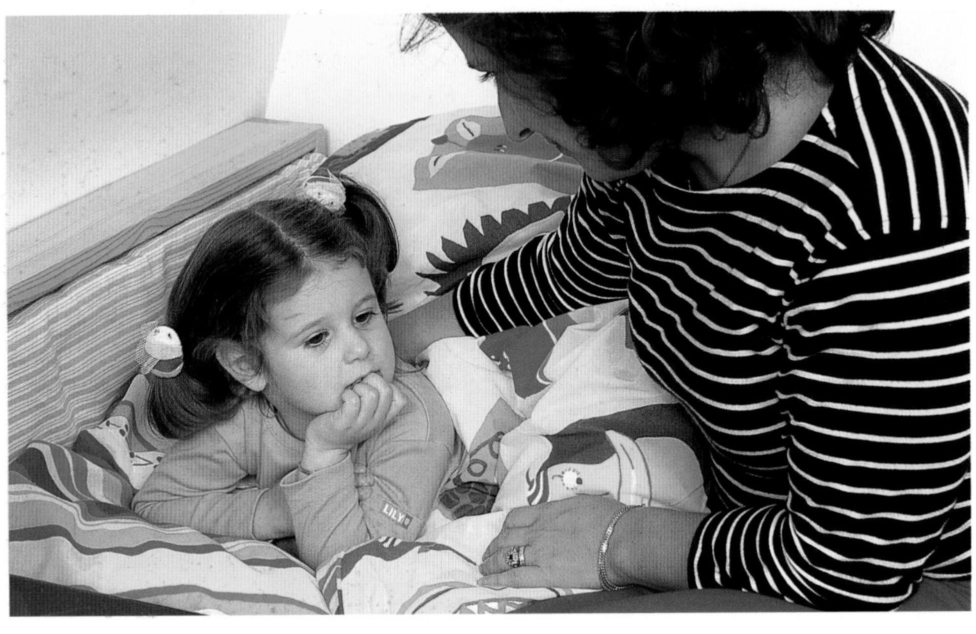

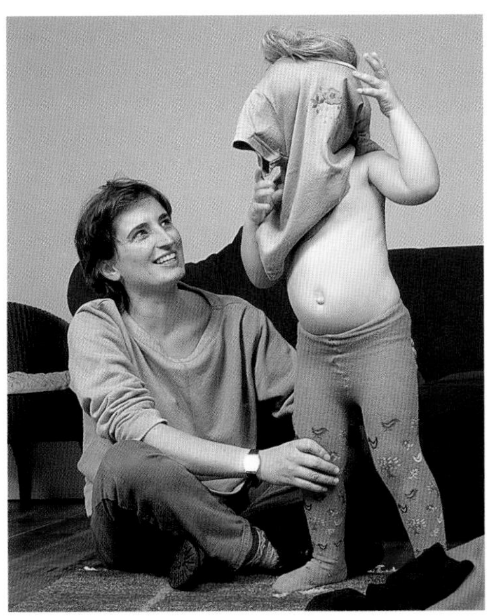

Left: Be patient while your child is learning to dress herself – if you help her too soon she may feel that you don't have confidence in her ability to do it correctly.

constant run of negative comments from you reduces his self-confidence, so find a way of expressing your ideas without leaving him to feel as though he is criticized all the time. Rules can be explained positively ('Be nice to your friends when they play with you' instead of 'Don't be horrible to your friends') and criticisms can be made without a totally negative slant ('I'm upset that you hit your pal because you're normally so friendly').

Show enthusiasm when he tries to be independent. The problem is that you can probably do things quicker yourself and your child's desire to manage on his own often slows things down. Dressing, for instance, takes much longer when he does it all by himself. That's why you need to give him plenty of time in these situations. If you know that putting on his vest and pants takes several extra minutes, make sure he starts dressing several minutes earlier than usual.

Top Tips

1. Read books with sociable themes. Try to find a story book that involves children sharing their toys and playing peacefully together. He'll enjoy listening to you read it to him and the theme helps him to think about his friendships.

2. Encourage board games. Following the rules of a game can be difficult, but it is a skill that your child learns through experience. You might need to supervise him and his friends when they are playing a board game, to ensure they stick to the rules.

3. Avoid toy guns and weapons. There is evidence from research which indicates that a child who plays with an 'aggressive' toy is more likely to play aggressively with his friends immediately afterwards. Toys and behaviour are connected.

4. Reassure him when he doesn't succeed. Your child cries, for example, when he realizes he can't complete a puzzle toy that his friend manages with ease. Show him the solution and remind him of all the things he can do.

5. Praise good behaviour. It's easy to fall into the trap of focusing too much on his negative actions. Don't forget to give him lots of praise and approval when he does behave appropriately to you, his siblings and his friends.

Below: Toy guns and weapons encourage aggressive behaviour among children, which may continue into other games, and so they should be avoided.

Q Why does my child stand there saying nothing when I catch him misbehaving?

A He probably doesn't know what to say and so chooses to keep quiet. But don't let his silence stop you from talking to him. Let him know that you disapprove and give him the reasons why you are annoyed with his behaviour. He listens to you even though he doesn't say anything.

Q Should I force my shy 4-year-old to go to parties?

A Try persuasion, not force. When he receives the next invitation to a party, strongly encourage him to go. Prepare him in advance by suggesting things he can say to the other children and give him loads of reassurance, as this helps to reduce his shyness. (You could even stay with him for a couple of minutes to help him settle – the party giver's mother won't object.) And after the party, tell him how proud you are of him.

Toys: board games, construction blocks, toy farm with animals and buildings, toy musical instruments, craft materials

Stimulating Social and Emotional Development: 4 to 4½ Years

Your child's friendships are now more stable, and petty arguments during play become less frequent. She understands the need for rules, not only for play but also for her behaviour at home – she wants to please you. You find that she is more outgoing with adults who talk to her, and she is able to take part in longer conversations with you.

FEARS

Research reveals that the majority of children this age develop a fear about something; girls tend to have more fears than boys. The most common childhood fear is of small, fast-moving animals – your child may be terrified when she discovers the hamster has escaped from its cage. Some children are afraid of failure.

If your child tells you she is afraid, treat her remarks seriously. Reassure her that she has nothing to be afraid of, and hold her hand as she confronts the focus of her anxiety. Her fear subsides once she realizes that she coped better than she expected.

Suitable Suggestions

Help your child to become an independent thinker, someone who doesn't simply follow her pals aimlessly without having her own ideas. It's better if she can make up her own mind, independent of group pressure. You can develop this characteristic by involving her in minor choices, such as selecting the games she wants to play next, the jumper she would like to wear today, or the snack she would like later this afternoon. Of course this doesn't mean that you always have to agree with her choice, but at least give her the opportunity to make her own decisions.

Another technique for encouraging your child to plan is to allow more flexibility in her routine. Of course daily routines remain important to her, but if she gives you a sensible reason for organizing her schedule differently then consider her request seriously. She responds positively when you offer her more freedom with decisions.

And let her voice her opinions, even if they clash with your views. Ask her to explain why she made a particular remark or why she likes a particular television programme. Establishing a dialogue of this nature gets your 4-year-old into the habit of thinking for herself. Her confidence improves when she has a say in finding solutions to problems and disagreements. In the long run, this makes her a more interesting, competent individual and more fun to be with.

Make sure she mixes with other children on most days, either through playgroup or nursery or through playing with them at home. Your child learns a great deal about herself, relationships and social skills just from playing with other children her own age. When she does invite friends to her

Below: By the age of 4 children have sufficient maturity to work out how to operate something and not to get frustrated if at first it doesn't work.

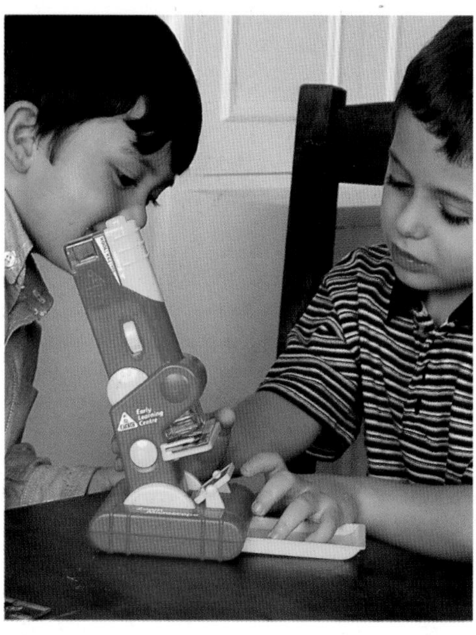

Right: There will now be continuity in your child's friendships as he becomes emotionally more mature and develops social skills.

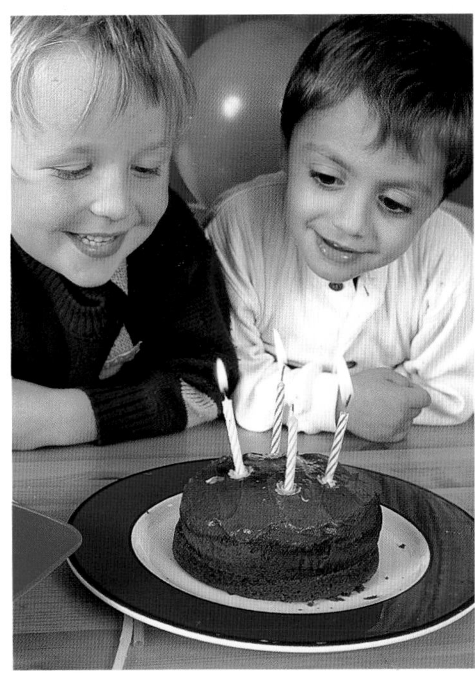

house to play, speak to her beforehand, suggesting that she draws up a rough plan of activities that they can work their way through. This keeps them busy, reduces boredom and increases everyone's enjoyment.

Remember that the aim of discipline is not to control your child but to teach her a system of rules that she can apply herself. When discussing your child's behaviour with her, offer a sensible explanation for the rules you set. For instance, going to bed at a reasonable time means that she feels good the next day, not hitting another child means that other child is unlikely to hit her, and comforting a tearful friend makes that child feel a lot better. She's old enough to understand the reasons underlying these rules and this increases the likelihood that she'll follow them.

Below: Good basic habits should now be well established and your child will understand the reasons for rules like washing his hands before meals.

Top Tips

1. Practise introductions. It's always difficult for your child to know what to say when she meets another child for the first time. That's why it is useful to practise introductions at home. Teach her to say, for example, 'Hello. Would you like to play with me?'

2. Set standards for her personal hygiene. She's old enough to take some responsibility for washing her hands and face regularly, for brushing her teeth, and for wearing fresh clothes. Check that she does this.

3. Reinforce her ambitions. If she wants, say, to be good at swimming, do what you can to arrange swimming lessons for her. This boosts her self-confidence and demonstrates that there are usually practical ways to achieve her personal aims.

4. Involve her when buying presents. It's good for your child's attitude to others to be with you when you choose a birthday card or present for someone else. Ignore any complaints of boredom and instead ask her advice when choosing.

5. Highlight strengths. It's good for your child to have spontaneous and unsolicited reminders of her positive characteristics. She'll feel so much better about herself when you mention to her, for instance, that she is interesting to talk to.

Q&A

Q How much more responsibility should my child assume for the family pet?

A At this stage, she should be able to feed the pet regularly. However, she needs your help when it comes to cleaning the pet's cage or tank.

Q I don't like my child's best friend. What can I do?

A Tread carefully – you can't stop her liking another child, and if you try that may actually strengthen their relationship. The most effective technique in this situation is actively to seek out other pals for her. Arrange for her to play with lots of friends, so that she doesn't stick to one child all the time.

Toys: dice games, bat and ball, animal and people play figures, medium-sized football, skipping rope, sand tray, doll's house

Stimulating Social and Emotional Development: 4½ to 5 Years

When you look at your child's social and emotional development compared to earlier in his life, you can see how much he has matured. He is confident, has lots of friends, talks to adults comfortably and is bursting with energy and enthusiasm. The start to infant class is not far off – and he's ready for this next exciting stage in his life.

Stealing

Young children steal for a variety of reasons: for excitement, to impress their friends, to get attention from their parents, and because stealing lets them have something that they can't get by other means. Whatever the explanation, your child knows that stealing is wrong and that he shouldn't do it.

Show strong disapproval if you find he has taken one of his younger sibling's possessions. The same applies if he takes something from his friend's house or his nursery, but try to return it discreetly without drawing public attention to it. Emphasize that other children won't want to play with him if they think he is in the habit of stealing from them, and point out that there is never any justification for this sort of behaviour.

Suitable Suggestions

Aim for your child to have a successful start to school. You may be surprised to realize that the most important characteristics to enable a child to progress in the infant class are not to do with reading, counting, spelling or writing. On the contrary – the child who settles best in his class is the one with good independence and social skills.

So encourage your child to be able to look after himself. For instance, he should be able to take off his jacket and hang it on a low peg, he should be able to attend to his hygiene and dressing needs when using the toilet, and he should be able to put on his trousers and shoes after any athletic activity at school.

Think about the school experience from his point of view. Try to imagine all the social and emotional challenges facing him (such as meeting new children, or asking the teacher questions) and practise these at home with him so that he is fully confident when he steps over the threshold of the classroom. Try not to make him anxious, however. Make these activities fun.

Right: Make sure your child can manage his outdoor clothes without help and is confident about using the toilet and washing his hands on his own.

Also give your attention to the more sophisticated social skills, especially those that are required for dealing with disagreements. After all, many of your child's class assignments will involve him in group work, in which he has to listen to others and cooperate with them. He needs to be able to get on with his classmates. Advise him that when he disagrees with someone, he should express his point of view calmly, listen to the

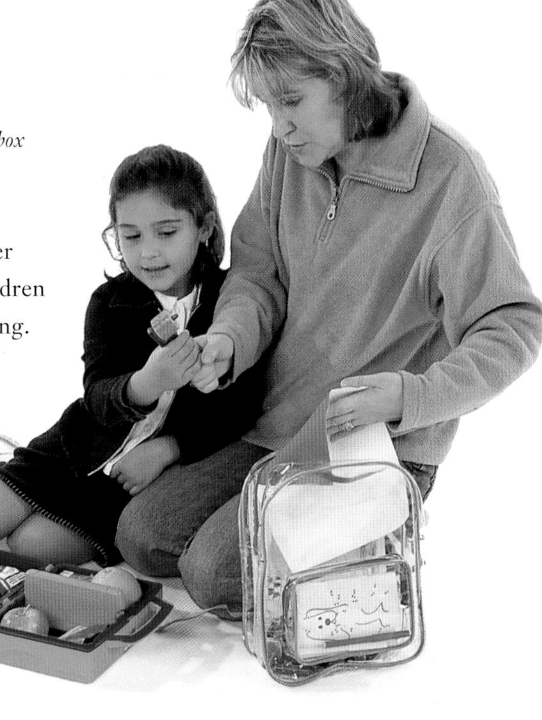

Right: Help to prepare your child for school by involving her in choosing her new bag, lunch box and things to put in them.

response and then in turn give a further reply if necessary. Conflict among children is best resolved by talking, not by yelling.

Make a point of seeking out some of the children who'll be in his class. You probably know them already if you live locally, but if you are new to the area, ask the school for advice on this matter. Arrange for some of these children to play with yours so that he is familiar with at least some of his classmates before the start of school.

Top Tips

1. Take him on a visit to his new school. Your child should lose any anxiety about starting school once he has visited it. Make sure that he sees around all the rooms, including the toilets, dining area and playground.

2. Reassure him that he'll cope. Explain that school is great fun and that he will manage all the activities in the classroom. Help him develop a positive attitude to school in order that he is enthusiastic and confident about it.

3. Teach him to be assertive, not aggressive. He needs to be able to stand up for himself, without appearing hostile. Explain that he can say 'no' to someone while still remaining calm and relaxed. Practise this with him.

4. Go out together to buy his school items. Take him with you to buy his school bag and lunch box – he probably wants to choose the ones that all his friends have. Let him also select the pencils, pencil case and crayons.

5. Believe in your child. If you have confidence in your child – if you believe he's a wonderful individual with tremendous potential – then he's more likely to believe in himself, too. And that's the best support you can give him.

Below: Talk to your child about school and what she will be doing there – this is an important new stage for her and if you are positive about it she will be, too.

Q Is this a good time to talk to my child about 'stranger danger'?

A Although you'll probably accompany him to and from school, he should be warned to be careful of strangers. In particular, tell him not to go off anywhere with a stranger or to take sweets from such a person. Tell him in such a way that he understands your message, without actually frightening him.

Q My child is nearly 5 years old but still expects me to do everything for him. How can I change this?

A Have higher expectations of your child. He has probably learned that if he stands there doing nothing, you'll eventually complete the task for him. It's time for you to stand back, do less for your child and encourage him to accept more personal responsibility.

Toys: pretend school items, board games, ball games, set of paramedic dolls, pretend post office, construction bricks

Index

D

E

F

G

M

N

O

Q

R

S

U

V

W

Y

Acknowledgements

Executive Editor Jane McIntosh
Editor Camilla James
Executive Art Editor Leigh Jones
Picture Research Jennifer Veall
Designers 2wo Design
Tony Truscott
Photography Peter Pugh-Cook
Stylist Aruna Mathur
Production Controller Louise Hall

First published in Great Britain in 2003 by
Hamlyn, a division of Octopus Publishing Group Ltd
2–4 Heron Quays, London E14 4JP

Distributed in the United States and Canada by
Sterling Publishing Co., Inc.
387 Park Avenue South, New York, NY 10016-8810

ISBN 0 600 60537 X

A CIP catalogue record for this book is available from the British Library

Printed and bound in China by Toppan Printing Company Ltd

10 9 8 7 6 5 4 3 2 1

Based on the previously published books *Bright Baby*, *Bright Toddler* and *Bright Child*